Mindful Aesthetics

Mindful Aesthetics: Literature and the Science of Mind

Edited by
Chris Danta and Helen Groth

B L O O M S B U R Y
NEW YORK · LONDON · NEW DELHI · SYDNEY

Bloomsbury Academic
An imprint of Bloomsbury Publishing Inc

1385 Broadway	50 Bedford Square
New York	London
NY 10018	WC1B 3DP
USA	UK

www.bloomsbury.com

Bloomsbury is a registered trade mark of Bloomsbury Publishing Plc.

First published 2014
© Chris Danta, Helen Groth and Contributors, 2014

Library of Congress Cataloging-in-Publication Data
Mindful Aesthetics : Literature and the Science of Mind / edited by
Chris Danta and Helen Groth.
pages cm
Includes bibliographical references and index.
ISBN 978-1-4411-0286-7 (hardback)
1. Literature and science. 2. Cognition in literature.
3. Philosophy of mind in literature. 4. Aesthetics in literature.
I. Danta, Chris, editor of compilation.
II. Groth, Helen, editor of compilation.
PN55.M54 2013
809′.93356–dc23
2013029976

ISBN: HB: 978-1-4411-0286-7
ePDF: 978-1-4411-8191-6
ePub: 978-1-4411-6252-6

Typeset by Integra Software Services Pvt. Ltd.
Printed and bound in the United States of America

Contents

Acknowledgments

The seeds of this volume were sown by a conference that explored cross-disciplinary dialogues between "science and literature," held at the University of New South Wales in 2010. We are indebted to both the Australasian Association for Literature and the University of New South Wales for supporting this event. We would also like to acknowledge the Australian Research Council, which has supported the research of a number of contributors in this volume, including our own. Thanks to our editor at Bloomsbury, Haaris Naqvi, for his unfailing support of the volume. Thanks also to Susan Danta, who provided us with invaluable assistance with the cover, and to Penelope Hone, whose thoroughness and insight has made a major contribution to the editorial process. Finally, we would like to thank our families for their patience and support.

Notes on Contributors

Brian Boyd, Distinguished Professor of English at the University of Auckland, has written on American, Brazilian, English, Greek, Irish, New Zealand and Russian literature, from epics, drama, poetry, fiction, nonfiction and translation to children's stories and comics. He is known especially for his many books on Vladimir Nabokov and on literature, evolution and cognition. His work has been translated into 17 languages and won awards on four continents. His next book is a co-translation and co-edition of Nabokov's *Letters to Véra* (2013). He is currently researching a biography of philosopher Karl Popper.

Claire Colebrook is Edwin Erle Sparks Professor of English at Penn State University. She has written books and articles on poetry, queer theory, feminist theory, literary theory, visual culture and contemporary European philosophy. Her most recent book is *Theory and the Disappearing Future* (2012), co-authored with Tom Cohen and J. Hillis Miller.

Hannah Courtney is a PhD candidate at the University of New South Wales, Sydney, studying narrative trickery in contemporary fiction. She is the author of "Narrative Temporality and Slowed Scene: The Interaction of Event and Thought Representation in Ian McEwan's Fiction" in *Narrative* (2013). She won the Graduate Student Prize at the 2011 International Society for the Study of Narrative conference.

Chris Danta is Senior Lecturer in English in the School of the Arts and Media at the University of New South Wales, Sydney. He is the author of *Literature Suspends Death: Sacrifice and Storytelling in Kierkegaard, Kafka and Blanchot* (2011) and the co-editor of *Strong Opinions: J. M. Coetzee and the Authority of Contemporary Fiction* (2011). He has also published essays in *New Literary History, Angelaki, Textual Practice, Modernism/modernity, SubStance* and *Literature & Theology*.

Paul Giles is Challis Professor of English at the University of Sydney. His most recent books are *Antipodean America: Australasia and the Constitution of U.S. Literature* (2013), *The Global Remapping of American Literature* (2011) and *Transnationalism in Practice: Essays on American Studies, Literature and Religion* (2010).

Helen Groth is Associate Professor and ARC Future Fellow in the School of the Arts and Media at the University of New South Wales, Sydney. She is the author of three books: *Victorian Photography and Literary Nostalgia* (2003), *Moving Images: Nineteenth-Century Reading and Screen Practices* (2013) and, with Natalya Lusty, *Dreams and Modernity: A Cultural History* (2013). She has also recently co-edited a special issue of *Textual Practice* (2012) on "The Uses of Anachronism."

Penelope Hone is a PhD candidate in the School of the Arts and Media at the University of New South Wales, Sydney. Her research concentrates on nineteenth-century English literature, with a particular interest in noise, new media and the form of the novel.

Stephen Muecke is Professor of Writing at the University of New South Wales, Sydney. He works with Indigenous groups in Broome (a new book is *Butcher Joe* (2011)) and on the Indian Ocean. *Contingency in Madagascar*, with photographer Max Pam, appeared in 2012 in the Intellect Books' Critical Photography Series.

Julian Murphet is Professor of Modern Film and Literature and Director of the Centre for Modernism Studies in the School of the Arts and Media, University of New South Wales, Sydney. He has published *Multimedia Modernism* (2009) and co-edited the collection *Styles of Extinction: Cormac McCarthy's* The Road (2011) and the forthcoming *Modernism and Masculinity* (2014), among others.

Paul Sheehan is Senior Lecturer in the Department of English at Macquarie University, Sydney. He is the author of *Modernism, Narrative and Humanism* (2002) and *Modernism and the Aesthetics of Violence* (2013). He has also recently co-edited a special edition of *Textual Practice* on "The Uses of Anachronism" (2012) and published essays on W. G. Sebald, Cormac McCarthy and Ralph Ellison, as well as several pieces on Samuel Beckett.

Mark Steven is a graduate student in English at the University of New South Wales, Sydney. His thesis is on the formal intersection between communism and modernist poetics. He has published on Celan, Faulkner, Poe and on the history of cinema, and has co-edited a book of essays, *Styles of Extinction: Cormac McCarthy's* The Road (2012).

John Sutton is Professor of Cognitive Science at Macquarie University, Sydney, where he was previously head of the Department of Philosophy. He is author of *Philosophy and Memory Traces: Descartes to Connectionism* (1998) and co-editor of *Descartes' Natural Philosophy* (2000) and of the international journal *Memory Studies*. Journals in which his recent papers appear include *Textual Practice*, *Discourse Processes*, *Philosophy Compass*, *Review of Philosophy and Psychology*, *Phenomenology and the Cognitive Sciences*, *Journal of Mental Imagery* and *Biological Theory*. His current research addresses social memory and collaborative cognition, point of view in imagery and memory, embodied cognition and skilled movement and (with Evelyn B. Tribble) cognitive history.

Evelyn B. Tribble is Professor and Donald Collie Chair of English at the University of Otago, New Zealand. She is the author of *Margins and Marginality: The Printed Page in Early Modern England* (1993), *Writing Material: Readings from Plato to the Digital Age* (with Anne Trubek, 2003), *Cognitive Ecologies and the History of Remembering* (with Nicholas Keene, 2011) and *Cognition in the Globe: Attention and Memory in Shakespeare's Theatre* (2011). She has also published scholarly articles in *Shakespeare*

Quarterly, Shakespeare, Shakespeare Survey and (with John Sutton) in *Shakespeare Studies* and *Textual Practice*. She is currently working on a project on "Ecologies of Skill in Early Modern England."

Anthony Uhlmann is Professor of Literature and Director of the Writing and Society Research Centre at the University of Western Sydney. His most recent books are *Samuel Beckett in Context* (2013) and *Thinking in Literature: Joyce, Woolf, Nabokov* (2011).

Charles T. Wolfe is a Research Fellow in the Department of Philosophy and Moral Sciences and Sarton Centre for History of Science at Ghent University and an associate member of the Unit for History and Philosophy of Science at the University of Sydney. He has published in journals such as *Early Science and Medicine, Perspectives on Science, Progress in Biophysics and Molecular Biology, Recherches sur Diderot et l'Encyclopédie, Dix-huitième siècle,* as well as in *Chimères, CTheory* and *Multitudes*. His edited volumes include *Monsters and Philosophy* (2005), a special issue of *Science in Context* on *Vitalism without Metaphysics?* (2008); *The Body as Object and Instrument of Knowledge: Embodied Empiricism in Early Modern Science* (edited with O. Gal, 2010); *The Concept of Organism* (with P. Huneman, special issue of *History and Philosophy of the Life Sciences*, 2010); *Vitalism and the Scientific Image, 1800–2010* (with S. Normandin, 2013) and *Brain Theory* (forthcoming). His current project is a monograph on the conceptual foundations of vitalism.

Introduction: Between Minds

Chris Danta and Helen Groth

In a famous passage in *Northanger Abbey*, Jane Austen's impassioned third-person narrator defines the form of the novel thus: "only some work in which the greatest powers of the mind are displayed, in which the most thorough knowledge of human nature, the happiest delineations of its varieties, the liveliest effusions of wit and humour are conveyed to the world in the best chosen language."[1] Austen is here defending the novel against its detractors in the 1780s and 1790s. The delicate understatement of the word *only* aside, she could not have put her case in stronger or more positive terms: the novel is valuable because it displays "the greatest powers of the mind," "the most thorough knowledge of human nature" and "the liveliest effusions of wit and humour." What is interesting to note from the perspective of this volume is that Austen chooses to defend the novel in terms that resonate with the work of cognitive and evolutionary literary scholars of the 1990s and 2000s.

In the last few decades, literary critics have increasingly drawn insights from cognitive neuroscience to deepen and clarify our understanding of the value of literature. Broadly speaking, these critics agree with Austen that literature is valuable because it reveals to us the powers of the human mind and knowledge of human nature. According to Jonathan Gottschall and David Sloan Wilson, in their 2005 collection *The Literary Animal: Evolution and the Nature of Narrative*, literature is "a vast, cheap, and virtually inexhaustible argosy of information about human nature."[2] But, to make their case for the value of literature, contemporary cognitivists draw upon very different empirical data than did Austen. As Alan Richardson puts it in his book *The Neural Sublime: Cognitive Theories and Romantic Texts*:

> Stephen Greenblatt opened his influential New Historicist study *Shakespearean Negotiations* with the memorable (and oft-paraphrased) statement, "I began with the desire to speak with the dead." My own paraphrase here might be, "I began with the desire to talk with my colleagues in psychology, linguistics, and neuroscience."[3]

Richardson's desire, like the desire of cognitive and evolutionary literary theorists more generally, is to put literary criticism on a firmer, more scientific footing.

One of the key ideas to emerge from the interdisciplinary hallway conversation currently taking place between literary critics and cognitive neuroscientists is the idea of mind-reading. As Lisa Zunshine writes in her book *Why We Read Fiction: Theory of Mind and the Novel*, "we engage in mind-reading when we ascribe to a person a certain mental state on the basis of her observable action (e.g., we see her reaching for a glass of water and assume that she is thirsty)."[4] Similarly, "Human beings are adaptively designed, as highly (and when need be, deviously) social creatures," notes

Richardson, "to search for and identify signs of intentionality, emotions, and belief states in others, primarily as revealed by the face and eyes, although blind people readily develop a sense of other minds through voice and touch."[5] It is possible, then, to translate Austen's stirring defense of the novel in *Northanger Abbey* into the modern parlance of cognitive science: novels are about mind-reading, which is to say, they are a rich source of evidence for how human beings search for and identify signs of intentionality, emotions and belief states in others. This cognitivist idea of the innate sociality of the human mind certainly applies well to the world of Austen's fiction. Her characters are constantly trying to read others' minds based on the various physical signals they receive from these others.

But the cognitive turn in literary studies has been equally generative and contentious. While cognitive literary studies has reinforced how central the concept of mind is to aesthetic practice from the classical period to the present, critics have questioned its literalism and selective borrowing of scientific authority. This collection presents both these perspectives as part of a broader consideration of the ongoing and vital importance of shifting concepts of mind to both literary and critical practice. It differs from recent collections that have sought to justify the viability of cognitive literary studies in two key ways: it creates a space for an open critical dialogue between cognitive and noncognitive models of mind and it is reflective and speculative, rather than field defining.

This collection also contributes to the forging of a "new interdisciplinarity," to paraphrase Richardson's preface to *The Neural Sublime*, that is more concerned with addressing how, rather than why, we should navigate the increasingly narrow gap between the humanities and the sciences.[6] Richardson speaks of the need to place one's "home disciplinary perspective into sustained, mutually vulnerable, and potentially transformative dialogue with the rival perspectives of colleagues trained in significantly different areas, with different methods and aims" (x). By bringing together perspectives from cognitive philosophers, historians and philosophers of science, literary theorists and literary historians to create an open, although sometimes, contentious dialogue across fields, our aim is to present multiple variations on the potentially transformative possibilities of what we have chosen to call *Mindful Aesthetics*. *Mindful* means "full of care; heedful, thoughtful."[7] By *mindful aesthetics* we refer to the careful and thoughtful application of the science of mind to literature. But, read in another way, *mindful aesthetics* also encourages more skeptical and theoretical reflections that interrogate the propriety of literature's relation to other systems of knowledge.

Critics of cognitive literary studies, of which there are some in this collection, have identified a perceived impulse to ahistoricism and an incipient conservatism that seeks to dial back the post-structural theoretical interventions of continental philosophy in the rush toward a pseudoscientific empiricism. In this scenario, cognitive theory represents the death of an aesthetics that embraces the uncertain, the unknowable and the inchoate meanings and difficult forms that render the literary distinct from the real. Questioning the elitism of this aesthetic stress on form and language over the psychology of reading, Blakey Vermeule has recently challenged the very grounds of the assumption that, to quote Paul de Man's famous theoretical edict, it is "not a priori certain that literature is a reliable source of information about anything but its own language."[8] Drawing on Alan Leslie's concept of decoupling, the ordinary human capacity that finds one of its earliest manifestations in the "reality-oriented play" of the child, Vermeule argues that intransigent distinctions between the literary and the real, and, correspondingly, the aesthetic and the empirical, are ultimately unhelpful if we want to begin to unlock the cognitive mechanisms that underlie why we care about literary characters.[9] Instead she suggests:

> Perhaps we could simply bracket the intense formalist interest in how to determine the boundaries between the fictional and the real and turn to other questions instead—questions that may explain some of the energy that we humans expend on people that we have never met and never will meet.[10]

These questions for Vermeule begin with unpacking how and why we "reason about other people" and discovering whether our "built-inference systems vary under different cultural and historical circumstances."[11] For instance, do some cultures foster a greater or lesser capacity to decouple the real from the unreal? Why do humans animate everything? How can narratives reveal the way the human mind is wired to tune into social information about other minds through psychological processes such as "concept representation, rules of inference, 'hot' cognition, and automatic processing," to invoke the social psychological terminology of Ziva Kunda.[12] Vermeule ultimately concludes that there is no sure fire system to account for why some narratives trigger or "activate our higher order mind-reading capacities" and others do not.[13] All we can do is extrapolate from the existing data that tells us that the history of modern literature from Samuel Richardson onwards has been paralleled by a persistent concern with why and how characters take on a life of their own and why readers, in turn, are drawn to selectively empathize and engage in what Vermeule describes as the evolved and elastic, yet ordinary human capacity of mind-reading.[14]

Vermeule's study reveals, like so many others working at the meeting point of psychology and literature, that literary history offers a rich yield of data about these alignments between literature and the mind, although there are quite significant differences in approaches to how to interpret that data. Mark Turner, for example, has challenged the focus on the historical and cultural at the expense of the embodied mind:

> literary criticism has given us a concept of literature as the product of circumstances...not as a product of the capacities of the human mind. We do not ask, what is the human mind that it can create and understand a text? What is a text that it can be created and understood by the human mind? These questions are not at the center or even the periphery of our critical inquiries.[15]

Turner's concern was that in the rush to read literature as an expression of an historical episteme, the essential and definitive characteristic of literature as a common human activity had been forgotten. If we choose to read literature in this way, as Patrick Colm Hogan has argued, we must stress the universal aspects of literature, a widening of the scope of critical inquiry that requires that we identify the intrinsic psychological characteristics that unite us, rather than fixate on the contingencies that differentiate one epoch, nation or culture from another. This claim leads Hogan, in Turner's wake, to assert that the study of literary universals should become a subfield of cognitive science. "Cognitive science," he argues, "can hardly claim to explain the human mind if it fails to deal with such a ubiquitous and significant mental activity as literature."[16] Correspondingly, Hogan contends cognitive science is equally vital to "the study of literary universals."[17]

Mark Turner's work exemplifies one of the ways in which the study of figurative language, and in particular metaphor, can be enlisted to investigate the predominantly unconscious workings of what he calls "the cognitive apparatus."[18] Turner's stated ambition in the introduction to *Reading Minds* is to reframe "the study of English so that it comes to be seen as inseparable from the discovery of mind, participating and even leading the way in that discovery."[19] Reading literature through this frame identifies patterns and structures that align literary language to the embodied experience of everyday life—to the stories we tell ourselves everyday as part of making sense of the world. "Narrative imagining," or story, as Turner so evocatively puts it in *The Literary Mind*, is "the fundamental instrument of thought."[20] Narrative structures our sense of time, allowing us to predict, plan and retrospectively explain. This inherently "literary capacity" is indispensible to human cognition and is the primary evidence that "the mind is essentially literary."[21] Literature, in Turner's terms, is thus transformed into a portable cognitive rhetoric that neuroscientists and computer scientists, as well as cognitive and evolutionary psychologists, can enlist to further their understanding of the stories, scripts and schemas that are integral to human cognition. Even the most fundamental quotidian experience of letting one's eye follow an object across a room, the fleeting attention paid to walking through a particular space, or drinking a cup of coffee should be understood as the way in which our minds construct "small spatial stories" as part of a universal human process by which we learn to distinguish, organize and adapt to our environments.[22] While Turner concedes that "cultural meanings" commonly "fail to migrate intact across anthropological or historical boundaries," he ultimately insists in *The Literary Mind* that the "basic mental process that make these meanings possible" are universal, regardless of the race, gender, class, ethnicity or historicity of individual bodies and minds and the stories they tell (11). In this sense, like Vermeule, Turner refuses the aesthetic distinction between the fictional and the real. Making meaning is a process that cannot be fixed or contained in an individual text, culture or geographic locale: "Meanings are not mental objects bounded in conceptual places but rather complex operations of projection, binding, linking, blending and integration over multiple spaces...meaning is parabolic and literary."[23]

Lisa Zunshine concludes in *Why We Read Fiction* that this affinity between literary and cognitive formation means that even when we misinterpret a novel in our desire to find points of identification with our own minds we still derive pleasure from engaging in what she calls our "Theory of Mind."[24] While she concedes that "getting it right" offers greater cognitive satisfaction that, in the case of a writer such as Henry James, allows the reader to go deeper into the connection between behavior and mind, Zunshine suggests that even a surface reading that misreads some or all of James' textual nuances can tell us much about our evolved adaptive compulsion to test the limits of our mind-reading capacities.[25] Expanding on this point, Zunshine suggests that we can extend the same cognitive approach to understanding the critical behaviors of a range of literary critics who, whether they recognize it or not, engage in a very similar form of cognitive engagement to an overzealous misinterpreter of James. Reflecting on the "variety of literary techniques that allow us to make a given text newly exciting precisely by reading more into its treatment" of the connections between body and mind, Zunshine observes that it seems "that a majority of literary-critical paradigms—be that paradigm psychoanalysis, gender studies, or new historicism—profitably exploit, in their quest for new layers of meaning, our evolved cognitive eagerness to construct a state of mind behind a behavior."[26] In this context aesthetics is something that one can "throw in" (20) as needed, as Zunshine does, through a citation of Wayne Booth's influential reading of *The Wings of the Dove*.

According to Zunshine, the nuance of Booth's critical observations on James' "beautifully realized human creatures" only serves to prove that the reader, in this case Booth, has passed the test of being a good, highly evolved reader:

> Why (so you pipe in happily), if a reader's mind-reading profile is constituted like Booth's, there is no doubt that it is "good" for him to be "tested" by *The Wings of the Dove*. At every step, the book is telling such a reader, as it were: "*These* immensely complex, multi-leveled, ethically ambiguous, class-conscious, mutually reflecting and mutually distorting states of mind you are capable of navigating. *This* is how good you are at this maddening and exhilarating social game. Did you know it? *Now* you know it!"[27]

It is difficult to see what role aesthetics plays in this mode of reading which is so keen to embrace the universal over the particular stylistics and contexts of individual writers and critics.

Yet, as Zunshine also notes, cognitive literary theory is a dynamic and diverse field, which also includes the more specific historical and aesthetic focus of critics such as Ellen Spolsky and Alan Richardson. Spolsky has observed that it is the job of cognitive studies "to begin to chart the emergence, manifestation and readability" of the "only temporarily stable relationships between the humanly universal and the culturally and individually specific, as coded and recorded in cultural artefacts."[28] Richardson's exemplary 2001 study *British Romanticism and the Science of Mind* provides a template for how this type of rigorous historical and aesthetic criticism can work in conjunction with the formulations of contemporary cognitive neuroscience. In his illuminating reading of "Coleridge and the new unconscious," for example, Richardson broke with the then conventional psychoanalytic encodings of memory and unconscious states in canonical Romantic works.[29] He also departed from deconstructive philosophical approaches to Coleridge's complex and multivalent conception of mind. Instead he offers a revelatory reading of Coleridge's seminal renditions of unconscious thinking or creativity—most notably in the introductory note to *Kubla Khan*—alongside the contemporary brain-based theories of the French materialist philosopher Pierre Jean George Cabanis, who contended that the mind is constantly active and embodied, whether we are awake, asleep or unconscious of how various sensations may be modifying our ideas and emotions.[30] Rather than reading Coleridge's famous introductory note to *Kubla Khan* as a performative ruse, Richardson reads Coleridge's claim that he composed the poem in an opium-induced dream-state as a confessional emanation of his engagement with Cabanis, as well as Erasmus Darwin's speculations on how opium reveals the involuntary nature of thought. Given this context, Richardson concludes that the longer one looks at the poem through the lens of Romantic brain science the more the introductory note to *Kubla Khan* resembles "a brain scientist's dream" in its implication of "a subject fractured into conscious and unconscious entities, the persistence of cognitive activity in the absence of conscious judgment and volition" and the "mind's susceptibility to and perhaps ultimate dependence on material changes in the body."[31] Richardson's finely observed reading of Coleridge's often contradictory and polemical engagement with his scientific contemporaries thus ultimately embeds the poet's work in a contemporary network of theories of cognition and perception, rather than obscuring historical, cultural and aesthetic differences in the drive to lock down the definitive patterns and schema of a universal reading experience.

More recently, Vanessa L. Ryan has developed upon this historical approach to the convergence between nineteenth-century literary formations and the science of mind in *Thinking without Thinking in the Victorian Novel*. Like Richardson, Ryan's concern is less with identifying universal patterns of literary materializations of mind and more with fleshing out the ways in which the works of individual literary writers, such as George Eliot, Wilkie Collins, Henry James and George Meredith, were imbricated in and imbued with the concepts of mind of their psychological peers, such as William Carpenter, George Henry Lewes and James Sully. As Ryan argues, the new mind-brain sciences of the nineteenth century moved away from the Cartesian understanding of thinking as synonymous with an awareness of one's essential self and toward a model of thought that sought to bridge the gap between mind and matter, self and environment. While Ryan identifies this concern with understanding how consciousness and subjective experience relate to the brain and the body as a shared one with contemporary cognitive and neuroscientific theory, her concern is to illuminate how Victorian fiction writers in particular played an integral role in grappling with a powerful new psychological paradigm:

> Victorian fiction writers went beyond the question of what the mind is to explore the dynamic experience of how the mind functions. Novelists during this period drew on new explanations of mind-body interaction to examine how we experience our minds, how that experience relates to our behavior and questions of responsibility, how we can gain control over our mental reflexes, and how fiction plays a special role in understanding and training our minds.[32]

The important point for Ryan here is that certain Victorian fiction writers managed to write about the problem of how the mind functions without at the same time subordinating their literature to science.

In a recent forum in *Critical Inquiry* on Literary Darwinism, Ryan criticizes evocriticism for doing just this:

> Literary Darwinism presumes a unified view of human nature that is ill-suited to account for individuality in literary writing and interpretation. Its attention to "a primary, literal order of representation" means that it cannot adequately address questions of form. Its view of literature as an adaptive function and its search for consilience subordinates the value of literature to the principles of evolutionary psychology.[33]

In trying to take stock of this point, we might return to the passage from Jane Austen with which we began. Austen notes with delicate irony that the novel is "only some work in which the greatest powers of the mind are displayed, in which the most thorough knowledge of human nature, the happiest delineations of its varieties, the liveliest effusions of wit and humour are conveyed to the world in the best chosen language." As this passage develops, the question of literary form becomes more important. If literature displays a thorough knowledge of human nature, is this knowledge the same as or different to that displayed by other modes of human enquiry? In what sense, that is, does literary form (the language chosen by the writer) affect the conclusions the writer draws about human identity?

This is ultimately an aesthetic question. As the *OED* reminds us, *aesthetics* is "the distinctive underlying principles of a work of art or a genre."[34] By *mindful aesthetics*, we also mean being mindful of aesthetic distinctions. And this means, among other things, paying attention to the literariness of literature. By contrast, Vermeule's call in *Why Do We Care about Literary Characters?* to bracket the intense formalist interest in how to determine the boundaries between the fictional and the real runs the risk of causing us to lose sight of the specificity of literature. There is a good reason why we commonly refer to literature as fiction: literature decontextualizes the reader by fictionalizing the reader's world. It is escapist. It takes us away from the familiar and toward the unfamiliar. But the thrust of much cognitive literary criticism is to concentrate on the return journey of the reader from the fictional to the real world and to figure literature as a form of recontextualization. It is the realist aesthetic of Jane Austen's novels that makes them so amenable to a cognitive approach. But what about novels that are more fantastical in their orientation? Or novels that document an aberrant or a fantastical state of mind? Are they immediately amenable to a cognitive approach? Something we mean to say with this collection is *mind the gap*. Be mindful, that is, of the difference between fiction and reality.

Why Do We Care about Literary Characters?: the title of Vermeule's book encapsulates the bias found in much cognitivist literary theory toward real-world rather than fictional-world experience. William Flesch had already asked this question at the beginning of the first chapter of his 2007 book *Comeuppance: Costly Signaling, Altruistic Punishment and Other Biological Components of Fiction*: "Why do we care about what happens in a fictional representation, to fictional characters, in a fictional world? What makes it possible for us to have a vivid emotional response to fictions?"[35]

Flesch's repetition of the word *fictional* here widens the gap between reality and fiction. The word that never appears in his or Vermeule's formulation of the question—*real*—is nonetheless the word that the question takes most for granted or that does the most work in it. Why do we *real* readers care about fictional characters? But what do we mean by *real*? The stakes here are ontological. When one proposes to discuss the biological or the evolutionary or the cognitive aspects of fiction, one is already working with a certain understanding of what reality is and what it means to be human.

An answer that cognitive literary theorists repeatedly give to the question of why we care about fiction and fictional characters is that human beings are incorrigibly prosocial creatures. Prosocial behavior is behavior "which is positive, helpful, and intended to promote social acceptance and friendship."[36] As Flesch explains:

> Even when given the opportunity to be free-riders, people tend not to be. We usually cooperate instead of maximising the net gain we can get out of the cooperation of others. We do this because of an increasingly complex attitude towards others: we have a native inclination towards altruism; we expect others to have such an inclination as well…. We tend to reward others who engage in genuinely altruistic behaviour, and to approve of anyone else who rewards them, and we tend to approve as well of others who punish antisocial behaviour or socially obnoxious behaviour.[37]

Flesch argues elegantly in *Comeuppance* that we have evolved to look for prosocial behavior in others and to reward such behavior. This evolutionary bent toward the prosocial, he suggests, directly influences our taste in literature: "We like characters who engage in effective altruistic behavior and we dislike their opposites."[38] Apparently, something we like even more than altruistic reward is altruistic punishment. An altruistic punisher is someone who promotes altruistic behavior by punishing another—a so-called free-rider—for acting selfishly. So here, in a nutshell, is Flesch's argument: we especially care about fictional characters when they act altruistically and when they punish altruistically.

Again, it is possible to respond to Flesch's argument from evolutionary biology by raising the aesthetic question of literary form. (Flesch admits at the end of his book that he hasn't "been discussing much the esthetics of narrative."[39]) In Flesch's schema, how do readers' reactions to altruistic punishment in literature differ from their responses to this phenomenon in real life? How should we account for the specificity of the discourse of literature in this regard? Flesch seems to envision readers as relatively passive in the sense that they respond to altruistic behavior in literary texts because they are naturally disposed toward prosocial behavior. But it is possible to present the process of aesthetic perception as being more active than this and more oriented toward the individual response of the reader. In his critical work from 1919 to 1921, *Toward a Philosophy of the Act*, Mikhail Bakhtin offers an alternative position to Flesch's. "In aesthetic seeing you love a human being not because he is good," writes Bakhtin, "but, rather, a human being is good because you love him. This is what constitutes the specific character of aesthetic seeing."[40] The movement Bakhtin here ascribes to aesthetic seeing is the opposite of the one Flesch traces in *Comeuppance*. It is from reality to fantasy rather than from fantasy to reality. We do not love someone because he is good (because he acts or punishes altruistically); rather, he becomes good through our perceiving of him. By emphasizing its individualist, relativist and fantastical elements, Bakhtin presents aesthetic perception as a more active process than Flesch does. For Bakhtin, readers do not just see their prosocial evolutionary natures reflected in the text. Rather, in some sense, they also actively create and re-create their own identity and the identity of the text through their aesthetic perception.

To be fair to Flesch, the truth of aesthetic perception is probably somewhere between his position and Bakhtin's. Aesthetic perception, that is, must involve the reader shuffling to and fro between states of activity and passivity. (In this regard, love is a particularly good metaphor for aesthetic sight.) Moreover, it would be wrong to overemphasize the role of individuality and fantasy in aesthetic perception. Readers are not free to create their identities or the identities of the texts they read. What is outside the text—our social, evolutionary, cognitive and biological natures—must in some way determine our sense of what is inside the text. The cognitive turn is at its most productive when it cautions us against adopting an overly negative or ironic understanding of literature or aesthetics à la de Man. The strength of Flesch's position is its very positivity and literality. The mechanisms of prosociality he describes no doubt play a vital role in our understanding of literature. But the point we want to stress here is that it is important for cognitive literary scholars to take the complexity of the aesthetic act into account when reading literature. For otherwise we run the risk of undervaluing the social agency of literature. Is there not a sense in which what is inside the literary text also determines who we are? As we have seen, Gottschall and Sloan Wilson describe literature as "a vast, cheap, and virtually inexhaustible argosy of information about human nature."[41] But when we read literature, we do not just read for information. The ontological exchange that takes place between the reader and the author of a literary text is a much more active and profound process than this formulation suggests. We also read literature to see how the author and the text challenge and even reshape our ideas of whom we are.

According to geneticist Alberto Piazza in an afterword to Franco Moretti's *Graphs, Maps, Trees: Abstract Models for Literary History*, "literary writing can be construed as a system that is not bound by the particular instruments it has itself created, and is therefore capable of metabolizing metaphors and ambiguities belonging to several systems of knowledge." Piazza then adds that the "system of scientific knowledge... is paradoxically very well suited to such a metabolising function."[42] The first part of the collection—"Theoria"—showcases a range of possible responses to Piazza's claim that literature is ideally suited to metabolize metaphors and ambiguities belonging to the system of scientific knowledge. Brian Boyd's field-defining work, most notably *On the Origin of Stories: Evolution, Cognition, and Fiction*, argues for the unique proximity of literature and psychology. Boyd contends that both literary writers and readers participate in a mutually recognized thought experiment that interrogates the ways in which human minds engage with the world and with one another. Polemically, Boyd dismisses both psychoanalysis and behaviorism, arguing that the mythic constructs of the former and the empirical literalism of the latter are irrelevant to literary studies. Cognitive psychology, by contrast, is the ideal scientific method to "investigate aspects of the mind" that literature reveals, specifically the emotions, imagination and memory. Boyd continues to make this case in the context of the work of Vladimir Nabokov in the opening essay of this collection, aptly entitled "Psychology and Literature: Mindful Close Reading."

In "Vitalism and Theoria," Claire Colebrook puts the counterargument to Boyd's exemplification of the cognitive evidence to be gleaned from scientific methods of mindful reading. Colebrook argues strenuously against what she characterizes as the antitheoretical vitalism of the turn toward science in literary studies and in particular embodied concepts of mind typified by the work of Andy Clark, George Lakoff and Mark Johnson. She claims that as "long as we would regard relations, texts, apparatuses, assemblages, distances, gaps or points of inertia as retrievable or reducible to the complexity of the lived we remain at the level of organic narrative (tracing relations from bodies) rather than theory." For Colebrook, then, the recent embrace of embodied cognition amounts to a rejection of theory—for theory is what necessarily maintains a critical distance from life. In "Continental Drift: The Clash between Literary Theory and Cognitive Literary Studies," Paul Sheehan continues Colebrook's polemic against vitalism. According to Sheehan, part of the remit of Cognitive Literary Studies is to cut the ground out from theory by returning to many of the claims proscribed by the latter—claims for universalism and objectivism, and for the primacy of biology over culture and empirical research over theoretical supposition. For Sheehan, as for Colebrook, continental theory is antivitalist in the sense that it identifies the literary as the noncoincidence of the laws of the body with the laws of the text.

In "Thinking with the World: Coetzee's *Elizabeth Costello*," Anthony Uhlmann critiques what he identifies as two foundational propositions within the emerging discipline of cognitive poetics—"that human consciousness provides an adequate model or analogue for both thought itself and the nature of the novel," and that "the kind of thought which emerges from human consciousness is built around metaphor." Arguing for the need to be aware of the limitations imposed by these propositions, Uhlmann considers the degree to which these approaches can provide an account for the specific "kind of thinking that takes place in literature." Drawing upon recent work on "distributed cognition" or "extended mind," Uhlmann then develops a reading of J. M. Coetzee's novel *Elizabeth Costello* that opens up a space for reflecting further on the relationship between literature and cognitive theory.

The second part of the collection—"Minds in History"—exemplifies how the history of brain science can inform contemporary debates about the nature of mind and the relationship between science and aesthetics. The four chapters in this part observe, albeit in varying ways, Anne Harrington's qualification that "a lively interest in the sciences of mind and brain in one's own era" does not justify using history as "a vehicle to hunt for the present in an earlier age."[43] Continuing the historical project undertaken by Alan Richardson, Athena Vrettos, Vanessa L. Ryan, Nicholas Dames and others, who have turned to eighteenth- and nineteenth-century dialogues between literature and the beginnings of experimental psychology, these chapters also speak across the disciplinary divide between literary history and the history and philosophy of science. In cognitive psychology externalizing the mind is synonymous with Andy Clark and David Chalmers' influential, albeit polarizing, concept of extended mind. Taking up Wittgenstein's challenge that one of the "most dangerous ideas" is that we "think with or in our heads" (*Zettel*), Clark and Chalmers model an idea of active rather than passive externalization, the cognitive integration of mind and world. Starting from Denis Diderot's description of the brain as "a book which reads itself," Charles T. Wolfe reconsiders Diderot's 1769 experimental novel *Rêve de D'Alembert* as an extension of his materialist account of "what brains do, and how much our mental, affective, and intellectual life is contained therein." Wolfe describes Diderot's novel as a "para-literary work," which can be enlisted to challenge more recent reductive materialist or psychophysical models of mind.

The next two chapters in this part make a historical claim for the significance of the psychological aesthetics of the late nineteenth-century evolutionary psychologist James Sully. Sully was a seminal figure in late Victorian psychological circles. He was an early editor of *Mind*, a friend and colleague of seminal figures writing on the new science of mind, such as George Henry Lewes, Alexander Bain and William James, and a prolific writer on a wide range of psychological subjects. He was also a typical Victorian polymath, writing essays on George Eliot, the relationship between art and psychology, literary dreams and the science of dreaming, and the increasingly vexed relationship, in his mind at least, between noise and civilisation. In "Muted Literary Minds: James Sully, George Eliot and Psychologized Aesthetics in the Nineteenth Century," Penelope Hone reads Sully's polemical essay on "Civilisation and Noise" alongside George Eliot's psychological interrogation of the noise of other's minds in *Middlemarch* and *Daniel Deronda*. Hone enlists Sully's "Civilisation and Noise" to examine the ways in which Eliot tests the aesthetic limitations of literary form. "The uniquely muting power Sully ascribes to Eliot's fiction reflects an idealized model of literary communication that Eliot herself engaged with in her early writing," Hone argues, was subsequently reconceived in line with more materialist conceptions of mind in her later novels *Middlemarch* and *Daniel Deronda*.

Sustaining the focus on Sully, but departing from his interest in noise and consciousness, in "The Mind as Palimpsest: Art, Dreaming and James Sully's Aesthetics of Latency" Helen Groth reads Sully's model of dream interpretation as both a continuation of his writing on the psychological function of aesthetic experience in two earlier essays that were published in *Mind* in the 1870s, "Art and Psychology" and "George Eliot's Art" and as a catalyst for reflecting on the limitations of the transhistorical approaches of some recent cognitive literary theory. In both his literary and dream interpretation, Sully attempts to isolate what is unique to fictional experience. Literary allusions pervade his dream analysis, functioning as devices that reveal both the psychological complexity of the dream and its value as a key to the relationship between conscious and unconscious modes of thought. Correspondingly, Sully interprets art, and more particularly the process of reading George Eliot's art, as a multichanneled mediation that transmits messages on different frequencies that the psychologically trained mind subsequently decodes.

In "The Flame's Lover: The Modernist Mind of William Carlos Williams," Mark Steven uses Williams' epic poem *Paterson* as the occasion to investigate a certain modernist conception of mind. As Steven notes, Williams' poem "frames itself as synthesizing scientific rigor with aesthetic pleasure, yet rigor immediately transforms the mind into an inaccessible object, concealed by the diaphanous veils of beauty, and so the poem's synthesis might have already proven to be a 'mindless' undertaking." In his close reading, Steven shows that Williams uses literary form to transform the discourse of science. Even though he is a medical doctor, Williams, as he says himself, does "not propose to be a scientist in [his] seeking of truth." For Steven, what the modernist poet-doctor Williams ultimately affirms as the truth of the mind is the falling to the earth of the absolute—the fleeting inseparability "of beauty and the thing, of science and the sensorial stain."

The third part of the collection—"Contemporary Literary Minds"—is united by its focus on contemporary literary practice, while sustaining this volume's interest in the dialogue across and between a variety of approaches to the dynamic relationship between literature and science. In " 'The Creation of Space': Narrative Strategies, Group Agency, and Skill in Lloyd Jones' *The Book of Fame*," John Sutton and Evelyn B. Tribble show how a reading of Lloyd Jones' *The Book of Fame* can contribute to the interdisciplinary study of literature and cognition. Sutton and Tribble argue that we can gain insights into the nature of skillful group agency, of distinct forms and distinct timescales, by treating *The Book of Fame* as a "brilliant evocation of features of collective thought, movement, and emotion that both everyday and scientific inquiry can easily miss."

Stephen Muecke, taking a very different approach to Sutton and Tribble, picks up on Clare Colebrook's insistence on the need for a nonvital textuality. Muecke asserts that it is through a reproductive capacity that texts (and other things) can be said to formally engage those vital relations that "keep them alive in their place." In "Reproductive Aesthetics," Muecke thus suggests a method for literary analysis that understands the vitality of things, including texts, through the reproductive partnerships into which they enter. Drawing on his own distinctive critical practice, which writes across the boundary between creative and critical practice, Muecke reflects on the reproductive parallels between poetic and biological modes of production. As he observes, "Poetry is one of the many ways in which humans foster an interest in each other; the interest in reproduction, we might say, involves the reproduction of interest."

The final two essays in the collection report on the intersection of literature and contemporary neuroscience but draw diametrically opposed conclusions about the productiveness of this intersection. In "Distended Moments in Neuronarrative: Character Consciousness and the Cognitive Sciences in Ian McEwan's *Saturday*," Hannah Courtney demonstrates how Ian McEwan's obsession with the cognitive sciences manifests not just in the content of his novels but also in their form. To show how the neuroscientific content of McEwan's novels shapes their form, Courtney identifies a new narrative technique that McEwan uses to elucidate the consciousness of his characters: the so-called slowed scene. In the slowed scene, as she describes it, an author or a narrator unnaturally distends a moving or timed moment in a narrative in order to make the reader aware of the relativity of time and of the minutest delineations of a character's consciousness.

By contrast to Courtney, in "A Loose Democracy in the Skull: Characterology and Neuroscience," Julian Murphet accuses the form of the novel of integrating neuroscience at the level of content, "without allowing that science's representations of the psyche, tethered at all points to an organic sublime, to interfere with its [the novel's] insipid and reactionary formal 'business as usual.' " Murphet's polemical claim is that we should turn to film rather than to literature to understand the aesthetic possibilities of recent advances in cognitive neuroscience. Appealing to Gilles Deleuze *Cinema 2: The Time-Image*, he argues that film "*thinks* brain science immanently, according to its own protocols, and yields for us a working image of the brain as an object of thought." The polemical note that Murphet sounds in his essay only confirms to us that, even some two hundred years after Austen felt impelled in *Northanger Abbey* to defend the form of the novel against its detractors, we can perhaps never take the psychological value of literature for granted.

Notes

1   Jane Austen, *Northanger Abbey*, ed. Susan Fraiman (New York: Norton, 2004), 23.
2   Jonathan Gottschall and David Sloan Wilson, eds., *The Literary Animal: Evolution and the Nature of Narrative* (Evanston, IL: Northwestern University Press, 2005), 197.
3   Alan Richardson, *The Neural Sublime: Cognitive Theories and Romantic Texts* (Baltimore, MD: The Johns Hopkins University Press, 2010), x.
4   Lisa Zunshine, *Why We Read Fiction: Theory of Mind and the Novel* (Columbus, OH: Ohio State University Press, 2006), 6.
5   Richardson, *The Neural Sublime*, 82.
6   Richardson, *The Neural Sublime*, x.
7   "mindful, adj.," *OED Online*, March 2013, Oxford University Press, http://www.oed.com/view/Entry/118740?redirectedFrom=mindful.
8   Paul de Man, *The Resistance to Theory* (Minneapolis, MN: University of Minnesota Press, 1986), 11.
9   Alan Leslie, "Pretense and Representation: The Origins of 'Theory of Mind,'" *Psychological Review* 94, no. 4 (1987): 412.
10 Blakey Vermeule, *Why Do We Care about Literary Characters?* (Baltimore, MD: The Johns Hopkins University Press, 2010), 18.
11 Vermeule, *Why Do We Care about Literary Characters?*, 18.
12 Ziva Kunda, *Social Cognition: Making Sense of People* (Cambridge, MA: MIT Press, 1999), 7.
13 Vermeule, *Why Do We Care about Literary Characters?*, 48.
14 Vermeule, *Why Do We Care about Literary Characters?*, 62.
15 Mark Turner, *Reading Minds: The Study of English in the Age of Cognitive Science* (Princeton: Princeton University Press, 1991), 16.
16 Patrick Colm Hogan, *The Mind and Its Stories: Narrative Universals and Human Emotion* (Cambridge: Cambridge University Press, 2003), 4.
17 Hogan, *The Mind and Its Stories*, 4.

18 Mark Turner, *Death Is the Mother of Beauty: Mind, Metaphors, and Criticism* (Chicago: University of Chicago Press, 1987), 9–10. Other early field defining studies include, George Lakoff's *Women, Fire, and Dangerous Things: What Categories Reveal about the Mind* (Chicago: University of Chicago Press, 1987); Mark Johnson, *The Body in the Mind: The Bodily Basis of Meaning, Imagination, and Reason* (Chicago: University of Chicago Press, 1987); and George Lakoff and Mark Turner, *More than Cool Reason: A Field Guide to Poetic Metaphor* (Chicago: University of Chicago Press, 1989).
19 Turner, *Reading Minds*, vii.
20 Mark Turner, *The Literary Mind* (New York: Oxford University Press, 1996), 4–5.
21 Turner, *The Literary Mind*, 10.
22 Turner, *The Literary Mind*, 13.
23 Turner, *The Literary Mind*, 57.
24 Zunshine, *Why We Read Fiction*, 4.
25 Zunshine, *Why We Read Fiction*, 25.
26 Zunshine, *Why We Read Fiction*, 25.
27 Zunshine, *Why We Read Fiction*, 21.
28 Ellen Spolsky, preface to Alan Richardson and Ellen Spolsky, eds., *The Work of Fiction: Cognition, Culture, and Complexity* (Aldershot: Ashgate, 2004), vii.
29 Alan Richardson, *British Romanticism and the Science of Mind* (Cambridge: Cambridge University Press, 2001), 39–65.
30 See Pierre Jean George Cabanis, *On the Relations between the Physical and Moral Aspects of Man*, trans. Margaret Duggan Saidi, ed. George Mora (Baltimore, MD: The Johns Hopkins University Press, 1981), 2: 547–8.
31 Richardson, *British Romanticism and the Science of Mind*, 51.
32 Vanessa L. Ryan, *Thinking without Thinking in the Victorian Novel* (Baltimore, MD: The Johns Hopkins University Press, 2012), 1.
33 Vanessa L. Ryan, "Living in Duplicate: Victorian Science and Literature Today," *Critical Inquiry* 38 (Winter 2012): 416.
34 "aesthetics, n.," def. 1a, *OED Online*, March 2013, Oxford University Press, http://www.oed.com/view/Entry/293508?redirectedFrom=aesthetics.
35 William Flesch, *Comeuppance: Costly Signaling, Altruistic Punishment and Other Biological Components of Fiction* (Cambridge, MA: Harvard University Press, 2007), 7.
36 "prosocial, adj.," *OED Online*, March 2013, Oxford University Press. http://www.oed.com/view/Entry/152981?redirectedFrom=prosocial.
37 Flesch, *Comeuppance*, 155.
38 Flesch, *Comeuppance*, 156.
39 Flesch, *Comeuppance*, 182.
40 M. M. Bakhtin, *Toward a Philosophy of the Act*, trans. Vadim Liapunov (Austin, TX: University of Texas Press, 1999), 62.
41 Gottschall and Wilson, eds., *The Literary Animal*, 197.
42 Alberto Piazza, "Evolution at Close Range," afterword to *Graphs Maps, Trees: Abstract Models for Literary History* by Franco Moretti (London: Verso, 2007), 95–6.
43 Anne Harrington, *Medicine, Mind, and the Double Brain: A Study in Nineteenth-Century Thought and Culture* (Princeton: Princeton University Press, 1987), 4.

Part One

Theoria

1

Psychology and Literature: Mindful Close Reading

Brian Boyd

Of all the sciences, psychology lies closest to literature. Literature in the broad sense, from epics to comics, from Homer to Homer Simpson, links to psychology because it both represents and appeals to human minds. Writers write precisely in order to *appeal* to human minds, and their main way to do so is to *represent* human minds engaging with the world, and especially with one another. Their works are thought experiments not only with human experience, with partly typical, partly unique personalities in situations partly typical and partly unique, but also with the anticipated responses readers, themselves partly typical, partly unique, will have to their accounts of particular imagined experiences. Writers are intuitive experimenters, at their best highly aware of readers' expectations of worlds, words and minds, and able to devise new experimental set-ups, new combinations of worlds, words and minds, to secure the attention, trigger the imagination and stir the emotions of readers in partly typical, partly unique new ways.

In the mid-twentieth century, when behaviorism and Freudianism dominated psychology, rats running mazes and pigeons pecking levers appeared to offer little for literature, and Oedipus complexes and death wishes paid little heed to scientific method. In the last 30 years, however, psychology has begun to investigate aspects of mind crucial to literary studies: emotions, including the social emotions; imagination; memory, including the memory of things more humanly meaningful than strings of arbitrary symbols; our understanding of other minds and our own; metarepresentation, our ability to track, shift and multiply perspectives; and much, much more.

Vladimir Nabokov (VN) has been literature's most gleefully recidivist anti-Freudian ("All my books should be stamped Freudians, Keep Out"), and no fan of behaviorism.[1] Nevertheless he once dismissed as "preposterous" Alain Robbe-Grillet's claims that his novels eliminated psychology: "the shifts of levels, the interpenetration of successive impressions and so forth belong of course to psychology—psychology at its best."[2] Later, when an interviewer reminded him of comment about Robbe-Grillet and asked, "Are *you* a psychological novelist?," he replied, "All novelists of any worth are psychological novelists."[3] Since we can safely assume that, to put it mildly, Nabokov did not consider himself a novelist of no worth, we can only conclude he considered himself a psychological novelist.

Psychology fills vastly wider channels now than when Nabokov, in the mid-twentieth century, refused to sail the narrow course between the Scylla of behaviorism and the Charybdis of Freud. It deals with what matters to writers, readers and others, with memory and imagination, emotion and thought, art and our attunement to one another, and it can do so in wider time frames and with tighter spatial focus than even a Nabokov could imagine. It therefore seems high time to revise or refresh our sense of the relations between literature and psychology. I want to consider Nabokov as a serious (and of course a playful) psychologist, partly because he's the author I know best, partly because he wrote more major masterpieces than any other writer over the last century, partly because he drew more intense portraits of psychological extremes, from Luzhin and Hermann to Humbert, Kinbote and beyond, than anyone else over the last century and partly because I think he had the keenest eye for the psychology of readers.

I offer no definitive chart of the terrain, just prompts to exploration. We could move in many directions, a fact itself a tribute to Nabokov's range and strengths as a psychologist: the writer as a reader of others and himself, as an observer and an introspector; in relation to the psychology he knew from fiction (Dostoevsky, Tolstoy, Proust, Joyce) and from nonfiction, from professional psychology (William James, Freud, Havelock Ellis); as a psychological theorist, in his fiction and nonfiction; and as a psychological "experimenter" in his fiction, running thought experiments on the characters he creates and on the effects he produces in readers. We could consider him in relation to the different branches of psychology, in his own time and now (abnormal, clinical, comparative, cognitive, developmental, evolutionary, existential, individual, personality, positive, social); in relation to different functions of mind, whose limits he happily tests (attention, perception, emotion, memory, imagination and pure cognition: knowing, understanding, inferring, discovering, solving, inventing); in relation to different states of consciousness (waking, sleeping, dreaming, delirium, reverie, inspiration, near-death experience, death experience). And we could consider what recent psychology explains in ways that Nabokov foresaw or all but ruled impossible to explain.

He used to tell his students: "the whole history of literary fiction as an evolutionary process may be said to be a gradual probing of deeper and deeper layers of life...the artist, like the scientist, in the process of evolution of art and science, is always casting around, understanding a little more than his predecessor, penetrating further with a keener and more brilliant eye."[4] As a young boy he desperately wanted to discover new species of butterflies, and he became no less avid as a writer for new finds in literature: not only in words, details and images, in structures and tactics, but also in psychology.

He declared, "Next to the right to create, the right to criticize is the richest gift that liberty of thought and speech can offer." He himself liked to criticize, utterly undaunted by reputation.[5] He especially liked to correct competitors. He was fascinated by psychological extremes, as his fiction testifies, but he deplored Dostoevsky's "monotonous dealings with persons suffering from pre-Freudian complexes."[6] He admired Tolstoy's psychological insight, and his gift of rendering experience through his characters, but while he availed himself of Tolstoy's techniques for scenic immersion, he sought to stress also, almost always, the capacity of our minds, whether as characters or readers, to transcend the scenes in which we find ourselves. Nabokov valued Proust's capacity to move outside the moment, especially in untrammelled recollection, but he allotted more space to the constraints of the ongoing scene than Proust. In *The Gift* he gives Fyodor some of Proust's frustration with the present, but he also locates the amplitude and fulfillment even here, for those who care to look. And where Proust emphasizes spontaneous, involuntary memory in restoring our links with our past, Nabokov stresses memory as directed by conscious search. He revered Joyce's verbal accuracy, his precisions and nuances, but he also considered that his stream-of-consciousness technique gave "too much verbal body to thoughts."[7] The medium of thought for Nabokov was not primarily linguistic: "We think not in words but in shadows of words."[8] Thought was for him also multisensory, and, at its best, multilevel. As cognitive psychologists would now say, using a computing analogy foreign to Nabokov, consciousness is parallel (indeed, "massively parallel"), rather than serial, so it cannot translate readily into the emphatically serial mode that a single channel of purely verbal stream of consciousness can provide.

Famously, Nabokov could not resist deriding Freud. And for good reason: Freud's ideas were enormously influential, especially in Nabokov's American years, but his claims hollow. Nobel laureate Peter Medawar, perhaps the greatest of science essayists, declared, in terms akin to Nabokov's, that Freudianism was "the most stupendous intellectual confidence trick of the twentieth century."[9] Nabokov saw the intellectual vacuity of Freudian theory and its pervasiveness in the popular and the professional imagination. He thought it corrupted intellectual standards,[10] infringed on personal freedom,[11] undermined the ethics of personal responsibility,[12] destroyed literary sensitivity[13] and distorted the real nature of childhood attachment to parents—as have all been amply confirmed by modern developmental psychology.[14]

Nabokov treasured critical independence, but he did not merely resist others: he happily imbibed as much psychology as he could from the art of Tolstoy and the science of William James. He also looked for himself. He was a brilliant observer not only of the visual and natural worlds but also of the world of human nature. We can see his acute eye for individuals throughout his letters and memoirs, and in others' recollections of *his* sense of *them*, even many years later, and of course in his fiction.

Let's turn there now: to the fiction, to one short passage from his longest, richest, raunchiest, most romantic and most comic novel, *Ada*, published in 1969, a passage a mere 67 words out of almost 600 pages. I want to interweave the psychology Nabokov observes and experiments with in his fiction and the modern psychology about whose possibilities he was so skeptical. I also want to show just how much psychological *work* the play of fiction can involve, or how much Nabokov's swift shifts *make* it involve.

Ada takes place on a parallel world that matches ours in geography but not quite in history, so that there are titled nobility, and a mix of English, French and Russian widely spoken, in North America, and in the 1880s swimming pools and Hollywood movies and petrol-powered flying carpets and a ban on electricity but certainly not on sex.

In *Ada*'s fourth chapter, we see 14-year-old Van Veen, the hero and narrator, at his first school, the elite public school (in the British sense) Riverlane; and we see him at for the first time, with the young helper at the corner shop, a "fat little wench" whom another boy at the school has found can be had for "a Russian green dollar." The first time, Van spills "on the welcome mat what she would gladly have helped him take indoors." But "at the next mating party" he "really beg[a]n to enjoy her . . . soft sweet grip and hearty joggle," and by the end of term he has enjoyed "forty convulsions" with her. The chapter ends with Van leaving to spend the summer at Ardis, with his "aunt" Marina, where he will fall in love with, and become the passionate lover of, his 12-year-old "cousin," Ada, in fact his sister. Here's our sample:

> In an elegant first-class compartment, with one's gloved hand in the velvet side-loop, one feels very much a man of the world as one surveys the capable landscape capably skimming by. And every now and then the passenger's roving eyes paused for a moment as he listened inwardly to a nether itch, which he supposed to be (correctly, thank Log) only a minor irritation of the epithelium.[15]

Nabokov writes fiction, not psychology, but this typically exceptional passage depends on, depicts and appeals to psychology. Passages like this, and psychology, have much to offer each other.

The "elegant first-class apartment" and the "gloved hand" make the most of a cognitive bias, the contrast effect: our minds respond to things much more emphatically in the presence of a contrast. Through the suddenness of the switch, Van and VN contrast the tawdriness of the "fat wench" possessed "among crates and sacks at the back of the shop" with the opulence of the train and Van's fine dress (I.4: 33).

"One feels very much a man of the world": we can all recall and imagine sudden moments of self-satisfaction, especially at points where life clambers up a level in childhood and adolescence. We can unpack this several ways.

Life-history theory in recent evolutionary biology focuses on species-typical patterns of development and their consequences across species[16]—although before life-history theory showed our human life patterns in a comparative light, we knew the importance of, and the unique delay in, the onset of human sexual activity. Psychology analyses this long neglected emotion. Now it explores even the social emotions, like those associated with status. Taking a step up on the staircase of life marks a rise in status, and recognizing that boosts levels of the neurotransmitter serotonin in the brain. This rise in turn, past puberty, raises the inclination to sexual activity—as in Van, on his way to Ardis; he wakes up there early the next morning to a "savage sense of opportune licence" (I.7: 48) when, in his skimpy bathrobe, he encounters the 19-year-old servant Blanche.

In "*one's* gloved hand . . . *one* feels very much a man of the world," Van invites us to a common human emotion through the generalizing pronoun "one." We take this appeal to shared experience for granted, and recognizing shared experience and wanting to are at the basis of fiction, and the social life fiction feeds on. But psychology should do more than just take these facts for granted: it should help us explain them.

Mirror neurons, discovered in the 1990s, fire in the same part of my motor area that would be activated if, say, I grasped something, when I merely *see* someone else grasping. This unforeseen component of neural architecture, especially elaborate in humans, helps us to understand and to learn from others, and perhaps to cooperate or compete with them.[17] We also have from infancy a far stronger motivation to share experience than have other animals, even chimpanzees: think of an infant's compulsion to point, to draw others' attention to something just possibly of interest. This heightened motivation to share experience seems to lay the foundation for human ultrasociality.[18]

We understand the actions of others when we see them, by partially reactivating our own experience of such actions, stored in our memories.[19] But more than that, we also attune ourselves to others' actions and empathize with them, unless we perceive them as somehow opposed to us. Over the last 15 years, psychology has begun to study the remarkably swift and precise ways we attune ourselves rapidly, and often unconsciously, to what we see in others.[20] Van and Nabokov appeal here to our shared experience, to our recollection of our pride in reaching a new stage in life, like learning to walk, starting school or, here, mastering the rudiments of sex.

Research in grounded cognition in recent neuroscience shows that thought is not primarily linguistic, as many had supposed, but multimodal, partially reactivating relevant multimodal experiences in our past, involving multiple senses, emotions and associations.[21] Just as seeing someone grasp something activates mirror neurons, even hearing the *word* "grasp" activates the appropriate area of the motor cortex.[22] Our brains encode multimodal memories of objects and actions, and these are partially reactivated as percepts or concepts come into consciousness.

Nabokov rightly stressed that imagination is rooted in memory: indeed, that was the very point of entitling his autobiography *Speak, Memory*. Since the early 1930s it has been known that we store episodic memories, memories of our experiences, as *gist*, as reduced summaries of the core sense or feel of situations, rather than all their surface details.[23] Our stored knowledge of past situations and stimuli allows us later, as it were, to unzip the compressed file of a memory and to reconstruct an image of the original. Recent evidence shows that memory's compression into gist evolved not only to save space on our mental hard drives but also to make it easier to activate relevant memories and to recombine them with present perception or imagination of future or other states not experienced.[24] If memories were stored in detail and the details had to match exactly, mental search would be slow and rarely successful. But once memories have been compressed into gist, many memories can be appropriate enough to a new situation or a new imaginative moment to be partially reactivated, as it were, according to their common mental keywords or search terms.

Minds evolved to deal with immediate experience, and although human minds can now specialize in abstract thought or free-roaming imagination, we still respond most vividly and multimodally to immediate experience. For that reason more of our multimodal memories can be activated by language that prompts us to re-create experience, as fiction does, rather than more abstract, less personal, less sequential texts.[25] Nabokov was right to insist on the power of the specific in art to stimulate the imagination. Here, he and Van appeal to the groundedness of cognition through their use of details like the velvet side-loop and the gloved hand to activate our multimodal memories of the look and feel of gloves, velvet and side-loops in trains or cars.

So far I have stressed how these first few words appeal to what we share in experience. But despite its appeal to what we share, the passage also implies different kinds of distance. There's the distance between Van as adult narrator—as by this stage we already know him to be, despite his third-person presentation of young Van as character—and Van as a 14-year-old feeling himself "very much a man of the world." The word "one," which generalizes from his situation, as if adolescent Van can now grandly sum up a new truth he has reached from his lofty vantage point of experience, can only seem absurd to Van many years later, after much more sexual exploration than a few furtive convulsions with a shopgirl. As a nonagenarian narrator, he can see a 14-year-old's pride in his experience as proof of his past self's relative innocence. But that distance between Van as character and Van as narrator *also* sets up something for us to share with Van as narrator: we have all reflected ironically later in life upon satisfactions that had seemed robust when we first felt them. We see here how memory compression into gist may help us retrieve a whiff of similar episodes we have experienced or witnessed.

But apart from this multiple appeal to what we share, Van and especially Nabokov behind him also know that his way of wording his recollection will also establish a different kind of distance between Van and his readers. Many readers never travel first class, and few males, however "elegant," now wear gloves on a summer's day. Van, in his "elegant first-class compartment," with his gloved hand in a velvet loop, has a strong element of dandified class-consciousness mingling with his pride at being "very much a man of the world." The generalizing pronoun "one," which on one level invites readers to share a common experience, on another also discloses Van's intellectual pride in arriving at the new generalization, and his foppish indulgence in his sense of superiority to others. The upper-class English use of "one" applied to oneself, seen as a mark of high-toned speech, reinforces the snobbery that amplifies Van's self-satisfaction and complicates the appeal to our identification with him—although we too will recognize moments when we have felt superior to others.

We're not far into this passage yet. Let's move on one clause: "one feels very much a man of the world as one surveys the capable landscape capably skimming by." Here Van and VN comically evoke our human tendency to see the world through the tinted lenses of our emotions, or even to project our emotions onto what we perceive. "Capable" applies legitimately only to agents; Van and VN absurdly apply it to the landscape, and then, adverbially, to the way the landscape skims past Van's train window. Narrator and author know the comedy of twice misapplying this term, which suits only Van's sense of himself, to the landscape. Nabokov suddenly confronts us in this surprising, vivid, ironic, amusing way with an instance of our human tendency to project our emotions onto our world. Psychologists study this kind of projection through priming, in terms, say, of what we notice or think of first if we have been primed with (just exposed to) either positive or negative images. Yet despite the comedy of Van's emotional "priming," Nabokov and Van also appeal to our imaginations through our memories, in that landscape "skimming by."

We're hurtling along now, at the last sentence already: "And every now and then the passenger's roving eyes paused for a moment as he listened inwardly to a nether itch." Van and VN activate our own multimodal memories and awareness: our proprioceptive sense (our awareness, from inside, of our body positions and sensations) of the ways our eyes move as we attend to an inner discomfort or pain, and our memories of others glancing sideways in thought or hurt. The surprise and yet the naturalness of the metaphor, *"listened* to a nether *itch,"* trigger another multimodal activation (roving eyes, inner ears, touch) of multimodal memories of monitoring our inner sensations—and perhaps arise out of the synesthesia that Nabokov rendered so exactly in *Speak, Memory* that his description has become a classic of synesthesia studies.

But Van, attending to this nether itch, supposed it "to be (correctly, thank Log) only a minor irritation of the epithelium." We are invited to infer that Van has a few momentary worries about a venereal disease he could have contracted from the "fubsy pig-pink whorelet" at the shop near his school, and that some time later, when the itch does not recur, he confirms to himself that there was no cause for alarm (I.4: 33). Nabokov stresses the importance in the development of modern fiction of writers' learning to trust readers' powers of inference, because we prefer to imagine actively, to see in our mind's eye much more than what the page spells out explicitly. We intuit Van's concern through our familiarity with his context: because we now share that common ground with him, things *don't* have to be spelled out for us to infer the whole situation, and that successful inference further confirms our sense of the ground we share with Van.

Van's unfounded fears of venereal disease may add another note of comedy, but they also prepare us structurally both for (1) the romance of love and sex with Ada at Ardis, where Van's train is taking him, a romance highlighted by contrast with the schoolboy lineup for paid sex, and for (2) the tragic aspects of Ardis as sexual paradise, not least in the venereal disease that, through Blanche, enfolds itself into the romantic myth of Van and Ada at Ardis.

This brief paragraph, immediately accessible, immediately evocative of multiple senses, emotions and memories, typically embodies a multiple awareness: of Van at the age of 14 on the train; of him a little later that summer, when he can feel sure he has not caught a venereal disease; of him as a much older narrator recalling his young self and inviting his readers to sense what we share with him, but also to recognize young Van's cocky sense of what makes him privileged and apart. As narrator Van evokes and reactivates the experience, yet he also sees himself from outside: "And every now and then *the passenger's* roving eyes paused." Psychologists distinguish between a field and an observer relationship to an experience or a memory: an inner view, as if amid the field of experience, and an outer view, observing oneself as if from outside. Ordinarily we experience life in the "field" condition; but precisely because we can compress memories into "gist," we can also afterwards recall our experience as if from the outside, as in the radical recombinations of our memories in our dreams. As we read, we also tend to toggle or glide between imagining ourselves within the experience of a focal character—Van seeing the landscape swimming by, or listening to his nether itch—and an outer view—seeing Van with gloved hand in the velvet side-loop.

A number of times in his works Nabokov makes explicit one of his personal psychological observations, about the casual, insignificant impressions suddenly locked into permanent memory when they happen to be caught in the forehaze of a major change. Here he does not refer explicitly to the forehaze, but that's what he portrays: Van is unaware that the visit to his "cousins," from which he does not expect much, will transform his life—and of course will cast an entirely different light on his pride in being a man of the world merely because of a few paid ejaculations with a fubsy whorelet.

As re-readers we can be highly conscious of the structural role of this scene, of the contrasts between Van in the shop with the pig-pink wench and, at Ardis, in passionate embrace with Ada; or between the cheap whorelet and the fancy whores he later resorts to when away from Ada, or when he flees Ardis, appalled at her infidelity; or between the whorelet and the comically fleeting anxiety about venereal disease that she causes Van and the venereal disease that Blanche, the prime celebrant of the romance of the Veen venery at Ardis, tragically passes on to her child.

Ada's complexities and charms invite multiple re-readings, and re-readers can sense all these multiple contexts surrounding the immediate scene. We also seek to explain anything unaccounted for by its local or larger context. I had laughed at the "capable landscape capably skimming by" but never felt it problematic. But a circle of Nabokov scholars who meet in Kyoto every month to read more of *Ada* recognized something in the conjunction of "capable" and "landscape" that anyone who knows the English eighteenth century well should recognize. Van and VN allude here to the greatest of English landscape architects, Lancelot "Capability" Brown (1716–83), particularly appropriate since Ardis, where Van is headed, is an eighteenth-century estate, whose grounds display the kind of gentle naturalness Brown introduced, between earlier English formality and later Romantic preferences for the wild and sublime. I find the fact that Van and VN smuggled this allusion in, and that I didn't see it, but that it was eminently discoverable, very funny. Nabokov loves the psychology of attention, of memory, of discovery and of humor.

On re-reading we can be aware not only of what we know now but also of what we were being led to expect or being mentally and emotionally prepared for on a first reading, or what the author has devised to work one way for first-time readers and more richly still for re-readers. We are immediately aware here of Van as 14-year-old character, and less vividly but still consciously aware of him as mature narrator looking back with amusement but also with pleasure at his young self, and of the intricate combination of appeal to shared experience and proud Van's sense of his own specialness. And after discovering the hidden as well as the overt joke in "capable," we can also recall our discovery of the allusion, and our state of innocence before the discovery. We can be aware of multiple times and levels: Van (1) here in June 1884, (2) a few weeks later, when he can be sure he has picked up no disease from the shopgirl, (3) recalling this in later life (4) and at the moment of writing this; (5) Nabokov behind Van Veen and, then, readers, (6) when reading it for the first time, and recalling train journeys we have taken or stages in life we have triumphantly reached, (7) re-reading, and placing the scene in relation to Ardis and even (8) expert enough to see the landscape architect hidden in the landscape.

Think how different this is from our experience as readers of Tolstoy characters on trains. In Tolstoy we seem to enter immediately into the minds and experience of the focal characters, because he conjures up all the relevant elements of the situation, the physical presence, the personalities of those involved, the interactions between them and relevant information about their past relations. Our imaginations seem contained entirely within the scene: we feel ourselves within the space the characters occupy. But Nabokov prefers to evoke and exercise our recognition of the manifold awareness of consciousness: the different Vans here, character now, character slightly later, narrator much later, felt from inside or seen from outside; the different appeals to recognize what we share and what holds us at a distance from Van; the awareness on re-reading of the appeal to first-time readers and to our accumulated knowledge of the rest of the book on re-reading, or our awareness of specific puzzles we can now recognize as puzzles because we have seen their solutions. Tolstoy also builds up scenes gradually, coordinating characters' actions and perceptions. Nabokov speeds us into his railroad scene without warning, without explicitness (only "first-class compartment," "skimming" and "passenger" specify the situation), without lingering (the scene ends here) and without spelling out the when or where until we infer them at the beginning of the next chapter. He has confidence in our pleasure in imagination, inference and orientation.

Clinical, comparative, developmental, evolutionary and social psychology over the past 30 years have devoted a great deal of attention to Theory of Mind and to metarepresentation.[26] Theory of Mind is our capacity to understand other minds, or our own, in terms of desires, intentions and beliefs, and metarepresentation, our capacity to understand representations *as* representations, including the representations other minds may have of a scene.[27] While some intelligent social animals appear to understand others of their kind in terms of desires and intentions, only humans have a clear understanding of others in terms also of what others *believe*, and factor beliefs effortlessly into their inferential systems. By adolescence, we can readily understand four degrees of intentionality: A's thoughts about B's thoughts about C's thoughts about D's. As adults, we start to make errors with, but we can still manage, five or six degrees: our thoughts as re-readers, say, about our thoughts as first-time readers about Nabokov's thoughts about Van the narrator's thoughts about Van's thoughts at Ardis about Van's thoughts on the train to Ardis.

Nabokov finds fascinating the multilevel awareness of the mind, and worked to develop it in himself and in his readers and re-readers—as he discusses most explicitly through Fyodor in *The Gift*, his greatest Russian novel, written in the 1930s. Fyodor deliberately sets himself exercises of observing, transforming, recollecting and imagining through the eyes of others. Frustrated at earning his keep by foreign language instruction, he thinks, "What he should be really teaching was the mysterious thing which he alone—out of ten thousand, a hundred thousand, perhaps even a million men—knew how to teach: for example—multilevel thinking"—which he then goes on to define.[28] The very idea of training the brain in this way, as Fyodor does for himself, as he imagines teaching others, as he learns to do for his readers, as Nabokov learned over many years to do for *his* readers, fits with neuroscience's recent understanding of brain plasticity, the degree to which the brain can be retrained, fine-tuned and redeployed.[29]

Play has been nature's main way of making the most of brain plasticity. It fine-tunes animals in key behaviors like flight and fight—hence the evolved pleasure animals take in chasing and frisking, and in rough-and-tumble fighting, which is nature's way of ensuring they'll engage in this training again and again. In *On the Origin of Stories* I look at art as a development of play, and as a way of fine-tuning minds in particular cognitive modes that matter to us: in the case of fiction, our expertise in social cognition, in Theory of Mind, in perspective-taking, in holding multiple perspectives in mind at once.[30] As I made that case, I was not thinking of Nabokov, but he takes this kind of training of the mind—perception, cognition, emotion, memory and imagination—more seriously, and more playfully, than any other writer.

I have used one brief and superficially straightforward example from *Ada* to show how much psychological work we naturally do when we read fiction, and perhaps especially when we read Nabokov's fiction, and how much light psychology can now throw on what we do naturally when we read fiction.

Literature's aims differ considerably from those of research psychology. Nevertheless literature *draws on* human intuitive psychology (itself also a subject in recent psychology), and *exercises* our psychological capacities. Literature aims to understand human minds only to the degree it seeks to move human minds. It may move readers' minds, in part, by showing with new accuracy or vividness, or at least with fresh particulars, how fictional minds move, and by showing in new ways how freely readers' minds can move, given the right prompts. Psychology too wants to understand minds, both simply for the satisfaction of knowing and also in order to make the most of minds, to limit mental damage or to extend mental benefits. It uses the experimental method. We can see fictions too as thought experiments, experiments about how characters feel, think and behave, and about how readers feel, think and behave, and how they can *learn* to think more imaginatively, feel more sympathetically and act more sensitively. Fictions are experiments whose results will not be systematically collected and peer-reviewed—and then perhaps read by a few psychologists—but will be felt vividly by a wide range of readers.

Nabokov thinks that at their best art and science meet on a high ridge. Psychology, after wandering along wrong paths to Freud Falls or the Behaviorist Barrens, has just emerged onto a ridge that affords rich vistas. Nabokov may have doubted psychology could crest this particular ridge, but I think he has met science there.

Notes

1 Vladimir Nabokov, *Bend Sinister* (New York: Time-Life, 1964), xviii.
2 Vladimir Nabokov, *Strong Opinions* (New York: McGraw-Hill, 1973), 80.
3 Nabokov, *Strong Opinions*, 174.
4 Vladimir Nabokov, *Lectures on Russian Literature*, ed. Fredson Bowers (New York: Harcourt Brace Jovanovich/Bruccoli Clark, 1981), 164–5.
5 Nabokov, *Lectures on Russian Literature*, ii.
6 Nabokov, *Lectures on Russian Literature*, 104.
7 Nabokov, *Strong Opinions*, 30.
8 Nabokov, *Strong Opinions*, 30.
9 Peter Medawar, *Pluto's Republic* (Oxford: Oxford University Press, 1982), 140.
10 Nabokov, *Strong Opinions*, 47.

11 Vladimir Nabokov, "Interview with Anne Guérin," *L'Express*, 26 January 1961.

12 Nabokov, *Strong Opinions*, 116.

13 Nabokov, "Interview."

14 See the work of Bowlby and Hrdy: John Bowlby, *Attachment*, vol. 1, *Attachment and Loss* (Harmondsworth: Penguin, 1971); Sarah Blaffer Hrdy, *Mothers and Others: The Evolutionary Origins of Mutual Understanding* (Cambridge, MA: Belknap Press of Harvard University Press, 2009).

15 Vladimir Nabokov, *Ada or Ardor: A Family Chronicle* (New York: McGraw-Hill, 1969), I.4: 33.

16 See Michael Muehlenbein and Mark V. Flinn, "Patterns and Processes of Human Life History Evolution," in *Mechanisms of Life History Evolution: The Genetics and Physiology of Life History Traits and Trade-offs*, eds. Thomas Flatt and Andreas Heyland (New York: Oxford University Press, 2011), 153–68.

17 Marco Iacoboni, *Mirroring People: The New Science of How We Connect with Others* (New York: Farrar, Straus and Giroux, 2008).

18 Michael Tomasello, *Origins of Human Communication* (Cambridge, MA: MIT Press, 2008).

19 Lawrence W. Barsalou, "Grounded Cognition," *Annual Review of Psychology* 59 (2008): 617–45.

20 Daniel Goleman, *Social Intelligence: The New Science of Human Relationships* (New York: Bantam, 2006).

21 Barsalou, "Grounded Cognition."

22 Lisa Aziz-Zadeh and others, "Congruent Embodied Representations for Visually Presented Actions and Linguistic Phrases Describing Actions," *Current Biology* 16, no. 19 (2006): 1818–23.

23 Frederic C. Bartlett, *Remembering: A Study in Experimental and Social Psychology* (Cambridge: Cambridge University Press, 1932).

24 Daniel L. Schacter and Donna Rose Addis, "The Cognitive Neuroscience of Constructive Memory: Remembering the Past and Imagining the Future," *Philosophical Transactions of the Royal Society B* 362 (2007): 773–86.

25 John Tooby and Leda Cosmides, "Does Beauty Build Adapted Minds? Toward an Evolutionary Theory of Aesthetics, Fiction and the Arts," *SubStance* 30, nos. 1–2 (2001): 6–27.

26 Rebecca Saxe and Simon Baron-Cohen, *Theory of Mind* (Hove: Psychology Press, 2006; repr. 2007); Dan Sperber, "Metarepresentations in an Evolutionary Perspective," in *Metarepresentations: A Multidisciplinary Perspective*, ed. D. Sperber (Oxford: Oxford University Press 2000), 117–38.

27 I first proposed the centrality of Theory of Mind to fiction in Brian Boyd, "The Origin of Stories: *Horton Hears a Who*," *Philosophy and Literature* 25, no. 2 (2001): 197–214. Lisa Zunshine also makes Theory of Mind central to fiction in *Why We Read Fiction: Theory of Mind and the Novel* (Columbus, OH: Ohio State University Press, 2006), but drew on a very limited portion of the scientific research and misinterpreted the fictional examples, as I note in "Fiction and Theory of Mind," *Philosophy and Literature* 30, no. 2 (2006): 571–81. Zunshine replied in 2007, as did I in turn. See Lisa Zunshine, "Fiction and Theory of Mind: An Exchange," *Philosophy and Literature* 31 (2007): 189–95. See also the sophisticated work of Maja Djikic: Maja Djikic and others, "On Being Moved by Art: How Reading Fiction Transforms the Self," *Creativity Research Journal* 21 (2009): 24–9.

28 Vladimir Nabokov, *The Gift*, trans. Michael Scammell with the author (New York: Putnam, 1963), 176.

29 Norman Doidge, *The Brain That Changes Itself: Stories of Personal Triumph from the Frontiers of Brain Science* (New York: Penguin, 2007).

30 Brian Boyd, *On the Origin of Stories: Evolution, Cognition, and Fiction* (Cambridge, MA: Belknap Press of Harvard University Press, 2009).

2

Vitalism and Theoria

Claire Colebrook

The very notion of mindful aesthetics pulls in two directions. On the one hand, aesthetics provides a path beyond mind, if mind is taken in a Cartesian, cognitive or intellectualist sense. In a tradition that goes back at least as far as Gilbert Ryle's criticism of mind as a "ghost in the machine" and that draws on Romantic criticisms of the reifying intellect, it is claimed that the poetic and attuned comportment to the world is primary.[1] In the beginning is the engaged feeling or lived relation with the world, *from which* the logical and calculative intellect emerges. It is a mistake to ask how we come to know the world, for we are always already in the world—feeling, acting, creating, desiring and imagining—with knowledge, doubt and the notion of the subject being late (possibly pernicious) add-ons. This notion of a proper connectedness has come to the fore recently in philosophical and neuroscientific appeals to the Buddhist notion of mindfulness, the most significant being Varela, Thompson and Rosch's supposedly Heideggerian claim for mindfulness and the freedom of being selfless:

> The point of mindfulness/awareness is not to disengage the mind from the phenomenal world; it is to enable the mind to be fully present in the world. The goal is not to avoid action but to be fully present in one's actions, so that one's behaviour becomes more positive and aware.... To be progressively more free is to be sensitive to the conditions and genuine possibilities of some present situation and to be able to act in an open manner that is not conditioned by grasping and egoistic volitions.[2]

Mindful aesthetics would be a retrieval of this responsive, affective, embodied and felt engagement with the world, and would be in line with a general turn to mindfulness (in the sense of care or broadened awareness) that is critical of mind (in the sense of the separate subject or intellect).

In this chapter, I suggest that we might ask about the ways in which aesthetics today precludes any mindful vanquishing of mind: what if there were something in the very tendency of what has come to be known as art that intensified the Cartesian separation of mind? I would begin by parsing the opposing tendencies of mindful aesthetics by pointing out two directions in current work on art and its relation to mind or the intellect.

In a number of fields—cognitive archaeology, neuroscience, evolutionary psychology and various appropriations of Darwinism by the humanities—a certain reversal has taken place: aesthetics is not, as it was for Kant, a way of thinking about a specifically subjective capacity for *form* (where form is a synthesizing activity that gives our world and what we intuit order). Rather, there is something like a forming tendency (such as our capacity to discern patterns or our capacity to bond with other living beings by the use of common refrains or rituals), and it is from that broader living potential shared by humans and nonhumans that formal language and mind emerges. Works of art, far from indicating a capacity to think form as such, as a purely subjective indication of our supersensible potential for abstraction and synthesis, would be an intimation of what the human intellect shares with all life. With mindful aesthetics, form is not that which we impose upon the world; the world itself gives form, and it is from that general forming or mindful mode of the world that thinking and human minds become possible. Consider this contrast: for Kant and post-Kantian aesthetics it is art that discloses a gap or separation from the world. We cannot know the world as it is in itself, and the work of art (or our experience of nature as ordered and capable of being studied as lawful and regular) indicates that in addition to the world in itself there is something like judgment, or a way of experiencing the world as it would be for a subject in general.[3] This is not the actual subject but an imagined and projected "any subject whatever." By contrast, recent reactions against this formal and subjective aesthetics claim that art is not distant from the world but indicates our emergence from the world. V. S. Ramachandran's principles of aesthetics explain art by referring to the human brain's capacities to discern patterns or tendencies that would be crucial for survival; if we admire a sculpture of female form, it is because it intensifies qualities in the female body that would serve our genetic survival, or if we find patterns pleasing, this is because the brain is fitted to solve problems and discern order.[4] For Stephen Mithen, the human capacity for music does not indicate some power of humans to enjoy the purely formal relations among sounds, evidencing their status as subjects freed from bodily interest; on the contrary, in the beginning—for all animals—sound served to create social bonds and unifying affects, and it is from there that language and human cognition emerged.[5] From within the domain of what is left of literary studies, Brian Boyd has suggested that narrative is a survival strategy, and in so doing he has shifted the focus of literary studies away from the 1980s' attention to nonsemantic properties (the sounds or material inscriptions of text) toward a consideration of literature in a broader field of cognition.[6] If "text" in the 1980s, after theory, was a way of thinking about what Derrida referred to as an "untamed genesis,"[7] or what de Man described as materiality (a mindless rogue force beyond all synthesizing and organic life), then today textuality and aesthetics have an opposing function.[8] If there are art works it is supposedly because life *extends* itself into narrative and musical systems; we can always intuit life's purposiveness by looking at art objects as evidence of life's (not the subject's) forming power. If there are subjects it is because of an artfulness in life, and not vice versa.

One way of thinking about art in the twenty-first century would be to see aesthetics today as retrieving or turning back to mindful life, where mind is not some distinct privilege of the human species. This constant, shrill and insistent sense of returning mind to life, and defining life as always already tending toward art, creativity, communication and mindfulness, occurs just as evidence for art's detachment from life and life's potentiality for destructive incommunicability presents itself. Why now in the era of the anthropocene would we be insisting on mindful aesthetics (where mind signals a mode of empathetic concern and connectedness), when a certain mode of mind today appears as a distinctly human event, and where what has come to be known as aesthetics or the production of works of art indicates a certain "a priori deadness"?[9] We can see this in both "high" art and popular culture. Are we not becoming less and less capable of reading the archive of artworks that supposedly extends and maximizes life? Are not works as various as *Titus Andronicus, American Psycho* and *ITSOFOMO* more and more demanding and less and less capable of circulation and consumption? Does not the concrete matter of distinct artworks and their untranslatability indicate a divergence rather than a mindfulness of life? Far from life being some interconnected, self-furthering, self-creating and communicating whole, and far from this expressive and living expansiveness extending itself via art, it might be better to view art as an indication of life's tendency toward splitting and diremption?[10] More specifically, today the widespread production of postapocalyptic film and literature is anything but adaptive and beneficial to life's furtherance: insofar as these works represent the world's end they do so by myopically remaining within familial narrative frames (such as Cormac McCarthy's *The Road*, where the father and son wander a post-nuclear-family landscape, mourning the mother's death, finding a hint of redemption with the concluding scene of a possible renewal of family life). Films such as *Children of Men, The Day the Earth Stood Still* and *Contagion* entertain the possibility of an end and destructiveness of life, and yet also present human and remarkably romantic and personal resolutions to the crisis of life. The disaster film genre provides a managerial strategy for dealing with impending trauma, providing a solution in advance for any posed threat. At the same time, there is something that is mindless and countervital in the aesthetic, a potential in the art object for detachment, and this is so in the broadest definition of art. Either art is somehow at odds with the shared sense and meaning we make of the world, providing some resistance to the easy management of "the lived," or art, in granting meaning to life, precludes the human species from confronting its violent disjunction from life. Rather than striving to return art to life, imagining that life extends itself fruitfully and mindfully into its own proliferating future, it might be worthwhile today to recall art's relation to theory.

The vital turn

A new vitalism has been proclaimed, both explicitly in a series of turns to "affect," "life," "matter" or the "brain"—all of which would be *after* theory or after the linguistic turn—and implicitly in a series of accounts of the emergence of mind from life.[11] This seemingly recent and radical embrace of life that sets itself against a diagnosed history of Western intellectualism is, I would argue, yet one more reactive retreat to the figure of the bounded organism, a figure that operates as a seductive lure that precludes thinking. Nowhere is this relapse into organicism (and a moralism of the organism) more evident than in a series of gestures that would return "high" theory back to its more vital precursors. As an example, we might cite the return to a Heidegger of "being-in-the-world" that would efface Derrida's, Foucault's, Deleuze's or Stiegler's Heidegger of folds, *poiesis*, death and the *Zwiefalt*[12]; or the widespread mobilization of the Merleau-Ponty of the flesh and lived body against Merleau-Ponty's late forays into "wild being"[13] or, finally, various returns to the Bergson before Deleuze, or the Husserl before Derrida. Both of the last two retreats are offered by Mark Hansen, who argues that Deleuze and Guattari failed to pay sufficient attention to the bounded condition of the organism in their development of Bergson's philosophy of becoming.[14] He also argues that Husserl's location of temporal syntheses *within* transcendental subjectivity is to be preferred over any "misreading" (such as Stiegler's) that would see time as possible only if supplemented by technical prostheses. This assertion of the primacy of the "lived" over the merely technical (where *techne* would be perniciously detached from embodiment) allows Hansen to provide aesthetic criteria elevating (to name just one example) the media experiences of the art of Bill Viola over the less "enabling" work of others:

> By opening the imperceptible in-between of emotional states, what I shall hereafter call affectivity, to some kind of embodied yet intentional apprehension, Viola's *Anima* exemplifies the capacity of new media to broker a technical enlargement of the threshold of the now, to intensify the body's subject-constituting experience of its own vitality, or, borrowing terminology from Maurice Merleau-Ponty (to whom I return below), to expand "the thickness of the pre-objective present" that comprises the very ground for experience as such.[15]

Hansen's sophisticated critiques are expressions of a broader "post-theory" attack on theory, in which something like a general "mindfulness" (or attention to dynamic and creative processes) allows for an exit from the supposedly dead systems of theory. Indeed, one of the ways of reading the widely used notion of the "turn" at present would be to see these various movements as both redemptive and antitheoretical. The "affective" turn questions the notion that feelings, emotions and embodiment would always be mediated by systems; the "performative" turn places constitutive dynamism and force in the body, rather than the linguistic systems that make explicit reference to the body; the "inhuman turn" demands that we no longer see language as some privileged system for thinking about the world; the "cognitive turn" would enable us to think about the living brain and not locate systems in some disembodied system of signification. The "theological turn," for all its call to divinity, is nevertheless also a means of granting some sort of life or spirit beyond linguistic systems. All these "turns" are not so much turns *back* to some pure origin. Rather they take part in what one might refer to as a general commitment to mindfulness (or the notion that we only have systems that are seemingly detached because life itself extends itself). Art should, if one accepts the desirability of the "turn," be a restoration of technical matters and systems to their living conditions of emergence, while what is left of theory ought to be the intuition of the genesis of that flowing forth of art from living bodies.

I would suggest that the very concept of *mindful aesthetics* should provide an occasion for problematization and decoupling. If there is something like aesthetics as a general process of sensing or sensations, then it would be best thought of as at odds with mindfulness or the commitment to the dynamic interconnectedness of the world and life. Aesthetics would be able to yield something like the detachment of sensation, as that which is released from mind's synthesizing powers. This is given in Kant's theory of reflective judgment, in which both beauty and sublimity are felt as that which is not yet brought into organizing and theoretical knowledge, while mind is that which can only know the world relationally, or from its own point of view. The current turn to mindfulness is, then, a reaction against the detachment of mind as a representing and organizing subject opposed to a passive and not yet organized (and yet proto-ordered) sensation. The turn to "mindfulness" attributes all those qualities that had been enclosed within mind or the subject to life in general, and turns to a reality that is dynamic and mindful in its capacity to generate relations beyond that of a supposed human finitude. Humans, in turn, would not be constructors or mediators of an external reality, but always already caught up in a world with which they are inextricably intertwined. Mindfulness would, then, be destructive of a certain notion of aesthetics that attended to aesthesis (or the sensations that are felt in their processes of formation in any work of art) and would also be opposed to "mind" or any notion of the separation of thinking from the world. In this respect, too, mindfulness would be opposed to theory, or the assumption of the distance between thinking and what is given. Mindfulness, with its insistence on the unexceptional, connected, embodied and dynamically attuned relatedness of the human would be a way of overcoming theory's excessive blindness to history, embodiment and life. Andy Clark redefines the brain not as the basis for mind as subject but as a connected and extended network:

> The brain fascinates because it is the biological organ of mindfulness itself. It is the inner engine that drives intelligent behaviour. Such a depiction provides a worthy antidote to the once-popular vision of the mind as somehow lying outside the natural order. But it is a vision with a price. For it has concentrated much theoretical attention on an uncomfortably restricted space; the space of the inner neural machine, divorced from the wider world which then enters the story only via the hygienic gateways of perception and action. Recent work in neuroscience, robotics and psychology casts doubt on the effectiveness of such a shrunken perspective. Instead it stresses the unexpected intimacy of brain, body and world and invites us to attend to the structure and dynamics of extended adaptive systems.... The mind itself, if such a vision is correct, is best understood as the activity of an essentially *situated* brain: a brain at home in its properly bodily, cultural and environmental niche.[16]

Drawing more specifically on Buddhism, and tying this to Heideggerian phenomenology, theorists of embodied cognition insist on the connectedness of the world:

> Experiences flow, and they flow sensibly or coherently, bound by memory and a feeling of accumulation. The posit of a self, or better, a person makes sense if we

think of mindfulness, introspection or phenomenology as an activity performed by a changing system—a continuous and for now relatively self-contained changing system—on itself. Over time, both the "observer," the system, and what is "observed," the system's experiences are ever-changing. Nothing stands still, nothing stands in a stable relation of observer to observed. We are just as Heidegger insists beings-in-time.[17]

What I would suggest, against such arguments for the extension of mind, is that the vital order, or the figure of organic life as a bounded unity whose motility accounts for relations, is an effect of refusing or denying theory, and it is this countertheory maneuver that is blindly anthropocentric. As long as we regard relations, texts, apparatuses, assemblages, distances, gaps or points of inertia as retrievable or reducible to the complexity of the lived, we remain at the level of organic narrative (tracing relations from bodies) rather than theory.

Even if vitalism were a specifically modern phenomenon, setting itself against Cartesian mechanism, philosophy has always been both enabled by and yet constitutively defined against an implicit or proto-vitalism. When Descartes explicitly articulates a distinction between thinking mind and extended matter, he is immediately met with a charge of denying the spirit and divinity of the world;[18] and, as Heidegger points out, Descartes' "subject" is just one more metaphysical mode of grounding all beings on a founding Being.[19] Anti-Cartesianism, or the vitalist insistence on one unified and creative life, pre-exists Descartes and continues, today, in both avowedly anti-Cartesian declarations of "Descartes' error" and in broader reactions against the detachments of theory, language, technology and instrumental reason. On the one hand, it is precisely because Western philosophy sets itself against sophistry, or the circulation of the mere force of rhetoric without animating intent or reason, that philosophy will always be driven by the notion of a return to the proper sense from which language (as *techne*) emerged. Justification is an essentially vital imperative whereby one does not simply submit to a norm but searches for that norm's legitimacy. This legitimation is not simply the agreement achieved through present consensus or opinion but anticipates what *would be* legitimate and justifiable for any living reason. Justification is at once theory, or the detachment from what *simply is* for the sake of a reflection on the broader contexts of possibility and genesis, at the same time as it is also a retrieval of a law or norm's vital originating sense. As long as *techne* or any system of norms, rules or conventions are seen as (properly) continuous extensions and modes of flourishing of the lived body, there will always be a vital imperative to ground technologies and structures in their origin. Philosophy would be, as a process of legitimation and grounding, an ongoing process of revivification. On the other hand, philosophy—as theory—is also marked by a resistance to reducing truth to that which emerges empirically from psychophysical minds and would, in this respect, be distinct from psychologism, historicism or recent forms of cognitive archaeology. True thinking occurs not when one is located within the lived and accepted narratives and figures of one's time but when the very opacity and mythical nature of lived figurations are confronted and reflectively justified. To argue as Lakoff and Johnson do, that thinking emerges from a metaphorics of the lived body—that happiness is "up" or that thinking is "grasping"—not only restricts the range of metaphor to those that emerge from the lived body; such a theory of genesis must occlude the *figure* of metaphor itself.[20] For metaphor is only conceivable if we have installed ourselves within an imaginary of a mind that molds its world: the image of the body that shapes and makes sense of its own mind and world is itself figural and cannot provide some ultimate pre-imaginary reality. Who or what is this shaping, and what is its border and temporality? Can it be theorized in the sense of being intuited in its very possibility?

Here, then, is the double bind of theory: philosophy is *praxis*, grounded in the ways and forms of life from which its questions emerge (and is therefore vital). At the same time, philosophy must also be *theoria*, not simply a doubling of the lived but a justification and decision about how one *ought* to live. Not only does this strange double of *praxis-theoria* mark out a series of philosophical names (such as Aristotle versus Plato, Hume versus Kant, MacIntyre/Nussbaum versus Rawls), it also splits "theory" from within. One way of thinking about the invasion of theory into nonphilosophical disciplines is as a curious opening of a philosophical question that could not be addressed within philosophy itself. Consider two proper names in this regard: Derrida and Deleuze. In his early work on Husserl, Derrida insisted that Husserl was asking *the* philosophical question *par excellence*.[21] If the very meaning of truth demands an ideality or temporality that transcends any single context, how also does one account for the opening to the infinite, the genesis of the universal? Such questions were philosophical but would, necessarily, not be answerable as long as one remained within the ground of transcendental subjectivity. Philosophy's own genesis, its formation of questions about absolute origins, could never be accountable from within the world, nor from within the bounds of the thinking subject. Deleuze also noted that philosophy has always been a question of beginnings, even if every attempt to open philosophy properly would fall back upon an "image of thought."[22] If the proper names of Deleuze and Derrida appear to divide theory, with Derrida often being characterized as a textualist of high theory and Deleuze as a vitalist—the former detaching texts from their social conditions, the latter failing to consider the rigor of truth—this might indicate a certain symptom.[23] *Theoria* and *vital praxis* appear as distinct terms, often with a supposedly proper temporal order.[24] And yet both terms or tendencies always call up their other in a manner that cannot be ordered into narrative. Theory cannot be placed before praxis, as though one could act only with the possession of an already given logic (as in certain forms of rationalism, idealism, social constructivism or structuralism); nor can there be a silent and self-maintaining praxis, at one with itself, that would then be followed by the abstraction of theory. Such narrative scenarios would presuppose an original organic whole: either a body that faces the world, before action, blessed already with all the organs of cognition, *or* a body that is an act unto itself that may subsequently develop a self-distancing of theory. As an example of the former—of a body that is intrinsically "theoretical" and that ought to orient its theory toward the practices of living—one might consider the tradition of the primacy of the discursive: we only know the world as it is given to us through our cognitive or linguistic categories and can therefore only work within this constructedness. Judith Butler's early theory of the heterosexual matrix as the condition for forming one's identity via already given gender norms continues a tradition of seeing the world as possible only through some mode of mediation.[25] By contrast, and this was evidenced in early criticisms of Butler's work as overly linguistic, there has been a return to the body and the lived.[26] As an example one could cite any "anti"-theory, whether that be a call to ground theory in contexts and politics or to surpass theory with an attention to embodiment, affect, living systems, history or (most recently and most reactively) Darwinism.[27]

Both in its etymology, which refers to looking, and in its traditional philosophical articulation, *theoria* emphasizes a distance or detachment from the world, in contrast with the (perhaps ideally) unreflective engagement of praxis. This is why Kant insists that we can *think* about certain ideas—God, freedom, immortality—but only have theoretical knowledge about what is given to us as finite beings who must relate to a world that is different and distant. In this respect, certain forms of redemptive or attuned vitalism would refuse theory's insistence on mediation. In its current mode vitalism is evidenced not only in a series of retreats, relapses or returns that occur "after theory," it also dominates cognitive science and neuroscience: both disciplines are now dominated by a rejection of cognition as some sort of centered logic in favor of the embeddedness of knowledge in embodied and dynamic life.[28] Just as Descartes' insistence on the distinction between a merely extended substance and thinking life elicited a series of counterclaims for the divine mindfulness and spirit of the world of matter, so today the godless and disenchanted world of mere matter is countered by appealing to the rich life and spirit of things, matter, life, objects and all things nonhuman.

Far from being a late-nineteenth-century reaction to industrialization and mechanization, an appeal to life has always existed alongside and contaminated philosophy's striving for a metaphysical transcendence from which life might be judged. Philosophy, often from within philosophy itself, has been criticized for being too abstractly theoretical—too focused on knowledge and cognition as ideal systems rather than the practical life from which any such systems must emerge. And it is often literature, especially in today's post-theoretical climate, which is appealed to as a point of cure from the overly formal or technical nature of a philosophy that has become increasingly logic-oriented. It is often the case, particularly in the "post-continental" writings of Richard Rorty, Martha Nussbaum and Jürgen Habermas, that the rigid reason of foundationalist theory is tempered or overcome by an appeal to literature as a vehicle of sympathy, creativity or lifeworld disclosure.[29] Habermas insists that philosophy is *not* literature and that its proper mode is theoretical (in the sense of being distanced) and yet such theory and reflection must not become disengaged or alienated from the lifeworld, a lifeworld that "we" can recognize as a lifeworld though literature. Habermas' appeal to the "lifeworld" is both typical of a perennial criticism of the disengaged intellect and also indicative of a new mode of counter-theoretical vitalism that has the supposed sanction of science: gone is the Romantic or mystical opposition to the rationalization of the world. Instead, science itself offers new theories of living systems and self-organizing matter that have been embraced by the humanities both as a way of legitimating philosophy's insistence on meaning and sense and as a way of "putting mind and world together again."[30] It is cognitive science that has itself been critical of the cognitive model, turning to aesthetics, animal intelligence, Buddhism and embodiment to overcome its Cartesian prison.

There has, since the very suggestion of the theoretical ideal, always been a criticism of theory as a deadening of the life of praxis. The clearest early articulation of this comes from Aristotle, who criticizes the Socratic life of *eironeia*, arguing that an excessive distance from the polity fails to achieve the golden mean of a life that realizes itself through a full actualization of all its powers, social as well as rational.[31] This sense of the theoretical, distanced and ironic self as a *negation* of one's properly active, political and social being was rearticulated by Cicero and has remained a constant in counter-rationalist philosophy ever since.[32] There has always been an intense vitalist underpinning *and* undermining of theory. In its first articulations, Aristotle grounded our theoretical duties on a model of life. That is to say: we theorize because of the type of living beings that we are.[33] It is because we are political and social animals, oriented to speaking in common, that we are not mere physical organisms but rational beings possessing the potential to think about what we (and any other being) *ought* to be. Each being is defined by its proper potential, and *ought* to actualize that potential if it is to achieve its proper definition. Because human life is defined by its capacity to intuit first principles—its capacity to see not simply what *is* the case but also what *ought* to be— we ought to reason; not to do so would be a negation of our life's proper and defining potential. Such ideals are rearticulated today by neo-Aristotelian philosophers, such as Philippa Foot, who also insist that our moral, social, communicative and reflective being *can* be grounded on our living being, not because we are innately rational and reflective, but because we are at our most human when we exercise this potentiality.[34] If ideals of life as properly realizing its potentiality have underpinned the tradition of *theoria*, they have also been used to undermine the theoretical ideal. If life is essentially expansive, creative, active and self-maintaining, how do we explain a life that fails to realize itself? How do we explain the need to return thinking to life? If life is so very vital, why did it subject itself to the rigidity of Cartesian reason?

One answer comes in the form of the intellect or theoretical power, which is deemed to be an extension of life's vitality at the same time as it tends toward disengagement. Well before Romanticism criticized the murdering dissection of the intellect by appealing to a plastic imagination that was not detached from the life of the world, the ideal of living praxis has frequently acted as a challenge to *theoria*. When Descartes defined the world as so much extended matter that could be known and mastered lawfully, a vitalist countertradition emphasized a spirit that flowed through being, irreducible to the quantifying and calculating laws of mechanism. Closer to our own time we might think of Heidegger, for whom life begins properly as unfolding disclosure, and only subsequently (and parasitically) falls into the *epistemological* attitude of *theoria*, so that logos becomes logic. For Heidegger, before we can ask how or why the world exists we are always already in the world, and if we wish to ask the profoundest questions we should not begin with the distance and disengagement of theory, but go back to the speaking and living from which that distance emerges. Heidegger does not, like Bergson, attack the intellectual power for its reification and loss of intense life; and, unlike Bergson, he does not imagine that we could so enliven our perception as to achieve a unique concept for each experience. But he does insist that there is a horizon of sense that is inadequately imagined as the representation of the world by some separate and knowing mind. Theory ought not to be abandoned, for it is not a question of becoming one with life as the simply vitalist tradition will imagine. Rather, we should recognize that the condition for theory, for the sense we have of the world, is not a cognitive glance at *what* this or that being is. Sense—or the world considered as a meaningful domain of being—emerges from being in the world; against the idea of language, ideas or cognition as a system through which the world is grasped, and against the idea of theory as a reflection or critique of those systems, categories or concepts, Heidegger offers an account of language as an emergent practice. Language is neither a representation nor logic imposed on the world, nor an innate grammar or a system of categories, but an "equiprimordial" event that occurs in the coming to presence of the world, and our relation to that revelation through speaking with others. Heidegger is, then, perhaps the most significant philosopher for thinking about the relation between vitalism and theory, and this is because he is critical *both* of a *Lebensphilosophie* that would account for the genesis of sense as a simple continuation of life and of a rationalism or logic that would be the pre-condition of the world: language is not the world itself but the world *as* this or that lived, unfolded and intended dwelling. For Heidegger it is *poiesis* or the placing into separateness of language that allows us to rethink the opening of the world.

Heidegger will be critical of any supposed return to life or bios, for that would be one more metaphysical and disclosed foundation forgetful of its emergence from a specific sense or dwelling of the world. But if Heidegger is critical of a vitalist affirmation of life or bios, he is also no less enamored of a critical philosophy that would stress the language, system or concepts *through which* we view the world. Heidegger's critique of Kant is that while Kantianism recognizes that the world lived is not the world in itself, Kant fails to ask the question of that unfolding, genesis or emergence of the world *as being*. Instead, Kantianism takes one being—the mind and its categories—as the position from which theory is undertaken. In the famous Husserlian attack on Kantianism, Eugen Fink argued that Kantianism began from the mind and its experience of the world without accounting for the emergence of the world.[35] In its Heideggerian form, this criticism of beginning questions from the mind in relation to the world went beyond Husserl's insistence on turning back to consciousness and sense for the disclosure of the world. Indeed, Husserl's intellectualism—his assumption that the unfolding of the world was primarily undertaken by a transcendental subjectivity oriented toward knowledge and apodictic presentation—was the target not only of Heidegger's critique but also Levinas' and Derrida's later departures from phenomenology.[36] Life does not begin as *knowledge*; the first relation is not a striving toward theory or the intuition of essences. Thought is not understood if it is imagined primarily as a will to know, and as a will to know that which remains the same and true for all time. Rather, thought emerges from praxis, being in the world, or an exposure to alterity. The world is not a thing, whose sense I then determine. In the beginning is the relation or trace. We do not possess a logic through which we encounter the world, for logic is a subsequent reification of *legomenon* or speaking about. Asking the question of Being, or the question of how it is that we are situated in relation to a world that we can question, is neither a return to the world as it is (for the emergence of language comes not from life itself but from our living of that life), nor is it a return to the world as it is lived. If we begin to ask questions from the world as it is already disclosed, we fail to ask the question of disclosure or unfolding.

It is this problem of *genesis and its relation to theory* that I will return to in the conclusion of this chapter. For now what I would like to note is the complexity of Heidegger's relation to vitalism. Heidegger is frequently mobilized as a cure by a number of philosophers in the supposed wake of both analytic philosophy and the "linguistic turn": before there is anything like a system, grammar or logic—before mind as something like a computer—there is a relational comportment toward the world that is embodied and dynamic rather than centered and formal. Like Husserl before him, Heidegger was critical of historicism, psychologism and the various forms of *Lebensphilosophie* that would render language thoroughly immanent to, and continuous with, life. He did, however, also criticize the neo-Kantianism of his day that began with categories or some form of logic. So there are two sides to Heidegger: antivitalist in relation to simple emergence and antilogicist in relation to Kantianism. It is the anticognitive, antirepresentationalist and existential Heidegger that has been taken up in the new vitalism that accounts for language as an emergent property. What I want to explore in the rest of this chapter is not the question of the fidelity to Heidegger in current philosophy and cognitive science, but the normative image of life that dominates the uses of Heidegger and the forgetting of Heidgger's *poetic* understanding of language—a *poiesis* that is intensified in post-structuralist theory and which is directed against the normative images of life that dominate Western metaphysics.

It is perhaps not surprising that a certain mobilization of Heidegger has been used to shift philosophy away from models of centered cognition and theoretical detachment and representation toward vitalist affirmations of a life that is properly considered as embodied, practical, self-maintaining, *autopoetic* and homeostatic.[37] Heidegger is not the only grand European philosopher celebrated by this postanalytic turn to life. Antonio Damasio has, for example, used Spinoza's concept of conatus, or a life that strives to preserve in its own being, to argue for a self that begins with emotions (or essential self-maintaining responses to its environment), which are then registered as feelings, ultimately allowing for a sense of self.[38] Morality is not, as Kantianism proper would have it, effected from the recognition that we must give a law to ourselves. It is an emergent property, actualized when our brain's capacity for principles is exercised in social networks.[39] The use of Heidegger by recent philosophers and cognitive scientists is more significant, though, precisely because Heidegger also opens up a divergent tradition of post-structuralist thought. Heidegger can be appealed to both by those who want to appeal to an ideal of the self as originally practical and self-maintaining—the autopoetic model—*and* by those philosophers who are at the heart of "literary theory." This dual possibility of reading Heidegger as a harbinger of both embedded pragmatism *and* the distance, difference and difficulty of a language that shines in its own right is no accident, and stems from a tendency that goes well beyond the Heideggerean corpus. It cannot be explained away by pointing out that the cognitive science Heidegger is the Heidegger of *Being and Time*, while literary theory has been influenced by the later work in *The Origin of the Work of Art*. There is, I would suggest, a necessary bifurcation that is best thought of through the notion of literary theory: as literary, our practices of reading concern already given textual objects, emerging from and circulating in our lifeworld; as *theory*, we are always in relation to those textual objects that demand to be read, and that are not immediately and continuously living without the labor of reanimation that theory enables. (We are all familiar, through teaching, of the book that is immediately read—the *Wuthering Heights* that students already know and love as a romance, or the William Blake that circulates in the general public as so much cutesy wisdom; it is theory as distance or estrangement that must deaden that too lively object and recall the event of distancing that reading entails but often ignores.)

We can return to consider in slightly more detail the Heidegger of the philosophy of cognitive science: this is the Heidegger of Hubert Dreyfus, Michael Wheeler, Andy Clark, Jeff Malpas and Maturana and Varela. I'll begin with the cognitive scientists first and then move back to the philosophers who add Heidegger to their own appeals to embodied life as the true path to understanding cognition. For Maturana and Varela, it is a mistake to think of the organism as a being that somehow has to perceive *the* world.[40] Rather, each living being's world is a system of relatively stable responses, all of which are oriented not toward representation but to self-maintenance or autopoesis. Organisms are not self-sufficient beings that encounter a world and *then* respond; rather, in the beginning is the response, or the establishing of some relation that allows for something like "a" life. Cognition as we usually understand it is not only belated—occurring after we have already disclosed a world through orientation, reaction, dwelling and response—it is also an inaccurate and truncated notion. Our thinking does not take the form of representation that would then be contemplated for the sake of deciding what to do; thinking is distributed. Philosophical sense of this is made by Dreyfus, who draws upon phenomenology's concept of intentionality. The mind is not something that then has to picture or represent the world, for the mind is always *of* its world and has no being other than this relation.[41] It is from this relational model of the mind—not as a thing that must impose or create a logic but as an orientation that produces a logic or grammar through interaction—that the way is paved for embodied and decentered cognition. Andy Clark's catchy title, *Natural Born Cyborgs*, captures a far more radical anti-Cartesianism than Dreyfus' insistence on intentionality.[42] Not only is it the case that there is no such thing as mind in itself, for the mind is nothing other than the sense and relation it bears to the world in which it lives; the sense and orientation of the world are not located in the mind. The body has response networks which are readily adaptive and self-maintaining and do not require a rule or intention from which orientation takes place. Clark makes two key points distinguishing his own approach from traditional or computational theories of mind. The first is the notion of distributed cognition: actions are undertaken without (necessarily) the intervention of concepts or explicit intentions. If we want to build a system that walks, for example, it would be laborious and futile to make a robot that had a central computer directing the mechanical parts. What would work, though, is a mechanism whose parts could respond to the environment. What we need to model are not instructions but interactions. The second more significant concept is that of an originary supplement, leading to the "extended mind." If someone asks us if we know the time, we answer "yes" because we have a watch that would deliver such information. The mind is not a container within which knowledge is held but is always already a cyborg; it extends beyond the body's boundaries to include potential mechanisms. We are thinking when we use a pencil and paper to perform long division, and we are desiring when we compose a shopping or Christmas list. The mind is not centered but extended, and we can see recent commercial mobilizations of this insight. Our Amazon homepage does not read our mind (or what is present) but provides maps of what we will want based on past responses; and it is likely that if we act on those supposedly "likely" choices—if we purchase Kate Grenville because we previously bought John Banville—that our ongoing suggestions and desires will not have originated from the mind (or body) itself but from a mindful body attached to a responsive machine.

The self is naturally prosthetic: this sounds, initially, like Derrida.[43] In the beginning is not the thing or the self but the relation or the difference. Perhaps it is this proximity to post-structuralism that has encouraged recent work on Deleuze to turn happily to the natural sciences and to theories of embodied and extended cognition.[44] The key difference, though, between cognitive science's appeal to a vital and immanent Heideggerianism and what I would defend as post-structuralism and literary theory is the latter's critique of normative life. I would like to conclude, then, with two other ways of thinking the Heideggerian turn. First, we can recall Derrida's quite distinct argument for the supplemental or prosthetic nature of life, which cannot be confined to language as some additional *extension*. Second, I would also like to draw attention to Deleuze and Guattari's definition of art as a monument, as detached from its originating intent and the lived.[45] For Derrida the supplement or prosthesis is not an extension of intentional life. Rather, the possibility of the supplement, *techne*, writing or prosthetics redefines life as always already made possible by death. If it is the case that one lives, goes through time, makes one's way in the world, understands one's self to be a self, then this self-maintenance and living on is possible only through that which does not live, cannot be intended and decided and always remains radically distinct from, and resistant to, self-incorporation. This is why deconstruction was never a philosophy of language. All those features assigned to language (or the tool or prosthesis) already invade the supposed self-sufficiency of embodied life. What was at stake in deconstruction was the non-self-presence of life to itself. The body that lives on—the lived body of phenomenology whose world is given through possibility and action—can only be close to itself through some element, trace or work that is not its own. The ongoing synthesis of time, that I live this "now" as mine, is possible only with a sense that *this* here is before me, that there is a difference between here and there, before and after, self and world; and for Derrida it is that *différance*—not the difference between one body and another but the marking or tracing of a sense *that there is difference*—that constitutes the "scene of writing." Literature is the putting into relief of that marking out or tracing: so before literature says *what* is the case, literature presents a saying, or *that there is speaking*. This is why all literary reading is directed not to meaning but the putting into meaning, which essentially cannot be seen as the extension of a voice or wanting to say (*vouloir dire*). Once articulated, the literary object circulates—is quoted, copied, repeated and re-read. It is because the work is not attached to the author that it demands to be read; it lives on only because its life is not self-present.

The present is haunted by these dead literary objects; we live, breathe and think through an archive that is not our own and that requires our retrieval of sense, even if every retrieval is also a difference and disjunction with the work itself. For all their differences with regard to life, philosophy and metaphysics, we can draw some connection here between Derrida's insistence on the scene of writing and Deleuze and Guattari's definition of the work of art as that which allows sensations and affects to stand alone. In Deleuze's own work, the cinematic eye is perhaps the clearest example of Deleuze and Guattari's criticism of an active vitalism. The striving of life to extend and maintain itself requires deterritorialization, or (to use Bergson's terminology) the creative and explosive difference that is life also allows for an element of conservation or nonproduction in order to live on.[46] An organism lives by responding to difference, but lives on also by reducing difference and diminishing the intensity of its life for the sake of a future. Technologies, such as the concepts we use to perceive the world as a causal ordered network, maintain sameness through time, and allow us to decrease the effort of thinking and living. We become ourselves, that is, human organisms, by abandoning part of ourselves to technologies of perception and articulation. Life, therefore, requires, in its organic form, an element of inactivity, sameness or nonlife. The eye that sees the world as an extended and continuous whole remains dead to certain influxes, folding and selecting what it responds to according to its body's needs. Even so, that very *techne* of deterritorialization allows for the possibility of counteractualization or higher deterritorialization. The very unit that imposes itself on the world, allowing for a diminution of difference, can open up worlds and timelines beyond the present. In Bergson's case, if I can have morality by imagining every body as the same as mine and therefore an extension of my interest, I can also imagine a purely virtual body that is not present. In this case, a difference of degree (or the extension of the body via morality) shifts into a difference in kind (a deterritorialized or disembodied spirit). I could act, not for the sake of man with whom I am in sympathy, but for one who is not present, not given, not within time. For Deleuze, it is the *poiesis* of art objects— or their technical existence beyond the body and mind of their creator—that opens perceptions of a world not lived, and affects of a world not felt. The camera that extends the eye allowing us to see more, recognize more and take part in a shared world can also detach itself from recognizing and synthesizing life.

Theory, I would conclude, is just the intensification of that dehumanizing and lifeless point of view that imagines words not as messages addressed to us, but as objects not immediately invested with life and intentionality. Theory is that gaze or look that addresses the object not as a thing of this world but as the provocation to destroy our sense of the world and open up a world of sense. Theory enables us to think of aesthetics, not as the art of the perceiving and feeling body, but as the capacity for *aesthesis* to exist beyond the lived. This allows us to conclude by rethinking the relation between art praxis and theory, which I would now like to suggest is an impossible but productively contrary relation. Consider two quotations from William Blake (who is also often read as a vitalist, with his emphasis of returning systems to their act of creation, *and* as an antivitalist, with his creation of singular poetic artifacts that refuse communicability, circulation and consumption). First we might think of the often-quoted aphorism from *The Marriage of Heaven and Hell* that "everything that lives is holy." In one sense this takes us back to life, as the ultimate horizon of all holiness; divinity is not above and beyond life but immanent to life. On the other hand, everything that lives is *holy*; holiness or the sense that there is always more than the merely given haunts all life, which is never given as fully present. A second aphorism bears the same structure: "all deities reside in the human breast." All deities can be seen as emerging from the imagination; but the human breast also harbors deities, or spots of divinity that transcend our presence to ourselves.[47] This doubleness in Blake, like the doubleness in Heidegger, is neither accidental nor avoidable. Insofar as we live—insofar as we are beings who speak in common and therefore dwell in and with literature—we are also beings haunted by theory: for life is never at one with itself, but lives on only by submitting itself to that which operates with an insistence and resistance that is excessively literary.

Notes

1 Gilbert Ryle, *The Concept of Mind* (Chicago: University of Chicago Press, 1949). See also, Jonathan Bate, *The Song of the Earth* (Cambridge, MA: Harvard University Press, 2000).
2 Francesco J. Varela, Evan Thompson, and Eleanor Rosch, *The Embodied Mind: Cognitive Science and Human Experience* (Cambridge, MA: MIT Press, 1992), 123.
3 Jean-François Lyotard, *Lessons on the Analytic of the Sublime: Kant's Critique of Judgment, Sections 23–29*, trans. Elizabeth Rottenberg (Stanford: Stanford University Press, 1994).
4 V. S. Ramachandran and William Hirstein, "The Science of Art: A Neurological Theory of Aesthetic Experience," *Journal of Consciousness Studies* 6 (1999): 15–51.
5 Steven J. Mithen, *The Singing Neanderthals: The Origins of Music, Language, Mind and Body* (London: Weidenfeld and Nicolson, 2005).
6 Brian Boyd, *On the Origin of Stories: Evolution, Cognition, and Fiction* (Cambridge, MA: Belknap Press of Harvard University Press, 2009).
7 Jacques Derrida, *Writing and Difference*, trans. Alan Bass (Chicago: University of Chicago Press, 1978), 157.
8 Paul de Man, *Aesthetic Ideology*, ed. Andrzej Warminski (Minneapolis, MA: University of Minnesota Press, 1996), 70.
9 J. M. Bernstein, "'Readymades, Monochromes, Etc.: Nominalism and the Paradox of Modernism,' in 'Rethinking Beauty,'" *Diacritics* 32, no. 1 (Spring 2002): 83–100.
10 Jennifer Doyle, *Hold It against Me: Difficulty and Emotion in Contemporary Art* (Durham, NC: Duke University Press, 2012).

11   Steve Fuller, Marc de Mey, T. Shinn, and Steve Woolgar eds., *The Cognitive Turn:*
     Sociological and Psychological Perspectives on Science (Dordrecht: Springer, 1989);
     Todd F. Davis and Kenneth Womack, *Mapping the Ethical Turn: A Reader in Ethics,*
     Culture, and Literary Theory (Charlottesville, VA: University of Virginia Press,
     2001); Dominique Janicaud, *Phenomenology and the "Theological Turn": The French*
     Debate (New York: Fordham University, 2000); Patricia Ticiento Clough, "The
     Affective Turn: Political Economy, Biomedia and Bodies," *Theory, Culture & Society*
     25, no. 1 (2008): 1–22; Gregor McLennan, "The Postsecular Turn," *Theory, Culture*
     & Society 27, no. 4 (2010): 3–20; Richard Shustermann, "Postmodernism and the
     Aesthetic Turn," *Poetics Today* 10, no. 3 (1989): 605–22; Maxine Sheets-Johnstone,
     The Corporeal Turn: An Interdisciplinary Reader (New York: Academic, 2009); Ursula
     Heise, "The Posthuman Turn: Rewriting Species in Recent American Literature,"
     in *A Companion to American Literary Studies*, eds. C. F. Levander and R. S. Levine
     (Oxford: Blackwell, 2011); Peter Dirksmeier and Ilse Helbrecht, "Time, Non-
     representational Theory and the 'Performative Turn': Towards a New Methodology in
     Qualitative Social Research," *Forum Qualitative Sozialforschung/Forum: Qualitative*
     Social Research 9, no. 2 (2008).
12   Michael Wheeler, *Reconstructing the Cognitive World: The Next Step* (Cambridge, MA:
     MIT Press, 2005).
13   Shaun Gallagher, *How the Body Shapes the Mind* (Oxford: Clarendon Press, 2005);
     Humberto J. Maturana and Francisco J. Varela, *The Tree of Knowledge: The Biological*
     Roots of Human Understanding (Boston: New Science Library, 1987).
14   Mark Hansen, *Embodying Technesis: Technology beyond Writing* (Ann Arbor, MI:
     University of Michigan Press, 2000), 206.
15   Mark Hansen, "The Time of Affect, or Bearing Witness to Life," *Critical Inquiry* 30,
     no. 3 (Spring 2004): 589.
16   Andy Clark, "Where Brain, Body and World Collide," *Material Agency: Towards*
     a Non-Anthropocentric Approach, eds. Carl Knappett and Lambros Malafouris
     (Dordrecht: Springer, 2008), 1.
17   Owen Flanagan, *The Problem of the Soul: Two Visions of Mind and How to Reconcile*
     Them (New York: Basic Books, 2002), 209–10.
18   Jonathan Israel, *Radical Enlightenment: Philosophy and the Making of Modernity,*
     1650–1750 (Oxford: Oxford University Press, 2001).
19   Martin Heidegger, *What Is a Thing? trans. W. B. Barton Jr. and Vera Deutsch* (Chicago:
     H. Regnery Co., 1967).
20   George Lakoff and Mark Johnson, *Metaphors We Live By* (Chicago: University of
     Chicago Press, 1980).
21   Jacques Derrida, *Edmund Husserl's Origin of Geometry: An Introduction*, trans. John
     Leavey Jr. (Lincoln, NE: University of Nebraska Press, 1989).
22   Gilles Deleuze, *Difference and Repetition*, trans. Paul Patton (New York: Columbia,
     1994).
23   Bill Martin, *Matrix and Line: Derrida and the Possibilities of Postmodern Social Theory*
     (Albany, NY: SUNY Press, 1992), 100; Scott Lash, "Life (Vitalism)," *Theory, Culture &*
     Society 23, nos. 2–3 (2006): 323–9.
24   As an indication of this torsion, one might consider the dubious status of what
     would count as the other of praxis. One opposite is theory, so that a certain Marxist
     political tradition would ground all general theoretical claims in the working
     relations of bodies; another opposite would be *poiesis*, so that praxis is action that

remains bound to living bodies while *poiesis* creates a distinct and detached object; yet another opposite would be *techne*, so that praxis remains tied to intended outcomes while *techne* is a threatening means (and with *theoria* in turn aligned with active reasoning contemplation in opposition to a merely technical, repeatable and enervated circulation of systemic tokens); and there would finally be an opposition between praxis and *physis*, with the former being the properly human condition that propels "our" species being into speech and labor while the latter remains in itself. For relatively recent discussions of praxis and its various others, one might consider the highly moral accounts of Agamben and Taminiaux. The point to be drawn from the ways in which these oppositions and their dominant axiology generate conflict is not only that theory and praxis can only be defined relationally but that the distinction is narrative and normative: in the beginning is praxis as a properly organism-extending manner of achieving ends, and this closeness to life can be enhanced by *theoria* as the contemplation that allows "us" to intuit our proper ends or can be perverted by theory if contemplation itself becomes a practice unto itself. See Giorgio Agamben, *The Man without Content*, trans. Daniel Heller-Roazen (Stanford: Stanford University Press, 1999), 68; and Jacques Taminiaux, *Poetics, Speculation, and Judgment: The Shadow of the Work of Art from Kant to Phenomenology*, trans. Michael Gendre (Albany, NY: SUNY Press, 1993).

25   Judith Butler, *Gender Trouble* (New York: Routledge, 1990).

26   Karen Barad, "Posthumanist Performativity: Toward an Understanding of How Matter Comes to Matter," *Signs: Journal of Women in Culture and Society* 28, no. 3 (2003): 801–31.

27   Joseph Carroll, "What Is Literary Darwinism: An Interview with Joseph Carroll," *Neuronarrative* (2009), http://neuronarrative.wordpress.com/2009/02/27/what-is-literary-darwinism-an-interview-with-joseph-carroll/.

28   Evan Thompson, *Mind in Life: Biology, Phenomenology, and the Sciences of Mind* (Cambridge, MA: Belknap Press of Harvard University Press, 2007).

29   Richard Rorty, *Consequences of Pragmatism: Essays, 1972–1980* (Minneapolis, MA: University of Minnesota Press, 1982); Martha C. Nussbaum, *Love's Knowledge: Essays on Philosophy and Literature* (New York: Oxford University Press, 1990); and Jürgen Habermas, *The Philosophical Discourse of Modernity: Twelve Lectures*, trans. Frederick Lawrence (Cambridge, MA: MIT Press, 1987).

30   Maurice Merleau-Ponty, *Phenomenology of Perception*, trans. Donald A. Landes (London: Routledge, 1962), 433.

31   W. Gooch, "Socratic Irony and Aristotle's 'Eiron': Some Puzzles," *The Phoenix* 41, no. 2 (Summer 1987): 95–104.

32   Claire Colebrook, *Irony: The New Critical Idiom* (London: Routledge, 1994).

33   Terence Irwin, *Aristotle's First Principles* (Oxford: Clarendon Press, 1988).

34   Philippa Foot, *Natural Goodness* (Oxford: Clarendon Press, 2001).

35   Eugen Fink, "The Phenomenological Philosophy of Edmund Husserl and Contemporary Criticism," in *The Phenomenology of Husserl: Selected Critical Readings*, ed. R. O. Elveton (Chicago: Quadrangle Books, 1970), 73–147.

36   Emmanuel Levinas, *Discovering Existence with Husserl*, trans. Richard A. Cohen and Michael B. Smith (Evanston, IL: Northwestern University Press, 1998).

37   Michael Wheeler and Julia Kiverstein eds., *Heidegger and Cognitive Science* (New York: Palgrave Macmillan, 2012); Mark Wrathall and Jeff Malpas eds., *Heidegger, Coping, and Cognitive Science* (Cambridge, MA: MIT Press, 2000).

38   Antonio R. Damasio, *Looking for Spinoza: Joy, Sorrow, and the Feeling Brain* (Orlando, FL: Harcourt, 2003).

39   Even Kantian constructivism has been adopted by recent theorists of emergence. Using John Rawls' notion that moral theory is based on abstract principles, and cannot be given in the generalization from concrete instances (à la Hume), Marc Hauser argues that there is a moral equivalent of the mind's potential for language and grammar, and that this capacity is grounded in the brain. See Marc D. Hauser, *Moral Minds: How Nature Designed Our Universal Sense of Right and Wrong* (New York: Ecco, 2006).

40   Maturana and Varela, *The Tree of Knowledge*.

41   Hubert L. Dreyfus, Stuart E. Dreyfus, and Tom Athanasiou, *Mind over Machine: The Power of Human Intuition and Expertise in the Era of the Computer* (New York: Free Press, 1986).

42   Andy Clark, *Natural-Born Cyborgs: Minds, Technologies, and the Future of Human Intelligence* (Oxford: Oxford University Press, 2003).

43   Bernard Stiegler, "Derrida and Technology: Fidelity at the Limits of Deconstruction and the Prosthesis of Faith," *Jacques Derrida and the Humanities: A Critical Reader*, ed. Tom Cohen (Cambridge: Cambridge University Press, 2001), 238–70.

44   William E. Connolly, *Neuropolitics: Thinking, Culture, Speed* (Minneapolis, MA: University of Minnesota Press, 2002).

45   Gilles Deleuze and Félix Guattari, *What Is Philosophy?* trans. Hugh Tomlinson and Graham Burchell (New York: Columbia University Press, 1994).

46   Henri Bergson, *Creative Evolution*, trans. Arthur Miller (London: Macmillan, 1911).

47   William Blake, *The Marriage of Heaven and Hell*, ed. Geoffrey Keynes (Oxford: Oxford University Press, 1975).

3

Continental Drift: The Clash between Literary Theory and Cognitive Literary Studies

Paul Sheehan

The relationship between science and literature over the last century has been multifaceted, contradictory and resistant to any one account or rationale. When it comes to science and literary theory, however, there is, if not a single narrative, then at least a persistent rhetorical tendency that stands out. Literary theorists throughout the century most often enlisted science to make their critical reflections more rigorous and exacting, to codify and compartmentalize and to give greater intellectual weight to the often-subjective task of literary interpretation and analysis. If this became the holy grail of critical reflection for much of the last century, up until the late 1960s, it was formalist theories of literary analysis that pursued it more vigorously than any other. Russian Formalism, the Prague Linguistic Circle and French Structuralism all, in their turn, sought to establish a "poetics that would be the equivalent of science."[1]

Leapfrogging several decades, to the end of the century, we can see how drastically the relationship, and the climate, has changed. Science and literary theory came together in a publicly visible way in 1998, when Alan Sokal and Jean Bricmont pointed out the abuses of scientific and mathematical terminology in the service of (in their words) a "cognitive and cultural relativism."[2] Lacan, Baudrillard, Deleuze and Guattari, Paul Virilio, Julia Kristeva and others were exposed as scientific pretenders—using terms they didn't fully understand, and making pronouncements that did not jibe with the data-heavy, evidential methods of empirical scientific enquiry. Even theory's defenders had to admit that many of the charges were not unjust, albeit while pointing out that the more sinister subtext of the enterprise—to discredit continental theory in a wider sense—did its authors no favors.[3]

In retrospect, what is most striking about Sokal and Bricmont's somewhat overdrawn and self-serving polemic is its blithe unawareness that the age of high theory had long since passed. In the new millennium, by contrast, there has been a noticeable shift in academic publishing—from survey books detailing what theory *is*, to elegies outlining what it *was*.[4] The death in 2009 of Claude Lévi-Strauss, the last surviving member of the Sixties generation, served as a stirring reminder of a time when theory truly mattered, when the stakes were so much higher than they are now. However, these obituaries for theory are not absolute; the current era may be regarded as "post-theoretical," but the term itself is ambiguous, and does not necessarily connote finality. Colin Davis, in *After Poststructuralism*, puts it succinctly. In terms of the corpus of high-theoretical texts, he writes, "we may come after them but we are not over them yet."[5] This statement is borne out in the current legacy of theory, which, I want to suggest, is three-fold.

In the first place, a new set of "master-thinkers," or figures of dissent, has arisen to take the place of the old. Though many of them have been active for several decades, their fame and influence is more recent. I refer here to Antonio Negri, Bruno Latour, Alain Badiou, Jean-Luc Nancy (and his erstwhile collaborator, the late Philippe Lacoue-Labarthe), Giorgio Agamben, Slavoj Žižek, Jacques Rancière and so on. These thinkers claim a very different heritage from their predecessors. Though power, ideology and desire are still high on the agenda—carrying in their wake those once-indomitable founders of discursivity, Nietzsche, Marx and Freud—there are other names to conjure with, more anomalous and unruly figures such as Mao Zedong, Carl Schmitt, Antonio Gramsci and St Paul.

Second, high theory may have emerged as a comprehensively and relentlessly *critical* form of thinking, suspicious of all authority, but it has itself become authoritative, respected, even canonical. That "respect" is evident enough from the fact that so many of the thinkers I have just named engage directly with their predecessors—Agamben with Foucault, Rancière with Barthes, Žižek with Lacan, Badiou with Deleuze (and Lacan) and so on. More broadly, critical precepts that were once subversive, once inextricably bound up with dissident forms of thinking, have become mainstream and institutionalized, exerting their *own* forms of authority. The notion of a textual unconscious, the fraught relationship between author and work, textual meanings that are no longer clear-cut but are instead provisional, heterodox, undecidable…these now uncontroversial critical precepts are all signifiers of theory's double-edged "success." It is double-edged because the shift from theory as *critique* to theory as *convention* means it has become normalized, perhaps even neutralized—given that its principal targets were the foundational assumptions of the Western philosophical and literary traditions, and the rigid, authoritative norms that have congealed around them. Theory, then, renders itself open to contestation—from without *and* within—as it never has before.

This brings me to the third marker of post-theory. The most concerted challenge to theory's rule has come not from the inner chambers of continental thinking itself, but from across the Channel in some instances, and across the Atlantic in others. Cognitive literary studies (CLS) is that challenge, an Anglo-American attempt to restore *mind* to the literary equation, as the necessary mediator between language and world. CLS begins from a literary-experiential foundation and imports from the vast array of cognitive sciences, including post-Chomskian and psycholinguistics, computer science, cognitive evolution, evolutionary psychology and biology and neuroscience.[6] By drawing on understandings of the "cognitive" and its focus on the brain/mind as a knowledge mediator, CLS explores how brain activity/mental functioning condition the writing, reading and interpretation of texts. The cognitive turn in literary studies represents, in short, an attempt to put literary analysis on a more empirical, scientific, physicalist footing, by adapting the tools and approaches of mind-embodiment science.

Cognitive studies branched out into a distinctively literary movement in 1998, following a Discussion Group on the topic at that year's MLA conference. The related subdiscipline of "cognitive poetics," however, had been developing since the early 1980s—a less critical-philosophical and more analytical-linguistic form of textual reflection.[7] And since the early 1990s, the adjacent field of cognitive-evolutionary literary studies has been on the rise, bringing Darwinist ideas about adaptation to the discipline.[8] According to some accounts of the genesis of cognitivist approaches to literature, it simply *had* to happen, as an inevitable backlash against continental theory and its excesses.

In the early 1990s, Mark Turner heralded the arrival of cognitive poetics with the declamation that contemporary critical theory had become a self-sustaining, mandarin practice "unrestrained by laws of entropy."[9] Several years later, Brian Boyd reiterated the sentiment: "Over the last few years," he wrote, "the Theory wave has started to break under the inherent weakness of its arguments and the strength of the welling counter-evidence."[10] And in the mid-2000s, Joseph Carroll recalled how, ten years earlier, he had become "profoundly dissatisfied with the irrationalism and textualism of the prevailing literary doctrines."[11] The charge-sheet is, by now, all too familiar: theory is too difficult, too speculative, too counterintuitive, "too continental." Even theory's defenders, such as Alan Richardson and Francis Steen, describe a "spreading dissatisfaction with the more bleakly relativistic and antihumanist strands of poststructuralism."[12]

It could be argued, then, that the relationship between the emergent field of CLS and the embattled domain of continental or post-structuralist theory is to a large extent a codependent one, in which neither can afford to ignore the other. What I want to do, in the remainder of this chapter, is to focus on the tensions that abide between the two camps, and to suggest that those tensions are too deeply embedded, and too unyielding, for there to be any *rapprochement*, let alone any kind of pact or truce. So I will be addressing not those enemies of theory, who want to see it shut down and banished from academe, but rather its cognitivist-based allies, who are working to incorporate theoretical concepts and tenets into their own reading strategies and practices.

Euphoric dreaming: The science of theory

As a way in to the theory–CLS debate, we might first consider the continental perspective on the cognitivist turn. To date, the only substantive response has come, not untypically, from Slavoj Žižek. In an article entitled "Lacan between Cultural Studies and Cognitivism," Žižek frames his response as a struggle between the skeptical, self-reflexive methods of cultural studies and the "cognitively" engaged scientific disciplines, with their quaint, logocentric belief in the graspability of truth.[13] As F. Elizabeth Hart has pointed out, Žižek's understanding of cognitivism is crude and tendentious; rather than engaging with the brain/mind paradigm on its own terms, he pursues a rhetorical stance that uses cognitivism as a stand-in for "science" *per se*, and for the truth-centered realism that is its remit.[14] More recently, in *The Parallax View*, Žižek has pointed out the folly of attempting to align cognitive science with psychoanalysis.[15] Žižek's animadversions, in fact, lend weight to the mistaken belief that continental theory is somehow *antiscience*, or that it rejects the scientific worldview in its entirety; a caricature that the Sokal–Bricmont polemic did nothing to ameliorate. This is clearly not the case, as I now want to show—although theory's relationship to science is more complex than just endorsement or rejection.

The generation of French thinkers immediately prior to the Sixties luminaries is notable for two historians of science, Gaston Bachelard and Georges Canguilhem, both of whom wielded enormous influence over their successors. Canguilhem was particularly important for the young Michel Foucault, becoming "one of [his] closest intellectual friends and allies."[16] He could be seen as providing the initial impetus for Foucault's lifelong project of tracking the internal regimes of power circulating among the discourses of science, particularly the human sciences (psychology, medicine, sociology, human sexuality). Further evidence can be gleaned from Roland Barthes, who, after the publication of *S/Z* in 1970, acknowledged the part he played in making literary criticism more scientific, even as he had moved decisively beyond it. "I passed through a euphoric dream of scientificity," he memorably remarked, as much as lamenting the fact that the dream remained unrealized.[17] And let us not forget that one of the most influential works of the 1980s, Jean-François Lyotard's *The Postmodern Condition: A Report on Knowledge*, was primarily a book about science and technology.[18] Though questioning the classical scientific method of seeking determinate truths, and espousing instead the systemic unpredictability and paralogical instability of postmodern science, Lyotard nonetheless took techno-scientific discourse seriously, and acknowledged its importance in an increasingly computerized world.

But perhaps the best statement on the complexity of the theory–science nexus comes from Jacques Derrida. His legendary *annus mirabilis*, 1967, saw the publication of three books, including a study of what he called the "science of grammatology." In an interview the following year, conducted by Julia Kristeva, he was asked, "[T]o what extent is or is not grammatology a 'science?'"[19] Derrida replied that grammatology, the "science of textuality," had vigilant deconstructive work to do, and that meant working within existing scientific discourses.[20] Grammatological practice, he writes, must "accentuate whatever in the effective work of science contributes to freeing it of the metaphysical bonds that have borne on its definition and its movement since its beginnings. Grammatology must pursue and consolidate whatever, in scientific practice, has always already begun to exceed the logocentric closure."[21]

Science, then, is hampered by its *counter*-scientific tendencies for making metaphysical claims, for striving to attain the determination of "logocentric closure." Derrida here cites positivism—the claim that only observable, quantifiable phenomena count as meaningful—and scientism—the expansion of scientific method to encompass the entire life-world—as the most egregious offenders. It should be clear, then, that scientific practice itself possesses the wherewithal to curb these totalizing tendencies, in a kind of aporetic makeover; and that in assisting in this process of "correction," grammatology is opening the way to alternative futures, and to shaping its own writerly potentialities. This is why, says Derrida, there is no simple answer to the question of whether or not grammatology is a science. "In a word, I would say that [grammatology] *inscribes* and *delimits* science; it must freely and rigorously make the norms of science function in its own writing; once again, it *marks* and at the same time *loosens* the limit which closes classical scientificity" (36).

Derrida also declares that grammatology must avoid the cardinal error of all attempts at going beyond classical science, which is to fall into what he calls a "prescientific empiricism" (35). This is a striking pronouncement given that classical science is, of course, founded on empirical methods. Derrida would appear then to be warning against the dangers of scientific method in becoming an end in itself, and closing off the reflexive thinking that fosters self-critique. However, the most damning theoretical dismissal of that method comes from Fredric Jameson, and his 1972 study, *Marxism and Form*. Jameson sets his sights on "Anglo-American empirical realism," which he describes as the "dominant ideology of the Western countries."[22] Jameson's Marxist orientation leads him to decry it for opposing the intellectual dexterity of dialectical thinking—an ironic echo of Hegel's critique of empiricism for its constrictive focus on the given—but his objections go much deeper than that.[23] Empirical realism instates a pernicious method of "separating reality into airtight compartments," which means that any critique of capitalism is displaced by rhetoric about "freedom"; that politics cannot be thought alongside history and that any questioning of the status quo can only be limited and partial, only brought to bear on that which is "discrete and immediately verifiable."[24] Social consciousness, in short, is permanently stunted by the poverty and inadequacy of the empirical outlook on reality.

But although these attitudes have been reiterated by post-structuralist critics, the case against empiricism is, like other aspects of theory-and-science, far from closed. Gilles Deleuze, for example, reworks empiricism for his own ends, using it to account for his conception of human existence. He writes, "[W]e will speak of a transcendental empiricism in contrast to everything that makes up the world of the subject and the object."[25] It is not the sensation of simple empiricism that he invokes, but "the passage from one [sensation] to the other as becoming, as increase or decrease in power."[26] For Deleuze, empiricism is akin to pluralism; instead of unity or totality he seeks out multiplicity, defined as "a set of lines or dimensions which are irreducible to one another."[27] And unlike orthodox empiricism, which involves the painstaking recording of data, based on certain precepts determined in advance, transcendental empiricism bypasses abstractions and generalizations—the starting points for rationalist philosophies—in order to ascertain the unruly actuality of experience. Deleuze calls it the "concrete richness of the sensible": pure, unmediated perception, sensation, imprinting of impressions, rather than reflections of experience.[28] It cogently defines his singular and severe modification of empirical method.

Science, then, is entangled in theory in convoluted and manifold ways—whether it be Derrida's crusade to rid scientific discourse of its metaphysical pretensions, through grammatological critique; Deleuze's goal of being more empirical than the empiricists; or more recent theoretical analyses of biopolitics that engage closely with the life sciences. To get to the nub of my argument, that theory and cognitivism are radically incompatible, I will first point out the irreconcilable philosophical differences between the two forms of thinking, and then demonstrate more specifically, via a case study, why a "cognitive-based poststructuralism" *in its current form* is inherently unworkable.

Language, epistemology and *différance*

Cognitivist approaches see language as something that issues directly from human activity, securing an intimate and agential bond between the two. Continental theory, by contrast, conceives of language as an impersonal archive, an indicator of alterity that can be steered in certain directions without being (even in any limited cognitivist sense) either instrumentalized or owned. It is not so much language *per se* that poses problems, however, as *mind*—or rather, mind's relationship to language, subjectivity and meaning. Mind, as one early cognitivist-literary study notes, is "the very site of meaning and creativity"—a move that restores *agency* to the thinking, perceiving, self-aware subject.[29] Theory's indifference to the biology of mind is, according to some cognitivist critics, its most serious weakness; this is, however, to overlook the philosophical underpinnings that shape its operations. Continental theorists have taken a keen interest in perception—think of Derrida's work on the ear in the *Grammatology*, for example, or in his tribute to Jean-Luc Nancy and touch—but when it comes to the mind, they do not accord it any special status, based on its cognitive processing capability.[30] Rather, theory treats the mind as the space of experience—and, importantly, as a *subject-less* experience, an impersonal opening that cannot be filled out with the consoling assurances of self-presence.

This is most pronounced when it comes to epistemology. In his "Report on Knowledge," aka. *The Postmodern Condition*, Lyotard offers a decidedly *noncognitive* understanding of knowledge in postmodernity. He refers to the "mercantilization" and the "exteriorization" of knowledge, something that is held at a distance from the "knower." He writes, "The old principle that the acquisition of knowledge is indissociable from the training of minds, or even of individuals, is becoming obsolete and will become ever more so."[31] Just as Lyotard insists on knowledge without a knower, Deleuzean empiricism describes, as we have seen, experience that takes place in the absence of a self-grounded subject. As a theoretical precept, this notion can be traced back to Georges Bataille and Maurice Blanchot, and their post-Nietzschean perorations on "inner experience" and "limit-experience."[32] In other words, it is one of the philosophical cornerstones of theory, this striving for a nonassimilable relation to an outside, an otherness, a *not I*, the task of which is necessarily ongoing. With theory, in short, *becoming* is raised over *knowledge* as an intervention in, or suspension of, the quest for mastery.

Continental theory deals for the most part with the immaterial—with the oblique, unconscious forces that channel power, desire and ideology, and that evade empirical capture. Theory operates, then, as a kind of symptomatology, reading culture and its discontents through a diagnostic lens. Its analytical horizon is the ripple effects generated by language, subjectivity, social formation and so on, by means of which it addresses more specifically hermeneutical questions of meaning and interpretation. If high theory found "materialist" applications in the age of protest, through the shocks, threats and euphorias that abetted the various 1960s movements (ignited by the *événéments* of May 1968), post-theory is fitted to a more disillusioned, disenchanted age. Taking shape after the breakup of the Soviet bloc, and the ostensive triumph of liberal capitalism, it confronts the waning of revolutionary hopes in the vertiginous, protean context of global postmodernity.

CLS represents a deliberate turn away from the historical, social and political conditions that shape the literary, toward the universal structures of cognition.[33] Moreover, its rise (though not its genesis) is in step with the principles of technological reason that underpin the Internet age. The latter was enabled by assimilating the logic of brain function to the logic of computer programming, which meant finding ways to map thought processes onto software programs. Or, reading this the other way around, we could say that the Internet has provided an interactive model for the convolutions of brain function, with disparate users as synaptic agents working in unison. "We have entered the age of life as information," writes Melinda Cooper, addressing "liberal war" in the new century.[34] Cooper affirms just how material the virtual is, how information is more tangible and graspable than, say, the coded murmurings of the unconscious. Cognitive approaches to literature thus provide a timely theoretical platform for a world bounded by digital flows and networked subjects.[35]

There would seem, then, to be an unbridgeable gap between cognitivist and continental attitudes to human experience. In terms of the CLS writers most invested in theoretical concerns, seeking to beget a cognitive-based post-structuralism, there are other incompatibilities. When they talk about theory, for example, they mean "high" or "pure" theory, which, in nearly all cases, comes down to just three names: Derrida, Foucault and Lacan. In particular, it is "Derridean deconstruction" that is most often taken as representative of "poststructuralism," of "French theory," or of "postmodern relativism" *tout entier*.

Ellen Spolsky's reading of Darwin and Derrida, in 2002, is a case in point, in which she argues for the productive compatibility of natural selection and deconstruction.[36] Spolsky makes no mention of a 1996 article by Joseph Carroll, a critic in the vanguard of cognitive-evolutionary literary studies, in which Darwinian adaptation is shown as radically *incompatible* with Derridean deconstruction. In a reversal of the usual denigrations of theory, which see it as bleakly deterministic, ceding nothing to free will, Carroll argues (with greater myopia and polemical disregard) that theory refuses to recognize the "constraints of biology," and that its political agenda is "anarchistic utopianism."[37] Spolsky, by contrast, lays claim to a sort of "third way," a limited autonomy that just happens to be enough for natural selection to do its work—in the fit between organism and environment—and for the Derridean "free play" that is the movement of *différance*, ensuring that meanings and referents can never properly, *fully* coincide.

Spolsky avers that "nothing could be more adaptationist, more Darwinian than deconstruction and post-structuralism, since both understand structuration...as an activity that happens within and in response to a specific environment.... Since the cultural/biological nexus is always in motion, it never exactly fits."[38] At the very least, this analogy poses intractable philosophical problems. Natural selection is a mechanism that conditions the survival and development of all animal species, and centers on those species' capacities for adaptation. *Différance*, however, concerns the Western habit of overvaluing the word/reason nexus (or *logos*)—an overvaluation that discloses, among other things, an ethnocentrism at the heart of our cultural systems.[39] By focusing solely on *function*, Spolsky draws attention away from the nonadaptationist—and, hence, counter-Darwinian—cast of deconstruction.

To count as "Darwinian," writes Spolsky, a theory must "account for systematicity, that is, for stability and predictability, while allowing the possibility of adaptive change."[40] In a Derridean or deconstructive context, "systematicity" and "change" are predicated on the repeatable or *iterable* potentiality of language (as Spolsky acknowledges).[41] Because of this potentiality, writes Derrida,

> a written syntagma can always be detached from the chain in which it is inserted or given without causing it to lose all possibility of functioning, if not all possibility of "communicating," precisely. One can perhaps come to recognize other possibilities in it by inscribing it or *grafting* it onto other chains. No context can entirely enclose it.[42]

Iterability thus implies *systematic* language usage, such that effective communication can take place between users, who are adept with its codes, and *changeable* language usage, in which inscriptions from one context (or "chain") can be grafted onto another, yielding a range of semantic possibilities not present in the original context. But "change" here, like Derridean change more generally, is not Spolsky's *adaptive* change, which has its basis in cognitive flexibility. When Derrida introduces the possibility of variation or transformation into his philosophical notations, it is invariably future-oriented, undecidable and/or reliant upon (as Paul Patton remarks) "a certain usage of the absolute or the unconditioned."[43] None of these epithets is applicable to Darwinian adaptation.

Spolsky's title is somewhat misleading, given that the implied collocation of "Darwin and Derrida" occupies barely a paragraph, and is vastly outweighed by more general remarks about post-structuralism and reading (textuality, figuration, representational systems, social structures). Nested amidst these conjectures is a somewhat questionable remark about Foucauldian historicity: "The variations and revisions for both Darwin and post-structuralists are neither divinely nor benignly directed. Here Darwin and Foucault must part company. Darwin would no more have attributed change to a malignant intention, as Foucault always seemed to, than to an angelic intention."[44] Outlining his Nietzsche-derived method of reading history, Foucault famously profiles the genealogist: "He must be able to recognize the events of history, its jolts, its surprises, its unsteady victories and unpalatable defeats—the basis of all beginnings, atavisms, and heredities."[45] As a view of the past, seen through the archive, this gives no hint as to intention, malignant or otherwise.

We might also note which parts of the literary sphere the most enthusiastic critics of cognitive-based post-structuralism occupy. Ellen Spolsky, F. Elizabeth Hart and Mary Thomas Crane are all early-modern specialists, with a particular interest in Shakespeare; and Alan Richardson's focus is British Romanticism and Jane Austen. It is not clear why so few modernist critics have come forward and brought cognitive-based approaches to bear on their field.[46] Given that modernist writing is, to a large extent, the provenance of continental theory, it is a surprising gap in the field, and something that belies the supposedly "universal" structures of mind that permit cognitive-oriented critics to theorize about literary works.

If we are, indeed, in a "post-theoretical" world, then any adequate assessment of theory's legacy must confront the possibility that the reconstruction of its history and poetics will look considerably different in the light of the cognitive turn. But just as there is a critical reluctance on the part of continental theorists to address that turn, so too do CLS advocates themselves display a major critical blind spot when it comes to theory. The persistent rolling-out of Derrida, Foucault and Lacan means there is no indication of the existence of, much less any kind of critical engagement with, the doyens of post-theory. This is a glaring oversight when many of the thinkers identifiable as post-theoretical are no less engaged with science than were their predecessors.

Alain Badiou has written at length and in great detail on what he calls the "science of being," and on the structures that underlie it.[47] In his study of the philosopher's work, Jason Barker stresses that "Badiou is above all...a mathematical philosopher, and no serious introduction to his work could bypass its scientific foundations."[48] Moreover, Badiou draws freely on the rationalist heritage of philosophy—a heritage that he is trying to revivify—in order to construct his own "meticulously rationalist system."[49] Badiou, in short, exemplifies the ongoing engagement of continental theory with science, even as he continues to be ignored by cognitivist-based critics. Were the latter to engage with such a thinker—indeed, with the intellectual challenge of post-theory itself—it is conceivable that the impasse identified above could be overcome.

Notes

1   Nicholas O. Warner, "In Search of Literary Science: The Russian Formalist Tradition," *Pacific Coast Philology* 17, nos. 1–2 (November 1982): 71. The exception to the formalist rule here is American New Criticism, once (wrongly) accused of making criticism more scientific, despite its avowedly antiscientific bent. In fact, it was the desire for a more *systematic* critical method that prompted comparisons with scientific practice, as John Crowe Ransom makes clear: "Criticism must become more scientific, or precise and systematic...It will never be a very exact science, or even a nearly exact one. But neither will psychology...It does not matter whether we call them sciences or just systematic studies; the total effort of each to be effective must be consolidated and kept going" (587). Ransom, "Criticism, Inc.," *Virginia Quarterly Review* 13, no. 4 (Fall 1937): 586–602. See also René Wellek, "The New Criticism: Pro and Contra," *Critical Inquiry* 4, no. 4 (Summer 1978): 618–9.
2   Alan Sokal and Jean Bricmont, *Intellectual Impostures: Postmodern Philosophers' Abuse of Science* (London: Profile, 1998), 1.
3   See John Sturrock, "Le pauvre Sokal," *London Review of Books* 20, no. 14 (16 July 1998): 8–9; and Jonathan Rée, "The Storm Is Put Back in Its Teacup," *Times Higher Education* 1, no. 340 (10 July 1998): 22.

4 This was first announced sporadically throughout the 1990s (Nancy Easterlin and
   Barbara Reibling, eds., *After Poststructuralism: Interdisciplinarity and Literary Theory*
   (Evanston, IL: Northwestern University Press, 1993); Frederick Crews, "The End of
   the Poststructuralist Era," in *The Emperor Redressed: Critiquing Critical Theory*, ed.
   Dwight Eddins (Tuscaloosa, AL: University of Alabama Press, 1995); Wendell V.
   Harris, ed., *Beyond Poststructuralism: The Speculations of Theory and the Experience
   of Literature* (University Park, PA: Pennsylvania State University Press, 1996);
   Thomas Docherty, *After Theory* (Edinburgh: Edinburgh University Press, 1996); and
   Martin McQuillan, *Post-Theory: New Directions in Criticism* (Edinburgh: Edinburgh
   University Press, 1999)) and then more urgently and resolutely in the new century
   (see Tom Cohen and others, eds., *Material Events: Paul de Man and the Afterlife
   of Theory* (Minneapolis, MA and London: University of Minnesota Press, 2001);
   Herman Rapaport, *The Theory Mess: Deconstruction in Eclipse* (New York: Columbia
   University Press, 2001); Valentine Cunningham, *Reading after Theory* (Oxford:
   Blackwell, 2002); Terry Eagleton, *After Theory* (New York: Basic, 2003); Michael
   Payne and John Schad, *life.after.theory* (London: Continuum, 2003); Ivan Callus and
   Stefan Herbrechter, eds., *Post-Theory, Culture, Criticism* (Amsterdam: Rodopi, 2004);
   and Gavin Kitching, *The Trouble with Theory: The Educational Costs of Postmodernism*
   (Sydney, NSW: Allen and Unwin, 2008)).
5 Colin Davis, *After Poststructuralism: Reading, Stories and Theory* (New York:
   Routledge, 2004), 5.
6 F. Elizabeth Hart, "The View of Where We've Been and Where We' d Like to Go,"
   College Literature 33, no. 1 (Winter 2006): 226.
7 See Reuven Tsur, *What Is Cognitive Poetics?: Papers in Cognitive Poetics* 1 (Tel Aviv:
   The Katz Research Institute for Hebrew Literature, Tel Aviv University, 1982).
8 I am grateful to Laura Salisbury for providing invaluable background information on
   literary cognitivism.
9 Mark Turner, *Reading Minds: The Study of English in the Age of Cognitive Science*
   (Princeton: Princeton University Press, 1991), 3.
10 Brian Boyd, "Jane, Meet Charles: Literature, Evolution, and Human Nature,"
   Philosophy and Literature 22, no. 1 (1998): 1.
11 Joseph Carroll, *Literary Darwinism: Evolution, Human Nature, and Literature*
   (New York: Routledge, 2004), xvi.
12 Alan Richardson and Francis Steen, "Literature and the Cognitive Revolution: An
   Introduction," *Poetics Today* 23, no. 1 (Spring 2002): 2.
13 Slavoj Žižek, "Lacan between Cultural Studies and Cognitivism," *Umbr(a): A Journal
   of the Unconscious* 4 (2000): 9.
14 F. Elizabeth Hart, "The Epistemology of Cognitive Literary Studies," *Philosophy and
   Literature* 25 (2001): 318–20. A less doctrinaire example of a continental theorist
   addressing the cognitive turn can be seen in Bruno Latour's review of *Cognition in
   the Wild*, Edwin Hutchins' 1995 study of "distributed cognition" in certain practical
   contexts. Hutchins draws on psychology and anthropology, rather than literary
   studies, but is nonetheless concerned with the cognitive aspects of cultural activity.
   Latour states that "Hutchins has redefined cognition in terms of coordination of
   representational media" (61), i.e., he has shifted the emphasis from the agential,
   mindful individual to the propagation and coordination of media representations—a
   shift that brings "cognitive anthropology" closer to the precepts of continental
   theory. My thanks to John Sutton for this reference. Latour, "Cogito ergo sumus! Or

Psychology Swept Aside Inside Out by the Fresh Air of the Upper Deck…," *Mind, Culture, and Activity: An International Journal* 3, no. 1 (1996): 54–63.

15 Slavoj Žižek, *The Parallax View* (Cambridge, MA: MIT Press, 2006), 175–9.

16 James Miller, *The Passion of Michel Foucault* (Cambridge, MA: Harvard University Press, 1994), 59.

17 Roland Barthes, "Réponses," *Tel Quel* 47 (Autumn 1971): 97.

18 Jean-François Lyotard, *The Postmodern Condition: A Report on Knowledge*, trans. Geoff Bennington and Brian Massumi (Manchester: Manchester University Press, 1979; 1984).

19 Jacques Derrida, *Positions*, trans. Alan Bass (Chicago: University of Chicago Press, 1981), 35.

20 Derrida, *Positions*, 34.

21 Derrida, *Positions*, 35–6.

22 Fredric Jameson, *Marxism and Form: Twentieth-Century Dialectical Theories of Literature* (Princeton: Princeton University Press, 1972), 367.

23 G. W. F. Hegel, *Hegel's Logic: Being Part One of the Encyclopedia of the Physical Sciences*, trans. William Wallace (Oxford: Clarendon Press, 1975), 61–3.

24 Jameson, *Marxism and Form*, 368.

25 Gilles Deleuze, *Pure Immanence: Essays on a Life*, trans. Anne Boyman (New York: Zone, 2001), 25.

26 Deleuze, *Pure Immanence*, 25.

27 Gilles Deleuze, *Dialogues II*, trans. Hugh Tomlinson and Barbara Habberjam (New York: Continuum, 2006), vi.

28 Deleuze, *Dialogues II*, 54.

29 Joseph M. Bizup and Eugene R. Kintgen, "The Cognitive Paradigm in Literary Studies," *College English* 55, no. 8 (December 1993): 849.

30 Jacques Derrida, *On Touching, Jean-Luc Nancy*, trans. Christine Irizarry (Stanford: Stanford University Press, 2005).

31 Lyotard, *The Postmodern Condition*, 4.

32 See George Bataille, *Inner Experience*, trans. Leslie A. Boldt (Albany, NY: SUNY Press, 1988), 39; and Maurice Blanchot, *The Infinite Conversation*, trans. Susan Hanson (Minneapolis, MA: University of Minnesota Press, 1993), 202–15.

33 Jonathan Gottschall, *Literature, Science, and a New Humanities* (New York: Palgrave Macmillan, 2008), 10–3.

34 Melinda Cooper, rev. of Michael Dillon and Julian Reid, "The Liberal Way of War: Killing to Make Life Live," *Radical Philosophy* 160 (March/April 2010): 52.

35 The Deleuzian inflection here is deliberate, if only to highlight how his work has been appropriated by acolytes of digital capitalism. Adam Schatz makes a good case for what he calls this "perversion" of his philosophy: "Indeed, the language of desire, multiplicity and all the rest is no longer the language of revolution. It is the language of cyberspace, and of neoliberal capitalism. Deleuze and Guattari's desiring machines, constantly seeking out new sensations, look a lot like today's permanently distracted consumers and websurfers" (12). Shatz, "Desire Was Everywhere," *London Review of Books* 32, no. 24 (16 December 2010): 9–12.

36 Ellen Spolsky, "Darwin and Derrida: Cognitive Literary Theory as a Species of Post-Structuralism," *Poetics Today* 23, no. 1 (Spring 2002): 43–62.

37 Joseph Carroll, "Poststructuralism, Cultural Constructivism and Evolutionary Biology," *Symplokē* 4, nos. 1–2 (Winter/Summer 1996): 215.

38 Spolsky, "Darwin and Derrida," 56.
39 See Jacques Derrida, *Of Grammatology*, trans. Gayatri Chakravorty Spivak (Baltimore, MD: The Johns Hopkins University Press, 1998), 3.
40 Spolsky, "Darwin and Derrida," 58.
41 Spolsky, "Darwin and Derrida," 50.
42 Jacques Derrida, *Limited Inc.*, trans. Alan Bass (Evanston, IL: Northwestern University Press, 1972), 9.
43 Paul Patton, "Future Politics," in *Between Deleuze and Derrida*, ed. Paul Patton and John Protevi (London: Continuum, 2003), 17.
44 Spolsky, "Darwin and Derrida," 57.
45 Michel Foucault, *The Foucault Reader*, ed. Paul Rabinow (Harmondsworth: Penguin, 1986), 144–5.
46 Performance studies is one area where modernist work *has* been addressed. See Bruce McConachie and F. Elizabeth Hart, *Performance and Cognition: Theatre Studies and the Cognitive Turn* (London: Routledge, 2006). And a recent study has brought cognitivist-based criticism to bear fruitfully on Imagist poetry. See Daniel W. Gleason, "The Visual Experience of Image Metaphor: Cognitive Insights into Imagist Figures," *Poetics Today* 30, no. 3 (Fall 2009): 423–70.
47 See Alain Badiou, *Being and Event*, trans. Oliver Feltham (New York: Continuum, 2005).
48 Jason Barker, *Alain Badiou: A Critical Introduction* (London: Pluto Press, 2002), 8.
49 Barker, *Alain Badiou*, 130.

4

Thinking with the World: Coetzee's *Elizabeth Costello*

Anthony Uhlmann

This chapter begins with a critique of two foundational propositions within the emerging discipline of cognitive poetics: first, that human consciousness provides an adequate model or analog for both thought itself and the nature of the novel; second, that the kind of thought which emerges from human consciousness is built around metaphor. I argue that we need to be aware of the limitations imposed by these propositions, and consider the extent to which they are capable of fully accounting for the kind of thinking that takes place in literature. I move from here to consider how one of the most interesting strands of cognitive psychology and cognitive science, "distributed cognition" or "extended mind" might be applied to ideas of literary practice.[1] I end by developing a reading of J. M. Coetzee's novel *Elizabeth Costello* to reflect further on these issues.

Recent advances in cognitive science have been seized upon by literary criticism, as these advances have in part moved away from narrowly rational understandings of thought processes (which reduce thinking to logic), in demonstrating that human cognition depends as much on embodied emotional responses and tendencies as upon logical processes.[2] A focus upon the brain and brain function has also been seen to offer evidentiary support for claims about thought processes, and as such these have been seen to add weight to claims made through literary criticism for the importance of literary production to human understanding.[3]

Influential theorists have emerged who have begun to adapt insights and concepts from cognitive science, cognitive psychology and philosophy of mind to an understanding of literary practice. Lisa Zunshine, for example, developing Mark Turner's concept of "mind-reading," which she pairs with "metarepresentation," argues that because we think and feel we believe others to think and feel and this process generates the fields of meaning we inhabit, as we are able to interpret the minds of others as working in similar ways to our own.[4] These capacities in turn, she suggests, make possible and are explored in works of fiction and our readings of them. Working at a more fundamental level, within the tradition of linguistics, philosophy and psychology, Lakoff and Johnson argue that the basis of all thinking is metaphor.[5] These metaphors are prelinguistic and formed from bodily experiences that emerge as frames of reference or models that they call "image schema," which condition and determine our understanding of the things we perceive.[6]

While not wishing to discount the important insights that might be developed through these methods, I wish to underline here that they involve the presupposition that the primary model for thought or mind with which we should work in considering the nature of literature is the human mind (understood as inseparable from the human body so that thinking always involves feeling).[7] In turn, then, the concept of thought is identified with human consciousness. For example, when one undertakes Zunshine's version of "mind-reading," one attributes (even as one recognizes it might be an erroneous attribution) the quality of a perceiving consciousness (which is always at base a consciousness of a self) to other people and even things.

These presuppositions are defensible and productive: much fiction does involve engagement with or representations of human consciousness. Furthermore, we do make use of the capacities Zunshine identifies in reading fiction. Yet the human and the human mind also clearly exist within a larger frame, as part of an immeasurably larger whole (Nature) that is not determined by or beholden to human consciousness. Second, a work of fiction is not a human mind, nor, as Boyd points out in his response to Zunshine's work, do works of fiction always engage with embedded processes of mind-reading or metarepresentation.[8]

What I wish to underline is that the particular model for thinking one might choose has important implications for the potential to account for or adequately read works of literature. I wish to argue that "thought" in literature, while often engaging with levels of human consciousness, is not solely confined to human consciousness. Rather, the model of thinking first offered by Spinoza, which decouples thought from human consciousness and sees it instead as involving the *ideas* of all relations of causation in Nature, offers a more thorough frame through which the kinds of thinking that occur in literature might be understood. Spinoza's thought *includes* consciousness; yet rather than being understood as special and separate from the rest of the universe (as a "dominion within a dominion") human consciousness is understood to come into being and function through the same kinds of causal processes that generate all being.[9] Furthermore, Spinoza describes three kinds of knowledge that are available to humanity that roughly correspond to the imagination or consciousness (the first kind); reason or scientific understanding (the second kind); and intuition or immediate understanding (the third kind).[10] I argue in *Thinking in Literature* that, rather than being limited to the imagination, literary works are able to make use of all three of these kinds of knowledge in developing their representations.[11]

Lakoff and Johnson's idea that thought is built upon the metaphorical structuring of concepts is elegant and suggestive and has been highly influential in the emerging field of cognitive poetics. It attempts to escape the confines of language by describing how image schema (which are determined by the bodily contexts and conditions we actually experience in the world) generate frameworks of meaning that are nonlinguistic.[12] Yet the frame of the metaphor and the notion that thought is built upon conceptual metaphors is asserted rather than proven. With regard to cognitive psychology and linguistics, it has been criticized by Keysar and others, who have developed reading-time experiments that "call into question Lakoff and Johnson's central claim about the relationship between conventional expressions and conceptual mappings."[13] Equally tellingly it has been criticized with regard to its philosophical consistency. Marina Rakova summarizes her critique of the model they develop by indicating that "the idea of metaphorical structuring of concepts turns out to depend crucially on accepting a kind of extreme empiricism which is unlikely to be true."[14] Further, the focus on metaphor limits how the theory might be applied to a reading of literature. Literature, and rhetorical theory, makes use of a wide range of figures and tropes: metaphor is clearly an extremely important figure, but it is only one among many. Lakoff and Johnson do discuss metonymy, in chapter eight of *Metaphors We Live By*, but leave aside the rest. *The Norton Anthology of English Literature*, for example, lists 22 Figures of Thought under Rhetorical Figures including metaphor and metonymy.[15] All of these figures involve relations between signs or across elements within texts, but they can by no means be reduced to metaphor.

So too, if we are being asked to develop an understanding of thought built upon science why limit our model to cognitive science alone? As Michel Serres affirms, the hard sciences (once based exclusively on physical causation) are all increasingly becoming interested in information and the flow of information through systems of signs that can be recognized in molecular interactions, in chemical reactions, in DNA and elsewhere. Indeed for Serres, as for Spinoza, thought occurs everywhere in the natural world.[16] He states, "Our classical sciences calculate relations of power and energy, forces, and causes of movements. In so doing, they remain on the entropic scale. But today these sciences also go on to describe in all things the storage, emission, reception, and processing of information."[17]

These processes are fundamentally not metaphorical; rather, they involve relations of information as well as physical causation or causal relations. In order to account for such levels of complexity, one might attempt to develop a molecular semiotics or a bio-semiotics, but such endeavors necessarily involve understandings of relations within matter rather than an understanding of metaphor.[18] Mathematics too, which is mobilized in many fields of scientific thought to account for and predict kinds of causal interaction, involves considerations of relations, rather than metaphor.

This is not to discount the importance of metaphor to human consciousness, but neither life, being, nor the novel is limited to metaphor. That is, rather than itself being a primary category, metaphor is a subcategory of relation, even within consciousness.

An engagement with cognitive science, nevertheless, will no doubt offer insights for the study of literature. Yet, with the reservations expressed above in mind, it becomes still more important to consider whether there might be limitations with some of the models developed through cognitive science, problems that might limit the extent to which they might be applied to an adequate understanding of literary practice.

Cognitive scientists such as Andy Clark have argued that a weakness with the models developed by most mainstream cognitive science is found in how "mind" is understood to relate to the singular human organism. That is, any "mind" is usually understood to exist within the skin and the skull of an individual. Clark and others who have developed an approach sometimes called "distributed cognition" and sometimes called "extended mind" seek to alter the definition of the mind to enable it to include interactions not just between agents (other human minds), but within contexts, which include objects and tools that assist these agents in their thinking processes. At first sight this approach seems to overcome some of the problems I have mentioned above: such an approach moves beyond a single consciousness and sees thought as taking place within the world as much as within individuals. Indeed, the variety of approaches bracketed together as "distributed cognition" or "extended mind" promise a fuller response to questions that examine the nature of cognition, approaches that might allow genuine engagement with the kinds of thinking both described and performed through literature and related art forms.[19] The points of correspondence are not yet fully or completely aligned, however. It is worth tracing some of the areas of correspondence and some of the areas of divergence between thinking as it emerges through and is presented in literature and the descriptions of thinking available through distributed cognition.

Theories of distributed cognition have, since Edwin Hutchin's seminal 1995 study *Cognition in the Wild*, attempted to bridge the gap between the brain and nervous system and the physical and interpersonal contexts that surround it.[20] The range of interests and concerns addressed by distributed cognition are usefully summarized by John Sutton:

> On Clark's view, we are intricately psychologically tangled with, and our minds projected out into, a range of cognitive objects such as instruments, media, and other people. When (for example) an academic is writing a paper, or an artist is working on an abstract artwork, the intelligent activity driving the process can include or span (as well as the brain and body) a notebook, a sketchpad, scraps of paper with old notes, a friend at the other end of a phone call, various files on computer or on paper with records from different earlier stages and so on. [...] What makes this a view about distributed *cognition* is the point that such mind-tools are not simply cognitive commodities, for the use and profit of the active mind: rather, in certain circumstances, along with the brain and body interacting with them, they *are* the mind.[21]

The particular strand of distributed cognition developed here (and Sutton shows how there are a range of views which fall under the more general heading of distributed cognition) is extremely plastic and has been effectively applied to an understanding of memory.[22] Sutton has made use of it to develop readings of creative works (see in particular his essay on *Memento*) and has outlined the importance of an interdisciplinary approach to a fuller understanding of the nature of cognition, stating that "neuroscience must be coupled with the social sciences, history, media theory, and so on if we are to get at objective accounts of our cognitive hybridity."[23] The question remains, however, as to how effectively it might be applied to an understanding of literary practice.

There is still something of a gap that renders immediate application of the theories, to the extent that they have currently been developed, to literary theory. This relates to the "action-oriented" nature of distributed cognition, which is "set up for the integration of a range of embodied and interpersonal goals or processes."[24] The idea of action, or doing, is extremely useful to a theory of interaction or a system that functions through (usually, a limited range of) interactions. Yet, as became apparent with J. L. Austin's "Speech Act Theory," theories of goal-oriented action do not easily fit with the idea of literary practice, because the goals of literary practice are often not immediately clear with regard to specified actions. For example, in Austin's view literary statements (such as an actor pronouncing the words "I do" in a dramatized wedding on stage) are not seriously intended, and so must be bracketed out of his theory because they do not accomplish an action.[25] While distributed cognition is quite different to the Speech Act Theory of Austin, the nature of the relation to literary form seems, at present, similarly difficult for it to engage with. The theory fits well with certain kinds of practice that relate to literature: for example, it could be very usefully applied to the process of writing, as described in the example Sutton offers above. It might also be usefully applied to the performance of literary texts as Evelyn B. Tribble has done with her work on Shakespeare's Globe. Tribble shows how actors in Shakespeare's time worked effectively with the contexts they inhabited, making use of prompts, for example, to facilitate the smooth running of a tight schedule of performances.[26] Yet notwithstanding this, I would argue that the theory does not yet fully account for the kinds of thinking that are presented through literary form.

Most works of literature (even those closely tied to lines of action or story) are not limited to a single line of action-oriented depictions but rather offer an overview of a range of perspectives and a more or less complex interplay of lines of action. The thought that is thereby expressed within the work is not the mind of an individual or group acting in the world, or not only that; but rather, a world is created which itself thinks.

While the kinds of thinking represented in fiction still largely revolve around human interactions and understandings (even when the subjects described are nonhuman), the extent of thought in literature is different and relates to meaning and the generation of feeling and meaning rather than the achievement of an action. Even action-based works of fiction (which dominate mediums of representation) have a wider frame than currently seen in distributed cognition. That is, while distributed cognition might focus on a major line of action that is planned, clearly organized and realized, such as piloting a ship into harbor, literary fiction shows both intentional actions and actions that are unintended or out of the control of the agents represented in the texts.[27] Further, while distributed cognition focuses on goals, on the achievement of intended actions, literature, even when it describes "actions," does not achieve real actions; rather, literature develops interrelated representations of actions and ideas that generate meaning or feeling about these actions and ideas. The end achieved by literature concerns the felt meaning of thoughts and events rather than the accomplishment of an action.

Beyond consciousness: Intertextuality

It is worth attempting to underline the points of critique set out above with reference to an example. The work of J. M. Coetzee underlines, first, how the kind of thinking apparent in novels cannot be reduced to human consciousness; second, how novels make use of relations that include but go beyond metaphorical relations; and finally, how the kinds of relations represented in fiction are concerned with questions of meaning and the generation of feeling and meaning rather than with real action.

While he works in other ways and with other themes, an important technique Coetzee uses to produce or generate meaning in his works is what he terms "doubling."[28] This process commonly involves the relation of the text he writes to other texts with which his text deliberately and often provocatively enters into dialogue through dissonance or error as much as through resonance and correspondence.[29] The term, then, applies to the kind of intertextual relations Coetzee develops. The titles and contents of some of his novels (for example, *Foe*, which enters into dialogue with Daniel Defoe's life and his novel *Robinson Crusoe*, and *The Master of Petersburg*, which enters into dialogue with Fyodor Dostoevsky's life and his novel *Demons*) already clearly direct readers to certain texts, while other texts he enters into dialogue with are less obvious. At times, however, he draws attention to these in secondary material: his interviews with David Attwell and his critical texts invite readers to read other works alongside his fiction. For example, in *Doubling the Point* he underlines the relation between his novel *In the Heart of the Country* and two films: Chris Markers' *La Jetée* and Andrzej Munk's *The Passenger*.[30] While he also mentions the importance of the South African *Plaasroman* in this interview, he only offers further clues to this question in an essay written a decade after the novel appeared.[31] These interests have been noted before, and intertextuality is a well-known technique in literary form (though Coetzee develops it in unexpected ways).[32] With regard to the arguments developed here, however, it becomes apparent that the nature of intertextuality underlines the inadequacy of using human consciousness as a model, or analog for the novel. While representations of human consciousness are important to Coetzee's works, intertextuality functions through the relation of one work to another, or several others. That is, meaning is generated through relations that are not in themselves representations of human consciousness.

Beyond metaphor: Relation beyond action (felt meaning)

In *Elizabeth Costello* ideas are continuously in play, but the nature of the play of these ideas is complicated by the form of the novel, which constantly refers them to other often contradictory forms. This aspect of the work tends to exasperate some readers. Peter Singer was asked to respond to *The Lives of Animals* (which would become Lessons Three and Four in *Elizabeth Costello*) when the two chapters were first presented by Coetzee as the Princeton Tanner lectures of 1997–98. In his response to Coetzee, which clumsily attempts to mimic Coetzee's form, Singer sees Coetzee's approach as amounting to a kind of trick, and states, "Call me old-fashioned...but I prefer to keep truth and fiction clearly separate."[33]

For those who like their truth and fiction clearly separated, then, Coetzee's form can be maddening, but the form itself is also related to the species of madness described in the coda to the novel: the letter from one "Elizabeth C." to Francis Bacon dated

September 11, 1603. In this letter Elizabeth Chandos (whom we relate to Elizabeth Costello through the shared first name and initial of the surname) refers to this species of madness, where one sign is always related to another sign, and absolutely everything feels meaningful.

The letter from Elizabeth C. begins with a quotation from another fictional letter written by the German writer Hugo von Hofmannsthal in 1906. Here von Hofmannsthal takes on the persona of Lord Chandos, a fictional friend to the great English scientist and writer Francis Bacon, in a letter supposedly written in 1603. In this letter Chandos replies to Bacon, who has asked Chandos why he has not seen any works published by Chandos in recent times, when he was at one time such a promising writer. Chandos writes to explain his strange affliction, which has stopped him from writing. This can be summed up in the passage Coetzee cites:

> At such moments even a negligible creature, a dog, a rat, a beetle, a stunted apple tree, a cart track winding over a hill, a mossy stone, counts more for me than a night of bliss with the most beautiful, most devoted mistress. These dumb and in some cases inanimate creatures press towards me with such fullness, such a presence of love, that there is nothing in range of my rapturous eye that does not have life. It is as if everything, everything that exists, everything I can recall, everything my confused thinking touches on, means something. (Hugo von Hofmannsthal, "Letter of Lord Chandos to Lord Bacon," 1902)[34]

It is worth pausing on this text, which is not written by Coetzee, but with which he enters into intertextual relation, to begin to consider the question of the nature of the relations described and how they generate a feeling of meaning. Following Lakoff and Johnson metaphor is at the heart of thought, yet the character Lord Chandos seems to be suggesting something subtly different here. He lists a range of creatures and things. These creatures and things are not used metaphorically, and nor is the meaning they convey, for Lord Chandos, achieved through metaphor. That is, they stand for themselves and not for something else. They are, however, related by Lord Chandos to two things: "a presence of love" and "life." It is these relations, to love and life, that charge these various things with meaning. Indeed, the feeling of meaning itself here becomes a third term of relation with the things Chandos perceives: "everything...means something." The feeling of meaning is not dependent on metaphor, then, but with a logic that seems tautological, on the relation to meaning itself. If something is felt to have meaning it is meaningful. The feeling of meaning itself, at least for Chandos, is in turn associated with the sense of love and the sense of life. These insights call into question the centrality of metaphor to thinking, or the generation of meaning in literature; rather, relation itself might be argued to be ultimately more fundamental, with metaphor being one kind of relation among others; it is an important kind of relation, but it is only one kind.

So too, this passage might be seen to underline the difference between the end of literature and the end of real action (as set out, say, in Speech Act Theory, or in theories of distributed cognition, which both, necessarily perhaps, privilege action in describing communication and thought outside of literary domains). Chandos laments his inability to act. The inability to act in turn is tied to the proliferation of meaning. Meaning emerges through the readings of things that seem to generate spontaneously from his perception of them. In effect, his problem is that the world has become a work of fiction: it is now, predominantly, meaningful. A strange consequence of this is that he is now no longer able to act upon it.

Entering into dialogue with Hofmannsthal's text and his fictional characters Coetzee then develops the character of Chandos' wife, who is mentioned briefly in the original letter. The character Elizabeth C. Coetzee invents here, then, answers von Hofmannsthal's character Lord Chandos and the ideas von Hofmannsthal develops. Yet the character of Elizabeth C. offers a subtly different understanding of the manner in which meaning is generated, which is both more explicit in the understanding it offers of the processes through which meaning is generated and connects a different set of associations, with meaning itself.

> All is allegory, says my Philip. Each creature is key to all other creatures. A dog sitting in a patch of sun licking itself, says he, is at one moment a dog and at the next a vessel of revelation. And perhaps he speaks the truth, perhaps in the mind of our Creator (*our Creator*, I say) where we whirl about as if in a millrace we interpenetrate and are interpenetrated by fellow creatures by the thousand.[35]

Coetzee here offers a reading of Hofmannsthal that distorts and extends Hofmannsthal's ideas. While he does not turn to metaphor, he turns to a mode that is broadly similar in structure, and which, like metaphor, might be raised up as a dominant mode: allegory. Allegory involves the relation of one set of signs to another set of signs; further, it relates one set of meanings (the meaning of the "vehicle") to another set of meanings (the meaning of the "tenor"). The relation between the two sets is, as de Man has argued, arbitrary, just as, following Saussure, the relation between the elements of the linguistic sign are arbitrary. This differs from metaphor, which involves a play of similarity and difference (two signs are related in the metaphor but one resembles, and so also differs from, the other). Here, then, for Coetzee, the power that generates meaning is an arbitrary relation that carries the feeling of meaning.

Continuing the logic of allegorical structure Elizabeth relates the creatures not to themselves (as Chandos does), but to some meaningful otherness: "a dog" becomes "a vessel of revelation" (229). Note here how the second term is already identified with meaning itself. One might write, "a dog becomes meaning." Coetzee's Elizabeth then goes further by drawing in the figure of the Creator. God, or Nature, following Spinoza's identification of these two, is that which exists of necessity, and that which brings into being. God is also traditionally called upon to grant or guarantee meaning. In effect, then, Elizabeth imagines a Nature imbued with understanding, with thought.

At last Elizabeth turns to a metaphor to sharpen or more fully convey her idea: "as if in a millrace" (229). We picture ourselves rushing in the stream that heads toward a millstone, which will crush and intermingle what passes through it. Yet the image that is being introduced through this metaphor is an image of relation itself: of the interpenetration of things. The metaphor serves to help us picture interpenetration, but the phrase "we interpenetrate and are interpenetrated by fellow creatures by the thousand" is not dependent on the metaphor of the millrace. Rather, the process of interpenetration, if a Creator who underwrites or guarantees meaning exists, is given as standing for itself without any metaphorical mediation. Indeed, the power of the sentence depends upon us feeling that this *might not be* a metaphor. Again, then, against Lakoff and Johnson, metaphor is not the dominant element in the generation of meaning here. It is relation itself, and the relation of a feeling of meaning to the thing encountered, which allows it to generate meaning. Coetzee's text, like Hofmannsthal's, further underlines how this disease of meaning generates an inability to act in Lord Chandos.

Other signs push forward, without obvious explanation: the letter from Elizabeth C., for example, is dated "This 11 September" (230). In 2003 (when this novel appeared), it was impossible to refer to this date without readers thinking of September 11, 2001: when the Twin Towers were destroyed by Al Qaeda in New York. This resonance, in turn, seems to signify or require interpretation. Perhaps it causes us to think of a time when meaning itself becomes uncertain. This time of uncertainty, in turn, might be further generalized to a time when we are confronted by the reality of death: the imminence or unavoidability of death (be it our own or those we love). This is a moment at which action fails, or action ceases. The kind of confrontation that results from this failure or ending necessarily makes us question what things mean. These processes of serious questioning, rather than engaging with metaphor, engage with or attempt to come to terms with things that are, things that stand for themselves.

This line of thinking is very relevant to this novel, which follows Elizabeth Costello as her mind descends into confusion as she approaches death. So this doubling of signs with signs, with every relation generating more meaning, could become, or could be considered, maddening, or madness. On the other hand, it could be understood to be a kind of power, precisely, the power of fiction, which leads to different kinds of understanding than those available through other more narrowly conceived systems of thought or easily reconciled with systems which concentrate on human action or agency. It is not limited to conscious thought, as Zunshine's work implies, but creates a world which itself thinks (with Spinoza's first, second, and third kinds of knowledge). Rather than being limited to metaphor, as Lakoff and Johnson's work affirms, it develops various relations between signs that generate a sense of meaning. Rather than being concerned with bringing about an action, as distributed cognition requires, it concerns itself with focusing on the nature of meaning itself.

Notes

1   See John Sutton and others, "The Psychology of Memory, Extended Cognition, and Socially Distributed Remembering," *Phenomenology and the Cognitive Sciences* 9, no. 4 (December 2010): 521–60; Andy Clark, *Being There: Putting Brain, Body, and World Together Again* (Cambridge, MA: MIT Press, 1997); Richard Menary, ed., *The Extended Mind* (Cambridge, MA: MIT Press, 2010).

2   See Antonio Damasio, *Descartes' Error: Emotion, Reason, and the Human Brain* (New York: Random House, 1994); Antonio Damasio, *Looking for Spinoza: Joy, Sorrow, and the Feeling Brain* (New York: Random House, 2004); Eric Eich and others, *Counterpoints: Cognition, Memory, and Language* (Oxford: Oxford University Press, 2000); Tone Roald, *Cognition in Emotion: An Investigation through Experiences with Art* (Amsterdam: Rodopi, 2007); and Frederic Perez-Alvarez and Carme Timoneda-Gallart, *A Better Look at Intelligent Behavior: Cognition and Emotion* (New York: Nova Science Publishers, 2007).

3   "Mirror neurons," while still controversial, have been seen to offer a model that will allow the development of a new concept of empathy. See Stein Braten, ed., *On Being Moved: From Mirror Neurons to Empathy* (Amsterdam: John Benjamins Publishing, 2007); and Gregory Hickok, "Eight Problems for the Mirror Neuron Theory of Action Understanding in Monkeys and Humans," *Journal of Cognitive Neuroscience* 21, no. 7 (July 2009): 1229–43. See also the work of Brian Boyd, who links the importance of pattern recognition, among many other elements in cognitive functioning and cognitive evolution to the development of and the importance of narrative.

4   Lisa Zunshine, *Why We Read Fiction: Theory of the Mind and the Novel* (Columbus, OH: Ohio State University Press, 2006); Mark Turner, *Reading Minds: The Study of English in the Age of Cognitive Science* (Princeton: Princeton University Press, 1991).

5   George Lakoff and Mark Johnson, *Metaphors We Live By* (Chicago: University of Chicago Press, 2003).

6   Mark Johnson, *The Body in the Mind: The Bodily Basis of Meaning, Imagination, and Reason* (Chicago: University of Chicago Press, 1987); George Lakoff, *Women, Fire, and Dangerous Things: What Categories Reveal about the Mind* (Chicago: University of Chicago Press, 1987).

7   My understanding of concepts from cognitive science and how they might be productively applied to literary theory has been greatly enhanced through engagement with a talented doctoral student, Gavin Smith, whose own work demonstrates how ideas from Zunshine and Lakoff and Johnson, among others, might be applied extremely effectively to an understanding of the nature of literature. Smith, however, deepens the readings developed by these thinkers by drawing upon work from philosophical Pragmatists such as John Dewey and William James.

8   Brian Boyd, "Brian Boyd responds [to Lisa Zunshine]," *Philosophy and Literature* 31, no. 1 (April 2007): 197.

9   Benedictus de Spinoza, "Preface to *Ethics*," in *The Collected Works of Spinoza, Volume 1*, ed. and trans. Edwin Curley (Princeton: Princeton University Press, 1985), Part III, 491–2. See also Chapter 1 in Anthony Uhlmann, *Thinking in Literature: Joyce, Woolf, Nabokov* (London: Continuum, 2011).

10   Spinoza, *Ethics*, Part II, Proposition 40, Scholium 2, 477–8.

11   Uhlmann, *Thinking in Literature*, 9–19.

12   Johnson, *The Body in the Mind*; Lakoff, *Women, Fire, and Dangerous Things*.

13   Boaz Keysar, Yeshayahu Shen, Sam Glucksberg, and William S. Horton, "Conventional Language: How Metaphorical Is It?" *Journal of Memory and Language* 43 (2000): 576.

14   Marina Rakova, "The Philosophy of Embodied Realism: A High Price to Pay?" *Cognitive Linguistics* 13, no. 3 (2003): 215.

15   Stephen Greenblatt, ed., *The Norton Anthology of English Literature*, 8th ed., vol. 2 (New York: Norton, 2006), A76–8.

16 Michel Serres, *Atlas* (Paris: Flammarion, 1997); Michel Serres, "Feux et Signaux de Brume: Virginia Woolf's Lighthouse," *SubStance* 116:37, no. 2 (2008): 110–31.

17 Serres, "Feux et Signaux," 127.

18 See, for example, Koichiro Matsuno, "Molecular Semiotics towards the Emergence of Life," *Biosemiotics* 1, no. 1 (April 2008): 131–44; Marcello Barbieri, "Biosemiotics: A New Understanding of Life," *Naturwissenschaften* 95, no. 7 (2008): 577–99.

19 See Menary, ed., *The Extended Mind*; Clark, *Being There*; Andy Clark, "Reasons, Robots, and the Extended Mind," *Mind and Language* 16 (2001): 121–45; and Andy Clark, *Supersizing the Mind: Embodiment, Action, and Cognitive Extension* (Oxford: Oxford University Press, 2008); Robert A. Wilson, *Boundaries of the Mind: The Individual in the Fragile Sciences: Cognition* (Cambridge: Cambridge University Press, 2004); and Frederick Adams and Kenneth Aizawa, *The Bounds of Cognition* (Oxford: Wiley-Blackwell, 2008).

20 See Itiel E. Dror and Stevan R. Harnard, *Cognition Distributed: How Cognitive Technology Extends Our Minds* (Amsterdam: John Benjamins Publishing, 2007).

21 John Sutton, "Representation, Levels, and Context in Integrational Linguistics and Distributed Cognition," *Language Sciences* 26, no. 6 (November 2004): 505–6. See also Clark, *Being There*; Clark, "Reasons, Robots, and the Extended Mind," 121–45; and Clark, *Supersizing the Mind*.

22 Sutton and others, "The Psychology of Memory."

23 Sutton, "Representation," 518.

24 Sutton, "Representation," 507.

25 J. L. Austin, Chapter 7 in *How to Do Things with Words* (Cambridge, MA: Harvard University Press, 1975).

26 Evelyn B. Tribble, "Distributing Cognition in the Globe," *Shakespeare Quarterly* 56, no. 2 (Summer 2005): 135–55.

27 Edwin Hutchins, *Cognition in the Wild* (Cambridge, MA: MIT Press, 1995).

28 See J. M. Coetzee, *Doubling the Point: Essays and Interviews*, ed. David Attwell (Cambridge, MA: Harvard University Press, 1992).

29 See Anthony Uhlmann, "J. M. Coetzee and the Uses of Anachronism in *Summertime*," *Textual Practice* 26 (April 2012): 747–61; and Anthony Uhlmann, "Realism and Intertextuality in Coetzee's *Foe*," in *Strong Opinions: J. M. Coetzee and the Authority of Contemporary Fiction*, ed. Chris Danta, Sue Kossew, and Julian Murphet (London: Continuum, 2011), 81–95.

30 Coetzee, *Doubling the Point*, 60.

31 J. M. Coetzee, "Farm Novel and *Plaasroman* in South Africa," *English in Africa* 13, no. 2 (October 1986): 1–19.

32 Intertextual strategies are frequently mentioned in passing before the critics pass on to other points. See, for example: Sue Kossew, *Pen and Power. A Post-Colonial Reading of J. M. Coetzee and Andre Brink* (Amsterdam: Rodopi, 1996), 12; James Meffen, "Elizabeth Costello," in *A Companion to the Works of J. M. Coetzee*, ed. Tim Mehigan (New York: Camden House, 2011), 173; David Attwell, *J. M. Coetzee: South Africa and the Politics of Writing* (Los Angeles, CA: University of California Press, 1993), 101–3; and Louise Bethlehem, "*Elizabeth Costello* as Post-Apartheid Text," in *J. M. Coetzee in Context and Theory*, ed. Elleke Boehmer, Katy Iddiols, and Robert Eaglestone (London: Contiuum, 2011), 20. Clarkson has closely examined the relation between Coetzee's fiction and his critical writing, and Murphet and Patton develop insightful arguments related to opinion and the status of truth and

how this involves the relation to other texts. See Chris Danta, Sue Kossew, and Julian Murphet, eds., *Strong Opinions: J. M. Coetzee and the Authority of Contemporary Fiction* (London: Continuum, 2011); Carroll Clarkson, *J. M. Coetzee: Countervoices* (London: Palgrave, 2009). Critics who have dedicated articles or chapters specifically to intertextuality or what Hayes calls "co-textuality" in specific novels include: Kenneth Pellow, "Intertextuality and Other Analogues in J. M. Coetzee's *Slow Man*," *Contemporary Literature* 50, no. 3 (Fall 2009): 528–52; Peter Horn, "Michael K: Pastiche, Parody or the Inversion of Michael Kohlhaas," *Current Writing: Text and Reception in Southern Africa* 17, no. 2 (2005): 56–73; Tisha Turk, "Intertextuality and the Collaborative Construction of Narrative: J. M. Coetzee's *Foe*," *Narrative* 19, no. 3 (October 2011): 295–310; Laurence Wright, "David Lurie's Learning and the Meaning of J. M. Coetzee's *Disgrace*," in *J. M. Coetzee's Austerities*, ed. Graham Bradsaw and Michael Neill (Farnham: Ashgate, 2010), 147–62; Jens Martin Gurr, "Functions of Intertextuality and Metafiction in J. M. Coetzee's *Slow Man*," *Anglistik* 18, no. 1 (March 2007): 95–112; Patrick Hayes, *J. M. Coetzee and the Novel: Writing and Politics after Beckett* (New York: Oxford University Press, 2010), 106–29.

33   J. M. Coetzee, *The Lives of Animals*, including reflections by Majorie Garber, Peter Singer, Wendy Doniger and Barbara Smuts (Princeton: Princeton University Press, 2001), 86.

34   Cited in J. M. Coetzee, *Elizabeth Costello* (New York: Knopf, 2003), 226.

35   Coetzee, *Elizabeth Costello*, 229.

Part Two

Minds in History

5

"The Brain Is a Book which Reads Itself": Cultured Brains and Reductive Materialism from Diderot to J. J. C. Smart

Charles T. Wolfe

Materialism, brains and discontinuity

Günther Mensching once observed that materialism is a "discontinuous tradition,"[1] which does not proceed by a transmission of doctrines, modified from generation to generation. Rather, each period founds a form of materialism on new bases, from theology onto natural history and emergent biology in the Enlightenment, biochemistry in the nineteenth century, physics in the mid-twentieth century and neuroscience ever since. Additionally, the ontological status of the brain is recognized in the eighteenth century as a key challenge in articulating a form of materialism. I shall focus on this problematic status of the brain as a starting point for materialists, notably Denis Diderot in the eighteenth century and the twentieth-century proponents of the "identity theory" of brain and mind (hereafter IT). Here, the discontinuity is not due to changing intellectual or sociocultural contexts ("it is possible to attend to contexts and to brains at once"[2]) but rather to differing *attitudes toward the brain*, which themselves imply differing conceptions of science, materialism and culture.[3]

Materialism has no essence or suprahistorical definition, as it reflects particular intellectual constellations (thereby rendering any "history of materialism," like Lange's, untenable[4]), but most generally, it is the view that everything that is real is material or is the product of material processes. More precisely, materialism takes two distinct forms: a more cosmological claim about the ultimate nature of the world and a more specific claim about how what is mental is in fact cerebral: how mental processes *are* brain processes. Now, both of these seem to indicate a privileged relation between materialism and scientific inquiry—a privileged *role* for scientific inquiry.

An amusing, mostly unknown linguistic residue testifies to the close relation between materialism and the sciences. Prior to becoming a philosophical term in the late seventeenth century with More, Cudworth and Leibniz, the word "materialist" originally referred to pharmacists, who prepared the *materia medica*: the traveler Pierre Belon noted in 1553 that "Les drogueurs ou matérialistes qui vendent ordinairement les drogues par les villes de Turquie, sont pour la plupart hommes Juifs" ["The druggists or materialists who ordinarily sell drugs in the cities of Turkey are for the most part, Jewish men"].[5] Indeed, from materialists as druggists to the "identity theorists" of brain and mind in the 1960s (whose name came from psychophysics), and the subsequent *doxa* of materialism as the handmaiden of neuroscience, the question of *which* science is in play is always relevant.

In the twentieth century, the predominant science in the vision of a privileged relation between materialism and scientific inquiry was physics. Materialism became synonymous with "physicalism": the entities that were considered to be real were those described in the physics of the time. But what about the status of brains, including within a physicalist scheme? An uneasy alliance then appears: is the materialist a brain theorist or a metaphysician bringing the rest of the world into line with physics? As David Lewis noted in his defense of the IT, "a confidence in the explanatory adequacy of physics is a vital part, but not the whole, of any full-blooded materialism. It is the empirical foundation on which materialism builds its superstructure of ontological and cosmological doctrines, among them the identity theory."[6] In fact, it has been observed that much of the identity theory—in its blend of logic, semantics and physicalism— conspicuously left out the messy details of neuroscience altogether.[7]

My topic is not physicalism but rather the second species of materialism, claims about minds and brains, within which I distinguish more active, "plastic" visions of the brain from more passive visions, the former being open to an integration of brain and culture, science and our fiction-making capacity. Denis Diderot was one of the first thinkers to notice that any self-respecting materialist had to address the question of what brains do, and how much of our mental, affective, intellectual life is contained therein. This is not simply the prototypical materialist attribution of thought to the brain, which occurs 50–60 years earlier in John Toland ("Whatever be the Principle of Thinking in Animals, yet it cannot be perform'd but by the means of the Brain"; thought is a property of the brain[8]), and Anthony Collins (consciousness is "a real Quality, truly and properly inhering in the Subject itself, the Brain, as Modes of Motion do in some Bodies, and Roundness does in others"[9]). But neither Toland nor Collins feels compelled to provide more neuroanatomic detail or speculation; implicitly, this is not part of the responsibility of the philosopher as they see it.[10]

In contrast, what is unique in Diderot may not be flagrant, after a generation of models of neural complexity, "uncertain systems" and "self-organization" (some of which even credit Diderot, as Gerald Edelman does, for his network concepts of brain and nervous system[11]): the recognition that *the brain presents a special explanatory and ontological challenge to the materialist* in a way that atoms, trees or polyps do not. This recognition leads Diderot to formulate a new kind of materialism, in which the nervous system in particular and network models in general, such as the harpsichord, play a constitutive role.[12]

After this the topic grew stale—more elegantly, "the nineteenth-century nervous system was less dynamic"[13]—with repeated, knee-jerk reiterations of psychophysical identity by "vulgar materialists" such as Ludwig Büchner and Carl Vogt, who obsessively asserted that knowledge of the nervous system fully explains mental life, most famously in Vogt's crude formulation that "thought is to the brain what bile is to the liver or urine to the kidneys."[14] Here, scientific practice is collapsed into materialism as an ideology. In the 1950s–60s, a group of primarily Australian philosophers, U. T. Place, J. J. C. Smart and D. M. Armstrong (with contributions from Herbert Feigl and David Lewis), took up brain-mind materialism afresh, under the name "identity theory," in the sense that they were arguing for an *identity* between mental processes and cerebral processes; they actually waver in between being brain theorists (with surprisingly little invocation of neuroscientific evidence) and being metaphysicians (bringing the rest of the world into line with physics).

If we contrast Diderot's materialism with that of the identity theorists, several notable features emerge, chief of which was that Diderot allows for a much more culturally saturated brain, which he describes as a book—"except it is a book which reads itself," and that he expressed his materialism in the form of an experimental philosophical novel, *Le Rêve de D'Alembert* (1769). Rather than just extracting abstract claims from his writings, I note that Diderot presents materialism (definitely not just the handmaiden of science then) in a literary or a paraliterary work, which plays on experimentalism both in science and in style.[15] I focus on two cases of materialism, both of which invoke the brain and the status of cerebral processes, although very differently: Diderot and the identity theory of mind. But some attention to history is called for.

Fluidity and spirits

The move from eighteenth-century "neurophilosophy" to twentieth-century philosophy of mind may seem a large historical leap, but there is not much *philosophical* reflection on brains in the interim. What, then, of brains prior to Diderot? Doubtless the most important earlier episode in the history of brains is the neuroanatomical work of Thomas Willis, professor of natural philosophy at Oxford and a founding member of the Royal Society.

Willis' 1664 *De cerebri anatome* is a fascinating and influential work, articulating an experimental program for a bold, unconstrained neuroscience, filled with animal spirits and typologies of souls, yet based on comparative anatomy. Despite propelling the brain to the fore, however, Willis does not specifically worry about its particular *status*, or its cultural embeddedness. That is, unlike Toland and Collins' *metaphysical* assertion of mind-brain identity or Locke's "I shall not at present meddle with the Physical consideration of the Mind,"[16] Willis opens up neuroanatomy as an unbounded playing field, *without* committing to any dangerous philosophical considerations on matter and mind. However, his emphasis on fluids, fermentation, the chemistry of life and the mobility of animal spirits cannot be understated in terms of a yet-unwritten history of brain plasticity. Plasticity notoriously is a go-between concept, spanning experimental neuroscience and social, psychological, linguistic accounts of development, and sometimes invoked to stress the brain's uniquely adaptive character.[17]

A useful distinction, to which I return below, is between more "dynamic" and more "static" visions of the brain. Willis definitely belongs in the former category, for he envisions the brain as a plastic, self-transforming, self-organizing entity, while opponents (but also later localizationist neuroscientists) see the brain as more of a passive mechanism—a lump of matter "of a clammy and unactive Nature and Substance; [which] seems as far as we can judge of it to be a meer passive Principle, as to the Acts of inward Sensation and Intellection," in the words of one Boyle Lecturer attacking Willis,[18] or a mere "Cake of Sewet or Bowl of Curds," unfit to perform our cognitive operations, in Henry More's words.[19] Robert Boyle seems to be directly responding to More when he declares that "there must be in the brain...far more of mechanism than is obvious to a vulgar eye, or even to that of a dissector"; this "seemingly rude lump of soft matter" which looks almost like "so much custard" in fact has "strange things performed in it,...partly by the animal spirits it produces..."[20] A vision of brain privileging transmission, dynamism, fluidity and motion, or even just allowing for "more of mechanism in it," is rather different from a "clammy nature," a "cake of sewet" or a mere "rude lump of soft matter." For after all,

> like Aphrodite, animal spirits would not be among those hypothetical entities which meekly hang around waiting to be observed. Making sense of the bits of the world which move might require a certain shimmying. Just as in late-twentieth-century sciences "nothing is less static than the nervous system," so the baroque internal edifices of the early modern neurophysiology of spirits were maintained only by motion.[21]

And while a more positivistic history of science would not find a lot of material in the next hundred years of proto-neuroscience (aside from imaginative constructs such as Hartley's "vibratory neuropsychology" and Albrecht von Haller's experimental study of the nervous system), these "baroque internal edifices" bear various fruit. Initially, the focus on animal spirits as explanatory of cognitive processes and thus behavior generates various embodied, clandestine appropriations of neuroscience.[22] Subsequently, this overdetermination of the plasticity of spirits leads to an emphasis on the cultural plasticity of neurology itself: "like the modern nervous systems it sought to describe, neurology proved itself to be particularly susceptible to absorbing the impressions, sensations and contaminations of the broader cultural discourses in which it was immersed."[23]

If we combine this gradual recognition of a cultural sedimentation of nervous systems with the fascination with nerves as explanatory of various disorders, we get what G. S. Rousseau called a new "neuromania" in the eighteenth century: "in some qualified senses...much of the eighteenth-century Enlightenment was one magisterial footnote on nervous physiology, a remarkable attempt to secularize cognition and perception through the brain and its vassal nerves."[24] An intriguing case of this neuromania, and a central one here, is Diderot.

"The brain is a book which reads itself": Diderot and plasticity

Just as the present chapter is not an exercise in the sociocultural history of brains, similarly, it does not focus on the cultural embeddedness of "neuromania" (including spirits, brains, nerves, fibers), however fascinating that might be. I accept that brains are culturally sedimented, permeated in their material architecture by our culture, history and social organization, and that this sedimentation is reflected in cortical architecture, as first seen by the Soviet neuropsychologist Lev Vygotsky in the early twentieth century. Vygotsky emphasized the brain's embeddedness in the social world, arguing that early social interaction leads to synaptic modifications. As his collaborator Luria put it, "Social history ties the knots that produce new correlations between certain zones of the cerebral cortex."[25] In today's language, "Our minds and brains are (potentially) subject to constant change and alteration caused by our ordinary developmental engagement with cultural practices and the material world."[26] This is materialism *sensu stricto*, as it is a description of the properties of brains. Similarly, in the case of Diderot, we have someone who is not only fascinated with literary incarnations of the spirits (like Laurence Sterne in *Tristram Shandy*) but is also engaged in natural-philosophical reflection on bodies, organs, nerves and brains—one is tempted to say "scientific" reflection but the very name for this part of Diderot's œuvre is a problematic issue.

Diderot's reflection on the activity of brains and minds spans a variety of publications, some of which we would regard as novels, others as scientific commentary and others as plain "philosophy." The question of genres in his work is an old favorite, also as regards the relation between literature and science. Key texts here are his 1749 *Lettre sur les aveugles* and his 1769 "dialogue" *Le Rêve de D'Alembert*, both of which seamlessly combine scientific speculation and literary experimentation. For present purposes, however, most relevant in addition to the *Rêve* is his *Éléments de physiologie*, which he worked on during the last two decades of his life, and did not publish.[27] I shall first discuss the *Rêve* before turning to the *Éléments*, which contains the key statement on the brain as a book.

Le Rêve de D'Alembert was one of Diderot's personal favorites among his works, and remained unpublished during his lifetime; he gave one copy to Catherine the Great as a gift. It is divided into three dialogues, all of which feature real individuals as fictional characters. The first, between Diderot and D'Alembert, covers traditional philosophical issues such as self and world, matter and thought, and God. The second and main dialogue involves the somnolent D'Alembert, the doctor Bordeu and Mlle de Lespinasse. It is based on the conceit of a delirious D'Alembert, raving in his sleep (in fact letting dream associations do the argumentative work for him as he accepts what he denied in the first dialogue), so that his companion, Mlle de Lespinasse, grows alarmed and summons the doctor to whom she reports D'Alembert's utterances. The rhetorical ingenuity is that D'Alembert has essentially uttered a series of rather concise materialist pronouncements, which Bordeu proceeds to explicate, carrying the reasoning much further, including in various science-fiction-like thought experiments. Mlle de Lespinasse is somewhat shocked at some of these, primarily on moral grounds, but gradually begins, in Socratic fashion, to ask increasingly pointed questions. The third dialogue is shorter again, and involves only Bordeu and Mlle de Lespinasse, reprising certain issues from the second dialogue, including biological and social aspects of monsters, and our material and sexual nature.

The *Rêve* articulates a network model of sensibility and a metaphysics of living, sensing matter to buttress it. Sensibility (*sensibilité*, a.k.a. "sensitivity"[28]) is the property of the network, which is described through a series of metaphors—a bee-swarm, a harpsichord, a spider…and, in the *Éléments*, a crawfish:

> the entire nervous system resides in the medullary substance of the brain, the cerebellum, the extended spinal cord, and the ramifications of this substance throughout various parts of the body. It is a crawfish [spider], the nerves of which are the legs, and which is affected in various ways according to the leg.[29]

The bee-swarm is more a metaphor of organismic unity (our organs compose a whole organism like bees compose a swarm); the harpsichord is a step closer to our key metaphor of the book:

> This organic faculty, by internally connecting the sounds within it, produces and preserves the melody therein. Suppose that the harpsichord has the power to feel and to remember, and tell me if it will not know and repeat of its own accord the airs that you have played on its keys. We are instruments endowed with sensibility and memory; our senses are so many keys that are struck by surrounding nature, and that often strike themselves…[30]

This emphasis on sensibility should also be understood as underscoring how organisms are not like the passive recording mechanisms which fascinated earlier natural philosophers: as Diderot exclaims, "What a difference there is, between a sensing, living watch and a golden, iron, silver or copper watch!"[31] Notably, "our key characteristics lie in our brains, not in our external constitution (*organisation*)" so that "in order to explain the mechanism of memory we have to examine the soft substance of the brain."[32] Memory is a product of our *organisation* (a term that here means our overall physiological configuration): "What is memory?…A certain [kind of] *organisation* which grows, weakens and sometimes is entirely lost," "a corporeal quality," an "organic faculty," the aggregate of all the sensations I have experienced.[33] This makes for a different kind of materialism, but so far, it does not seem that unusual: we are different from other material arrangements of particles because our key characteristics reside in our brains, which themselves are the locus of cognitive processes. What *is* different is Diderot's central choice of metaphor for the brain, in the *Éléments*:

> In order to explain the mechanism of memory we have to treat the soft substance of the brain as a mass of sensitive and living wax, which can take on all sorts of shapes, losing none of those it received, and ceaselessly receiving new ones which it retains. There is the book. But where is the reader? The reader is the book itself. For it is a sensing, living, speaking book, which communicates by means of sounds and gestures the order of its sensations; and how does it read itself? By sensing what it is, and displaying it by means of sounds.[34]

Diderot may be influenced here by the mysterious, heterodox Benedictine monk Léger-Marie Deschamps—they met several times in 1769, when Diderot was writing the *Rêve*, and Deschamps shared with Diderot his "clandestine" materialist treatise, *La Vérité ou le vrai Système*.[35] Deschamps wrote, "to read me, to hear me read is to become composed of my work, which then acts physically by the eyes or ears on the fibres of the brain, and raises them to a given tone, according to its impressions on them."[36]

In fact, Diderot seems to move between different positions concerning the brain, at different times: either our key characteristics are located in our brain or the brain is just "an organ like any other," "a secondary organ,"[37] "merely a secretory organ;"[38] this wavering on whether the brain is "special" or "an organ like any other" occurs within the *Éléments* itself. It is likely that these shifting attitudes toward the ontological status of the brain map onto Diderot's shifting views on whether or not one can defend any degree of anthropocentrism within a naturalistic universe: that is, if the brain is special, it allows for a form of naturalism in which humans are unique, and if it is an organ like any other, we find ourselves in a more thoroughgoing naturalism—albeit one in which all of matter is, actually or potentially, *living* matter.

Similarly, Diderot sees that the concept of sensibility allows him to integrate the reactive, representational capacity of mind (the nervous system, the brain as a "book which reads itself"), *while maintaining a thoroughgoing naturalism*: there are no properties which are not properties of natural beings subject to causal processes as specified in the natural sciences, although these properties may vary. Naturalism as physicalism is rather different from Diderot's reduction to matter as the bearer of vital properties. Yet these "network" properties are not properties of matter as such. Rather, they belong to a body–brain network (like the spider and spider web which Diderot views as forming one organic system), which he describes as "a system of actions and reactions."[39]

But Diderot's claims are not just "scientific," even if there are naturalistic elements in both his experimental prose and his physiological notebooks. One approach views Diderot as a proto-Bachelardian poet-metaphysician of the cosmos[40] (as in the *Rêve*'s "human polyps on Jupiter or Saturn"[41]), who leaps into associative freedom, beyond the constrained empirical studies of scientists like Haller and others. Some describe this speculative dimension, in which Diderot's scientific imagination can reach conceptual "places" that science cannot, as a kind of science-fiction or better, as Anne Vila does, as "a thought experiment on sensibility"—a thought experiment which instantly has material effects and is itself "materialized."[42] The other view, which focuses on the *Éléments*, is to view Diderot as a commentator on scientific studies of sensibility who remains at the level of fragments, unable to provide his own scientific theory—at best, a (materialist) philosopher accumulating information to support his metaphysics. I prefer the more sympathetic and expansive version of this view, which does not strictly demarcate his reflections on sensibility, brains, bodies and networks from a genuine, if speculative (vitalist) life science.

Read from this perspective, two key features of Diderot's cultured-brain materialism appear more sharply: first, that the inextricable relation between thought experiments and the "materialization" of such acts of the imagination is constitutive of his thought: he speaks of "undertak[ing] by means of thought what Nature does sometimes."[43] In an extended materialist universe (albeit one in which sensibility is

a basic property of matter), imagination and what Diderot calls "supposition" play a
key role: the *extension of materialist ontology*. Similarly, when he engages with debates
on biological generation, Diderot neither dutifully takes notes on experimental
scientific work nor wildly speculates on it; he seeks to extend the reach of materialist
ontology—here, as regards Life. The second feature is that he would not countenance
a straightforward linear explanatory scheme in which knowledge of brains is more
primary and more exact than knowledge of culture. He would not think that a
future neuroscience would enable us to "explain" cultural forms, as in some current
neuroaesthetics, which tells us that in reading prose, "the line 'He had leathery hands'
has just stimulated your sensory cortex in a way 'he had rough hands' can never hope
to."[44] His way of integrating "cultured brain plasticity" ("the brain is a book which
reads itself") with broader imaginative extensions ("human polyps on Jupiter") is not
like neuroaesthetics, either in its positivistic incarnation (neuroscience *explains art*)
or in its utopian incarnation (creating new circuits in art means creating new circuits
in the brain, in Deleuze-Guattari's phrase).[45] It is less unidirectional and mechanistic
than the former, more flexible in its explanatory schemes; but it is also less utopian
than the latter. In this it partly resembles the libertine and clandestine appropriation
of scientific discourse as found in the so-called Radical Enlightenment.[46]

It is both striking and puzzling that the kind of dynamism on display both in early
modern discourses of animal spirits and in Diderot's vision of a self-transforming brain
is absent from the birth of experimental neuroscience in the nineteenth century. As
Sutton politely notes, the nervous system here was less dynamic.[47] But it is significant
here, for it is a further attempt—and a novel one—to correlate cognitive function with
bundles of "spatially structured living matter,"[48] under the heading of *localization*.
Most visible in this project is the "pseudo-science" of phrenology, along with various
assertions of psychophysical or psycho-physiological identity—which belong more to
a militant rhetoric of science than to the messy reality of empirical research. It is a very
different kind of identity, or at least a different kind of identity *claim*, than that of the
Australian materialists discussed below.

From the material organ of the mind to blotches on the wall: Identity quarrels

The localization of mental functions in parts of the brain has been described as the closest
meeting point of experimental natural science and core issues of human nature, including
the mind-body problem.[49] More precisely, by the nineteenth century "most physiologists,
physicians, and naturalists would [largely] agree that, whatever the function embodied
and instantiated by some organ, the activity of this bodily part resided...in the portion of
living matter by which it was subserved,"[50] as in Ewald Hering's 1870 address, "Memory
as a general function of organised matter."[51] Yet the one "site" where the correlation of
bundles of matter and functional properties was not clear was the brain.

Franz Joseph Gall (1739–1828) sought to correlate detailed anatomical descriptions
of the brain with morphological features of the skull, and with observations on the

physical, measurable, nature of our mental and moral faculties—what he called "organology" and his colleague Johann Spurzheim more enduringly termed "phrenology" (a term Gall rejected).[52] Each mental faculty possessed its organ, the development of which could be analyzed by examining the external features of the skull. For Gall, the brain was the material organ of the mind, composed of a definite number of compartments, each of which is the seat of an intellectual faculty or sentiment. Each mental function corresponded to a part of the cortex: the features of the mind were determined by the configuration of the brain.[53] The mind was seen as "a set of functions instantiated by spatially circumscribed and mutually connected portions of neural matter."[54]

Despite its somewhat nefarious ideological dimensions, phrenology and related projects are important because they explicitly defend an empirical form of mind-brain materialism, which naturalizes or at least partly demystifies the mental. These are reflections on the material basis of cognition, based on the experimental investigations of brains—portions of neural matter. Notice that this approach is light-years removed from Diderot's "cultured-brain materialism," which emphasizes plasticity and the sociocultural embeddedness of the brain; but, like his approach and unlike the IT, to which I now turn, it is a straightforward set of *empirical* claims.

The identity theory (IT), the project to philosophically articulate the identity between cerebral processes and mental processes, is the paradigmatic expression of materialism in twentieth-century English-speaking philosophy.[55] Here, the goal is to resolve or eliminate some of the problems that have arisen for philosophy as a result of the "mind-body problem," in at least two disparate ways, which hang together, sometimes well, sometimes awkwardly: *empirically* (seeking to apply some of the scientific successes of previous generations to the status of the mind) and *logically* (what does it mean to say that a mental event might be *the same* as a brain event?). Crucially, the status of the brain here differs from Diderot's "book which reads itself," including with regard to the status of science.

Smart states a mild version of the "scientific" approach (as we shall see, Place has a stronger version, bordering on scientism):

> *That everything should be explicable in terms of physics* (together of course with descriptions of the ways in which the parts are put together—roughly, biology is to physics as radio-engineering is to electro-magnetism) *except the occurrence of sensations seems to me to be frankly unbelievable.*[56]

Indeed, the question of *what science* the identity theorists found their claims on will be significant: is it neurology? molecular biology? physics (which yields the idea of causal closure)? This is distinct from the logical aspect of the question: when we say a sensation is a brain process, are there two *kinds* of things which are related (and what is the nature of the relation), or is there only *one thing*? Of course, these can be unified, as in Armstrong's presentation of the IT as a solution to the mind-body problem, which can account for (1) the unity of mind and body, (2) the numerical difference between minds, (3) the interaction of mind and body, (4) the emergence of mind (e.g. in evolutionary terms) and (5) inner states.[57] But in fact the IT (as distinct from later neurophilosophy, which focuses more on points 4 and 5) chiefly works on the first three points, in very internalist terms.

What exactly is happening when I say, "I see an orange blotch"? Smart's 1959 article begins abruptly: "Suppose that I report that I have at this moment a roundish, blurry-edged after-image which is yellowish towards its edge and orange towards its center. What is it that I am reporting?"[58] He later explains that he wants to show "that there are no philosophical arguments which compel us to be dualists"[59]: if recent science shows that organisms can be understood as physico-chemical mechanisms, what about the mind? Smart suggests, cautiously, that we should start by rethinking the *language* we use to describe mental events, such as "I am in pain" or "I see an orange blotch on the wall." Our sensation and the corresponding brain process *might well refer to the same thing*, even if the logic of the two statements may be different.[60]

The IT seeks to strip the "mental" dimension from my report of, say, a sensation of orange, so that it becomes "There is something going on within me like what happens when a certain physical stimulus is present." However, Smart cannot commit to *which* physical event the mental event is like; it is a *contingent* identity. That is why the IT is topic-neutral, more of a place-holder than a robust materialist account, although he has left room for science to "fill in the gaps." Indeed, as "brain-imaging evidence begins to replace the subject's introspective report in determining the occurrence and nature of her conscious experience," Place feels that the IT moves closer to being a genuine, verifiable *scientific* theory, just as for Feigl, a "detailed account of brain-mind identities is a matter of future progress of psychophysiological research."[61]

To Smart, this is partly right and partly wrong. He agrees that the claim "sensations are brain processes" can be tested scientifically (recall Vogt's "The brain secretes thought *like* the liver secretes bile"), yet he does not want to make empirical claims, not least because of the difficulty of correlating complex, intentional mental states with patterns of neuronal activity: "conscious experiences must be processes involving millions of neurons, and so their important likenesses and unlikenesses to one another may well be statistical in nature."[62] And statistical correlation is an unlikely basis for identity.[63] In the end, statistical correlations and contingent relations do not sound too boldly materialistic, unlike Diderot's ontologically assertive materialism: he may have thought brains were special, *qua* "books which read themselves," but Diderot was nevertheless willing to make empirical, *material* claims about living matter as a whole, including sensibility, cognition and mental life.

There is a surprising absence of scientific detail in the IT—of embodiment. There are hints of DNA and neurology; but mostly, there is physics: materialism post-1950s is *physicalism*. How does one get from physics to the specific relation between brain states and mental states? Armstrong says it is a "good bet"[64]; in fact it is partly an inductive argument based on the past successes of reductionist approaches. As Bickle and others note, there were various plausible candidates for psychoneural identities in scientific literature before the IT: Hebb's *The Organization of Behavior* (1949) explains psychological phenomena in terms of known neural mechanisms and processes. But the IT primarily focuses on the *logic* of the "identity" between sensations and cerebral processes (although as noted, Place differs from Smart on this). The contrast with Diderot and other materialists should be apparent: here, there is no strong claim that locates mental life in a bundle of (neural, material, sensing) matter. However much Diderot employed metaphors, he was speaking about the mode of existence of *real brains*. To be clear, the issue is not *how much* is known about the brain: writing after Gall and Flourens, Place and Smart know, or could refer to, far vaster swathes of neurocircuitry than Diderot or *a fortiori* Collins; but they chose not to.

Nevertheless, whether in the form of contingent identity claims (Smart) or of explicit empirical claims to be filled in by future neurophysiology (Place), the IT is, broadly speaking, *scientism*, that is, a vision in which materialism is ultimately fatal to philosophy by serving as the handmaiden of science:

> [I]t would seem that the long reign of the philosopher as the professional in charge of the mind-body problem is finally coming to its end. Just as ... the origins of the universe used to be a theological problem and is now an astronomical one, so the mind-body problem is about to pass from the grasp of the philosopher into that of the neuropsychologist.[65]

It should be clear that Diderot's materialism is not of this sort, notably because of its speculative, fictional component. Indeed, materialism does not *have to be* a "handmaiden" of the natural sciences; conversely, science is not necessarily "the laboratory of materialism."[66]

The brain between scientism and fiction

Materialisms diverge as they address the status of the brain, between more plastic and aesthetically open models (Diderot and others) and more static, quantitative models (including phrenology and the IT). The difference is not between a specifically cerebral materialism and more disembodied models; Toland and Collins also explicitly identify cerebral processes and mental processes, as does nineteenth-century localizationism in more detail (although it is not necessarily *philosophically* materialist) and psychophysics. Diderot is distinctive in recognizing a kind of cerebral plasticity and self-organization, *and* insisting on their irreducibly *fictional* dimension. Is he then the "predecessor" of a more holistic trend running counter to "Australian" materialism? This was claimed in once-fashionable works seeking to unify aesthetic complexity and physics, like that of Prigogine and Stengers.[67] But if we make Diderot into the poster child of an "enchanted materialism" of fiction and embodiment, we lose sight of his own reductionism. However, Diderot (like Vygotsky, for whom "History, changing the human type, depends on the cortex; the new socialist man will be created through the cortex"[68]) and some contemporary cultured-brain theorists provide not just a materialist outlook, but one which acknowledges the self-organizing dimension of brains.

One might say that Diderot's is a *materialism without physicalism*, whereas the IT is a *materialism without embodiment*.[69] Somehow, for reasons that are partly intuitive

and affective (embodiment implies affectivity), it is embodied materialism that
recognizes the "plasticity" of the book which reads itself, in contrast to the older view
of the brain as merely passive. Unlike the "clammy and unactive Substance," the "meer
passive Principle,"[70] Diderot's more plastic vision of the brain is neither passive nor
mechanistic. Cultured-brain materialism is thus not a "scientism" or a denial of the
symbolic and valuative dimensions of life, contrary to the criticisms launched recently
by David Hawkes—which are almost identical to the charges brought in a 1933 article
by Raymond Ruyer, tellingly entitled "What is living and what is dead in materialism."[71]

Ruyer suggests a thought-experiment: imagine a law court as seen through the eyes
of a materialist. "The halo of meanings, essences and values" vanishes, and what is
left is the "functioning of a sort of complicated mechanics" whereby brains produce
articulations, which in turn generate vibrations in the air, and thereby modify other
nervous systems.[72] For Ruyer, materialism is a strange kind of reductionism which
denies the reality of social institutions, values and, of course, minds. Hawkes' similar
vision has been nicely challenged by John Sutton and Evelyn B. Tribble. They note
(without any particular focus on the status of brains) that materialism need not claim
that "only matter exists," but is instead "firmly pluralist" in its ontologies: "Even if all
the things that exist supervene on or are realized in matter, the materialist can still
ascribe full-blown reality to tables and trees and tendons and toenails and tangos and
tendencies"; an account including the brain need not exclude "memories, affects, beliefs,
imaginings, dreams, decisions, and the whole array of psychological phenomena of
interest to literary, cultural, and historical theorists."[73]

The materialism of the "cultured brain" is very much of this sort: it integrates the
brain and the affects, cerebral architecture and our aptitude to produce fictions. But it
is not enough to rebut these "antelapsarian" visions of a cold, dead materialism seizing
living value, sentiment and meaning in its embrace and reducing them to piles of
"clammy" matter (sewet, curds, etc.). For from the opposite side of the spectrum, some
"neuroaesthetic" thinkers claim to integrate materialism, brain science and art, but in
the flattest way: "I picture a future for writing that dispenses with mystery wherever it
can, that embraces the astounding strides in thought-organ research. Ideally, a future
where neuroimaging both miniaturises and becomes widespread, augmenting the craft
of authors, critics, agents and publishing houses."[74]

Despite its potential scientism, the IT is not as caricaturally restrictive as this; it
can indeed consider that our knowledge of mental life is filled in by the progress of
neuroscience (Bickle), or instead become a "heuristic identity theory."[75] Either of these
can preserve narrativity as a supervenient feature, in which selfhood emerges out of
stories my brain "tells itself": a "narrative self"[76] in which "consciousness is a property
I have by virtue of my brain's attributing it to me. My story doesn't have to cohere
completely to be useful."[77] Of course, this narrativity is a far cry from Diderot's way of
preserving a role for fiction within materialism.

How is this role preserved? The *embodied* character of Diderot's materialism means
that the brain has particular properties distinct from physical nature as a whole. It
is a brain embedded in culture, expressed in works where experimentalism is both
"science," literature and metaphysics. Does the cultured-brain materialist have to grant

special ontological status to the brain? Clearly, for the IT, the brain does not have an ontology; there is physics, and anything above, including biology and neuroscience, is like special kinds of radio engineering. In contrast, for Diderot, it does. But how can materialism maintain that the brain has an ontology without reintroducing "kingdoms within kingdoms" (as Spinoza described the erroneous belief that human nature is apart from the laws of nature as a whole)? If we over-ontologize the brain in order to not be mystical dualists or knee-jerk antiscientists, we may also run the risk of reconfiguring humanity as just "a cerebral crystallization."[78]

Notes

1   Günther Mensching, "Le matérialisme, une tradition discontinue," *Materia actuosa…Mélanges en l'honneur d'Olivier Bloch*, eds. M. Benítez, A. McKenna and others (Paris: Champion, 2000), 525; 513. All translations are mine unless otherwise indicated.

2   John Sutton, *Philosophy and Memory Traces: Descartes to Connectionism* (Cambridge: Cambridge University Press, 1998), 1. For the sociocultural history of brains see Anne Harrington, *Medicine, Mind, and the Double Brain: A Study in Nineteenth-Century Thought and Culture* (Princeton: Princeton University Press, 1987); Michael Hagner, *Homo cerebralis. Der Wandel vom Seelenorgan zum Gehirn* (Berlin: Berlin Verlag, 1997).

3   Another complementary discontinuity, whereby the nineteenth-century emergence of experimental neuroscience did not support *philosophical* materialism, is studied by Alexandre Métraux in his fine paper "The Emergent Materialism in French Clinical Brain Research (1820–1850). A Case Study in Historical Neurophilosophy," *Graduate Faculty Philosophy Journal* 22, no. 1 (2000): 161–89.

4   Friedrich Lange, *History of Materialism and Criticism of Its Present Importance*, trans. E. C. Thomas, 3 vols. (1866; 4th rev. ed., London: Kegan Paul, Trench, 1892).

5   Belon, *Observations de plusieurs singularités et choses mémorables*, cited in Olivier Bloch, "Sur les premières apparitions du mot 'matérialiste,'" *Matière à histoires* (Paris: Vrin, 1998), 22.

6   David Lewis, "An Argument for the Identity Theory," *Journal of Philosophy* 63, no. 1 (1966): 23.

7   John Bickle, Pete Mandik, and Andrew Landreth, "The Philosophy of Neuroscience," *Stanford Encyclopedia of Philosophy*, ed. Edward N. Zalta, http://plato.stanford.edu/entries/neuroscience/.

8   John Toland, *Letters to Serena* (1704; repr., New York: Garland, 1976), IV:7, 139; and John Toland, *Pantheisticon* ("Cosmopoli," 1720), 15.

9   Anthony Collins, *Reflections on Mr Clarke's Second Defence*, in Samuel Clarke, *The Works*, 4 vols. (1738; repr., New York: Garland, 1978), 3:818.

10 A different case is David Hartley's "vibratory" theory of mind and brain, in which small vibrations are impressed in the solid filaments of the nerves by external objects; sensations are transmitted by ætherial vibration to brain particles. Different vibrations represent different primary sensations, or "simple ideas" in the brain, which can become complex ideas through associations with other chains of vibrations (David Hartley, *Observations on Man, His Frame, His Duty and his Expectations*, 2 vols. (London: Richardson, 1749), 1:13–16).

11 Gerald Edelman, *Bright Air, Brilliant Fire: On the Matter of the Mind* (London: Allen Lane, 1992), 19–21.

12 On "vibratory" models of the nervous system, see Jamie C. Kassler, "Man—A Musical Instrument: Models of the Brain and Mental Functioning before the Computer," *History of Science* 22 (1984): 59–92; some discussion also in Sutton, *Philosophy and Memory Traces.*

13 Sutton, *Philosophy and Memory Traces*, 26.

14 Carl Vogt, *Physiologische Briefe*, 14th ed. (1847; Gießen: Rickersche Buchhandlung, 1874), 8:323.

15 Jean-Claude Bourdin, "Du *Rêve de D'Alembert* aux *Éléments de physiologie*. Discours scientifique et discours spéculatif dans *Le Rêve de D'Alembert*," *Recherches sur Diderot et l'Encyclopédie* 34 (2003): 45–69; Charles T. Wolfe, "Le rêve matérialiste, ou 'Faire par la pensée ce que la matière fait parfois,'" *Philosophiques* 34, no. 2 (2007): 317–28.

16 John Locke, *An Essay Concerning Human Understanding*, ed. P. Nidditch (1690; 5th ed., 1701; repr. Oxford: Oxford University Press, 1975), 2. Citations are from the Oxford edition. For a novel interpretation of empiricism as *a contrario* suffused with spirits, fancy, brain traces and other materialities, see John Sutton, "Carelessness and Inattention: Mind-Wandering and the Physiology of Fantasy from Locke to Hume," *The Body as Object and Instrument of Knowledge: Embodied Empiricism in Early Modern Science*, eds. C. T. Wolfe and O. Gal (Dordrecht: Springer, 2010), 243–63.

17 Compare Peter Huttenlocher, *Neural Plasticity: The Effects of Environment on the Development of the Cerebral Cortex* (Cambridge, MA: Harvard University Press, 2002) to Bruce Wexler, *Brain and Culture: Neurobiology, Ideology, and Social Change* (Cambridge, MA: MIT Press, 2006). Work from Atsushi Iriki's lab shows that training Japanese macaques in tool use over several months produces changes in neural activity: certain neurons respond to a rake as if it were an extension of the hand. See Atsushi Iriki, "Using Tools: The Moment When Mind, Language, and Humanity Emerged," *RIKEN Research Report* 4, no. 5 (2009), http://www.rikenresearch.riken. jp/eng/frontline/5850; and Laura Spinney, "Tools Maketh the Monkey," *New Scientist* 2677 (2008): 42–5. For more conceptual discussion of the "cultured brain," see Warren Neidich, *Blow-Up: Photography, Cinema and the Brain* (New York: Distributed Art Publishers, 2003); and Charles T. Wolfe, "From Spinoza to the Socialist Cortex: Steps toward the Social Brain," *Cognitive Architecture*, eds. Deborah Hauptmann and Warren Neidich (Rotterdam: 010 Publishers, Delft School of Design, 2010), 184–206.

18 John Hancock, *Arguments to Prove the Being of God with Objections against It Answered* (1706) in Anon., *A Defence of Natural and Revealed Religion*, 3 vols. (London, 1739), 2:243.

19 Henry More, *An Antidote against Atheism* (1653), in *A Collection of Several Philosophical Writings* (1662; repr., New York: Garland, 1978), 34. Citations are to the Garland edition; Sutton, *Philosophy and Memory Traces*, 144–8, citing More at 145.

20 Boyle, *The Christian Virtuoso* (1690) in Robert Boyle, *The Works of the Honourable Robert Boyle*, ed. T. Birch, 6 vols. (1772; repr., Hildesheim: Olms, 1966), 6:741. Citations are from the Olms edition.

21 Sutton, *Philosophy and Memory Traces*, 26.

22 On the clandestine appropriation of Willis, Malebranche and others, see Charles T. Wolfe and Michaela van Esveld, "The Material Soul: Early Modern Epicurean Strategies for Naturalising the Soul," *Conjunctions: Body, Soul and Mind from Plato to Descartes*, ed. Danijela Kambaskovic-Sawers (Dordrecht: Springer, forthcoming).

23　Introduction in Laura Salisbury and Andrew Shail, eds., *Neurology and Modernity: A Cultural History of Nervous Systems* (London: Palgrave Macmillan, 2010), 8.
24　G. S. Rousseau, *Nervous Acts: Essays on Literature, Culture, and Sensibility* (New York: Palgrave, 2004), 250.
25　Alexander Romanovich Luria, "Vygotsky and the Problem of Functional Localization," *Selected Writings of A. R. Luria*, ed. M. Cole (New York: M. E. Sharpe, 1978), 279. Iriki's recent research illustrates this; Neidich's "cultured brain" concept pushes the concept of plasticity further outside of experimental neuroscience.
26　Lambros Malafouris, "The Brain–Artefact Interface: A Challenge for Archaeology and Cultural Neuroscience," *Social Cognitive and Affective Neuroscience* (2010), doi:10.1093/scan/nsp057.
27　The title comes from Haller's influential physiology textbook, *Elementa Physiologiae* (1757–1766).
28　See Charles T. Wolfe, "Sensibility as Vital Force or as Property of Matter in Mid-Eighteenth-Century Debates," *Sensibilité: The Knowing Body in the Enlightenment*, ed. H. M. Lloyd (Dordrecht: Springer, forthcoming).
29　Denis Diderot, *Éléments de physiologie*, in *Œuvres complètes*, eds. H. Dieckmann, J. Proust, and J. Varloot, 25 vols. (Paris: Hermann, 1975), 17:355.
30　Denis Diderot, "*Rêve de D'Alembert*," in *Œuvres complètes*, 17:102. On the role of analogies in Diderot, including "network analogies" of the nervous system, see Anne Beate Maurseth's, *L'Analogie et le probable: pensée et écriture chez Diderot* (Oxford: Voltaire Foundation, 2007).
31　Diderot, *Éléments*, 335.
32　Diderot, *Éléments*, 326; 470.
33　Diderot, *Rêve de D'Alembert*, 101; *Éléments*, 335.
34　Diderot, *Éléments*, 470; cf. 237–8.
35　For Deschamps' influence see Vernière's note in Denis Diderot, *Œuvres philosophiques*, ed. Paul Vernière (Paris: Garnier, 1961), 300n1; and André Robinet, *Dom Deschamps* (Paris: Seghers, 1974), 45ff.
36　Léger-Marie Deschamps, *Œuvres philosophiques* (Paris: Vrin, 1993), 404; 385.
37　Diderot, *Éléments*, 467.
38　Diderot, *Éléments*, 353.
39　Diderot, *Éléments*, 337.
40　See for example, Ian Alexander, "Philosophy of Organism and Philosophy of Consciousness in Diderot's Speculative Thought," *Studies in Romance Philology and French Literature* (Manchester: Manchester University Press, 1953), 1–21.
41　Diderot, *Rêve de D'Alembert*, 125.
42　Anne C. Vila, *Enlightenment and Pathology: Sensibility in the Literature and Medicine of Eighteenth-Century France* (Baltimore, MD: The Johns Hopkins University Press, 1998), 74. Further discussion in Wolfe, "Le rêve matérialiste."
43　Diderot, *Rêve de D'Alembert*, 149.
44　Damien G. Walter, "What Neuroscience Tells Us about the Art of Fiction," 6 June 2012, http://damiengwalter.com/2012/06/10/what-neuroscience-tells-us-about-the-art-of-fiction/.
45　Contrast the more positivist vision of the brain's relation to culture in Semir Zeki, *Inner Vision: An Exploration of Art and the Brain* (Oxford: Oxford University Press, 1999) with the more fluid vision in Gilles Deleuze and Félix Guattari, conclusion to *Qu'est-ce que la philosophie?* (Paris: Minuit, 1991); and Neidich, *Blow-Up*.

46 The way in which eighteenth-century libertine literature, including Sade and Boyer d'Argens, appropriates "scientific" discourse and bends it to suit its own mutated-materialist ends (vital fluids, animal electricity, humoral determinism, and so-on) has been studied, and is not the topic of the present chapter. See Caroline Warman's, *Sade: From Materialism to Pornography* (Oxford: Voltaire Foundation, 2002) and the current research of Claudia Manta.

47 Sutton, *Philosophy and Memory Traces*, 26.

48 Métraux, "Emergent Materialism," 164.

49 Robert M. Young, *Mind, Brain and Adaptation in the Nineteenth Century: Cerebral Localization and Its Biological Context from Gall to Ferrier* (1970; rev. ed., Oxford: Clarendon Press, 1990), vi.

50 Métraux, "Emergent Materialism," 164.

51 Ewald Hering, "Über das Gedächtnis als eine allgemeine Function der organisierten Materie," *Almanach der kaiserlichen Akademie der Wissenschaften* 20 (1870): 273–8.

52 Hagner, *Homo cerebralis*, 99–118; Michael K. House, "Beyond the Brain: Sceptical and Satirical Responses to Gall's Organology," *Neurology and Modernity: A Cultural History of Nervous Systems*, eds. Laura Salisbury and Andrew Shail (London: Palgrave Macmillan, 2010), 41–58.

53 Gall, in Edwin Clarke and Charles D. O'Malley, *The Human Brain and Spinal Cord: A Historical Study Illustrated by Writings from Antiquity to the Twentieth Century* (Berkeley, CA: University of California Press, 1968), 477; Young, *Mind, Brain and Adaptation in the Nineteenth Century*, 12; Hagner, *Homo cerebralis*, 89–118. My summary is indebted to Métraux, "Emergent Materialism," 167.

54 Métraux, "Emergent Materialism," 183.

55 U. T. Place, "Is Consciousness a Brain Process?" *British Journal of Psychology* 47 (1956): 44–50. Herbert Feigl, *The "Mental" and the "Physical"* (1958; repr., Minneapolis, MA: University of Minnesota Press, 1967); J. J. C. Smart, "Sensations and Brain Processes," *Philosophical Review* 68, no. 2 (1959): 141–56; D. M. Armstrong, *A Materialist Theory of the Mind* (London: Routledge, 1968). IT-friendly ideas flourish in neuroscientifically augmented form in the Churchlands' "neurophilosophy" and John Bickle's work *Psychoneural Reduction: the New Wave* (Cambridge, MA: MIT Press, 1998); *Philosophy and Neuroscience: A Ruthlessly Reductive Account* (Dordrecht: Kluwer, 2003).

56 Smart, "Sensations and Brain Processes," 142. My emphasis added.

57 Armstrong, *A Materialist Theory of the Mind*, 75–6.

58 Smart, "Sensations and Brain Processes," 141.

59 Smart, "Sensations and Brain Processes," 143.

60 Smart, "Sensations and Brain Processes," 151.

61 U. T. Place, "We Needed the Analytic-Synthetic Distinction to Formulate Mind-Brain Identity Then: We Still Do" (paper, "40 Years of Australian Materialism," Department of Philosophy, University of Leeds, 1997). Thanks to Dr. M. C. Wright of the University of Leeds for providing me with a copy of Place's paper. Feigl, *The "Mental" and the "Physical,"* 90.

62 J. J. C. Smart, "Materialism," *Journal of Philosophy* 60 (1963): 656. Smart's version of the IT is thus more flexible than Place's.

63 Timo Kaitaro, "Brain-Mind Identities in Dualism and Materialism: A Historical Perspective," *Studies in History and Philosophy of Biology and Biomedical Sciences* 35 (2004): 629; 642. In his intriguing paper, which is orthogonal to this one, Kaitaro

suggests that the IT matches Charles Bonnet's dualism rather than Diderot's materialism. He notes that dualists such as Bonnet, in addition to referring to the seat of the soul, were often ultralocalizationists regarding the anatomical correlates of separate ideas, for they considered that there was a specific fiber or fibers in the brain for each idea. However, "the postulation of such identities in itself is not committed to dualism or materialism" (Kaitaro, 629).

64   Armstrong, *A Materialist Theory of the Mind*, 90.
65   Place, "We Needed the Analytic-Synthetic Distinction," 16.
66   Olivier Bloch, "Poursuivre l'histoire du matérialisme," *Matière à histoires*, 459.
67   Ilya Prigogine and Isabelle Stengers, *Order Out of Chaos* (London: Heinemann, 1984), 82–3.
68   Lev Vygotsky, *Pedologija Podrotska* (1929), cited in René van der Veer and Jaan Valsiner, *Understanding Vygotsky* (London: Blackwell, 1991), 320. Further discussion in Wolfe, "From Spinoza to the Socialist Cortex."
69   On Diderot and others as *embodied* materialists, see Charles T. Wolfe, "Forms of Materialist Embodiment," *Anatomy and the Organization of Knowledge, 1500–1850*, eds. Matthew Landers and Brian Muñoz (London: Pickering and Chatto, 2012), 129–44.
70   Hancock, *Arguments to Prove the Being of God*, 243.
71   David Hawkes, "Against Materialism in Literary Theory," *Early Modern Culture* 9 (2011), http://emc.eserver.org/Hawkes.pdf, forthcoming; Raymond Ruyer, "Ce qui est vivant et ce qui est mort dans le matérialisme," *Revue Philosophique* 116, nos. 7–8 (1933): 28–49.
72   Ruyer, "Ce qui est vivant et ce qui est mort dans le matérialisme," 28.
73   John Sutton and Evelyn B. Tribble, "Materialists Are Not Merchants of Vanishing: Commentary on David Hawkes, 'Against Materialism in Literary Theory,'" *Early Modern Culture* 9 (2011), forthcoming.
74   Walter, "What Neuroscience Tells Us about the Art of Fiction."
75   R. N. McCauley and William Bechtel, "Explanatory Pluralism and the Heuristic Identity Theory," *Theory and Psychology* 11 (2001): 736–60.
76   Daniel C. Dennett, "The Self as Center of Narrative Gravity," *Self and Consciousness: Multiple Perspectives*, eds. F. J. Kessel, Cole and D. L. Johnson (Hillsdale, NJ: Erlbaum, 1992), 275–8.
77   Drew McDermott, "Little 'Me' (on D. Dennett & M. Kinsbourne, 'Time and the Observer')," *Brain and Behavioral Sciences* 15, no. 2 (1992): 217.
78   Deleuze and Guattari, *Qu'est-ce que la philosophie?*, 197–8.

6

Muted Literary Minds: James Sully, George Eliot and Psychologized Aesthetics in the Nineteenth Century

Penelope Hone

Responding to the increasingly dissonant soundscape of a modernizing London, the psychologist James Sully identified noise as a perilous threat to the civilized mind in his 1879 essay "Civilisation and Noise."[1] Noting a tension between the noise generated by London's working class and the more refined sensibilities of the educated classes, he observes: "Our mixed population represents all stages of human progress in auditory sensibility. The man with finely set musical ear[s] has practically to live with barbarians who actually take pleasure in harsh and unlovely sounds, and with many more semi-civilised who are quite indifferent to such noises" (716). Of central concern is the unavoidable nature of modern London's "unlovely sounds." The "cultivated ear" (704) is vulnerable to the deleterious effects of an "increase of noise" that accompanies the "unchecked tendencies" of progress (711).[2] Psychologizing the effects of noise, Sully describes the dissonance of the modern soundscape as an irrepressible source of psychic shocks that threaten to disable the civilized mind.[3]

The severity of Sully's account of the effects of noise on modern consciousness, however, is contradicted in a later essay on George Eliot, which entertains the possibility of an unimpeded aesthetic communication between reader and text. In "George Eliot's Art" (1881), Sully suggests that Eliot's exceptional powers of discriminative sympathy provide a "transparent medium" between the minds she represents and the reader's mind.[4] The demands Eliot places on her readers' concentration, he suggests, implicitly train them to attend to the muted psychological landscape of her texts. Consequently, her writing aspires to a "subtle sympathetic contact" (undisturbed and noiseless) between the mind of the reader and the aesthetic consciousness of the novel. Sully's convergence of Eliot's literary aesthetics and the workings of consciousness conceivably overcomes the psychic disruptions of the modern soundscape. As this chapter will argue, however, the muting effects of Eliot's literary aesthetics exist in a productive tension with the noise of other minds and of modern life—an inescapable reciprocity that Sully implicitly concedes in his polemical "Civilisation and Noise."

Reading Eliot's aesthetics as responsive to new theories of mind in this period, this chapter enlists Sully's "Civilisation and Noise" to examine the ways in which

Eliot tests the aesthetic limitations of literary form. The uniquely muting power Sully ascribes to Eliot's fiction reflects an idealized model of literary communication that Eliot herself engaged with in her early writing. As the first section of this chapter suggests, however, this muted, or silencing, conception of a literary aesthetics is at odds with the materiality of the novel. Focusing on the nexus of sound and consciousness, this chapter asks how we might refocus our aesthetic understanding of Eliot's later novels, *Middlemarch* (1874) and *Daniel Deronda* (1876), as responding to shifting conceptions of a psychologized aesthetics that attends to the dissonant materiality of literary form.

The opening section of the chapter situates Eliot's literary aesthetics in relation to the science of mind. I then turn to Eliot's evocative, oft-quoted allusion to "that roar which lies on the other side of silence." The convergence of hearing and consciousness in this passage from *Middlemarch*, I suggest, effects an alteration in the way Eliot conceives of the novel as an aesthetic form. While this moment in *Middlemarch* might be exemplary of an alteration in Eliot's aesthetic formulation of the novel, I contend that this reformulation plays an integral role in the thematic and formal structure of *Daniel Deronda*. As the concluding section of the chapter suggests, the constitutive role noise plays in Eliot's final novel complicates Sully's idealization of her novels as mutable inscapes. Rather, the psychologized aesthetics at work in her final novel concedes to a literary soundscape that modulates the dissonant nature of literary mediation.

Eliot's muted aesthetics

Eliot's engagement with and contribution to nineteenth-century psychological and scientific cultural networks is well established.[5] Her friendships and alliances included central figures of British psychology such as George Henry Lewes, Herbert Spencer, Henry Sidgwick, Frederick Myers and Sully. Typical of her time, however, Eliot's intellectual interests were heterogeneous. As well as moving in scientific circles, she was a seminal early theorist of the novel as a high-minded aesthetic form.[6] As this section suggests, Eliot's unique position as both literary theorist and contributor to new science of mind reveals a more complex psychologized literary aesthetics than Sully's account of her "Art" might otherwise suggest.

Eliot's 1868 "Notes on Form in Art" provides a compelling example of the attendant relationship between literature and science in her work. In this (unfinished) essay, Eliot switches between a disquisition on aesthetic form and the boundaries of consciousness. Delving into conceptions of poetic (and literary) form through her understanding of the ways in which organic and inorganic matter are shaped by internal and external influences, she writes:

> Even taken in its derivative meaning of outline, what is Form but the limit of that difference by which we discriminate one object from another?—a limit determined partly by the intrinsic relations or composition of the object, and partly by the extrinsic action of other bodies upon it. This is true whether the object is a rock or

a man; but in the case of the inorganic body outline is the result of a nearly equal struggle between inner constitution and the outer play of forces...[7]

The essay starts as an inquiry into "'Form' as applied to artistic composition" (231). As we read on, however, the essay turns into a meditation on the struggle for self-determination, where the ego is positioned as a contested site between internal—or conscious—forces and external forces. Notably, Eliot enlists aesthetic forms such as poetry or literature as ideal moderators of this contested and unstable boundary.

Eliot expresses the dynamic between external forces, consciousness and aesthetic form most frequently as a sympathetic connection between reader and text.[8] Sympathy, Eliot writes, provides the "raw material of moral sentiment"[9] and the "subtlest essence" of the "raw material of culture."[10] In perhaps her most famous account of the aesthetic's role in providing such moral guidance, Eliot describes this sympathetic experience as an amplification of the senses: "The greatest benefit we owe to the artist, whether painter, poet or novelist, is the extension of our sympathies.... Art is the nearest thing to life; it is a mode of amplifying experience and extending our contact with our fellow-men beyond the bounds of our personal lot."[11] While art focuses the mind on the "right" moral sentiments, it also dulls the senses to external distractions, harmonizing the relationship between mind and body, reader and text. This is apparent in a particularly evocative review Eliot wrote for J. A. Froude's *Nemesis of Faith*:

> On certain red-letter days of our existence, it happens to us to discover among the *spawn* of the press, a book which, as we read, seems to undergo a sort of transfiguration before us. We no longer hold heavily in our hands an octavo of some hundred pages, over which the eye laboriously travels, hardly able to drag along with it the restive mind: but we seem to be in companionship with a spirit, who is transfusing himself into our souls, and is vitalising them by his superior energy, that life, both outward and inward, presents itself to us for higher relief, in colours brightened and deepened—we seem to have been bathing in a pool of Siloam, and to have come forth reeling.[12]

More than amplifying one's senses, the experience of reading stifles physical and psychological distractions. Both mind and body are suffused with and vitalized by, quite literally, a "spirit" encapsulated within the text. Far from a site of struggle (as alluded to in "Notes on Form in Art"), the self—"both inward and outward"—is harmonized through an aesthetic engagement that effectively mutes distractions that lie beyond the words printed on the page. In this respect, Eliot, like Sully, proposes an idealized and undisturbed form of literary mediation between reader and text: one which effectively modulates the contact between the disruptions of a chaotic "outer play of forces" and one's inner self.

Central to the aesthetic engagement Eliot proposes here is its selective, filtering nature. The experience of reading Froude's *Nemesis of Faith*, for example, is framed as a chance occurrence amidst "the *spawn* of the press" (the emphasis is Eliot's). Finding the right text is a process of careful selection, requiring the reader to discern the literary amidst the cacophonous proliferation of other less literary "silly novels." With the "wrong" kind of text, the reader becomes distracted by matters that lie beyond the words on the page. As the review above suggests, in such cases a reader becomes fatigued by the laborious visual concentration demanded by her reading and the book's burdensome size. The aesthetic engagement she describes here is at once a sensorial and social form of literary mediation. It signifies a mind consciously attending to the words on the page, undeterred by other distractions, and a reader capable of divorcing the text from the encodings of a dissonant cultural network.[13] This bifurcated model of response, in turn, generates an aesthetic space that distances the reader from everyday reality. Eliot's aesthetics (which locate the literary as a medium of transmission) thus paradoxically insist on a greater psychological proximity of reader and text, and a conscious distancing from, or muting of, the present.

John Picker has deftly shown the ways in which sympathy in Eliot's writing is indicative of an interest in the audible world and its effects on consciousness.[14] The immersive sympathetic engagement Eliot outlines between reader and text, he argues convincingly, can be read as a process of careful and discrete listening, where readers are capable of hearing only that which harmonizes with an appropriately attuned consciousness. In her seminal study, *Desire and Domestic Fiction*, Nancy Armstrong identifies precisely this dynamic in the Victorian novel. Armstrong notes the ways in which "fiction did a great deal to relegate vast areas of culture to the status of aberrance and noise," thus enforcing a (superficial) conception of cultural harmony on its readers.[15] The sympathetic aesthetic engagement noted here typifies the muting effects Armstrong describes. Moreover, such literary ambitions seem synonymous with Sully's articulation of a muted psychologized literary aesthetics. However, Eliot's sympathetic articulation of her work is an intrinsically flawed form of literary soundproofing.

The quieted mode of literary mediation Eliot idealizes runs counter to the nature of the novel as an artistic form. Take, for example, Jacques Rancière's and Mikhail Bakhtin's account of literary language and the novel as a form.[16] Expanding on Plato's *Phaedrus*, Rancière writes of the "mute" nature of literary language. Plato posits the orphaned nature of the written word; where speech is guided and controlled (both in utterance and reception) by its immanent relation to a speaker, writing is released from such control. The written word is necessarily detached, free to speak "to anybody without knowing to whom it had to speak, and to whom it had not. The 'mute' letter was a letter that spoke too much and endowed anyone at all with the power of speaking."[17] Rancière sees the orphaned state of the written word as a form of mute speech, a mode of communication understood by others but powerless to speak for itself. Incapable of determining who reads it and how it is understood, this mute speech "determines a partition of the perceptible in which one can no longer contrast those who speak and those who only make noise, those who act and those who only live…Literature discovers at its core this link with the democratic disorder of literariness" (15).

In literature, the written word is therefore more than a representational schema or simple communicative system. Sharing the discursive fields of science, art and politics (a discursive hybridity particularly pertinent for a writer such as Eliot), words are a chattering, noisy medium. This volubility only becomes more apparent when set to work within a medium such as the novel. As Mikhail Bakhtin argues, the novel does not represent language as "unitary, completely finished-off and indisputable" but "as a living mix of varied and opposing voices, developing and renewing itself."[18] Eliot's selective relegation of that which is not literary to a type of cultural spawn (or noise, as Armstrong suggests) implies that the novel is capable of operating as a contained discriminatory form. Yet as Bakhtin reminds us, the novel is "plasticity itself. It is a genre ever questing, ever examining itself and subjecting its established forms to review" (39).

While both theorists of the novel cited here differ in radical ways—the former injecting a radical politics into literariness itself, the latter more attentive to the inner dialogism of literary language—Rancière's and Bakhtin's theories coalesce so far as they allow a critical reframing of the nineteenth-century novel as a form inherently open to external voices and noises as a part of its mediation. The dialogic and disorderly nature of the novel is palpably at odds with Eliot's push toward a muted, or silenced, literary engagement.

As the following sections go on to discuss, however, Eliot was not unaware of this problematic aspect of her literary aesthetics. As I show in the following section, we can trace the emergence of what we might term a "metaphorics of noise" within *Middlemarch*. This signals, I argue, Eliot's cognizance of the dissonant nature of literary mediation. Moreover, it marks a corresponding shift in Eliot's framing of the novel from a psychological inscape to a more modulated literary soundscape.

Beyond silence

Middlemarch contains one of Eliot's richest psychological reflections on the mind as soundscape. Contemplating the often painful realization of the gulf between what we imagine to be and what is, the narrator observes:

> That element of tragedy which lies in the very fact of frequency, has not yet wrought itself into the coarse emotion of mankind; and perhaps our frames could hardly bear much of it. If we had a keen vision and feeling of all ordinary human life, it would be like hearing the grass grow and the squirrel's heart beat, and we should die of that roar which lies on the other side of silence. As it is, the quickest of us walk about well wadded with stupidity.[19]

Alluding to the novel's heroine Dorothea's failure to register the dreary reality of her new husband's character, the passage frames this gap in perception as a necessary protection. For while Dorothea's lack of insight is first described in tragic terms, Eliot's narrator ultimately expresses relief at the psychological filtering that even those most alive to the world possess.

This preference for filtering—or for a psychological inscape—can be read, therefore, as a compelling instance of Sully's psychologized aesthetics in Eliot's writing. References to hearing, roars and an acoustic space beyond silence exemplify Eliot's

particular attention to the effects of the audible world on consciousness. This focus on
the psychic imprint sound makes is further emphasized by Eliot's rhetorically charged
invocation of the term "frequency."

Read in its technical register, frequency refers to the vibrating undulation of sound
waves through the air. Both Hermann von Helmholtz and John Tyndall had published
and given public lectures on the physical properties of sound in the mid-nineteenth
century.[20] Moreover, Eliot was familiar with both men's work, as her *Deronda* notebooks
make apparent.[21] Tyndall and Helmholtz furthered our understanding of the ways in
which sound waves travel across the air and are received by the ear. It was in response to
these explanations of how sound travels and 'enters' into our minds that some nineteenth-
century psychologists contemplated whether consciousness might similarly travel
across the air. Central to such thinking was the tantalizing possibility that such 'waves
of consciousness' might permeate another's mind, effectively allowing us to tune into
another's psychological frequency.[22] Far from celebrating this possibility, however, the
above passage conveys a sense of relief at this developmental lack in the human psyche.

Alternatively, frequency also implies habit or repetitive patterns. In this sense, the
auditory implications of the passage move away from a psychologically vested notion
of tuning into another's thoughts. Instead, the sounds against which our minds must
be "wadded" are the minutiae of everyday life: the continual and rapid beating of a
mammal's heart, the seemingly never-ending process of grass growing. In the passage
from *Middlemarch*, Eliot therefore also seems to be suggesting that these elements of
everyday life in all their dullness and inanity combine to produce a deathly roar against
which quick minds must be protected.

Eliot's rather grim take on the potential risks to the self by the sonic inundation of
other's lives (referred to as "that element of tragedy") thus anticipates the equally bleak
future James Sully imagines for the civilized mind overwrought with the "violent" and
savage incursions of its modern soundscape. However, unlike Sully's civilized few who
are powerless to protect themselves, Eliot's passage implies that refuge might be found
through an effectively formed sympathetic engagement with art. In these terms, the
tragic element referred to in the above passage is twofold. On the one hand, tragedy
lies in Dorothea's failure to read her husband's mind effectively—to know his inner-
self. On the other, it refers to the fact that she has allowed the tawdry reality of her
domestic life to penetrate her emotional life and dull her senses from the beauty of her
surroundings. Dorothea's distraught realization occurs while honeymooning in Rome.
The same relics that served as inspiration for Ruskin and Pater are "unintelligible," and
of "an alien world" (124), to Dorothea. Like the inattentive reader Eliot describes in her
review of Froude's *Nemesis of Faith*, Dorothea's attention is distracted by an "outer play
of forces." Alienated and traumatized, she is unable to form a sympathetic connection
with the surrounding beauty—a failure to enlist art to filter the dissonant effects of a
harsher reality that Eliot's narrator judges harshly.

Yet—and crucially—this confident assertion of art's ameliorative, muting effects
is riddled with uncertainty. The passage is pervaded by indefinite terms such as
"perhaps," "if," "would" and "should." Thus, the possibility of an art form powerful
enough to silence any other frequency is only tentatively offered. Indeed following

such undulating conjecture, even the closing "As it is," which through its syncopated syllables imposes a rhythmic forcefulness, reads less as a statement of fact and more as a defensively framed proposition.

It is here that I think we see a metaphorics of noise manifest itself at the level of Eliot's language. For, the vacillating nature of this passage extends beyond what is said to also how it sounds. Correspondence between Eliot and W. G. Clark, founder of the *Cambridge Journal of Philology* and Shakespeare scholar, reveals Eliot's interest in the effect that the sound and rhythm of language had on the reader. In a letter discussing the sonic effect of prefixing extra syllables to words in poetry, Clark writes:

> I have been very much interested by what you say about English rhythm. I quite agree with you that judged by the ear the verse "Baptism seemed to" is quite long enough, although another syllable prefixed would not to my ear, make it too long…Rules, merely conventional, have a powerful effect, and a departure from any one of them arrests the reader's attention and interrupts his sympathy with the author and his full enjoyment of the sense.[23]

The focus here on the sonic aspects of poetry and how this affects a reader's engagement suggests—at the very least—a (shared) attention to the aural effects of reading. Clark's account of the way unorthodox prosodic rhythms arrest a reader's attention and break the text's flow also resonates with the striking altercations in rhythm in the passage from *Middlemarch*. Take, for example, the long and convoluted, rhythmically awkward opening sentences. Syntactically complex and ruptured by semicolons and Oxford commas, the overall effect is of a kind of rhythmic dissonance—one which reflects "that roar" to which the words themselves allude. Against this awkward, elongated syntax emerges the succinct, concluding "As it is." These staccato-like effects then dissolve into the muting softness of the alliterative sequence "walk," "well" and "wadded," tempering the preceding sibilance of "is," "quickest" and "us." All this alliterative harmonizing, however, is ultimately and resonantly disrupted by the stark dissonance of "stupidity." Elaborated in this detail, one can begin to see how Eliot's carefully managed acoustic disruptions operate on a linguistic level, implicitly and precisely violating the protective "wadding" that is meant to shield the reader from such intrusions.

These disruptions do not mark a defiance of any grammatical or narrative rules (as might be the case in the poetic form referred to in Clark's letter). However, such rhythmic disturbances do, I think, serve to arrest the reader's attention. By doing so, and as Clark suggests, they interrupt her "sympathy with the author and [her] full enjoyment of the sense" by drawing attention to the process of mediation: the literal words on the page. Far from an assertion of the capacity for fiction to relegate "aberrant" noise to the realm of the unheard, the sonic complexity of this passage suggests an intense focus on the individual mind's tenuous capacity to simultaneously maintain a quieted aesthetic experience that somehow transcends the disruptive materiality of the medium of literary language.

This passage from *Middlemarch* therefore captures a tension within Eliot's desire for a psychologized aesthetics that engenders an undisturbed engagement between reader and text. Such a tension anticipates Sully's account of the relationship between civilization and noise. Sully's essay develops from the somewhat hopeless realization that with civilization comes noise. Acknowledging that this noise can never truly be excised from the modern urban soundscape, he suggests the only solace to be found is the hope that "people as individuals and as a community can be got to understand that to inflict noise on others for the sake of personal enjoyment is an interference with their just rights" (720). After this hopeful conclusion, however, comes the following addendum, written in a final footnote:

> Since this paper was written a fact has come to the writer's knowledge which seems to tell against the hopeful conclusion he has here reached. If there is a place in the world from which one might expect noises to be excluded it is Oxford. In a university town, devoted to the most contemplative form of academic life, requiring, as its whole construction suggests, perfect quiet before all other things, a diabolical hooter now shrieks out its long piercing wail every morning at 5.40, and again at 6.0. In order that a handful of railway employés [sic] may receive a convenient reminder of their hour of work, the drowsy ears of hundreds of fatigued night readers must be thus murderously assaulted. (720)

Even in a town constructed precisely around the quiet pursuit of academic study, a noiseless environment is unattainable. Eliot's conceptualization of the literary text is similarly placed: fraught with the dissonant nature of its form, it relies on the discipline of the reader to follow her advice—to remain "wadded with stupidity" while reading— and so avoid the fatal effects of that noise that lies on the other side of (civilized) silence. Yet, owing to its repeated vacillations, Eliot's text also belies a nagging uncertainty as to the effectiveness, or even probability, of achieving such protection.

The conclusion of *Middlemarch* provides a similar parallel with Sully's essay. As the narrator notes, "there is no creature whose inward being is so strong that it is not greatly determined by what lies outside it" (514). Here Eliot evokes a sentiment previously expressed in "Notes on Form in Art"—that of the struggle between self-determination and the influence of external forces. There is, however, a subtle semantic shift. Earlier accounts of her psychologized aesthetics celebrate the capacity of the (reading) subject to be so engaged with an aesthetic form as to be muffled from the distractions of the external world. However, such an engagement is cast in doubt through the use of a double negative: "no creature…is not…." Infusing the text with a degree of pessimism, the narrator's observation makes apparent the futility of trying to withstand external pressures for the sake of an uninterrupted engagement with the text. In the context of a novel that, as Gillian Beer has famously argued, incorporates contemporary debates on evolutionary theory, Eliot's use of such terms as "strength" and "determination" can be read as evoking Darwin's own rhetoric.[24] Far from a Lamarkian notion of evolution, which proceeds from human will-power, this language is proper to a world of impersonal forces, of selection that results from interaction with the external environment. Here then, Eliot seems to suggest that the ability to dull one's senses in order to hear only the civilized voice of the novelist is, in evolutionary terms, a repudiation of one's own subsistence.

This closing observation in *Middlemarch* suggests a recognition of the anachronism involved in a psychologized aesthetic that seeks to suppress its modern soundscape. Having recognized the unfeasibility of a fully sympathetic engagement with the literary text, Eliot thus draws attention to the idealism vested in the notion of the text as a "transparent medium" which functions as a "subtle sympathetic contact" with the reader's mind.[25] As I have suggested, she does so in light of emerging discourses concerning the effects of noise on consciousness that Sully would later write on. This conceptual and temporal blurring between Eliot and Sully substantiates what Vanessa L. Ryan identifies as a "cross-pollination" between literary and scientific discourses in the late nineteenth century.[26] As we shall see, Eliot's incorporation of a "metaphorics of noise," which seeks to modulate the relationship between consciousness and the hubbub of the external world through her novels, is more fully developed in *Daniel Deronda*.

"Blent transmission" in *Daniel Deronda*

Where *Middlemarch* was received as a literary masterpiece, critical responses to *Deronda* were less effusive. The first serialized part of the novel, which promised the intrigues of a romantic drama involving the beautiful Gwendolen Harleth, her cruel suitor (then husband) Henleigh Grandcourt and the mysterious hero Daniel Deronda, was warmly received. However, this enthusiasm soon cooled. Midway through the second issue of the novel's serialization, Daniel rescues a young Jewish girl, Mirah, from drowning herself in the Thames. Seeking Mirah's sole remaining relation—her brother—Daniel befriends Mordecai, a Jewish visionary whose lifework is committed to founding a nation-state for the Jewish people. From this point onwards, Daniel and the narrative are gradually drawn away from the bewitching charms of Gwendolen and toward Mordecai's spiritual ambitions.

What followed was unprecedented in the English novel. Pushing the domestic psychodrama with Gwendolen to the side, Eliot allowed Mordecai extended passages in which to propound his Zionist vision and expand on his Kabbala-style spiritualism. Eliot's privileging of Mordecai's voice in the narrative was, as she explained to her publisher John Blackwood, intended to enrich her novel with "a much more complex character and a higher strain of ideas."[27] Thus shielding her narrative from character tropes "already used up," Mordecai served to inject into *Deronda* a "vivid" and elevating artistic effect (7:223). Notably, while his character was, at the time, anomalous in the English novel, the way in which Eliot frames his intended effect on readers remained within the already familiar bounds of her psychologized aesthetics.[28]

Central to Mordecai's aesthetic effect were the demands his sections exerted upon the reader. In contrast with the more "dynamic" Gwendolen sections that opened the novel, the idiosyncratic, nationalist visions Mordecai propounds, often in sermon-like style, did not make for easy reading.[29] Attuning oneself to Mordecai's voice required a fixed concentration, so much so that even sympathetic (and intellectually engaged) readers found this aspect of the novel difficult and at times tedious. While *Deronda* was well received by the Jewish community, who felt a "responsive thrill" from the novelist's earnest and careful treatment of their culture, the broader (English) reading public struggled with Jewish parts of the novel.[30] Blackwood, for example, observed that he was unable to read the novel with distractions around him.[31] Even Henry James—a writer who later became renowned for the demanding nature of his prose—qualified the Jewish parts of the novel as difficult; under the guise of a conversational review by three fictional readers of *Deronda*, James observes:

> Little by little I began to feel that I cared less for certain notes than for others. I say it under my breath—I began to feel an occasional temptation to skip. Roughly speaking, all the Jewish burden of the story tended to weary me…[32]

Tellingly, the different types of reading required by the Gwendolen and Mordecai plots are configured as a difference in volume by one contemporary reviewer, who writes, "when the end of the startling scenes of 'Gwendolen gets her Choice' is reached, the attention of the reader cannot be properly fixed upon the quieter Jewish episode which follows…"[33] This description of an audible shift from the "startling" Gwendolen scenes to the "quieter Jewish episode" reflects the particular style of reading that Mordecai's voice demands. Soliciting a deeper, more concentrated engagement with her novel, Eliot's character epitomizes a literary aesthetics that distances the reader from her surroundings, quieting any physical and psychologized distractions.

The distancing effect of Mordecai's voice is inflected by the narrative's insistence on his dissociation from contemporary English culture. Shying away from public places, Mordecai avoids the hustle and bustle of the surrounding metropolis; the external world, he observes, "narrows the inward vision."[34] Elsewhere, Mirah draws attention to Mordecai's cultural strangeness. Alluding to the difficulties he might face when enlisting Daniel as his spiritual inheritor she asks:

> Does it ever hurt your love for Mr Deronda that so much of his life was all hidden away from you, that he is amongst persons and cares about persons who are all so unlike us—I mean, unlike you?… it would be a trial to your love for him if that other part of his life were like a crowd in which he had got entangled, so that he was carried away from you. (657)

Particularly revealing is the distinction Mirah makes here between Mordecai and the Jewish community: "I mean, unlike you?" It is not simply that Daniel is a gentile but that Mordecai stands as an isolated, singular figure. His desire to insulate himself from his surroundings reminds us of the tension Sully draws attention to between the civilized mind and an increasingly noisy London soundscape. However, while Sully's essay offers a more bleak prognostication, Mordecai's character suggests that cultural insulation is tenable: despite the unlikelihood of Daniel—as an English gentleman—disentangling himself from a crowd of other persons and committing himself to Mordecai's singular vision, this is precisely what appears to happen. Gwendolen is exiled to a solitary life in Gadsmere; Daniel and Mirah follow Mordecai's dying wish and sail off to the East in search of a national center for the Jewish people. Thus promoting the Mordecai narrative, the novel seems to preference the muting, distancing psychologized aesthetics outlined at the outset of this chapter.

Yet, as John Blackwood's and Henry James' responses to the novel suggest, far from effectively absorbing the reader and transfiguring their conscious engagement with the text so as to silence all other distractions, the Mordecai sections were, by contrast, the least engaging. Moreover, and as I have argued, the suggestion of a literary text capable of quieting the mind and filtering out eternal distractions is at odds with the very form in which Eliot worked. While embodying a type of literary muting, Mordecai's character is also framed as a culturally incongruous—or indeed, anachronistic—fixture within the novel, one which is ultimately superseded by the eponymous Daniel Deronda.

Eliot's readers were particularly sensitive to the incongruity of Mordecai's voice within Eliot's literary text. Indeed the novel was, for the most part, criticized for reading less as a work of literary art and more as a sociopolitical tract. As the nineteenth-century literary critic George Saintsbury observes in a review of the novel printed in *The Academy*:

> The question here is whether the phase of Judaism now exhibited, the mystical enthusiasm for race and nation, has sufficient connexion with broad human feeling to be stuff for prose fiction to handle. We think that it has not... the "Samothracian mysteries of bottled moonshine" (to borrow a phrase from *Alton Locke*) into which Mordecai initiates Deronda are not thus connected with anything broadly human. They are not only "will-worship," but they have a provincial character which excludes fellow feeling. Poetry could legitimately treat them;... But... they are not the stuff of which the main interest or even a prominent interest, or anything but a very carefully reduced side interest, of prose novels should be wrought.[35]

Elsewhere admiring Eliot's "unparalleled" (253) capacities as a novelist, Saintsbury is emphatic in his judgment of Mordecai as a stylistic malapropism.

Crucially, Eliot was not so committed to the "higher strain of ideas" Mordecai represented as to be oblivious to the problems his character posed to her literary work. Frustrated by reports of readers and critics skipping over the Mordecai narrative (much as James' fictional reader does), she (famously) protested that she "meant everything in the book to be related to everything else" (7:290). Yet Eliot reveals a more tempered view in the privacy of her own diary: "What will be the feeling of the public as the story advances I am entirely doubtful. The Jewish element seems to me likely to satisfy nobody" (7:238).

Notably, while the narrative recognizes Mordecai's cultural distinctiveness, this is often framed in terms of anachronism—almost as though Eliot was acknowledging, in parallel, the fundamental incongruity of his character. We first meet Mordecai huddled at the back of a dark second-hand bookshop on a secluded backstreet in the Jewish quarter of London. He is reading "yesterday's *Times*" and surrounded by texts that have fallen out of circulation (385). Later, standing on Blackfriars Bridge contemplating the Thames, Mordecai's instinct is "to stand perfectly still." Positioned above one of London's main commercial channels, his appearance as an "illuminated type of bodily emaciation and spiritual eagerness" contrasts with the material nature of the bustling trade being conducted around him (492). These perspectives highlight his dissociation from contemporary surroundings, yet they do so with the suggestion of stagnation and decay. The lively cityscape contrasts with his skeletal, wasting physique. Elsewhere depicted as surrounded by the silent "dead letters" trapped in second-hand books, his character is far from infusing the text with an enlivening spirit, seeming instead to equate to a literal dead-end.

It is, however, through the contrasting figure of Deronda that Mordecai's stylistic malapropism is most apparent. Indeed, Mordecai is largely made known to the reader through his friendship with Daniel. Moreover, their friendship has been predominantly read as a complicit partnership. Uncertain of his place in the world, Daniel is uneasy with his upbringing as an English gentleman. After discovering that he is Jewish, however, this unease dissipates. He pledges his life to Mordecai, promising to act as his spiritual inheritor and fulfill the dying man's search for a Jewish nation-state. Yet, as critics such as Amanda Anderson and Brian Cheyette have noted, despite his apparent complicity Daniel distances himself from Mordecai's spiritualism.[36] Daniel's preference for distance is, however, different from the cultural distancing practiced by Mordecai. Less a desire for cultural filtration, or quieting, Daniel's dissociation from Mordecai's absolutism reinforces a more fundamental aesthetic impulse in Eliot's work. As the previously discussed passage from *Middlemarch* exemplifies, this impulse oscillates between the need to immerse oneself in the muted inscape of art and the equally potent recognition of the complex relationship between consciousness, its dissonant soundscape and the literary text. And, as we see, Daniel's necessary filtering of Mordecai's relentless drive to give voice to Jewish culture parallels Sully's recognition that noise is (and will remain) an unrelenting effect on modern consciousness.

Unlike Mordecai's disengagement from his metropolitan surroundings, Daniel effortlessly rambles around London's streets. He moves easily between the bourgeois drawing rooms of his uncle, the feminine domestic space of his friends and the Meyricks' sitting room and the working-class Cohen family—"typical" Jewish pawnbrokers who care for Mordecai. Indeed, it is, I think, Daniel's preference for the "external world" (as Mordecai so oddly puts it) that causes him to feel "strangely wrought upon" by Mordecai in the early stages of their acquaintance (494). Daniel's reaction to Mordecai here echoes the passage from *Middlemarch* examined earlier; Mordecai typifies that "coarse emotion of mankind" which has not yet had the dissonant modern soundscape "wrought into" its perceptive capacities. In the earlier novel such a cultural attunement is figured as potentially tragic. Here, however, it is Mordecai's failure to open his mind to the "external world" that seems displaced and strange to the more open-minded Daniel.

The distancing of the two characters from one another is further apparent in their differing capacities to mediate (and indeed, modulate) printed texts. While what Mordecai reads is out of date and out of print, Daniel actively engages with the news of the day. He is both a consumer of news, taking time to read the paper, as well as a contributor to it, helping his uncle with political correspondence. After discovering his Jewish origins, Daniel inherits a chest from his grandfather filled with ancient Jewish texts. Tellingly, when Daniel first accesses this chest of written treasures, his response is framed in modern terms; meeting the friend of his father responsible for handing over his inheritance, Daniel "seemed to himself to be touching the electric chain of his own ancestry" (721). To expand on Picker's suggestion that Eliot's novel presses toward the as yet unrealized possibilities of telephonic communication, Daniel experiences the content of these ancient texts as a form of proto-electronic communication.[37] Whereas Mordecai exemplifies an anachronistic literary style, Daniel's openness to alternate modes and methods of reading and receiving texts typifies the more "plastic" nature of novelistic prose.

This contrast between the two friends is also reflected in Daniel's attitude toward Mordecai's Kabbalistic faith. This faith contends that having found his spiritual inheritor, Mordecai's soul will live on in Daniel. Daniel, however, openly refutes this notion, as he explains to Mordecai:

I must be convinced first of special reasons for it in the writings themselves. And I am too backward a pupil yet. That blent transmission must go on without any choice of ours; but what we can't hinder must not make our rule for what we ought to choose. I think our duty is faithful tradition where we can attain it. (751)

This "blent transmission" serves, on the one hand, as a recognition of the (unspoken) influence two minds might have on one another, and thus as an appeasement to Mordecai. However, and in anticipation of twentieth-century media communication theory, it also acknowledges that such mediation is never wholly separated from its surroundings.[38] Insisting on the priority of the written word, Daniel resists the immersive "marriage" of minds Mordecai's spiritual faith envisages, in favor of a far more publicly legible form of communication (751). His association between "the writings themselves" and "faithful tradition" locates cultural learning within a more socially determined register, recognizing the porous nature of texts and their capacity to contain traces of the past.[39] Daniel's resistance to Mordecai's voice and his recourse to a more resonant form of communication is indicative, I think, of Eliot's conflicted relation to the dissonant nature of mediation, no matter how inspired. Indeed, the above passage could also be read as the author's own recognition that reading must always involve a blent transmission: readers will always, for example, add their own "noise" to the purity of the words inscribed on the page.

This recognition of the dynamic nature of the literary text is reiterated in the closing pages of the novel. Far from the pure transmigration of souls Mordecai anticipates, his death occurs amidst a host of other events: Daniel's marriage to Mirah and their departure from England; Daniel's uncle's approval of his career choice, religion and wife; the Meyricks' shared heartbreak at losing their friend; and Gwendolen's poignant farewell letter to Daniel. Typical of the Victorian novel, the multiplicity of events incorporated in the closing chapter seeks to bring together the strands of a complex, multitiered narrative. Such multiplicity contrasts with the idiosyncratic bent of Mordecai's desires, and of the anachronistic nature of his literary voice within the novel. The singleness of Mordecai's voice is finally counterpoised by the incorporation of lines from Milton in the closing epilogue:

> Nothing is here for tears, nothing to wail
> Or knock the breast; no weakness, no contempt,
> Dispraise or blame; nothing but well and fair,
> And what may quiet us in a death so noble. (811)

In the guise of an epitaph, Mordecai's relegation to the quietness of death seems to imply a significant remediation of his message, locating it at once within novelistic (the narrative's closing lines) and poetic discourse. However, by transliterating Milton's poem into novelistic discourse at this pivotal moment in the narrative, Eliot also effectively incorporates another writer's voice into her text. By doing so, she thus exemplifies the "plastic" nature of literary form. This closing epitaph is therefore also continuous with the novel's stress on Daniel's capacity to mediate a variety of voices. Moreover, it marks Eliot's implicit engagement with a psychologized literary aesthetics that necessarily modulates the dissonant relationship between one's inner consciousness and the external world. Like Sully's weary discovery that silence is a growing anachronism for modern consciousness, Eliot recognizes here the necessity for a literary aesthetics to effectively modulate, rather than mute, the incumbent noise of the modern soundscape.

Notes

1 James Sully, "Civilisation and Noise," *Fortnightly Review* 24, no. 143 (November 1878): 704–20. Hereafter cited in text.
2 For a detailed account of nineteenth-century attitudes toward the changing soundscape, see John Picker's, *Victorian Soundscapes* (Oxford: Oxford University Press, 2003). See also John Picker's, "Aural Anxieties and the Advent of Modernity," *The Victorian World*, ed. Martin Hewitt (New York: Routledge, 2012), 603–19.
3 For an account of emergent conceptions of the physiological impact of emotions in the nineteenth century, see Jill Matus, *Shock, Memory and the Unconscious in Victorian Fiction* (Cambridge: Cambridge University Press, 2009).
4 James Sully, "George Eliot's Art," *Mind* 6, no. 23 (July 1881): 378.
5 Seminal studies include Gillian Beer's, *Darwin's Plots: Evolutionary Narrative in Darwin, George Eliot and Nineteenth-Century Fiction*, 3rd ed. (1983; repr., Cambridge: Cambridge University Press, 2009) and George Levine's, *The Realistic Imagination: English Fiction from* Frankenstein *to* Lady Chatterly (Chicago: University of Chicago Press, 1981). More recently, Vanessa L. Ryan's chapter on Eliot in *Thinking without Thinking* makes apparent the ways in which the author's in-depth depictions of character illuminate the complexities of the emerging field of psychology. *Thinking without Thinking in the Victorian Novel* (Baltimore, MD: The Johns Hopkins University Press, 2012). Michael Davis and Nicholas Dames have also re-examined

Eliot's aesthetic incorporation of, and contribution to, emerging theories of the mind. Michael Davis, *George Eliot and Nineteenth-Century Psychology: Exploring the Unmapped Country* (Aldershot: Ashgate, 2006); Nicholas Dames, *The Physiology of the Novel: Reading, Neural Science, and the Form of Victorian Fiction* (Oxford: Oxford University Press, 2007).

6   See, for example, her early essays: "The Natural History of German Life," *Westminster Review* (July 1856): 51–6; 71–2; "Silly Novels by Lady Novelists," *The Westminster Review* (October 1856): 442–61; and "Notes on Form in Art" (unpublished in her lifetime, written 1868). All are reprinted in George Eliot, *Selected Essays, Poems and Other Writings* (Oxford: Oxford University Press, 1990) and all references to these essays are from this edition.

7   Eliot, *Selected Essays*, 234.

8   Indeed, the centrality of sympathy as an aesthetic construct in Eliot's work has long been recognized. See, for example: A. H. Miller, *The Burdens of Perfection: On Ethics and Reading in Nineteenth-Century British Literature* (Ithaca, NY: Cornell University Press, 2006); Rae Greiner, "Sympathy Time: Adam Smith, George Eliot, and the Realist Novel," *Narrative* 17, no. 3 (October 2009): 291–311; Forest Pyle, "A Novel Sympathy: The Imagination of Community in George Eliot," *NOVEL: A Forum on Fiction* 27, no. 1 (Autumn 1993): 5–23 and Elizabeth Deeds Ermarth, "George Eliot's Conception of Sympathy," *Nineteenth-Century Fiction* 40, no. 1 (June 1985): 23–42.

9   Eliot, "Natural History of German Life," *Selected Essays*, 110.

10   Eliot, "Silly Novels by Lady Novelists," *Selected Essays*, 156.

11   Eliot, "Natural History of German Life," *Selected Essays*, 110.

12   Eliot, "J. A. Froude's *The Nemesis of Faith*," *Coventry Herald and Observer* (16 March 1849); repr., *Selected Essays*, 265. The emphasis is Eliot's.

13   Categorizing a cultural network as an increasingly noisy environment draws from historico-cultural accounts of the relationship between the novel and mid- to late-nineteenth-century print culture, such as Matthew Rubery's, *The Novelty of Newspapers: Victorian Fiction After the Invention of the News* (Oxford: Oxford University Press, 2009) and Leah Price's, *The Anthology and the Rise of the Novel: From Richardson to George Eliot* (Cambridge: Cambridge University Press, 2000).

14   See Chapter 3 in Picker's, *Victorian Soundscapes*.

15   Nancy Armstrong, *Desire and Domestic Fiction: A Political History of the Novel* (Oxford: Oxford University Press, 1987), 24.

16   Jacques Rancière, "The Politics of Literature," *SubStance, Issue 103*, 33, no. 1 (2004): 10–24; M. M. Bakhtin, *The Dialogic Imagination: Four Essays*, trans. Carl Emerson and Michael Holquist (Austin, TX: University of Texas Press, 1981).

17   Rancière, "The Politics of Literature," 14–15.

18   Bakhtin, *The Dialogic Imagination*, 49.

19   George Eliot, *Middlemarch* (New York and London: W. W. Norton & Co., 1977; repr., 2000), 124. All references are to this edition and hereafter are cited in text.

20   Hermann Von Helmholtz, *The Sensations of Tone as a Physiological Basis for the Theory of Music* (New York: Longmans, Green and Co., 1875). Tyndall's lectures are reprinted in John Tyndall, *Sound: A Course of Eight Lectures Delivered at the Royal Institution of Great Britain* (New York: D. Appleton, 1867).

21   See, for example, the physical science section of Eliot's Berg notebook, particularly 99v, 100 and 100v; repr., *George Eliot's Daniel Deronda Notebooks*, ed. Jane Irwin (Cambridge: Cambridge University Press, 1996), 20–1.

22 This cross-conscious tuning might be otherwise referred to as telepathy. As Roger Luckhurst's *The Invention of Telepathy: 1870–1901* shows, the "invention" of telepathy in the late nineteenth century emerged out of new theories of psychology. See in particular, Luckhurst's account of the psychological society of Great Britain between 1875 and 1879. Luckhurst, *The Invention of Telepathy: 1870–1901* (Oxford: Oxford University Press, 2002), 47–51.

23 W. G. Clark to George Eliot, 18 November ND (estimated 1870s), George Eliot and George Henry Lewes Collection, Beinecke Rare Book and Manuscript Library.

24 Beer, *Darwin's Plots.*

25 Sully, "George Eliot's Art," 390; 391.

26 Ryan, *Thinking without Thinking,* 154.

27 George Eliot to John Blackwood, 25 February 1876, *The George Eliot Letters,* ed. Gordon S. Haight (New Haven, CT: Yale University Press, 1955), 7:223. Hereafter cited in text.

28 Representations of Jewish characters throughout the nineteenth century fell almost exclusively under the realm of derogatory cultural stereotypes. Typical examples include Dickens' Fagin in *Oliver Twist* (1838) and George Du Maurier's Svengali in *Trilby* (1894).

29 Eliot's use of word "dynamic" to describe Gwendolen in the opening pages of the novel was remarked upon as a particularly modern appropriation of what was previously considered a distinctly scientific word. As Blackwood remarks in a letter to Eliot, "dynamic" was still "a *dictionary* word to so many people." 10 November 1875, *Letters,* 7:183.

30 Anon. to George Eliot, 31 August 1876, George Eliot and George Henry Lewes Collection, Beinecke Rare Book and Manuscript Library.

31 Blackwood writes to George Henry Lewes, "One cannot rightly read Deronda while people are talking and moving about." 2 March 1876, *Letters,* 7:227.

32 Henry James, "*Daniel Deronda*: A Conversation," *The Atlantic Monthly* 38, no. 230 (December 1876): 686.

33 "Novels of the Week, *Daniel Deronda,*" *Athenaeum* (29 April 1876): 593.

34 George Eliot, *Daniel Deronda* (London: Penguin Books, 1995), 521. Hereafter cited in text.

35 George Saintsbury, "Literature: *Daniel Deronda,*" *The Academy* 227 (9 September 1876): 254.

36 Amanda Anderson, *The Powers of Distance: Cosmopolitanism and the Cultivation of Detachment* (Princeton: Princeton University Press, 2001); Bryan Cheyette, *Constructions of "the Jew" in English Literature and Society: Racial Representations, 1875–1945* (Cambridge: Cambridge University Press, 1993).

37 Picker, *Victorian Soundscapes,* 104.

38 One of the basic tenets of information theory is the impossibility of pure mediation: noise will always be attached to the message.

39 Juan Suarez writes of such traces as "stains" on text in *Pop Modernism: Noise And the Reinvention of the Everyday* (Urbana, IL: University of Illinois Press, 2007), 12–13.

7

The Mind as Palimpsest: Art, Dreaming and James Sully's Aesthetics of Latency

Helen Groth

The late Victorian evolutionary psychologist James Sully was actively engaged in the socio-intellectual networks that generated a broader public engagement with psychological subjects in the latter decades of the nineteenth century, including the nature of consciousness, unconscious cerebration, evolutionary psychology, animal intelligence and dreams. He published prolifically and diversely in the major periodicals of the day, the *Cornhill Magazine*, the *Fortnightly Review* and the *Nineteenth Century*, served as editor of one of the field-defining psychological journals of the period, *Mind*, and ultimately moved into the university system in his later career, taking up the Grote Professorship of the Philosophy of Mind and Logic at University College, London, a position that he held from 1892 to 1903. During this time he also made a considerable contribution to the emerging field of child psychology. Sully's evolutionary conception of the dream as a palimpsest, which he formulated in his 1893 essay on "The Dream as a Revelation," would also prove influential for Freud, who cited Sully in his introduction to *The Interpretation of Dreams*.

The following chapter reads Sully's model of dream interpretation both as a continuation of his writing on the psychological function of aesthetic experience in two earlier essays that were published in *Mind* in the 1870s, "Art and Psychology" and "George Eliot's Art," and as a catalyst for reflecting on the limitations of the transhistorical approaches of some recent cognitive literary theory. In both his literary and dream interpretation, Sully attempts to isolate what is unique to fictional experience. Literary allusions pervade his dream analysis, functioning as devices that reveal both the psychological complexity of the dream and its value as a key to the relationship between conscious and unconscious modes of thought. As with his work on the dream as palimpsest, Sully interprets art, and more particularly the process of reading George Eliot's art, as a multichanneled mediation that transmits messages on different frequencies that the rational mind subsequently decodes. Responding to critics of Eliot's didacticism, Sully insists that it is precisely this impulse to teach and illustrate that infuses her work with "colour and determines the quality of the after-impression" it leaves on the reader's mind.[1] Indeed, for Sully, Eliot's didacticism constitutes her most significant challenge to those who wish to judge her work solely against limiting aesthetic criteria such as, "the delight in things as wonderful, beautiful, sublime, or mirth-provoking, and in their far-reaching harmonies" (378).

Putting questions of beauty and pleasure to one side, Sully turns to what he views as the "wider questions" Eliot's work raises, such as:

> What is the special distinguishing function of the modern art of fiction? What is its relation to the other arts?...I am not concerned with appreciating her exact rank as a novelist. I wish only to estimate the conception of her art which is not only latent in every work, but which now and again comes to the surface, shaping itself into an explicit utterance. (378)

Aesthetic evaluations or appreciations may be able to measure the surface effects of beauty, but they cannot decipher the latent conceptual and social networks that shape the novels of a writer such as Eliot, according to Sully. Instead, one must attune one's ear to the "message" she transmits "through a medium which is now commonly recognized as a form of art" (378). One must, in other words, actively interpret the novel as a specific process of mediation that connects apparently disparate forms of social phenomena despite its appearance of aesthetic autonomy.

In the subsequent pages of his essay on Eliot, Sully invites the psychologically attuned readers of *Mind* to decode this subliminal message by applying an alternative interpretive model that, to adapt Fredric Jameson, restores "to the surface of the text the repressed and buried reality" of its psychological unconscious.[2] For Sully, this means revealing the psychological underpinnings of Eliot's artistic vision, which he felt had been obscured by the critical focus on the superficies of beauty and form. Sully's primary focus was the "function of fiction," an emphasis which Vanessa L. Ryan has argued foreshadows recent interdisciplinary work by cognitive literary theorists, such as Lisa Zunshine's *Why We Read Fiction* and Blakey Vermeule's *Why Do We Care about Literary Characters?* Ryan rightly observes that reading Sully's work historicizes these critics' predominantly transhistorical examinations of how "theories of consciousness inform our understanding of the process and function of reading fiction," and the ways in which "fiction itself might provide a key to new theories of consciousness."[3] Unlike these critics however, Sully's conception of the psychological function of art and literature never loses sight of the literary specificity of Eliot's work and of its place within a historical network of writers interested in the relationship between literature and mind, including Eliot's partner, as well as Sully's friend and mentor, George Henry Lewes. Learning about the mind through Eliot's vivid characterization of "the subconscious region of mental life, the domain of vague emotion and rapid fugitive thought" is, for Sully, not an end in itself but an interesting by-product of reading her work "that leaves a kind of after-effect that remains when the more exciting stage of the impression produced by the particular presentiment is passing away" (393).

Literary palimpsests and psychological reading

In his autobiographical reflections Sully describes George Eliot's charismatic presence at the regular Sunday afternoon gatherings at the house she shared with her partner George Henry Lewes in uncharacteristically mystifying terms:

If Lewes amused his company by jocosities, George Eliot enfolded her auditors in an atmosphere of discriminative sympathy. She had a clairvoyant insight into mind and character, which enabled her to get at once into spiritual touch with a stranger, fitting her talk to his special tastes and needs, and drawing out what was best in him.[4]

Given Sully's skeptical attitude to the clairvoyant methods of contemporary psychical researchers, including those of his friend William James, his attribution of clairvoyant powers to Eliot seems inconsistent with his deep admiration for her work. The underlying distinction he is making here, however, is that her ability to reveal the latent depths of human personality through the medium of her characters primarily emanates from this "discriminative sympathy" rather than from an extensive knowledge of the science of mind (266). Her exceptional capacity to read the minds of those around her is in this sense unquantifiable—a mysterious art of an inspired medium. Eliot's "suggestive observations" assume a more material form for the nonmetaphysically inclined, according to Sully, when channeled through the medium of the novel, revealing a large intuitively "scientific insight into character and life" (378).

In contrast to his mystifying evocation of Eliot's authorial persona, Sully observes, her characters and plots are everyday, ordinary specimens that are "in no sense preternaturally endowed with admirable excellences: nor are they extraordinarily weighted with unlovely vices" (379). Their scientific value for the psychologically inclined reader lies beneath the surface, in the silent rhythms and unexpected dissonances of their thoughts and motivations, as Sully observes: "We have presented to us fragments of lives, in which the forces at work lie almost entirely within the familiar characters and the familiar circumstances which she paints, and her plots are just the development of these latent forces" (379). Consequently the key to the vivid illusion of solidity and movement that Eliot generates is derived from her understanding of the "deep-lying conditions" of this effect (380). Unlike so many of her contemporaries, Eliot achieves a "higher kind of artistic characterisation" by investigating "the complexity of the mental organisation" of individual minds (381). Sully describes Eliot's vision "passing below the surface" in contrast to the "shallow observer" who is unable to detect what is really taking place beneath the skin of her characters (382). Consistent with her particularizing style, Eliot herself observes of the interplay of surface and depth characteristics in *Middlemarch*: "Our vanities differ as our noses do: all conceit is not the same conceit, but varies in correspondence with the minutiae of mental make in which one differs from the other."[5] Indeed Beth Tressler has argued that Eliot's embrace of the fluid models of consciousness of peers such as Herbert Spencer and Henry Holland aligns her conception of authentic representation with those aspects of mind that are most difficult to control, objectify and classify.[6]

Spencer observed in *The Principles of Psychology* that human consciousness was defined by flux and differentiation: "consciousness can neither arise nor be maintained without the occurrence of differences in its state. It must ever be passing from some on state into a different state. In other words—there must be a continuous differentiation of its states."[7] George Henry Lewes likewise stressed differentiation and flux, coining the phrase "streams of consciousness," which is often and erroneously attributed to William James' *The Principles of Psychology*.[8] In *The Physiology of Common Life*, Lewes wrote of "the general stream of Consciousness" as both the process of the mind moving between conscious and unconscious, voluntary and involuntary states, and "the general stream of Sensation which constitutes his [the reader's] feeling of existence—the consciousness of himself as a sensitive being."[9] Both of these processes in Lewes's framework combine to capture not only the dynamic generative movements of consciousness but also its neurological basis in the senses and physical world.

Sully agreed with both Spencer's and Lewes' accounts of the complex interdependency between differential states of consciousness, although Sully's writing on the dream as a revelation of the nature of mind marked a significant departure from Lewes in particular. Freud, remarking on the alignment of his and Sully's interest in the differentiation between the manifest and latent content of dreams, inadvertently summed up the distinction between the two friends. Lewes, while interested in the dream as a neurological phenomena, would never have spoken of the dream as "palimpsest" as Sully would do in the following passage, which Freud positively cited in full in *The Interpretation of Dreams*:

> It would seem then, after all, that dreams are not the utter nonsense they have been said to be by such authorities as Chaucer, Shakespeare and Milton. The chaotic aggregations of our night-fancy have a significance and communicate a new knowledge. Like some letter in cipher, the dream-inscription when scrutinized closely loses its first look of balderdash and takes on the aspect of a serious, intelligible message. Or, to vary the figure slightly, we may say that, like some palimpsest, the dream discloses beneath its worthless surface-characters traces of an old and precious communication.[10]

Freud reads Sully's work as an interpretive turning point that expanded the significance of the dream beyond the physiological reductionism of Victorian psychology. The dream for Sully emanates from the mind's mythologizing impulses, creating the illusion of narrative coherence out of a chaotic assemblage of remembered images, while transforming the dreamer into the reader/spectator of their own potentially revelatory streams of consciousness.

Writing of Maggie Tulliver, Sully describes Eliot's underlying preoccupation with the convergence of streams of "obscure moral tendencies, nascent forces, which though they mingle with and help to colour the currents of thought and action, never come into the distinct light of self-consciousness, because circumstances have never supplied the stimulus needed to develop their full energy" (382). Described circumstances or environment, another key word for Sully, provides the stimulus that brings previously hidden or unconscious aspects of an individual character's mind to the surface of Eliot's writing. The fictional mind in this sense resembles a palimpsest. A character, like a personality, can only be perceived as "a concrete living whole when we attach it by a network of organic filaments to its particular environment, physical and social" (382). For Eliot the intricately detailed spaces in which her characters live out their everyday lives are literal extensions of their inner life—the carpenter's shop, the mill, the dairy, the village church. According to Sully, the "artistic value" of these microscopic representations of living continuities between people and their material environments, like Eliot's incremental building of characteristics into complete psychological portraits, lies in the revelation of the ways in which the "germ of individual character" emerges out of "the habitual channels of the emotions, the direction of the aims, the form of the obligations," which are, in turn, shaped by the invisible contours of "unwritten laws" (383).

Abiding by the "unwritten laws," however, does not condemn Eliot's characters to the crudely drawn outlines of social or class-based stereotypes Sully contends. Their dynamism and solidity arise from Eliot's drive to teach her readers how to feel by "the extension of our sympathies"—as she argues in "The Natural History of German Life."[11] Reading Eliot thus resembles a form of "psychological analysis," according to Sully, but of a specific fictional kind (388):

By psychological analysis in fiction is meant the unfolding of the inner germs of action, the spreading out before the eye those complicated activities of imagination and desire, impulse and counter-impulse, which are conduct in the process of becoming.... Our author lifts the invisible history to a prominent position, partly because the visible history as soon as it becomes intricate cannot be understood apart from it: partly, too, no doubt, because the inner history, the lyric flow of inaudible emotions, and the keen dramatic oppositions of invisible desires and aversions, beliefs and doubts, has a deep interest of its own for the sympathetic mind. (388)

Sully footnotes this densely packed observation with a further clarifying distinction that seems to diminish the psychological value of Eliot's characterization just at the point in his essay where he is most intent on making his case. Distinguishing Eliot from Balzac, whom he observes had an "excessive leaning to psychological analysis for its own sake," Sully describes Eliot's process of narrating "a history of a character" as more of a "genetic method" of presentation (388). He also uses terms like "quasi-scientific" (388) and "sympathy" to isolate what distinguishes Eliot's art from that of her predecessors such as Fielding and her peers who, "by repeating the shibboleth 'Art for art's sake,' would seem to aim at erecting art into a kind of metaphysical absolute, 'a thing-in-itself' out of all relation to the minds which dare to be impressed and delighted by it" (392). Ultimately, he concludes that the specificity of her art lies in her sympathetic powers of communication, which reveal the previously invisible and inaudible, to the eyes of the inquisitive sympathetic reader.

Notably, for Sully, the aim is not to reduce Eliot's characters to functional psychological exempla or universal data, but rather to reveal the close intertwining of Eliot's language with the questions of volition, the organic development of mind or embodied mind and the connections between modes of consciousness that preoccupied her psychologically inclined contemporaries. Drawing on Alan Richardson's historical approach to the affinities between Romantic aesthetics and the then-new science of mind, when read in context, Sully's reading of Eliot's work allows us to identify a constructive "consonance" between past and present approaches to what particular works of literature can teach us about the nature of mind. As Richardson stresses, the objective is to find points of comparison not identity:

> Recent work on the brain and mind can help scholars to perceive distinctions, register nuances, and appreciate moral and philosophical repercussions that might have seemed non-existent, elusive, or simply not worth pursuing a few decades ago. It can also help reveal how certain issues and questions are identical to those that have come to occupy cognitive scientists at the turn of the twentieth century. How could they be? Rather, the connections between, say adaptationist accounts of mind and the hypothesis of a modular brain, or anti-dualistic cognitive theories and an emphasis on the unconscious and emotive aspects of rational thought, have returned in a different but comparable manner.[12]

Richardson, like Nicholas Dames, Vanessa L. Ryan and a growing list of historically oriented scholars to which this chapter is indebted, consequently provides new ways of thinking about the technical history of literary forms that were forged out of complex patterns of what Dames aptly describes as "interdisciplinary collaboration and friction."[13]

Accordingly, while Sully may have spoken in evolutionary terms of art as needing to appeal to the "human susceptibilities" of the "most highly developed man," this does not equate to reducing Eliot's characters to a mimetic reflection of an adaptationatist cognitive predisposition to acquire "social information" through reading fictional minds as if they were real, which Blakey Vermeule has suggested is one of the primary transhistorical rationales for "why we care about literary characters."[14] Sully was undoubtedly interested in what George Eliot's characters could teach him about the mind, but this interest is always tempered by a sense of the irreducibility of Eliot's insights to a purely scientific model of mind. He consistently stresses the inaccessibility of Eliot's representations of mind to "the ordinary reader" (389), in contrast to the reader "representing the advanced wave of man's intellectual and moral development" (393). Her novelistic representations of mind resemble palimpsests and demand rigorous interpretive decoding of complex layers of allusion and descriptive technique. In this sense, Sully's psychological theory of modern fiction also diverges from Lisa Zunshine's conception of "fictional narrative as an artifact in progress—an ongoing thousands-years-long experimentation with our cognitive adaptations."[15] For Sully, there is a profound distinction between the evolution of aesthetic form as an apogee of human civilization, and the broader evolutionary claims Zunshine makes for all forms of fiction as permutations "of our evolved cognitive eagerness to construct a state of mind behind a behavior."[16] Modern fiction remains a distinct, often perplexing, medium of knowledge and experience for Sully, as opposed to the drive to critical and cognitive transparency that underlies Zunshine's collapse of all literary and literary-critical paradigms into permutations on one transhistorical and transgeneric "theory of mind." Fiction does more than facilitate experimentation with mind-reading, Sully suggests. It creates a space for reflecting on the rational limitations of art and the scientific preoccupations of modern life.

One of Sully's central preoccupations, elaborated in his earlier essay "Art and Psychology," is to isolate what is specific to aesthetic experience more generally—what sets it apart from other forms of experience. He found metaphysical conceptions of art's unique properties sterile and unintelligible to what he calls "the non-metaphysical mind."[17] Consequently he writes dismissively of the "unscientific condition of art-theory" and those who worship beauty in "the delightful haze which all emotion throws about its object and which is rudely dispelled by the full vigour of intellectual action" (467). There must, he argues, be a way of writing scientifically about art that allows for its "proverbial subjectivity and uncertainty" (468), its close connection to "social conditions and historical development," and to the principles "of taste and canons of art which apply to a particular nationality in a particular period" which are, in turn, "wholly inapplicable to the rest of mankind" (470).

The answer lies, he suggests, in delimitation, in isolating and abstracting characteristics from "the processes of art" that are amenable to scientific analysis (470). He concludes that the "aim of aesthetics might accordingly give an account of the nature and the growth of the artistic impulse in so far as it can be regarded as a separate factor in social activity and progress" (471). Dealing scientifically with "art-problems" would thus involve a more extended consideration of the "effects of art" that belong "to the more complex and variable phenomena of the human mind, that is to say, to phenomena which involve the more intricate and subtle influences of social contact, and which present numerous and wide fluctuations, answering to the many distinguishable stages of a society's intellectual and moral development" (471). Sully argues that the basis of this approach already exists in "every far-reaching critic" who is "an unconscious, if not a conscious, psychologist" when he or she engages with art's potential to reveal the complexity of human emotion—such moments, he suggests, touch on "principles which are *axiomata media* in psychological science" (471).

In line with his reading of George Eliot, however, the "final end of art" he conceded, could not be "settled by psychological principles but at most by an induction from the facts of art" (472). Psychology may provide the artist with the "*proximate* conditions of his effects" (472), but the question of artistic technique falls beyond science's scope. Reading psychologically for Sully involves addressing the larger social questions raised by art, which can be conducted in two ways "either by laying down definite laws of emotional susceptibility or intellectual activity" or "by determining the nature and origin of some particular mode of aesthetic feeling" (473). Sully illustrates this with a series of "art-problems": for example, the tension between the formal demands of poetry and music, such as rhythm, and the mediation of "comparatively formless" emotions like anger or disgust, "which by its very violence defies the restraint that is inseparable from all order" (474). In such instances, aesthetic forms "bend and mould" themselves to emotions that "resist all pressure" to align with "the fixed laws of rhythm and melodic arrangement" (474). Psychological interpretation in this context serves as a revelatory mechanism that exposes the tension between order and chaos that is intrinsic to the artistic process.

The art of dreaming

Sully's dream interpretation is equally concerned with the generative interplay between chaos and order, surface and depth. This final section reads Sully's model of dream interpretation as a process of interdisciplinary reading that preserves the parallel streams of literature and the science of mind. Fictionality is an intrinsic component of dreaming for Sully, which he, in turn, defines as a mode of unconscious thought. In this context, when it is the dream, not modern fiction, which is the central object of inquiry, literature does function as a source of individual examples of dreaming, whether it be George Sand dreaming of flying or the temporal and spatial distortions of De Quincey's opium-infused dream sequences. Drawing on an established nineteenth-century practice of citing literary sources to animate and dramatize the science of dreaming, of which Coleridge's *Kubla Khan* and De Quincey's *Confessions of an English Opium Eater* were among the most popular, Sully exploits a shared literary repertoire to mediate his scientific theory to a general audience, while maintaining the distinction between discursive modes.[18]

The expansive associative networks of the dream must always be drawn back into the realm of rational explanation according to Sully, which means that thinking continues beyond the limits of sleep. While "entering dreamland" may involve a certain degree of regression to more elemental or primitive emotions, Sully insists, in "The Dream as a Revelation," that dream activity is nevertheless the product of an evolved mind formed by the various histories of human experience.[19] This experiential dimension, which includes the collective memory of familiar stories and events, becomes manifest when the dreaming mind attempts to explain and understand the most fanciful occurrences, a sign, Sully argues, that the dreamer remains a "rational animal" (356). While the superficial "kaleidoscopic transformations of the dream," or "jumble of the nocturnal phantasmagoria," may run seemingly illogical scenes together, according to Sully's evolutionary model of the mind as palimpsest, the dream "strips the ego of its artificial wrappings and exposes it in its rude native nudity. It brings up from the dim depths of our sub-conscious life the primal, instinctive impulses, and discloses to us a side of ourselves which connects us with the great sentient world" (358).

Far from being a risk to the self, the dream reveals otherwise submerged layers of the mind, which Sully elaborates through a series of literary anecdotes:

> Southey tells us that he dreamt again and again of killing Bonaparte. George Sand, when a girl, more girl-like, dreamt that she took the tyrant in aerial flight to the top of the cupola of the Tuileries and remonstrated with him. We may assume, perhaps, that in each case the dream was the expansion and complete development of a vague fugitive wish of the waking mind. (358)

Reading passages such as this also highlights the affinities between Sully's rhetoric of repression and wish fulfillment and the taxonomy of Freudian psychoanalysis. Certainly, one can see parallels between Sully's account of the ego's repression and sublimation of primitive desire or instinct and Freud's dialectical model of psychic life. Freud, like

Sully, associated the dream with a regression to infantile or archaic thought, drawing on nineteenth-century evolutionary terminology when elaborating the entangled histories of the individual and the race or species.[20] But Sully's concept of the dream as wish fulfillment varies considerably from Freud's theory of the manifest content of the dream as a proxy of a latent wish.[21] Southey and Sand's dreams are fairly uncomplicated instances of wish fulfillment, whereas for Freud the wish lurks beneath the manifest content of dreams, latent and divergent from the apparent meaning of the dream. As Freud puts it, "A dreamer's relation to his wishes is a quite peculiar one. He repudiates them and censors them—he has no liking for them, in short."[22]

To return for a moment to Sully's reflections on Eliot's psychological characterization, consistent with the primary focus on the relationship between literature and psychology, Sully's treatment of the aesthetics of the unconscious mind in Eliot's work far exceeds his analogical gestures to Sand and Southey in the above passage. Sully informs his readers, for example, that Maggie Tulliver's lapses into unconscious thought or reverie in *The Mill and the Floss* open up a space for a more layered forensic analysis of consciousness that privileges the latent movements of the psyche over the often clichéd banalities of manifest content. He speaks of her relish for "exposing the inconsistencies of character" and transgression of "the current canons of art" (382). Eliot, unlike her less scientific peers, transforms her art into a forensic instrument that reveals the double nature of the self and mind. "The dominant impulses," or what she calls in one place "the persistent self," are crossed and complicated by antagonistic forces which may for a time seem to carry the day: meanwhile the persistent self, we clearly perceive, "pauses and awaits us" (382). What is of interest to Sully is that these deeper "organic roots of personality" are "rarely known even to the individual" character in Eliot's work (382). They remain "obscure" or latent in "the subconscious region of metal life," often never coming "into the distinct light of self-consciousness, because circumstances have never supplied the stimulus needed to develop their full energy" (382).

Sully's preoccupation with the interplay between layers of unconscious thought in Eliot was paralleled in each new iteration of his dream theory, which moved closer to the model of depth psychology that ultimately emerges in "The Dream as a Revelation." [23] This involved a corresponding shift away from the reference points that he had used to navigate his way toward the serious study of dreams in his early work, such as the associationist philosophies of mind of John Locke and Dugald Stewart, and closer to the work of the German psychologist William Wundt and influential French physician and dream theorist Louis Ferdinand Alfred Maury.[24] The following section explores the implications of these transitions in the context of the evolutionary psychology of Herbert Spencer, which was so integral to his concept of a scientific aesthetics.

Sully, like Spencer, advocated a form of "genetic psychology," the study of the evolution of mind, from its "savage" lower stages in children and so-called primitive peoples to the higher stages of the civilized adult mind. He was, however, loathe to embrace the experimental methods and questionnaires that were becoming the standard tools of his profession, favoring trained observation, in the case of children, and introspection for adults, to protect the spontaneity of his subject's responses.[25]

Also diverging from the strictly physiological account of mind favored by Lewes, Sully
urged his readers in "The Laws of Dream-Fancy" to consider not only the structural
processes of dreaming but also the sensory and emotional catalysts that generate the
vivid illusions of the real that the dreamer mistakes for objective realities. Sleep, he
contends, opens up the mind to reveal "apparently forgotten images of persons and
places" that "no discoverable play of association" can explain (543).

As the title suggests, one of the primary motivations of "The Laws of Dream-Fancy"
is to discover an order in the seeming chaos of dreams:

> It is commonly said that dreams are a grotesque dissolution of all order, a very chaos
> and whirl of images without any discoverable connection. On the other hand, a
> few claim for the mind in sleep a power of arranging and grouping its incongruous
> elements in definite, even though very unlife-like, sensuous representations. Each
> of these views is correct within certain limits; that is to say, there are dreams in
> which the strangest disorder seems to prevail, and others in which one detects
> the action of a control. Yet, speaking generally, sequences of dream-thought are
> determined by certain circumstances and laws, and so far are not haphazard and
> wholly chaotic. (544)

The failure to detect the invisible ties or "emotional vibration(s)" that interlink our
"dream-pictures" lies with the interpreter, according to Sully (545). In contrast to
the conscious connections made in waking thought that allow us to rationalize
resemblances, classify objects and ascribe purpose to events, in sleep the "slightest
touch of resemblance" may spark new successions of ideas or set off inexplicable
transformations of familiar scenes and faces—"transformation scenes" as he calls
them (545).

Refusing to accept that dreaming necessarily requires an abeyance of will, Sully
agreed with the seminal dream work of Alfred Maury, that volition plays a vital role
in fully developed dreams that actively exercise the attention of the dreamer. This
attentiveness involves seeking both "unity and consistency among the heterogeneous
elements of dream-consciousness" and the drive to achieve "emotional harmony"
(549). Dreaming thus becomes a form of selective aggregation and integration, in
which the dreamer continually adapts and connects "pre-existing groups of images" to
"every new dream-object" through a process of retrospective association, adaptation
and fusion (550). Magnification and exaggeration stimulate this "fusibility," as Sully
calls it, blending "images of a certain colour" into "composite images" that "transcend
in impressiveness those of our waking experience" (554).

Citing Darwin's correlation of "bodily irritation" and "mental perplexity," Sully
exemplifies how conscious experience of states of grief or elation, are hyperbolically
rendered in dream form as part of apparently random associative sequences that only
retrospectively cohere in the mind of "the reflective dreamer" (552). So while the
"higher intellectual activities" may be suspended while the mind dreams, returning to
"the primordial state of intelligence and mental development, as we see it in children
and some of the lower animals," this is mitigated in the mature adult mind, according

to Sully, by the dream images drawn from a larger field of emotional experience, including from books recently read or works of art encountered (555). In this sense dreaming, like reading a book, or viewing a work of art, involves a generative interplay between conscious and unconscious streams of thought that ultimately privileges order over chaos, likeness over difference.

Sully expands upon these theories in his study of *Illusions*, published over a decade later. Nodding to Lewes's analogy between reverie and dreaming, which Eliot also exploited as a fictional device, Sully distinguishes the dream as a complete and persistent illusion, in contrast to the transitory drift of attention of the daydream.[26] Sully speaks of the sleeper as "possessed" and "tied down" by "an image or group of images" that "lord it over" the mind "just as the actual impression of waking life" (138). What the eye and mind of the dreamer choose to fixate upon and interpret is nevertheless shaped by "the person's character, previous experience [and] ruling emotions" (147). Sully insists throughout "that during sleep every man has a world of his own," a stress on heterogeneity that consistently puts the onus on the interpretive process, both within and beyond the dream (147). In a section devoted to dream interpretation, Sully returns to the "exaggerated mode of interpretation" colored by emotion, again alluding to Lewes on this subject, while warning against the reductive typification of dream symbols by Albert Scherner in his *The Life of Dreams*, as Freud would do in his more extensive discussion of the absurdity of Scherner's claim that the symbolism of the house provides the standard scaffolding for all physiologically induced dreams (149).[27] In the case of a woman dreaming of sex, for example, Scherner suggested that the woman might begin by dreaming of a wet narrow courtyard along which she must travel "to take a gentleman a letter," but like all dreams generated by specific somatic impulses the dream imagination ultimately "throws aside its veil" to reveal "the organ concerned."[28]

Such literalism, Sully argued, verged on the absurd, discarding the complexity and hidden meanings of the dream in favor of the obvious and superficial.[29] He nevertheless maintained Scherner's symbolic interpretation was consistent with the "intellectual impulse to connect the disconnected" that dreams inspire, which was, in turn, intrinsic "to the very foundations of our intellectual structure" (175). Sully uses the term "dream-construction" to describe this process, which is fundamental to his theory of the dream as revelation of the "deeply rooted habit of the mind" (177). Accordingly, the logic of interpretation shapes the dream both while it is taking place and in retrospect, as the dream transforms according to the intrinsically human "impulse to arrange," harmonize and rationalize (177).

These theories are most fully realized in Sully's essay "The Dream as a Revelation," to which I will now turn. Published in the *Fortnightly Review*, this seminal essay was addressed to a general audience in the manner of "The Laws of Dream-Fancy," which appeared in Leslie Stephen's *Cornhill Magazine* over 20 years before. While Sully had long made his reputation as a distinguished contributor to *Mind*, he remained committed to the broader dissemination of psychology in both the press and the schools, the latter reflecting his pivotal role in the emerging field of child psychology.[30] Like Lewes, who facilitated many of his first introductions to key figures in Victorian psychology and science, including Alexander Bain, Herbert Spencer and Charles Darwin, Sully was a formidable professional networker. He was on intimate terms with John Tyndall, George Romanes, Thomas Huxley, Robert Louis Stevenson, George Meredith, George Eliot, John Addington Symonds (the younger) and Leslie Stephen, to name but a few of his connections. He was also familiar with key figures in the Society for Psychical Research, such as Henry Sidgwick, William James and, to a lesser extent, Frederic Myers and Edmund Gurney, although this did not translate into an enthusiastic embrace of their metaphysical tendencies. As he notes in his profile of James in *My Life and Friends*, he remained unconvinced by the embrace of the hypothetical in *The Will to Believe*, and expressed reservations about Sidgwick's speculative turn of mind.[31]

Sully recounts one of his own dreams to exemplify the "kaleidoscopic transformations" that dissociate external from internal sensations:

> I once dreamt of seeing an intimate friend of my youth. Moved by a childish impulse of tenderness, I put out my hand to touch his face, and, lo, I found it to be a mosaic. The impression of the cold hard surface in place of the softness and warmth of the skin, brought no shock, and what is odd, the initial caressing feeling persisted. (357)

Simplifying "the complex patterns of consciousness" and emotion, to paraphrase Sully, this impulsive gesture brings to light "forces and tendencies" that are hidden under "the superincumbent mass of the later and higher acquisitions"—reason, for example, or the conscious observation of the rules of adult civility that would impede reaching out to touch an old friend's face in the manner of a child (357). The transformation from expected warmth to the cool hard surface of the mosaic registers the intrinsic unreality of the dream, even though in accordance to the laws of dream exaggeration, the sensation of the caress persists and takes on the semblance of the real. To quote Sully, "This unveiling during sleep of the more instinctive layers of our mental life may be seen in the leaping forth into full activity of some nascent and instantly inhibited impulse of thought or feeling of the waking hours" (358).

The "revival of concrete experiences, of what we call memory," is also integral to the restorative powers of the dream, summoning immediate and remote images, the latter proliferating with age (360). Citing De Quincey's opium-charged dreams of minutest incidents of his childhood, Sully complicates the temporality of dreaming still further, speculating that many of the strange faces and scenes that inhabit our dream-life are "handed down from a remote past" even though we may not recognize them as recollections (360). These tidal returns of images from the "swiftly receding past" also challenge the dreamer's creative agency within the dream, temporarily disabling the higher brain functions of rational interpretation and revealing "the overlaid strata of old experience" (361). Dreams thus constitute "a second revived life, which intersects and interrupts our normal waking life" (361).

Developing this idea further, Sully speaks of the dream as conserving the "successive personalities" of the dreamer (362) and of reinstating our "dead selves," which are literally "undeveloped, rudimentary" versions of the self that ordinarily "belong to the hidden substrata of our mental being" (363). Censored and driven back by our "daily collision with our surroundings," it is these aspects of the self that are often the most vital and definitive aspects of an individual personality, as Sully concludes: "The particular personality, which we have developed, which is all that our friends know of us, is a kind of selection from among many possible personalities, a selection effected by the peculiar conditions of our environment" (363). It is this dimension of dreaming that culminates in the passage cited in Freud, which insists that the "chaotic aggregations of our night-fancy have a significance and communicate new knowledge" (364). While they may have diverged on the nature of this new knowledge and the mode of interpretation required to bring "these dream-disclosures" to light (364), to use Sully's terminology, the idea of the dream as key to the complex nature of human personality that took shape in "The Dream as a Revelation" came closest, as Freud conceded, to his hypothesis regarding the latent content of dreams than any other in the existing literature on the subject.

Sully's dream theory, like his aesthetic theory, thus privileges the process of interpretation, while stressing its necessary selectivity. While his dream theory clearly shares contemporary cognitive theoretical preoccupations with narrative as intrinsic to the patterning and rhythms of everyday thought, he makes a distinction between these evolving forms of structural sequencing and the particularities of aesthetic and psychic experience. While art and fiction are important touchstones for Sully for thinking through the definitive characteristics of the dream and other psychological phenomena, they nevertheless retain their integrity as discrete objects of knowledge that can never be entirely amenable to empirical analysis. Typifying the dynamic cross-pollination between literature, art and science in the Victorian period, Sully's work also emanates from a transitional period which ultimately saw the divergence of the professions of psychology and literary criticism, which those who have embraced the recent "cognitive turn" in literary studies are seeking to correct. For this reason alone, his work serves as an illuminating historical example of the enduring fascination with the question of why we continue to read fiction, and what that reveals about us and the culture and time in which we happen to be living.

Notes

1 James Sully, "George Eliot's Art," *Mind* 6, no. 23 (July 1881): 382. Hereafter cited in text.
2 Fredric Jameson, *The Political Unconscious: Narrative as a Socially Symbolic Act* (London: Routledge, 1981), 20.
3 Vanessa L. Ryan, *Thinking without Thinking in the Victorian Novel* (Baltimore, MD: The Johns Hopkins University Press, 2012), 14.
4 James Sully, *My Life and Friends: A Psychologist's Memories* (London: T. Fisher Unwin, 1918), 264.
5 George Eliot, *Middlemarch* (New York and London: W. W. Norton & Co., 1977; repr., 2000), 96.

6   Beth Tressler, "Waking Dreams: George Eliot and the Poetics of Double
    Consciousness," *Victorian Literature and Culture* 39 (2011): 490.
7   Herbert Spencer, *Principles of Psychology*, 2 vols. (New York: D. Appleton, 1906), 2:300.
8   This misattribution is most common amongst scholars of literary modernism.
    Judith Ryan, for example, claims that James was the "creator of the term 'stream of
    consciousness,'" *The Vanishing Subject: Early Psychology and Literary Modernism*
    (London: University of Chicago Press, 1991), 1.
9   George Henry Lewes, *The Physiology of Common Life*, 2 vols. (London: Blackwoods,
    1859–60), 2:63; 66.
10 Sigmund Freud, "The Interpretation" of Dreams in *Standard Edition of the Complete
    Psychological Works*, trans. James Strachey, 24 vols. (London: The Hogarth Press,
    1953–74), 5:135.
11 George Eliot, "The Natural History of German Life," *George Eliot: Selected Essays,
    Poems and Other Writings*, ed. G. Eliot (Oxford: Oxford University Press, 1990), 110.
12 Alan Richardson, *British Romanticism and the Science of Mind* (Cambridge:
    Cambridge University Press, 2001), 3.
13 Nicholas Dames, *The Physiology of the Novel: Reading, Neural Science, and the Form of
    Victorian Fiction* (Oxford: Oxford University Press, 2007), 6.
14 Blakey Vermeule, *Why Do We Care about Literary Characters?* (Baltimore, MD: The
    Johns Hopkins University Press, 2010), 14.
15 Lisa Zunshine, *Why We Read Fiction: Theory of Mind and the Novel* (Columbus, OH:
    Ohio State University Press, 2006), 27.
16 Zunshine, *Why We Read Fiction*, 25.
17 James Sully, "Art and Psychology," *Mind* 1, no. 4 (October 1876): 467.
18 Gillian Beer seminally identified this practice in "Parable, Professionalization, and
    Literary Allusion in Victorian Scientific Writing," *Open Fields: Science in Cultural
    Encounter*, ed. Gillian Beer (Oxford: Oxford University Press, 1996), 196–215.
19 James Sully, "The Dream as a Revelation," *Fortnightly Review* 53, no. 315 (March
    1893): 355. Hereafter cited in text.
20 Freud, *Standard Edition of the Complete Psychological Works*, 5:548–9.
21 Richard Wollheim describes Freud's concept of the dream as "the proxy of the wish"
    in *Freud* (London: Fontana, 1991), 74.
22 Freud, *Standard Edition of the Complete Psychological Works*, 5:580–1.
23 James Sully, "The Laws of Dream-Fancy," *Cornhill Magazine* 34, no. 203 (November
    1876): 536–55; "The Laws of Dream-Fancy," *Mind* 2, no. 5 (January 1877): 111–12;
    and Chapter 7 in *Illusions–A Psychological Study* (London: Kegan Paul, Trench & Co,
    1887). References to *Illusions* are hereafter cited in text.
24 Louis Ferdinand Alfred Maury (1817–92) was a French physician and experimental
    psychologist, whom Freud also cites in *The Interpretation of Dreams*. He coined the
    term "hypnagogic hallucinations" to describe the illusions generated when the mind
    is in the transitional state between waking and sleeping. His work notably inspired
    Salvador Dali's "Dream Caused by the Flight of a Bee around a Pomegranate a Second
    Before Awakening."
25 Lyubov G. Gurjeva provides an excellent account of Sully's divergence from the more
    experimental inclinations of his peers in "James Sully and Scientific Psychology,
    1870–1910," *Psychology in Britain: Historical Essays and Personal Reflections*, eds. G.
    C. Bunn, A. D. Lovie, and G. D. Richards (London: The British Psychological Society,
    2001), 72–94.

26 In addition to Vanessa L. Ryan's discussion of Eliot in *Thinking without Thinking in the Victorian Novel*, see Jill Matus, *Shock, Memory and the Unconscious in Victorian Fiction* (Cambridge: Cambridge University Press, 2009) and Michael Davis, *George Eliot and Nineteenth-Century Psychology* (Aldershot: Ashgate, 2006).

27 Freud observes of Scherner's "symbolizing imagination" that while it had no utilitarian application and disobeyed all "the rules of research," it still deserved to be examined as emanating from a long tradition of symbolic dream interpretation, "The Interpretation of Dreams" in Freud, *The Standard Edition of the Complete Psychological Works*, 4:87.

28 Cited in Freud, *The Standard Edition of the Complete Psychological Works*, 4:86.

29 Freud observes of Sully that "he was more firmly convinced than any other psychologist that dreams have a disguised meaning", *The Standard Edition of the Complete Psychological Works*, 4:60.

30 Lyubov G. Gurjeva discusses this aspect of Sully's career in detail in "James Sully and Scientific Psychology." This emphasis on childhood and the nexus of psychology and pedagogy is also reflected in the following works by Sully: *Outlines of Psychology with Special Reference to the Theory of Education* (1884); *Teachers' Handbook of Psychology* (1886); *The Human Mind: A Text-Book of Psychology* (1892); *Outlines of Psychology* (1892); *Studies of Childhood* (1895); and *Children's Ways* (1897).

31 Sully, *My Life and Friends*, 321; 285. Hereafter cited in text.

8

The Flame's Lover: The Modernist Mind of William Carlos Williams

Mark Steven

The foremost recurring image in William Carlos Williams' *Paterson* represents The Great Falls of the Passaic River, New Jersey. From their vantage we behold the entirety of this modern epic compressed into a singular vision of suspended gravity:

> That the poem,
> the most perfect rock and temple, the highest
> falls, in clouds of gauzy spray, should be
> so rivaled   .   that the poet,
> in disgrace, should borrow from erudition (to
> unslave the mind): railing at the vocabulary
> (borrowing from those he hates, to his own
> disfranchisement)   .
> —discounting his failures   .
> seeks to induce his bones to rise into a scene,
> his dry bones, above the scene, (they will not)
> illuminating it within itself, out of itself
> to form the colors, in terms of some
> back street, so that the history may escape
> the panders
> .   .   accomplish the inevitable
> poor, the invisible, thrashing, breeding
> .   debased city[1]

Take note of the grammatical arrangement giving shape to this image. The conjunctional "that" which begins each of the first two clauses hangs syntactically unfulfilled, lingering expectantly: it is left behind once the auxiliary verb "should" plunges its subjects ("the poem," "the poet") into the infinitive flow of their object clauses ("be so rivaled," "borrow from erudition"). Repetition only compounds the deferral of syntactic destination as

* My thanks to Julian Murphet and Sean Pryor for help with this chapter.

"that" doubles the "perfect" poem with the "disgraced" poet who is caught, in lieu of grammatical closure and artistic purpose, "discounting his failures," powerless "to unslave the mind," which remains hog-tied to the words themselves. Those two clauses thus begin to read like exclamations or apostrophes; and then, hanging airborne like the cartoon coyote, the poet momentarily defies gravity—"seeks to induce his bones to rise into a scene/his dry bones, above the scene"—before plummeting, inevitably, toward the "debased city" below.

My immediate sense of this correspondence between grammar and gravity is that *Paterson* is situating itself within the "clouds of gauzy spray" cast off by a modernist poetics, circa 1949, as it first encounters "the highest falls" of the twentieth-century's letters. Its sentences have materialized at a moment when late modernism was ostensibly giving way to an aesthetics of postmodernism, wherein "the mind" and the "debased city" to which it is destined would first be appropriated by Williams' own protégé, Allen Ginsberg: "I saw the best minds of my generation destroyed by madness," his era-defining poem begins, "starving hysterical naked,/dragging themselves through the negro streets at dawn looking for an angry fix."[2] But there is a parallax view to Williams' image: at once we are presented with either side of the fall, before and after, the modern and the postmodern, briefly held in place by the tensile parabola of words. This reading finds support in the fact that the poem and its poet together hold a curiously Janus-faced outlook on literary history. Gazing backward, *Paterson* carries the legacy of the modernist fathers' collective achievement; and forward, Williams remains bound to the future of modernism by a sense of filial duty to at least one poet two decades his junior. Directly addressing Ezra Pound, Williams declares, "Your interest is in the bloody loam, but what/I'm after is the finished product" (37). "April!" that month so significant to T. S. Eliot's most celebrated work, is glimpsed off "in the distance/being hanged" (72). "What meeting you meant to me," Williams was writing to Louis Zukofsky as early as 1928, "was at first just that Pound had admired your work…I was happy to find a link between myself and another wave of it…The thing moves by a direct relationship between men from generation to generation."[3] There is a muted exuberance to this sentence but, when read against those disenchanted allusions from *Paterson*, it would seem as though Williams is holding back on a palpable sense of ending. Gravity is yet to catch up with our poet.

But perhaps there is something else at stake here that is more important than the eventual loss of colleagues, friends and allies, and perhaps it is being felt even more acutely than the architectonic collision of eras. Fredric Jameson is certainly attuned to whatever irreconcilable energies are at work within this poem:

> William Carlos Williams' *Paterson* is…a modern epic that knows in its deepest structural impulses—unlike its great models in the pocket epics of Pound and Eliot, and in ways quite unlike the naïveté of cognate efforts like Hart Crane's *Bridge*—that it must not succeed, that its conditions of realization depend on a fundamental success in failing, at the same time that it must not embody any kind of will to failure either, in the conventional psychology of the inferiority complex or in the willful self-crippling of the accident-prone or the writer's block.[4]

Though we might fault Jameson's sharp distinction between modern epics (for *The Waste Land* and *The Cantos* are often described in similar terms), his verdict on *Paterson* itself remains accurate. Yet still, if we are going to demonstrate this poem's singular achievement or the individual logic of its "failure," our challenge will be to do so from within and against the broadly defined field of modernism. According to T. J. Clark, modernism could never, as it intended, translate the "shock of the material world" into a "new and fully public language."[5] "Its greatest artists," replies Charles Altieri, "were those who most intently and intensely revealed that failure in their work"[6] If Williams really is engaging the fact that no literary form is capable of fully relating "the material world" in prose or verse, then surely we must begin by asking what kind of materials are to be arraigned by his own hand; and, if we think about Williams' vocation as well as its various emphases in his poetry, an answer tentatively though unambiguously presents itself: Williams trained in, practiced and wrote about physiology. Considering this professional commitment and its possibly "failed" transposition into literature, let us approach *Paterson* via its disjunctive synthesis of poetry's aesthetic ambitions with the epistemological objectives of physiological science.

That poets use science as an analog for their own compositional accuracy is well known. Daniel Albright—whose *Quantum Poetics* maps this phenomenon in the work of Eliot, Pound and W. B. Yeats—suggests that the atomizing vocabulary of modernism implies its poets' collective fantasy "that each constituent element of a poem belongs to some domain of Absolutes, of valid equations, where there exists a unique picture, or unique prosodic rhythm, or unique trope, exactly equivalent to the feeling the poet wishes to evoke."[7] In this view, he says, scientific knowledge would allow for poets to apprehend and explore the prepsychical origins of the poem, because composition would have only endowed the hitherto inaccessible mind that produced it "with an electric charge of signification."[8] But where Eliot, Pound and Yeats variously embraced the scientific nomenclature, Williams would be far more hesitant about the role science had already come to play in literature. In his own words, published in 1919, "the scientist does not realize beforehand that he is deceived in his solidities while the artist knows the fleeting nature of his triumphs before they come. Therefore," he says, "I do not propose to be a scientist in my seeking of truth."[9] Despite this rhetoric, he too appropriated the vocabulary of science—or, in his case, physiology—as we encounter it throughout the entirety of his oeuvre. Within this context, however, the scientific idiom would operate quite differently and far less favorably than it had in the works of Eliot, Pound and Yeats. Here, words like "accuracy," "clarity," "rigor" and "stability" are all made to resonate with the restrictive force of master-signifiers, conjuring the discursive strength of science while simultaneously foreclosing on poetry's potential affirmations of the mind, which Williams always envisaged, paradoxically, as residing in an imperceptible state of permanent flux. "Rigor of beauty is the quest. But how will you find beauty," read the first lines of *Paterson*, "when it is locked in the mind past all remonstrance?" (3). The poem thus frames itself as synthesizing scientific rigor with aesthetic pleasure, yet rigor immediately transforms the mind into an inaccessible object, concealed by the diaphanous veils of beauty, and so the poem's synthesis might have already proven to be a "mindless" undertaking. "The vague accuracies of events dancing two/and two," we read 20 pages later, "with language which they/forever surpass—" (23). And here, when the empirical, scientific event is coupled with poetic language, their relationship is framed by oxymoron and the elusory: "accuracy" is made to feel decidedly "vague."

One of this chapter's implications will be that what sustains Williams' self-consciously grammatical weightlessness beyond the laws of physics, and what then culminates in the poet and poem's inevitable plummet, is that literary form is being deployed in *Paterson* to transformatively engage another discourse: namely, science. What we are encountering here is the granular materials of Williams' verse resisting the force of gravity—whose logic has been apprehended scientifically by Galilei, Newton, Eötvös and Einstein—and by doing so the poem discloses something we will soon recognize as the elusively "unslaved" mind. Before we can make that assertion, however, the critical task will be to account for this relationship between poetry and science as it plays out across Williams' epic more generally. Where my approach differs from existing scholarship is on the point (best made by John Hidebidle) that scientific knowledge might "serve in spite of failure as an example of the process of living and enduring life, a process in which diagnosis, both as science and as magic, has a continuing and central place."[10] I will be arguing, differently, that the relationship between Williams' poetic truth and the discursive truths of science (which, for Hidebidle, operate jointly as a kind of "medico-literary diagnosis") is all the more inimical and, if combined, their integration will have to be treated as a formal dialectic, governed by the process of mutual transfiguration. To this end, my chief claim will be that to fully register and make good on the disjunction of poetry and science is to generate a uniquely dialectical mode of literary expression that privileges and affirms the life of the mind only by transforming the science with which it engages. To suggest that *Paterson* has merely internalized its own historical location at the tail end of a movement or even its place within a world that is increasingly subject to the axiomatics of science would be to neglect a significant aspect of this poem—namely, that its so-called "failure" may well be its misinterpreted attempt to affirm against these antecedents something very particular and for it to do so in unfamiliar terms.

Antiphilosophy and modernism

"Believe me," Alain Badiou has written on the unbridled efficacy of science by the close of the twentieth century, "inane ethical committees will never provide us with an answer to the following question: 'What is to be done about this fact: that science knows how to make a new man?' And since there is no project everyone knows there is only one answer: profit will tell us what to do."[11] When Williams first conceived of *Paterson*, modern physiology had already appointed itself with the phylogenetic task of mapping the cellular, anatomical and sensorial composition of hominid forms. When operating under this modality, science will be viewed as the practical and pragmatic valence to philosophy's production of ontological "truths," all of which are variously wagered on the inviolable *a priori*. This is not the universal rule of science and philosophy—but it is, to be sure, the operational mode of all scientific and philosophical "positivism," the inflexible endorsement of logical methodologies and the consequential reduction of knowledge and values to what is measurable. "The gesture of scientific honesty," Theodor Adorno once argued, "which refuses to work with concepts that are not clear and unambiguous, becomes the excuse for superimposing the self-satisfied research enterprise over what is investigated."[12] Perhaps it is because of these territorializing superimpositions that Williams categorically opposed the migration of both scientific and philosophical methodologies into the domain of literary aesthetics. "For after all," he would come to reflect by 1930, "science and philosophy are today, in their effect upon the mind, little more than fetishes of unspeakable abhorrence. And it is through a subversion of the art of writing that their grip upon us has assumed its steel-like temper."[13] For Williams, then, literature is nothing less than a battleground for contesting rights to "the mind," that sovereign locus of all cerebral and imaginative endeavors.

These comments made by Williams resonate powerfully with an intellectual tradition whose most celebrated exponents have posthumously rallied under the banner of "antiphilosophy," a detour through which should help us appreciate what is at stake for the dialectic of *Paterson*. This term—coined by Tristan Tzara in 1920, redefined by Jacques Lacan in the mid-1970s and resurrected more recently within Badiou's genealogical exegesis—nominates those treatises whose chief objectives are to critically traduce philosophical fetishism and to posit, in the place of that discipline's logical schemata, a series of truths that are not mortgaged to empirical facts but engendered by their own material conditions:

> For the antiphilosopher the pains and ecstasies of personal life bear witness to the fact that the concept haunts the temporal present all the way to include the throes of the body. And as for not being a drudge, a mere tutor, a grammar prig or pious guardian of temples and institutions, this is a duty to which the antiphilosopher devotes himself with all the extreme violence of his opinions about his peers, the philosophers.[14]

If philosophy and science share an ambition for truth as defined by objective totality, and if that is why both disciplines fall under the weight of Williams' censure, then surely it will be instructive for us to approach *Paterson* from within the genre of antiphilosophical writing. Here, truth has been reclassified as that to which neither philosophy nor science claim access: "We feel that even when all *possible* scientific questions have been answered," writes Ludwig Wittgenstein, "the problems of life remain completely untouched. Of course there are then no questions left, and this is the answer."[15] But supposing there is an ontological core to this scientific investigation, it is precisely this—a quicksilver essence that eludes all inquisitions—which we shall follow Williams in naming "the mind." "I am not playing at being paradoxical by claiming that science need know nothing about truth," says Lacan. "But I am not forgetting that truth is a value that (cor)responds to the uncertainty with which man's lived experience is phenomenologically marked..."[16] The scientific worldview will thus be seen, from this perspective, to occlude truth by neglecting that phenomenal interface between the imperceptible mind and its lived experiences. But how, then, are we to make good on this connection and thereby affirm the absolutely ineffable with or within material forms?

In the greatest works of modern antiphilosophy, in Friedrich Nietzsche's *Thus Spoke Zarathustra*, Wittgenstein's *Tractatus Logico-Philosophicus* and Lacan's *Écrits*, the fragile demarcation between expression and ideation gives way to concepts in which content is fixed to and contingent upon the stylization of their form. The written word presents itself not as a merely constitutive medium but as a physiognomy of the imagination itself. So much is readily discernable from these books' metatextual emphases on written subjectivities and, in particular, on the protopsychical impact of a stylized prose. Recall Nietzsche's faithful observance of the aphorism ("In the mountains the shortest way is from peak to peak, but for that one must have long legs. Proverbs should be peaks, and those who are addressed should be great and tall"); Wittgenstein's accumulating series of propositions as cognitive steps whose ascending reader "must, so to speak, throw away the ladder after he has climbed it"; and, obviously, the multiple accents on style in Lacan's "writings," whose opening words are these: "The style is the man himself."[17] If science manufactures the discursive constraints that would ensnare an otherwise active mind, then the object-lesson of these books is that a stylistically burnished form keeps thought alive against the grain of philosophical and scientific reification, obviating positivism and generating truths by way of its own epiphenomenal dissonance. The very concept of antiphilosophy thus depends upon its ideas pursuing their own materiality and vice versa—which is, of course, a concept shared by literary modernism.[18]

It was Stéphane Mallarmé who inaugurated this concept—or perhaps even desire— with his insistence that (in Hugh Kenner's paraphrase) "poetry is made not of ideas but of words," and with his remarks that poetry "will, fatally, assume, according to precise laws and insofar as it is possible in a printed text, the form of a constellation. The ship will list from the top of one page to the bottom of the next, etc."[19] Every idea in Mallarmé remains irreducibly bound to a formal substrate—the book, its pages, their words—which it makes over in its own image while transforming itself in accord with these materials. An engagement with this particular materialism, with the typographical medium of words as both responsive to and responsible for the mind's hidden energies, also guided Pound from imagism ("Direct treatment of the 'thing' whether subjective or objective") into vorticism ("Every conception, every emotion presents itself to the vivid consciousness in some primary form") while fueling his lasting enthusiasm for the Chinese ideogram, each one "a vivid shorthand picture of the operations of nature."[20] If Pound's influential deployment of the ideogram is founded on the misunderstanding that each calligraphic lexeme is in fact a pictorial image, an iconographic writing wherein the relationship between signified and signifier, the mind and its materials, is properly motivated, then we should begin to see at least one of the reasons why so many modern poets admire the fine art of painting: the artwork's sensation never has to be translated into the symbolic abstractions of poetry; like the affective "aura," it is immanent to the accretion of oil on the canvas, manifestly bound to its own unique, talismanic object.

Williams was particularly indebted to Paul Cézanne, whose embodiment of this virtue the poet maintains in contradistinction to art's mimetic replication of philosophical and scientific positivism:

Today where everything is being brought into sight the realism of art has bewildered us, confused us and forced us to reinvent in order to retain that which the older generation had without that effort.

Cézanne—

The only realism in art is of the imagination. It is only there that the work escapes plagiarism after nature and becomes a creation…. Invention of new forms to embody this reality of art, the one thing which art is, must occupy all serious minds concerned.[21]

Observe any number of Cézanne's mature or final works and you will see exactly what Williams is suggesting here. To focus on one exemplary case, however, it is with the *Bathers* painting composed between 1895 and 1906 that we come face to face with this embodiment of the mind. Try to internalize at once the massive distortions of the reality principle operating so close to this painting's surface, with limbs transmuting into sexual objects, with every shadow simultaneously concealing and disclosing the workings of libido, and with each bather so clearly energized by some strange and isolating hypostasis. All of this, Williams would suggest, attests to the dynamic interchange of the mind and its materials, the artistic surcharge of truth itself, a stylistic economy which T. J. Clark has been keenest to describe:

Let me present you, say Freud and Cézanne, with a fully and simply physical account of the imagination. Let me show you bodies thoroughly subject, as we agree they must be, to the play of phantasy; that is, deformed and reconstituted at every point by the powers of mind. But let them appear as they would in a world where all the key terms of our endless debate—imagination, mind, body, phantasy, and so on—would be grasped, by the bodies and imaginations themselves, as descriptions of matter in various states. Then the world would truly be remade in representation. All of the mind's previous attempts to imagine its own deforming power would look pallid by comparison. Pallid because they did not understand what that power was *of*.[22]

Williams surely understood these strange powers of the mind, what they were of, and that the only way to hold faithful to them would not be with science but with art; and indeed, I will not be the first to observe that what Williams learned from Cézanne (and, as we shall see, from Freud as well) is that the mind's full powers are more actively present to the artwork itself than in the psychoanalytic discourse surrounding either.[23] And so, as Williams would have it in a poem whose title, "Cézanne," indicates it is dedicated to the painter: "art is all we/can say," he writes, "to reverse/the chain of events and make a pileup/ of passion to match the stars."[24] Here, Williams is situating his own stylistic ambitions within a collective campaign for art to outflank its competitors in a passionate bid for the mind—Cézanne, it seems, would be his commander elect; and his Mallarméan battle cry, trumpeted all throughout *Paterson*, is this: "no ideas but in things."[25]

It is thus that modernism reset the concept of poetry—which had been thought of, since Hegel, as a kind of universal abstraction—in simultaneously aesthetic and material terms, both subjective and objective, that would together keep the mind beyond the threshold of positivist comprehension; and it is, we should now recognize, a concept which finds its ideational correlative in the discourse of antiphilosophy. "For the beginning is assuredly/the end," Williams writes in the Preface to *Paterson*, "since we know nothing, pure/and simple, beyond/our own complexities" (1). The ordering, displacement or even censorship of these complexities is what would characterize the mind of scientific positivism. But "one must still have chaos in oneself to give birth to a dancing star," Nietzsche warned us. "Beware!" cautions Zarathustra (in words that return, like the hereditary trait of some distant ancestor, in Williams' poem to Cézanne): "The time approaches when human beings will no longer give birth to a dancing star."[26] It is with the dying glimmer of those very stars that I wish to see Williams' poetry light up, against the darkling sky of a singular modernity, and form a constellation. But just as soon as we voice that very possibility its supposition clashes, frustratingly, with the formal pragmatism and logical positivism inborn to so many of Williams' aphoristic mutterings. "Prose may carry a load of ill-defined matter like a ship," he once wrote. "But poetry is a machine which drives it, pruned to a perfect economy. As in all machines, its movement is intrinsic, undulant, a physical more than a literary character."[27] What therefore remains unknown are the requisite materials and formal stylizations that antiphilosophical thinking has urged us to acknowledge and which have the potential to recalibrate this reified "machine" in the name of an artistic mind. If that mind's indices are manifest in Cézanne's play of shape and color, Mallarmé's book, Pound's ideogram and Zarathustra's embodiment of celestial chaos, then to what profane entity shall we anchor the mind of *Paterson*?

Beautiful thing

In his autobiography, Williams notes that when "they ask me, as of late they so frequently do, how I have for so many years continued an equal interest in medicine and the poem, I reply that they amount for me to nearly the same thing."[28] More openly than anywhere else in Williams' body of work, *Paterson*'s eponymous speaker can be seen to occupy the same subject position as his author, yet he still

> envies the men that ran
> and could run off
> toward the peripheries—
> to other centers, direct—
> for clarity (if
> they found it)
> loveliness and
> authority in the world— (36)

Williams and Dr. Paterson bear fidelities to the "clarity" that has been associated with science and exploited by other poets, to the anachronistic and ultimately sentimental ideal of a "loveliness" in poetry and to an "authority in the world" resulting from either of the two. But, as independent modes of discursive production, scientific clarity and poetic loveliness are presented here as incompatible; they are driven apart by a parenthetical wedge whose insecurely subjunctive content ("if/they found it") speaks to the serious unlikelihood of any "authority in the world" resulting from the augmentation of either loveliness by clarity or clarity by loveliness. We might even conjecture that those whom Williams envies have been untroubled in their sprint toward "the peripheries" of poetry and the centers of science—perhaps he is even thinking of Albright's "quantum poets," spatially inverting their allegorically nuclear interiority—who liberally borrowed from this other discourse so as to illustrate their literary endeavors. The dialectic between science and poetry begins here, with the realization of their extensive incompatibility and the requisite mediations that will necessarily attend to their combination; and so, instead of writing anything like the other poets' waves of energy and particles of radiation, their sensible mechanisms and vortical turbines, Williams would posit an exceptional literary form upon which Dr. Paterson bestows the name "Beautiful thing."

"Beautiful thing" is a gendered personification of the mind's elements and energies together externalized and recombined by way of complex prosopopoeia. Emanating from her is the same destructive semblance brought to life in Arthur Symons' "Modern Beauty," whose opening sextet grants her the impossible interiority implied by poetic lyricism:

> I am the torch, she saith, and what to me
> If the moth die of me? I am the flame
> Of Beauty, and I burn that all may see
> Beauty, and I have neither joy nor shame,
> But live with that clear light of perfect fire
> Which is to me the death of their desire.[29]

But where Symons' poem offers only the abstract sign of beauty itself—a foresworn predecessor of Yeats' "terrible beauty"—its "perfect" form untrammeled by "desire" resonates all too harmoniously with the moral category of the "beautiful soul." For Hegel, "beautiful soul" refers to the unforgiveable embodiment of an abstraction, to a beauty devoid of depth or substance: "It lacks the power to externalize itself, the power to make itself into a Thing, and to endure being."[30] Though it would be difficult to demonstrate what Williams knew of Hegel, if much at all, we can still say with certainty that, for Williams, "beautiful" and "soul" fit together into the paradigmatic register of pure idealism. "What is beauty but a ghost?" asks the poet. "Beauty has no form but it is expressed in form."[31] "In this transparent purity of its moments," writes Hegel of the beautiful soul, "its light dies away within it, and it vanishes like a shapeless vapor that dissolves into thin air."[32] But if "beauty" refers to the outmoded experience of aesthetic pleasure, to the delightful encounter with an ideal semblance no matter how ghostly or vaporous, what shall we make of this emphatically earthbound noun, "thing," to which it has been attached?

If the "thing" has its own philosopher, then that philosopher's name will undoubtedly be Martin Heidegger. According to Heidegger, "things" unite upon themselves the fourfold of earth and sky, divinities and morals; their process of "thinging" is what grounds the sublime essence of imagination in variform sublunary particulars. "Men alone, as mortals, by dwelling attain to the world as world," he writes. "Only what conjoins itself out of world becomes a thing."[33] Yet science for Heidegger (as with Nietzsche, Wittgenstein and Lacan) has reduced the mysterious thing to a "nonentity," obliterating its "thingness" so as to replace that quality with the solely objective, physical, or physiological fact of "objects."[34] Along these lines we shall do well to reevaluate Williams' superficially straightforward riddle, from 1948, comprising just a title and two quatrains:

The Thing
Each time it rings
I think it is for
me but it is

not for me nor for
anyone it merely
rings and we
serve it bitterly
together, they and I[35]

Like Heidegger's "thinging of things," here the thing rings (or, to fully appreciate the titular rhyme, it "things," loudly announcing itself to a community of pronouns) but no connection is made between the anaphoric "it" and the mortals that have been reduced to bitter servitude. This, a verse that so effortlessly reflects the negative experience of modernity, knowingly orbits around a mere object stripped of its gestational and generative force; like beauty, the "thing" is a dead end for literature's pursuit of the mind. But why, then, would Williams seek to combine two superannuated concepts into his poetic "machine," one a deeply reactionary and antimodern mode of experience and the other which is improbable to attain and likely impossible to express?

My hypothesis is that beauty might reactivate the deadened "thing" while the "thing" might simultaneously fulfill the hollow sign of beauty—and, if this is true, then "Beautiful thing" has the potential to redeem its two constitutive fragments under the sign of a modernism that had rightly disabused itself of beauty and from within a modernity that has all but eradicated the "thing." Given the role of paradox in this conception, perhaps we shall now understand why Williams would eventually challenge the mind itself with the following series of chimerical imperatives: "the imagination must adorn and exaggerate life, must give it splendor and grotesqueness, beauty and infinite depth."[36] Jameson might be thinking of any one realization of these formally disjunctive combinations, of a grotesque splendor or an infinitely deep beauty, when he charges the topography of Williams' "failed" poem with manifesting "a telluric or chthonic reality which is also, from the inescapable standpoint of a

debased commercial modernity, a meretricious figment of the poetic imagination."[37]
This "meretricious figment" could very well be a truth of the mind and so a truth
accessible not to positivism but via "the poetic imagination," opened up to literature by
the chiasmic energies of a paradox and forced into presentation, as we shall now see,
from the domain of its dialectical antipode.

Supernova poetics

Let us turn, finally, to Part II of Book Three, "The Library," an episode in which
Paterson (to borrow Jameson's description) "tries to think its archival past in terms of
a conflagration as immense and catastrophic, as world-historical, as that of the library
of Alexandria."[38] Dr. Paterson's trip to the Library comprises multiple events used to
allegorize the mind and its tempestuous relation to Beautiful thing, all of which derive
from three catastrophes that struck the city of Paterson, between 1902 and 1903, when
half the town was destroyed: first by fire, then by flood and later by a freak tornado.
Welcoming devastation, Williams announces: "So be it" (117). Little wonder, given this
allegorized mind has already been anesthetized to a point near expiration. "The Library
is desolation," muses Dr. Paterson, "it has a smell of its own/of stagnation and death"
(100). To enter the Library is compared to encephalon autopsy: thought is shrouded
by "a slowly descending veil/closing about the mind/cutting the mind away," and, in
a clinical pun on the scalpel's slice, the rule is loudly announced on a line to itself:
"SILENCE!" (101). The mind's elements are dead unto themselves, wholly subject to
the physiologist's scalpel, and so it is that we have entered the cataleptic consciousness
of scientific reification.

   "Give it up. Quit it. Stop writing," some disembodied authority insists. "'Saintlike' you
will never/separate that stain of sense" (108). The disclosure of this sensorial stain leads
Dr. Paterson to an hallucinatory tryst with Marie Curie, celebrated pioneer of radioactive
science, the very thought of whom erupts into an unmistakably sensual, sexual and
yet ultimately dissonant desire: "Never. Never the radiance," desire precludes rigor;
"quartered apart, unapproached by symbols," rigor then mutilates desire (108). This
violent interplay between physical desire and physiological science drives Curie into Dr
Paterson's unconscious, from where she will reemerge several books later in a sexual
fantasy that surely trumps the studiously scientific analogies of Eliot, Pound and Yeats:

> —a furnace, a cavity aching
> toward fission; a hollow,
> a woman waiting to be filled
> —a luminosity of elements, the
> current leaping!
> Pitchblende from Austria, the
> valence of Uranium inexplicably
> increased. (176)

A now unrestrained desire superimposes the radioactive combustion chamber with the woman's body, "waiting to be filled," and thereby instantiates the periphrastic conversion of scientific research into a full-blooded desiring-production. We might even read the subtext of these lines as an obscene letter to Mina Loy, a known object of Williams' own affections, who famously hailed Gertrude Stein's ability "to extract/a radium of the word."[39] Whereas Loy's futurist poetics would restage the rationalized mechanization of desire ("the lucid rush-together of automatons," she calls it[40]), Williams' verse gallantly charges off in the opposite direction, returning to those "automatons," the madness of a libido that mechanical positivism would do away with. "I had a passionate desire to verify this hypothesis as rapidly as possible," wrote Mme Curie on the discovery of radium, and so we should know the desire belongs to her as well.[41] But this tremendous "return of the repressed," a seismic irruption of desire from the realm of science, will not take place until much later in *Paterson*, for any such encounter is surely prohibited within the Library, to which we must now return.

What should be retained from this projected fantasy, however, is the irrepressible centrality of sexual hunger to Williams' poem; and indeed, that craving should be kept in mind if we are to appreciate why Beautiful thing has been gendered female and made to resound in forms that are decidedly feminine. In an explanation as to why, within the psychoanalytic traditions of Freud and Lacan, woman is described as a symptom of man, Slavoj Žižek refers to "the well-known male chauvinist wisdom," that "women are impossible to bear, a source of eternal nuisance, but still, they are the best thing we have of their kind; without them, it would be even worse. So," he concludes, "if woman does not exist, man is perhaps simply a woman who thinks that she does exist."[42] It is repeated here only because the conception describes a subjunctive ontology whose contingent forces are revealed exclusively from within the space of sexual torsion. We might already suspect that Williams is attuned to this primitive code and its modern institutionalization, but here is the definitive moment, an instance of verse that oscillates uncomfortably between physiological diagnosis and lascivious aggression:

> TAKE OFF YOUR
> CLOTHES! I didn't ask you
> to take off your skin. I said your
> clothes, your clothes. You smell
> like a whore. I ask you to bathe in my
> opinions, the astonishing virtue of your
> lost body (I said).
> —that you might
> send me hurtling to the moon
> .   .   let me look at you
> (I said, weeping)
> (104–5)

Our initial temptation accedes to the old cliché that this patient's beauty is only skin deep: to set eyes upon the vestibule of her anatomy is to simultaneously encounter the scent of whoredom and the "lost body" of a ruined maidenhead. That reading might even ramify into an argument that Dr. Paterson is rerouting his libido through a scientifically reified and institutionally sanctioned breed of chauvinism. However, it would neglect the decisive fact that he is also entranced by a "virtue" so powerful it makes the mechanical monster "weep." We should therefore be reading this "smell/like a whore" as the redemptive de-reification of the imago of beauty. What Freud called the "olfactory stimuli" dethrones the sentimental idiocy of the beautiful soul—and simultaneously circumscribes the detachment of a positivist—by arresting the senses with an "astonishing virtue" that no poetry can ever hope to capture.[43]

Dr. Paterson's experience of this revitalized beauty is best inscribed in verse as an epic firestorm that violently transforms the Library over and through which it blazes. Books are incinerated or made illegible, "the ink burned, metal white," and a familiar semblance presents itself:

> Come overall beauty. Come soon. So be it.
> A dust between the fingers. So be it.
> Come tatterdemalion futility. Win through.
> So be it. So be it. (117)

But Williams and Dr. Paterson immediately concede the "tatterdemalion futility" of this impossible paragon, conjuring away the ideal of an absolute beauty (whose progenitors would include Symons' "perfect fire" and Yeats' "terribly beauty"). Given the already pronounced fetish quality of whatever supplements the absolute in this poem, we should certainly not shy away from reading that first verb, "come," in the sense by which it was popularized in the novels of James Joyce and D. H. Lawrence: here it sounds nothing like a plaintive beckoning, but precisely as though Dr. Paterson is willing his lover's climax, striving to substantiate her beautiful semblance with some other quality, a bodily presence, the blazoned crescendo of her own materiality.[44] This, the iridescent amalgam of materialism and the mind, is the only beauty we are permitted to know under modernism:

> Our feeling, dazzled, flutters like a flock of birds in the woman's radiance. And as the birds seek refuge in the leafy recesses of a tree, feelings escape into the shaded wrinkles, the awkward movements and the inconspicuous blemishes of the body we love, where they can lie not in safety.[45]

"Beautiful thing," we thus read, "your/vulgarity of beauty surpasses all their/ perfections!" (119). And here, in this moment of ecstatically internalized immolation, "intertwined" with the fire is a vision of her: "An identity surmounting the world, its core." She overcomes "the world" and its mortal poet ejaculates into the inferno, "from which we shrink squirting little hoses of/objection—and I along with the rest, squirting/ at the fire" (120). Beauty has aroused the desiring body and that body, now a "thing," has fulfilled a depthless beauty; and suddenly, the two are presented as one, fastened together by a tightly wound sequence of gerunds, repetitions and alliterations: "Rising, with a whirling motion, the person/passed into the flame, becomes the flame—/the flame taking over the person" (121). "How," asked Yeats in a poem that is echoed here, "can we know the dancer from the dance?"[46] For Williams, who would never dream of such knowledge, it is by embracing this very inseparability—of beauty and the thing, of science and the sensorial stain—that we shall affirm the mind in its fleeting singularity.

Is this episode a "meretricious figment of the poetic imagination," the stylistic signature of a mind heated to arousal? This we cannot know for certain. What we do know, however, is that these lines present an "authority in the world," but it is an authority that has welded itself to "the pains and ecstasies of personal life," and which forcefully submits the mind to "the throes of the body." The scientific rigors of (Mme Curie's) inspection deliver the "thing" to a beauty it has not heretofore properly known; and that "thing" is at once the woman in the passion of her research and the woman whose "astonishing virtue" is simultaneously her smelling "like a whore." This is not a contradiction, a fault in Williams' conception; it is a paradox that is the very key to his modernism, wherein beauty and science are together redeemed by the dialectical mediations of an improbable "thing." As such, the *Paterson* fireball is an artistic event: it formalizes the unpredictable trajectory of a "dancing star," a mnemonic vision of the mind; and with it, for just a moment or two, Williams manages to "reverse/the chain of events and make a pileup/of passion to match the stars." It is, finally, the inversion of a now recognizable image, upending those gravitational forces with which we began:

> And for that, invention is lacking,
> the words are lacking:
> the waterfall of the
> flames, a cataract reversed, shooting
> upward (120)

Notes

1   William Carlos Williams, *Paterson* (Middlesex: Penguin, 1963), 80. Hereafter cited in text.
2   Allen Ginsberg, *Howl and Other Poems* (San Francisco, CA: City Lights Books, 1956), 9. The city of Paterson is mentioned in line 12 of *Howl*—"incomparable blind streets of shuddering cloud and lightning in the mind leaping toward poles of Canada & Paterson, illuminating all the motionless world of Time between," (10)—and, in an introduction penned by Williams, the senior poet writes of Ginsberg: "When he was younger, and I was younger, I used to know Allen Ginsberg, a young poet living in Paterson, New Jersey, where he, son of a well-known poet, had been born and grew up" (7).
3   Quoted in Neil Baldwin, "Zukofsky, Williams, and *The Wedge*: Toward a Dynamic Convergence," *William Carlos Williams: Man and Poet*, ed. Carroll Franklin Terrell (Maine: National Poetry Foundation, 1979), 130.
4   Fredric Jameson, *The Modernist Papers* (London: Verso, 2007), 5.
5   Quoted in Charles Altieri, "Can Modernism Have a Future?" *Modernism/modernity* 7, no. 1 (2000): 131.

6   Altieri, "Can Modernism Have a Future?" 131.

7   Daniel Albright, *Quantum Poetics: Yeats, Pound, Eliot, and the Science of Modernism* (Cambridge: Cambridge University Press, 1997), 4.

8   Albright, *Quantum Poetics*, 5.

9   William Carlos Williams, "Notes from a Talk on Poetry," *Poetry* 14, no. 2 (1919): 214. This is quite similar to Zukofsky's (probably unfair) charge that Eliot seemed to think that minds elaborately equipped with specific information, like science, always must confuse it with other specific information, like poetry. That may be the case with unfortunates. The point, however, would be not to proffer solemnly or whiningly confusions to the confused, but to indicate by energetic mental behavior how certain information may be useful to other information, and when the divisions which signalize them are necessary. Louis Zukofsky, *Prepositions: The Collected Critical Essays of Louis Zukofsky, Expanded Edition* (New York: Horizon Press, 1967), 15.

10 John Hildebidle, "Take off Your Clothes: William Carlos Williams, Science, and the Diagnostic Encounter," *Modern Language Studies* 17, no. 3 (1987): 28.

11 Alain Badiou, *The Century*, trans. Alberto Toscano (Cambridge: Polity, 2007), 9.

12 Theodor Adorno, *The Positivist Dispute in German Sociology*, trans. Glyn Adey and David Frisby (London: Heinemann Educational Books, 1976), 73.

13 William Carlos Williams, *Imaginations* (New York: New Directions, 1971), 349.

14 Alain Badiou, *Wittgenstein's Antiphilosophy*, trans. Bruno Bosteels (London: Verso, 2011), 69.

15 Ludwig Wittgenstein, *Tractatus Logico-Philosophicus* (London: Routledge, 1961), 88.

16 Jacques Lacan, *Écrits*, trans. Bruce Fink (New York: Norton, 2006), 63.

17 Friedrich Nietzsche, *Thus Spoke Zarathustra*, trans. Adrian Del Caro (Cambridge: Cambridge University Press, 2006), 28; Wittgenstein, *Tractatus Logico-Philosophicus*, 89; Lacan, *Écrits*, 9. Lacan takes these words from Georges-Louis Leclerc, Comte de Buffon, though his conception of style is far closer to that of Arthur Schopenhauer, who wrote: "Style is the physiognomy of the mind, and a safer index to character than the face." Arthur Schopenhauer, *The Art of Literature*, trans. T. Bailey Saunders (Mineola, NY: Dover, 2004), 11.

18 Bruno Bosteels and Justin Clemens have both written on the literary dimension of antiphilosophy. See Bosteels, "Radical Antiphilosophy," *Filozofski vestnik* 29, no. 2 (2008): 155–87 and Clemens, "To Rupture the Matheme with a Poem: A Remark on Psychoanalysis as Antiphilosophy," *Trauma, History, Philosophy*, eds. Matthew Sharpe, Murray Noonan, and Jason Freddi (Newcastle, FL: Cambridge Scholars Press, 2007), 308–12.

19 Hugh Kenner, *The Pound Era: The Age of Ezra Pound, T.S. Eliot, James Joyce and Wyndham Lewis* (London: Faber and Faber, 1972), 130; Stéphane Mallarmé, *Selected Letters of Stéphane Mallarmé*, ed. and trans. Rosemary Lloyd (Chicago: Chicago University Press, 1988), 223.

20 Ezra Pound, *Literary Essays of Ezra Pound*, ed. T. S. Eliot (New York: New Directions, 1935), 3; Ezra Pound, "Vortex, Pound," *Blast*, 1 (10 June 1914): 153; Ernest Fenollosa, *The Chinese Written Character as a Medium for Poetry*, ed. Ezra Pound (San Francisco, CA: City Lights Books, 1936), 8.

21 William Carlos Williams, *The Collected Poems of William Carlos Williams*, 2 vols. (New York: New Directions, 1991), 1:198.

22 T. J. Clark, *Farewell to an Idea: Episodes from a History of Modernism* (New Haven, CT: Yale University Press, 2001), 147. Emphasis in original.

23 Charles Altieri, "'Ponderation' in Cézanne and Williams," *Poetics Today* 10, no. 2 (1989): 373–99. For a counterpoint to this, Jacques Rancière has argued persuasively that the regime of art is defined by articulations between visual forms and the words that surround them. See Jacques Rancière, *The Future of the Image*, trans. Gregory Elliott (London: Verso, 2007), 69–89.

24 Williams, *Collected Poems*, 2:377.

25 For an excellent genealogy of this phrase see Emily Lambeth-Climaco, "'This Rhetoric Is Real': William Carlos Williams's Recalibration of Language and Things," *William Carlos Williams Review* 28, nos. 1–2 (2008): 35–53.

26 Nietzsche, *Zarathustra*, 9.

27 William Carlos Williams, *Selected Essays of William Carlos Williams* (New York: New Directions, 1969), 256.

28 William Carlos Williams, *The Autobiography of William Carlos Williams* (New York: New Directions, 1967), 286.

29 Arthur Symons, *Images of Good and Evil* (New York: Woodstock Books, 1996), 118.

30 G. W. F. Hegel, *Phenomenology of Spirit*, trans. A. V. Miller (Oxford: Oxford University Press, 1977), 399–400.

31 William Carlos Williams, *The Embodiment of Knowledge* (New York: New Directions, 1974), 163. See Carl Rapp, *William Carlos Williams and Romantic Idealism* (Hanover: Brown University Press, 1984).

32 Hegel, *Phenomenology of Spirit*, 400.

33 Martin Heidegger, *Poetry, Language, Thought*, trans. Albert Hofstadter (New York: Harper and Row, 1971), 180.

34 Heidegger, *Poetry, Language, Thought*, 168

35 Williams, *Collected Poems*, 2:167.

36 Williams, *Imaginations*, xviii.

37 Jameson, *The Modernist Papers*, 14.

38 Jameson, *The Modernist Papers*, 35.

39 Mina Loy, *The Lost Lunar Baedeker*, ed. Roger L. Conover (New York: Farrar, Straus, and Giroux, 1996), 94.

40 Loy, *The Lost Lunar Baedeker*, 40.

41 Cited in Susan Quinn, *Marie Curie: A Life* (Reading, MA: Perseus Books, 1995), 150.

42 Slavoj Žižek, *The Sublime Object of Ideology* (London: Verso, 1989), 75.

43 Sigmund Freud, *The Future of an Illusion, Civilization and Its Discontents, and Other Works*, ed. and trans. James Strachey (London: Vintage, 1961), 99–100.

44 See Joyce ("Suppose you got up the wrong side of bed or came too quick with your best girl," 619; "I never came properly till I was what 22," 911) and Lawrence ("We came off together that time," 140; "when I'd come and really finished, then she'd start on her own account," 210). James Joyce, *Ulysses* (London: Penguin, 1992) and D. H. Lawrence, *Lady Chatterley's Lover* (London: Penguin, 1993).

45 Walter Benjamin, "One Way Street," *Selected Writings: 1913–1926*, volume. 1, ed. Marcus Bullock and Michael W. Jennings (Cambridge, MA: Harvard University Press, 1996), 449.

46 W. B. Yeats, *Selected Poems*, ed. Timothy Webb (London: Penguin, 1991), 153.

Part Three

Contemporary Literary Minds

9

"The Creation of Space": Narrative Strategies, Group Agency and Skill in Lloyd Jones' *The Book of Fame*

John Sutton and Evelyn B. Tribble

We began to float and to achieve a kind of grace that had become second nature, like language or riding a bike.

—*The Book of Fame*[1]

Early in Lloyd Jones' *The Book of Fame*, a novel about the stunningly successful 1905 British tour of the New Zealand rugby team known as the "Originals," one of the players turns to music to represent the ease with which they defeated English sides in their first two matches:

> One night Frank Glasgow sat down at the piano and composed music to describe the English style of play; it went—plonkplonkplonkplonk, plonk.
>
> You heard that and saw the English shift the ball across field, one two three four stop and kick for touch.
>
> To describe our play Frank came up with this number—dum de dah dum de dah bang whoosh bang! whoosh dum de dah clicketty-click bang! whoosh dah.(37)

Jones represents here both the nature of skilled group action—in the form of a "music new to English ears"—and the difficulties of capturing it in words. The novel's form is as fluid and deceptive, as adaptable and integrated, as the sweetly shaped play of the team that became known during this tour for the first time as the All Blacks, scoring 830 points in 32 matches while conceding only 39. Employing a dazzling array of narrative strategies, and a sensuous, highly wrought style that blurs distinctions between prose and poetry, heightened to match the exquisite precision of his subjects' movements, Jones incorporates lists, repetitions, menus, newspaper reports and materials from diaries and scrapbooks, along with metaphors from and links to contemporary arts and news events in "that year" when "Einstein and Matisse caused a stir" (167). While the novel is thus "bedded in research," it is a product of mindful aesthetics with a focus on shared expertise, imagination, embodied agency and skilled vision.[2] It, therefore, differs dramatically from revisionist or sociological, historical treatments of the tour.[3] Jones revels in the spaces created by the scant records, such that "the imagination slips easily into the gaps" (177).

In literary criticism and theory as in the cognitive sciences, sport has struggled to be seen as a legitimate area of inquiry. In literary studies, sport has either been relegated to the area of genre fiction or seen as a cover for some other, more important subject such as postcolonial identity. While *The Book of Fame* certainly demands reading in terms of "the snare of history" (51) as much as do Marina Warner's *Indigo*, Joseph O'Neill's *Netherland* or Shehan Karunatilaka's *The Legend of Pradeep Mathew*, it also treats sport on its own terms as a rich world, a set of bodily skills and an honest profession in itself.[4] Introducing his edited collection of New Zealand sports writing *Into the Field of Play*, Jones contested easy dismissals of the subject:

> I've always felt that sport in our neck of the woods was closer to a taste or colouring in the landscape—best viewed as a number painting that connects the small boy with his racquet playing on the street, with the old man at the club, the trophies, ladders and newsletters and fixture listings in Thursday night's paper, to the televised event at Wimbledon. And only once you begin to list such things and make the connections, you begin to realize just how big the catchment is, and how few of us escape it—and, more lamentedly, how few of us choose to write about it.[5]

So sport in *The Book of Fame* is a concentrated arena inhabited by extraordinary athletes whose "industry was football and experiments with space" (73). Both writers and cognitive theorists are increasingly aware of the wide "catchment" area of sport and embodied intelligent action in general. They embrace the challenge of understanding those who dedicate years to arduous training in unique, culturally specific activities with intense ideological, affective and motivational force.

In writing a book on this subject, Jones faces two problems. First, the narrative as received from historical sources is almost too good: a group of men unknown to the public and to each other travel from the other side of the world, crush their hosts at every turn and introduce a new style of the game to an awed audience. The material almost writes itself, but might do so unfortunately into that most clichéd of sports narratives: the triumph of the underdog. Second, skilled action confronts writers with the problems of "languaging experience,"[6] which Jones confronts in an essayistic manner, proliferating metaphors to convey both the richness and the slipperiness of his subject. Because of the innovative strategies by which Jones responds to these challenges, a reading of *The Book of Fame* can contribute to the interdisciplinary study of literature and cognition, exemplifying genuinely two-way "exchange values."[7] On the one hand, we can gain insights into the nature of skillful group agency, of distinct forms and at distinct timescales, by focusing on the precise forms taken by the All Blacks' creation of space. Here, we treat *The Book of Fame* as a brilliant evocation of features of collective thought, movement and emotion that both everyday and scientific inquiry can easily miss. On the other hand, we can also read back into the novel a subtle, fascinated interrogation of the mechanisms by which small groups form, evolve and act. In this more ambitious mode of analysis, we use independently motivated theoretical concerns to help us see real features of the literary work that might otherwise remain invisible.[8]

The Book of Fame is narrated in the first-person plural, by and through a superficially undifferentiated "we." The story is told collectively, as or for the "twenty-seven in our party," from manager George Dixon to the Invercargill bootmaker Billy Stead, from the captain Dave Gallaher, "a meatworks foreman," to Jimmy Hunter, who "farmed in Mangamahu, north-east of Wanganui" (9). Although James Wood claims that "successful examples" of stories told in the first person plural "are rare indeed,"[9] critics have discussed a surprisingly rich and varied range of "narrative fiction in the first person plural,"[10] though to our knowledge Jones' novel has not yet been assessed in this context. First-person plural narratives exemplify a core variety of "collective narrative agents"[11] and of "social minds in the novel,"[12] and some critical literature on these topics draws directly on research and theories of joint action in social ontology and cognitive science: our reading of *The Book of Fame* too hones in on its subtle treatment of group agency.

But the 1905 "Originals," who acquired the name "All Blacks" either through a typographical error in a report that they played as if they were "all backs" or because of what the Devon *Express and Echo* called "their sable and unrelieved costume," were no ordinary group.[13] The embodied skills of a successful sports team, as of dancers or musicians working together, constitute a unique form of collective action, and Jones' novel models a variety of strategies for representing such skilled joint activity. In their practice sessions on the SS *Rimutaka*, pumpkins bought in Montevideo are rearranged on the deck to model "possible lines of attack" in service of "the creation of space" (18) and from the time of scoring their first points on English soil, as Jimmy Hunter takes "a sweet transfer" from Billy Stead and "spins free" of the defense "as easy as passing through a revolving door," they realize collectively in action that "space was our medium/our play stuff," that "space can be wooed."[14]

In what follows, we focus on the relationship between skillful performance and collective action. These topics fall outside the ambit of much current work by literary theorists using cognitive research, who have instead tended to focus upon theory of mind and modularity, metaphor and blending, emotion and empathy, consciousness and concepts, representation and so on. But skilled performance and collective action nevertheless comprise surprisingly lively research fields across the sciences, from neuropsychology to philosophy of mind and cognitive anthropology. These areas of inquiry may provide even more productive avenues for future work in the interfield of literary and cultural theory and the cognitive sciences.

Skill and group agency in the cognitive sciences

Expert sportspeople share with dancers, acrobats and musicians extraordinary capacities for skillful movement in complex, changing settings. Their actions are, at times, perfectly shaped for the current situation. Even unforeseen challenges, requiring unplanned responses, can elicit extraordinary precision and timing in the control of unfolding action sequences. In open team sports, for example, two or more teammates can baffle a defensive line by magically meshing the direction and pace of their movements so as to create gaps or elude their markers. No matter how high speed the sport or performance, movements can seem to flow effortlessly, as if there was all the time in the world to inhabit each moment fully. Such expertise of course rests on arduous training, on long histories of experience sculpting grooved bodily routines. But in constantly adapting their skills to present demands, and fitting performance to the needs of each audience and situation, skillful performers reveal in their mindful bodies a kind of intelligence in action that remains as mysterious to theory and science across the disciplines as it is to the struggling novice. For all the rage about embodied cognition, for all the resources poured into sport science, for all the wishful dreams of a future neuroaesthetics, we have no integrated theoretical grip on the nature and mechanisms of skilled movement. Neither disappointingly abstract philosophical work on embodiment nor scientific data gathered in artificial lab settings far from the complex ecologies of practice can match what we fleetingly glean about the experience of expert performance from the occasional unusually articulate practitioner.

Arguably, both the difficulty of objective study of skill and the rarity of sustained informative phenomenological report are to be expected. On many views of expertise, its processes are pre-eminently tacit, not just inarticulable but inaccessible, and only likely to be disrupted by any attempt to tap, probe or inspect them. Effective descriptions of skilled movement may thus have to be indirect, the more so since sports narratives are often rife with clichés. Yet experts and coaches or teachers do develop and employ their own rich ways of talking and thinking about their activities. It is difficult for outsiders—fans, journalists, researchers or critics—to tap what may be peculiar, subculturally specific communicative forms that run "beyond the easy flow of everyday speech."[15] Alongside ethnography, the subtler tools of creative writers and artists might offer different imaginative access to the more or less silent springs of skilled action.

Such considerations about the priority of the tacit realm in embodied performance also perhaps explain why both the philosophy and the sciences of mind have tended to focus more on disorder and breakdown than on extraordinary skills, on dysfunction rather than heightened function. Yet honed expertise lies at the heart of characteristically human cognition in action, and is a fundamental, rich basis for mindful aesthetics in literature and culture. How can we find ways to study both the skills of the elite performer and the more widespread but still flexible and often exquisite everyday skills involved when people cook and drive, tend gardens and homes, make clothes and pots and blankets, write programs and tell stories? As we suggested above, literary researchers interested in skilled action can critically engage with a range of ongoing research programs on skill in the sciences of mind. Indeed expert movement, like memory, is an exemplary topic with which to combat the persisting caricature of the cognitive sciences as irretrievably marred by universalizing rationalist individualism. Far from privileging the detached or disembodied reflective planning of action, major current theorists of skill who differ on many other points argue that the strategic (or "cognitive" or "higher-order") control of action decreases dramatically or disappears as skills are developed to expert levels. In cognitive psychology and sport science, this point may be couched in terms of the increasing automaticity or "proceduralization" of skilled performance.[16] In philosophical traditions springing from Ryle or from phenomenology it may be described as the intuitive development of "know-how" or motor intentionality.[17] In Hubert Dreyfus' phenomenology of expert performance, for example, "mindedness is the enemy of embodied coping."[18] Such views radically privilege the silent or disappearing body of the expert, predicting that performance is all but traceless, produced by embodied mechanisms so divorced from attention and awareness that memory can get no grip. For Dreyfus, "an expert's skill has become so much a part of him that he need be no more aware of it than he is of his own body,"[19] while Beilock and Carr find evidence of "expertise-induced amnesia" in laboratory versions of sporting tasks.[20]

But such strong reactions against intellectualism have been criticized in turn for evacuating intelligence entirely from the body, and dividing doing from knowing. They thus leave unexplained experts' abilities to cope effectively with significant complexity or perturbation in their field.[21] While the forms of thinking in question must be highly dynamic, expert musicians and sportspeople do maintain ongoing online awareness of and strategic control over certain changing aesthetic or competitive features of their performance.[22] Among a recently burgeoning array of work on these topics in philosophy and cognitive theory, notable strands aim at identifying the key dimensions on which distinct forms of skillful action may vary,[23] and at more experience-near investigations of the embodied phenomenology of expert movement.[24] In our view, this kind of lively debate, which spans a range of methods and traditions in a field of cognitive science which is perhaps less high profile than others, affords inviting space for new critical moves from literary, historical and cultural theorists.

Similar opportunities arise in debates about group agency and group cognition. Humanities researchers sometimes assert that such notions, and allied ideas like collective memory, can only be used metaphorically, because mind, memory, agency and cognition are individual capacities. James Young prefers Jeffrey Olick's term "collected memory" to "collective memory," because "societies cannot remember in any other way than through their constituents' memories"[25]; in assessing Alan Palmer's extensive cognitive-literary studies of "thought that is not located in an individual mind," Patrick Hogan comments that "unfortunately, it is difficult to say just what this might mean" and that "cognitive science offers no help here."[26]

To the contrary, ideas with such difficult ancestry do indeed elicit widespread suspicion, due both to individualist assumptions in psychology and to political concerns about the top-down imposition of homogeneity and groupthink in our managerialist culture.[27] But with the ongoing advances of movements *within* the cognitive sciences which treat mentality as situated, distributed, dynamical and embodied,[28] there are substantial and expanding traditions of research both in empirical psychology and cognitive neuroscience and in philosophy and social ontology, which precisely theorize and study small group cognition, memory and action as emergent phenomena distinct (in a sense that obviously requires clarification) from the cognition, memory and action of the individuals who compose the group. On the one hand, considerable progress has been made on the metaphysical issues of just what "emergence" amounts to here. The intuition that a robust form of group cognitive process needs to be more than the sum of its constituent members' cognitive processes has been rendered more precise. Enthusiasts for and critics of stronger theoretical notions of group or collective cognition are increasingly able to agree on key concepts and requirements for resolving the debate even where they remain divided on how those concepts apply to actual cases.[29] On the other hand, empirical studies of strong forms of joint action and collaborative cognition in dyads, small groups and teams flourish in mainstream contemporary cognitive science.[30]

For current purposes, rather than summarizing the debates and available positions here, we point to an under-noticed difference between two broad directions of investigation into group agency. Some accounts focus on more formal and explicit mechanisms of cooperation, addressing, for example, public expressions of joint policy, belief or intent by institutionalized groups such as committees or organizations. Central topics in this field of social ontology include the possibility of stark divergence or discontinuity between the beliefs or attitudes of the group and those of its members, the kinds of open or mutual knowledge required to ground the formation of a "plural subject," and the challenges of maintaining consistency in collective decision-making over time.[31] In these traditions, the medium of group agency is typically taken to be linguistic, in the form of public representations.[32] While this approach offers some hope of identifying principles in common across smaller and larger groups, an alternative starting point is to focus on less easily articulable mechanisms. These lines of enquiry are not incompatible, of course, and we will suggest below that it would be a mistake to neglect explicit mechanisms of group formation. But when thinking and acting in the "we-mode," members of small groups may rely on more tacit kinds of shared action representations to ground strong forms of cooperation, by way of a range of collective socio-cognitive processes which were significant driving forces in the history of our species, supporting cross-generational apprenticeship learning and newly stable means of cultural transmission.[33] Embodied interaction and mutual alignment occur in small groups by way of a range of nonverbal processes including gesture, facial expression, posture and patterns of movement.[34] If such dynamic forms of coordinated movement and cognitive interdependence are likely to be essential components of highly skillful cases of collective action like team sports, they will also require distinctive, subtle methods and vocabularies to identify, study and describe.

Skilled action in *The Book of Fame*

Such vocabularies might well be found in fiction and literary analysis as much as in reports from laboratory or ethnographic settings. In eschewing conventional first- or third-person narration, Jones uses alternative strategies to introduce his cast of characters, emphasizing these details of embodied movement and of glimpsed habits and quirks. The plural narrator of *The Book of Fame* tells us that it was "in such small telling ways, through gesture and anecdote," that the New Zealanders departing on the long voyage to England "revealed ourselves to one another" (10). Even while "the larger sense of who we were hadn't yet forged itself," mutual recognition gradually emerges across the party of the men's patterns of humor, expressions, bodily comportment, dress, moods and personalities:

> The bookworm in Billy Stead
> Mona Thompson's fondness for setting his hat brim at a low tilt
> Eric Harper's learned ways with cutlery and table napkins
> [...] Jimmy Hunter's habit of closing his eyes and touching his nose
> whenever praised
> [...] the way George Tyler would butter his toast and afterwards, lick
> each finger tip.

Some are "jovial and spry at breakfast"; others emerge as "lags and wisecrack artists": some turned a tall story over "stone by stone" while others "sat back and enjoyed it like music" (10–11). On seeing filmed "shadows of themselves" in a London theater, and overcoming initial bewilderment at how "Fred looked like Fred, Billy Wallace like Billy Wallace, Jimmy Hunter himself but only more so," the tourists notice not only "what a mess the lineouts were in" but also "things, personal things, previously intimate to ourselves. Fred Newton scratching himself...Massa closing one nostril to blow snot out the other" (59–60). By the time of the journey home months later, the forms of *habitus* that have become shared and mutually recognized second nature within the group expand to include taste and temperament, manners and character, preferences and passions:

> McDonald's dainty way of drying himself, first towelling his feet, then
> each toe—not something you ordinarily see in a big man
> Cunningham's love of shovelling coal into the stoker of the SS *Rimutaka*
> Seeling's refusal to do the same [...]
> Those who preferred black tea with one sugar [...]
> the early nighters
> the insomniacs [...]
> The impulse of some to stop and pat a mangy dog
> and the single-minded haste of others. (168–9)

These embodied and nonverbal forms of alignment and mutual understanding form a dynamic but enduring foundation for shared identity and collective action.

Even at the outset, the individual skills of the members begin to form particular combinations: "Cunningham's singing and Frank Glasgow's piano playing; it only took a snatch of a melody from Cunningham for Frank to produce the whole works" (11). Such interactive cross-cuing, in any medium, signals the kind of interdependence in cognition and action that characterizes the plural subject, one operating as what Daniel Wegner calls a "transactive memory system": such a system consists of the distinctive, often highly specialized memories or skills of the individual members of the group, plus a sufficiently shared understanding of how those capacities are distributed so that appropriate information or performances can be filled in or created as required.[35] Just as a family, a group of friends or a long-standing couple may together remember something that none of the individuals could recall alone, so even forgetting can be fluent in a group with a rich enough shared history.[36] The New Zealanders' support play reminds one commentator of the way skilled actors can work around a lapse on stage: "to watch the 'Hamlet'-clad lot retrieve a failure is almost as interesting as the excitement at their customary swooping or rush of attack... There is always somebody under-studying for the time-being the player is hors de combat. Into the breach the new 'artist' without a second's hesitation goes" (44).[37] To exemplify the "moral advantages from combination" after months together, the narrator cites

> the time at a hoi polloi dinner that Carbine forgot the word
> he was searching for & George Smith chimed in
> beautifully
> with a connected subject. (170)

Such complementarity also operated on the field. Jones is quoting Gallaher and Stead's 1906 book *The Complete Rugby Footballer on the New Zealand System*, written for £50 each in the aftermath of the tour, in which these "moral advantages" of combination are illustrated by the case "when a player is making a great and difficult individual effort and is closely attended during this risky period by a trusty colleague ready to take the ball from him at the moment that his own possession of it becomes untenable."[38] This takes much longer to say than to do, and Jones employs varied tactics for dealing with the clunkiness of words for these mysterious interactive group processes that just occur and are gone. On first landing in England, the team find themselves displaying ball skills and making unprepared jokes for the waiting reporters: "It was amazing how quickly we found our voice and style, without thought so it seemed, like the wilfulness of water or the way light will bounce off in every direction at once" (25). Although such capacities for joint action are built partly on forms of unconscious mimicry and creative imitation which are also found in some other animals, humans are unusual in also easily performing "complementary instead of identical actions" in service of some broader shared or emergent goal which requires differentiated contributions from each group member.[39] Below we underline the heterogeneity and internal differentiation of even as integrated and coherent a group as this, a feature which we think undermines some standard concerns, both conceptual and political, about the idea of group agency. Here we stress again that such specialization or uniqueness is bodily at the same time as it is cognitive, as must be the case in a team game involving so many distinct demands and requirements on players in different positions as does rugby.

The team's integrated style of play is articulated in both mechanical and organic terms in the contemporary sources that Jones threads profusely through the novel. One report says, "They work together like the parts of a well-constructed watch. Wherever a man is wanted, there he is!" (36). Against England, another newspaper comments, the pack or scrum displayed a "corporate instinct," playing "like eight men with one eye" (98). In the central and shortest chapter, "How We Think," the players consider "the shape of our game" and see "an honest engine," with Billy Stead describing the "glorious feeling" of gliding outside a man:

> The English saw a tackler
> we saw space either side
> The English saw an obstacle
> we saw an opportunity […]
> The formality of doorways caused the English to stumble
> into one another and compare ties
> while we sailed through (75)

Radically new possibilities for group action emerge as "a matter of arrangement, of getting the combinations right" (72), manifesting in such uncanny mutual anticipation as in the "Taipu move" when Jimmy Hunter finds a man as he "props inside his opposite and flicks the ball back on his inside" (171). They gain a kind of knowledge that is

> inexact
> a feeling
> of shape & movement
> that understanding of trees in a high wind
> of knowing what to do
> having been there before & all that
> The simplest of ideas gained & held on to
> from things
> that move together
> in a loose shambling way—or
> what others like to call
> harmony (169–70)

Against Ireland, the novelty of the New Zealand system was so glaring that "it felt as though we were playing two different codes. We saw the paddock as an ever-changing pattern of lines. The Irish, on the other hand, saw the field as a sort of steeplechase, covered with low barriers and walls which as far as they were concerned were there to smash into": as Jones foreshadows much of the subsequent history of clashing rugby cultures across southern and northern hemispheres, the tourists "longed to tell them what they were doing wrong" (89–90).

In addition to music, early cinema, visual art and theater, the players compare themselves to other kinds of performers—Savade the lion-tamer who advises them on working the crowds to "share your joy," acrobats and jugglers and tightrope walkers, the "farcical acts of the Italian circus" (106) and "the non-verbal humility of world strongman Eugene Sandow and his assistants studying us in our baths following victory over Middlesex" (153). These are all apt parallel performance forms, for this team sport revolves not only around tactics and "ideas of space and longing" but also around strength, balance, flexible anticipation, drill and repetitive scrum work (133). Such physical skills ground the embodied confidence that springs from just knowing what to do together, each man able to move "instinctively into that space cleared for him," as a speechless Billy Stead still does in front of the waiting Invercargill crowd on his return home (162).

The art of movement, Jones describes, in part rests on body memory, which is a distinctive kind of procedural or skill memory: "what we knew was intimate/ as instinct or memory" (73–4). As we have noted, expertise in sport as in dance and music must rely heavily on such nonverbal mechanisms of alignment, on routine and habitual skill, on grooved and tacit knowhow. In these procedural forms of memory, movement history (both individual and shared) animates present action within the novel demands of a current situation, drawing on past experiences by improvising on their basis rather than reproducing their content.[40] Know-how of this kind is not explicitly *about* the past experiences in which it was actually gathered. Whereas personal or autobiographical remembering, even of a highly reconstructive variety, can bring specific past events to mind *as* past, in performing on the basis of skill memory we need not be aware at all of any particular past episode from which our embodied capacities derive.[41] Psychologists sometimes sharply distinguish such procedural memory from anything that can be consciously accessed or verbally articulated, pointing further to widespread practitioners' lore about the disruptive effects on movement skill of sudden intrusions of consciousness or thought.[42] From such a perspective, it might appear that the New Zealanders' individual and collective skill memory—the "kind of grace that had become second nature"—should be seen as pure and thoughtless intuition or habit, "like riding a bike," the motion of tuned bodies that in action come, in a certain sense, out of time (37).

The animal and material comparisons Jones employs seem at first blush to fit this picture of dynamic sports performance as pure presence. The New Zealanders are eels, wasps and monkeys, the backs like mercury (39–40). To explain how "it has all to do with space, finding new ways through," Freddy Roberts compares "the course of a spooked hare," and watches

> the spired rooftops
> as a flock of starlings
> switched shape and direction (66–7)

Even off the field, wandering the streets, or with "the boys milling outside the hotel steps," "they appeared to move together, like a herd bound by a solid core that knows and only wants itself for company" (134). And in a key passage at the end of the chapter on "How We Think," Billy Stead is again "describing the various character of space": "there was the fox outside Cambridge which he'd seen turn and run this way and that, in and out of the hounds pursuing it—a life-saving understanding of space instantly lost to memory" (76). So one form of self-organization in the collective is produced by the aggregation of such individual animal instincts. Such flocking behavior and "swarm intelligence" is widely studied in the contemporary cognitive sciences, with tools from the physics and biology of phase transitions in collective behavior applied to both social and cognitive phenomena in human crowds and populations. Surprisingly complex collective effects can arise when individual animals or agents are following fairly simple rules.[43]

Although this kind of model clearly connects with the ideas of distributed cognition and group agency toward which we are working,[44] it captures only one relatively restricted form of emergence, and therefore cannot fully account for the kind of mindful collective action that Jones represents. Groups with a rich shared history possess an extensive repertoire of shared and possible actions quite unlike the patterns produced by the aggregation of instinctual flocking behaviors. Such flock or swarm systems, in a real sense, are not mindful at all at the collective level: no real learning or memory is required of the individual animals, and each of them is assumed to follow the same set of options, with the group behavior emerging by mere aggregation. But in two main respects the skillful group agency invoked in *The Book of Fame* is of a very different sort: first, in the composition of the group and the relation between the group and its members, and second in the availability of explicit and self-reflective mechanisms of group identity-formation in addition to these more low-level or automatic processes.

First, the New Zealanders are in no way a homogeneous group. We have noted the idiosyncratic habits and differences in personal style that shape their mutual discovery, but Jones also continues to stress the disparate individuals and subgroups constituting the collective. There are "the Otago boys" and "the big men," the farmers and the loose forwards. Onboard ship, when staring out at a new landmass they are "trying to make up our minds about South America"—not "our mind" (17). Again, in a team sport like rugby it is obvious that the relation between group members must be one of complementarity rather than identity or even similarity, even when at another level of description they can rightly be seen in action as "fifteen sets of eyes/ pairs of hands and feet/ attached to a single/ central nervous system" (67). So Jones' narrative "we," the plural subject, is not incompatible with genuine plurality and diversity among its components; and he creates space and voices for many of the unique individuals.

Group agency of this kind in no way effaces the person, just as the coherence and shared commitments of the whole can coexist with stray and even conflicting beliefs and desires among the parts. This point about genuine group agency has both ideological and cognitive implications, which we address briefly in turn. There is a worry that concepts like group cognition, collective memory, joint agency and plural subjectivity spring from and play into a specific late capitalist drive to render individuality obsolete and to subsume us all into and under the unity, strength, values and mission of our institutions. Joshua Ferris, who employs "we" narrative to striking effect in his office novel *Then We Came to the End*, explains in an interview his reaction to the way "companies tend to refer to themselves in the first-person plural": in his book, "you see just who this 'we' really is—a collection of messy human beings—stripped of their glossy finish and eternal corporate optimism. It returns the 'we' to the individuals who embody it, people with anger-management issues and bills to pay, instead of letting the 'mystic we' live on unperturbed in the magic land promoted by billboards and boardrooms."[45] But in these novels as in our organizations, the existence of genuine internal diversity and complexity in a collective does not entail that the group level is somehow unreal, or will dissolve under individualist reduction.

Back in cognitive theory, one of the most promising recent lines of argument for group cognition and collective agency, by Georg Theiner and colleagues, relies on a well-developed scheme in philosophy of science for understanding mechanistic explanation across levels.[46] The mechanists typically work outward from case studies in biology or neuroscience to capture the exact sense in which certain kinds of wholes can be more than the sum of their parts while still not becoming ethereally disconnected from those parts. They focus on the arrangement or *organization* of those components.[47] They stress the contextually sensitive activities and processes in which those organized components engage: "emergence" here is given technical precision by identifying it as the failure of aggregation.[48] Roughly, to the extent that the behavior of a complex, multilevel system (whether biological or social) does not change when its component parts are exchanged or altered, then it is a merely aggregative system that does not exhibit emergent behavior, and it can be explained entirely in terms of the aggregated or merely juxtaposed action of its separable components. The more the system's behavior changes with such changes to its parts, the more it exhibits genuine emergence. These are matters of degree, so we have a spectrum of possibilities rather than a sharp distinction between a mere aggregate and a genuinely emergent collective system. Theiner persuasively applies this mechanistic framework to the case of groups. The nature and extent of emergent collective action in any group depends both on the unique nature of the group members and on the particular ways in which they relate to each other over time (the ways the components are organized or arranged).[49]

We suggest that this interlevel analysis of emergence in groups is particularly well suited to the case of elite sporting teams. Visiting Oxford, the New Zealanders compare the qualities of their homeland: "what we realized was this—it was a matter of arrangement, of getting the combinations right" (72). In a passage Jones takes directly from Gallaher and Stead, Billy Stead notes that despite their preference on the field for attacking in numbers with a shared strategy, opportunistic solo efforts have their place: "We in New Zealand are great sticklers for our orthodox systems of combination, but at the same time we do not prohibit individualism...Our attitude is one of unofficial and very guarded approval."[50]

In addition to this internal complexity and heterogeneity, there is a second respect in which the kind of group agency exhibited by the New Zealanders clearly departs from the animal collective, and from reliance solely on instinct and routine in a more mindless embodied present. As in any such long-term human group, even one so identified by and with its expert physical skills, there is also an explicit and self-reflective dimension to their group formation and identity. This arises in the earliest phases of forging "the larger sense of who we were" (10). In contrast to modern elite sports teams, many of the squad had not played together before the tour: as Gallaher and Stead tell us, it was only on embarking that "for the first time did many of the team see and know each other," for they had been "chosen from the extreme north and from the extreme south, and between these points there is a distance of twelve hundred miles."[51] So Jones can start at this point, picking up on and transforming his sources' statement that during the early "dreadful Antarctic storms...we studied the game very deeply, and made ourselves thoroughly sympathetic with each other in all matters."[52] He has them emerging from their places "of bush-creeping isolation" (10), winning at cricket against the passengers and crew—"us against 'the world'" (11)—and realizing that "being nowhere in particular, and without traditions to adhere to, we could be whatever or whoever we chose" (13).

On the long slow sea passage, "with whole days to kill...we were in danger of going our separate ways until Mister Dixon called us together" (14). Jones has Dixon, the manager, "propose that, from now on, all knowledge and experience would be pooled": the world is to be named afresh together, "to create 'an atmosphere' where we might share and share alike" (14). In a heightened passage, the players share not just tobacco and stories and "whatever we happened to carry in our pockets or in our thoughts" but also "small descriptive features" about their wives and girlfriends at home, donated into this masculine social space, "thus allowing them to construct and furnish their own visions," in select fragments evoking particular women's movements and styles and expressions which Jones sustains through 16 examples over two pages (14–16). So while there are times when the men say little, or tire of each other's company and part on their days off, or try not to look too closely into each other's faces, on many other occasions verbal and deliberate communication explicitly enhances sense of themselves as a collectivity. There is no tension, therefore, but a deep complementarity between the tacit and the explicit features of group process: between the easy grace of embodied interaction achieved together on the field and the openly expressed, mutually accessible common knowledge of their joint commitments on which theorists of social ontology like Margaret Gilbert have tended to concentrate. Certainly they have pooled their wills in the way Gilbert sees as essential for the genuinely plural subject, a process which gives rise to characteristic sets of norms, obligations and expectations within this community.[53] A richly described case like this, in Jones' treatment, can indeed remind theorists that all these levels and processes coexist within a group. The team's activities essentially involve both nonconscious routines and explicit declarations, both the embodied joy of successful joint action as they open up another defensive line and the off-field analysis of a tougher game in which "the space we usually basked in just wasn't there" (43).

Another explicit dimension of group identity can be identified in the team's collective attempts to assess their place in the world: in England, in history and in *The Book of Fame*. On initial arrival in the old country, "we weren't sure how to place ourselves in that scene outside our window," and only gradually do the players "try to insert themselves" (30). They first begin to situate themselves not through language, but through recognizing familiar "mannerisms and transactions of the people...the way a barman with one neat action sweeps the bar top dry before setting down a pint of Guinness," the

same measuring sideways glance out of an Irishman's face
when a leg pull was on … That was us as well. (31)

Within weeks, after a string of triumphs, they share a new confidence:

England felt like a place specially created
for us to excel. (53)

At the National Portrait Gallery, among "the famous faces which seemed to want
us to know them," they find one hall displaying "famous groups…Men of Science
Living in 1807–8/ Swinburne and his Sisters": but "none like us" (54–5). Their early
surprise at being the center of attention ("we'd catch them looking at us, measuring
and evaluating" (32)) shifts as win follows win until "we'd moved from the world of
ordinary men." Fame has many aspects. One is sheer joy:

we were the stuff of the shop window
What children's birthdays are made of […]
We were the place smiles come from.

Or "a shoal of brilliantly coloured flying fish" (42) "a thing of wonder," like "sword-
swallowing Moroccans" (168). Another is curiosity in comparison, as the New
Zealanders check their daily allotment of lines in *The Times* and track notables in other
domains and their "attempts to ascend the greasy pole."[54] Another is commodification,
as trophy hunters grab their old cufflinks, signatures and train tickets, as their images
appear on "postcards hawked about town" (57–9). Fatigue at the effort of being
themselves produces a countervailing yearning for the inanimate, appreciating

those things
which are utmost and confidently themselves
a lily flat on a pond
the pattern of wallpaper in an empty hotel room
the last tree in a paddock (61)

or at least to be free of human time and projects like the Serpentine ducks who

did not appear to crave a crowd—
there was no scoreboard, no tally. (103)

Only a mindful collective could thus dream of escaping mental life.

Fame is the heart of the explicit self-conception that emerges through the New
Zealanders' shared experience as they "changed people's lives" (107) and "introduced
new ideas to Europe" (167). Only when exhausted on the long voyage home, between
two lives, "somewhat betwixt, lame in our deckchairs, like old folk sharing memories," do
they amass examples and assemble "this story we'd created for ourselves" (151), collating

the trip's novel experiences and telling incidents into some sort of version that might last, that might stick in memory right through to the end of the night of the 1955 reunion in

> a crowded city bar on Lambton Quay
> two old men driven into a smoky corner
> unnoticed. (173)

They can only imperfectly compare themselves to other groups inhabiting worlds "bound by the same elemental fear & wonder," as they think

> of Roman galleys
> pulling on oars out to the wide ocean. (172)

Finally, fame also brings and then intensifies the possibility of failure, the shadow of and behind their shared commitments. The novel is given shape in part by "the irresistible attraction of defeat," by Wales' controversial 3–0 victory in Cardiff, the New Zealanders' only loss. As they sense "what defeat might be like" they feel "blind terror": afterwards, "none of us could imagine laughter again except as something that might happen to other people," and they dream of "a place where there's no such thing as fame" (123). Even though the team recovers to win their final four club matches, "everything we did took a crucial second longer," and "no one spoke of grace anymore. It was like it had been rubbed from our limbs" (125).

Although we have been discussing more explicit and more implicit forms of action and group process separately, they are, as we noted, intimately intertwined. What group members say and think and remember is grounded in and colored by what they do. Reflective and articulated self-conceptions at both individual and team level coexist with various ways of understanding "the things you see but can never tell about" (157). The latter kind of inarticulable awareness is not thereby essentially inner or private: it too can be shared or mutual, another form of common knowledge. To underline the point that different rhythms and timescales thus operate simultaneously and (usually) cooperatively in skillful group agency, we finish by briefly considering Jones' evocations of cross-temporal phenomena and of the ways that memories of different kinds interanimate. The novel is full of "moments." But rather than being static snapshots of isolated, disconnected events, many of these moments are in motion, drifting and reassembling.

Early on the voyage out, Bill Cunningham senses the rhythm of his ordinary miner's life as already "distant, like a place inhabited by cousins once visited as a child. While you've never gone back you can't forget it either" (13). On reaching England, the New Zealanders map it against old templates, trying "to locate something of what our parents had said, or a vista passed down by our grandparents. One or two of the players argued with the view" (22). It takes many reminders running back and forth between past and present for them to be able "to disassemble what we saw from what we knew or had heard or read" (22). Just as personal or autobiographical remembering is often a compilation or assemblage of many different sources,[55] so perception and emotion in the present are often shot through with memory. On hearing a familiar sound of wood on wood, Bunny Abbott "hears doors creaking in the bush—he blinks—and seeing it's England, colour enters his cheeks," while O'Sullivan "has the muddled idea that he's been here before" (23–4). In the midst of their unquenchable successes, dulled by their routines, sudden moments transport the players far away again:

> a baby's cry sending Stead's thoughts to Invercargill [...]
> a dog's bark causing the ears of Deans and Hunter to twitch
> and the exact hour in the hills registering in their eyes. (80)

These are ordinary memory phenomena, elicited both explicitly by letters from home and by just being confronted by the difference between those old "homebaked moments" and the present: struggling with homesickness on a gray day in West Hartlepool, Jimmy Hunter broke the silence—"How's this. In Mangamahu, on a hot day, the gorse bushes explode" (80–1). On the "black night crossing" to Ireland, we "drifted off to thoughts of home," eyes sometimes tearing at a specific memory, of smells—bacon fat, or deer—or of merely "looking out at the back yard with its chore list" (87). As Jimmy Hunter watches the crowds gather for the England game at Crystal Palace, a single shaft of memory plummets him to other times and places, as "the sound of a bellbird echoing from afar, across oceans, has him looking past these English trees to the heavily dressed branches of an elm brushing back the hurrying brown water of the Wanganui" (96). In further showing the ways that memory muddles time, Jones deploys lists and fragments, patchy sequences of items and experiences that connect as psychology rather than narrative. In the novel's final pages, memory drifts, across later wars and other stories. This is just what cannot happen for Billy Stead's fox, the one running this way and that in and out of the hounds pursuing it: unlike the New Zealanders' creations, its "life-saving understanding of space" was "instantly lost to memory" (76). Human memory and action are not entirely traceless.

Though all the versions of a complex and structured sequence of events and joint actions like a long-gone rugby tour are incomplete and partial, a novel such as this illuminates the space of multiple possibilities and of play. Both skill and group agency, we have suggested, are intriguing theoretical topics in their own right, ones which deserve more serious attention across the disciplinary spectrum. This one literary treatment of skilled collective action by Lloyd Jones offers a rich case study for mindful aesthetics. The point here is not simply to apply research in the cognitive sciences to a literary text; indeed, as should be clear from our discussion of the literature, there is no "settled science" of skilled group activity, but rather an assemblage of contentious, conflicting and emerging attempts to probe this often experienced but poorly understood phenomenon. In this context, fiction can be read as a form of skilled vision in itself.

Acknowledgments

Our thanks to the editors, and for discussion of related issues to Wayne Christensen, Greg Downey, Andrew Geeves, Doris McIlwain and Kellie Williamson.

Notes

1   Lloyd Jones, *The Book of Fame* (Auckland: Penguin, 2000), 37. Hereafter cited in text.

2   Christina Grasseni, "Skilled Vision: An Apprenticeship in Breeding Aesthetics," *Social Anthropology* 12, no. 1 (2004): 41–55.

3   Caroline Daley, "The Invention of 1905," *Tackling Rugby Myths*, ed. G. Ryan (Dunedin: University of Otago Press, 2005); Greg Ryan, *The Contest for Rugby Supremacy* (Christchurch: Canterbury University Press, 2005); Douglas Booth, "Sites of Truth or Metaphors of Power? Refiguring the Archive," *Sport in History* 26, no. 1 (2006): 95.

4   Marina Warner, *Indigo* (London: Vintage, 1992); Joseph O'Neill, *Netherland* (New York: Vintage, 2009); Shehan Karunatilaka, *The Legend of Pradeep Mathew* (Minneapolis, MN: Graywolf Press, 2012).

5   Lloyd Jones, *Into the Field of Play* (Auckland: Tandem Press, 1992), 9–10.

6   Maxine Sheets-Johnstone, *The Corporeal Turn* (Exeter: Imprint Academic, 2009), 363.

7   Mark J. Bruhn, "Introduction: Exchange Values: Poetics and Cognitive Science," *Poetics Today* 32, no. 3 (January 2012): 403.

8   John Sutton, "The Feel of the World: Exograms, Habits, and the Confusion of Types of Memory," *Memento*, ed. Andrew Kania (New York: Routledge, 2009): 65–86.

9   James Wood, *How Fiction Works* (New York: Farrar, Straus and Giroux, 2008), 3.

10 Amit Marcus, "A Contextual View of Narrative Fiction in the First Person Plural," *Narrative* 16, no. 1 (January 2008): 46–64.

11 Uri Margolin, "Telling in the Plural: From Grammar to Ideology," *Poetics Today* 21, no. 3 (Autumn 2000): 591–618.

12 Alan Palmer, "Social Minds in Fiction and Criticism," *Style* 45, no. 2 (Summer 2011): 196–240.

13 Ryan, *The Contest for Rugby Supremacy*, 77–8.

14 Jones, *The Book of Fame*, 33–4; 75; 171.

15 Sheets-Johnstone, *The Corporeal Turn*, 336.

16 J. R. Anderson, "Acquisition of Cognitive Skill," *Psychological Review* 89, no. 4 (1982): 369–406; Sian Beilock and Thomas H. Carr, "On the Fragility of Skilled Performance: What Governs Choking under Pressure?" *Journal of Experimental Psychology: General* 130, no. 4 (2001): 701–25.

17 Gilbert Ryle, *The Concept of Mind* (Chicago: University of Chicago Press, 1949); Hubert L. Dreyfus, "Intelligence without Representation—Merleau-Ponty's Critique of Mental Representation," *Phenomenology and the Cognitive Sciences* 1, no. 4 (2002): 1–18.

18 Hubert L. Dreyfus, "The Return of the Myth of the Mental," *Inquiry* 50 (2007): 353.

19 Hubert L. Dreyfus and Stuart E. Dreyfus, *Mind over Machine: The Power of Human Intuition and Expertise in the Era of the Computer* (New York: Free Press, 1986), 30.

20 Beilock and Carr, "On the Fragility of Skilled Performance," 703.

21 John Sutton and others, "Applying Intelligence to the Reflexes: Embodied Skills and Habits between Dreyfus and Descartes," *Journal of the British Society for Phenomenology* 42, no. 1 (January 2011): 78–103.

22 Roger Chaffin and Topher Logan, "Practicing Perfection: How Concert Soloists Prepare for Performance," *Advances in Cognitive Psychology* 2 (2006): 113–30; John Sutton, "Batting, Habit and Memory: The Embodied Mind and the Nature of Skill," *Sport in Society* 10, no. 5 (2007): 763–86.

23 Brian Bruya, *Effortless Attention* (Cambridge, MA: MIT Press, 2010); Barbara
    Montero, "Does Bodily Awareness Interfere with Highly Skilled Movement?" *Inquiry*
    53, no. 2 (2010): 105–22; Giovanna Colombetti, "Varieties of Pre-Reflective Self-
    Awareness: Foreground and Background Bodily Feelings in Emotion Experience,"
    Inquiry 54, no. 3 (June 2011): 293–313.
24 Jaida Kim Samudra, "Memory in Our Body: Thick Participation and the Translation
    of Kinesthetic Experience," *American Ethnologist* 35, no. 4 (November 2008): 665–81;
    Dorothée Legrand and Susanne Ravn, "Perceiving Subjectivity in Bodily Movement:
    The Case of Dancers," *Phenomenology and the Cognitive Sciences* 8, no. 3 (June
    2009): 389–408; Kath Bicknell, "Feeling Them Ride: Corporeal Exchange in Cross-
    Country Mountain Bike Racing," *About Performance*, no. 10 (2010): 81–91; Kenneth
    Aggerholm, Ejgil Jespersen, and Lars Tore Ronglan, "Falling for the Feint—An
    Existential Investigation of a Creative Performance in High-Level Football," *Sport,
    Ethics, and Philosophy* 5, no. 3 (2011): 343–58; Greg Downey, "Balancing between
    Cultures: Equilibrium in Capoeira," in *The Encultured Brain: An Introduction to
    Neuroanthropology*, eds. Daniel H. Lende and Greg Downey (Cambridge, MA: MIT
    Press, 2012), 169–94; Doris McIlwain and John Sutton, "Yoga from the Mat Up: How
    Words Alight on Bodies," *Educational Philosophy and Theory* (2013): 1–19, forthcoming.
25 James Young, *The Texture of Memory: Holocaust, Memorials, and Meaning* (New
    Haven, CT: Yale University Press, 1993), xi; Jeffrey K. Olick, "Collective Memory: The
    Two Cultures," *Sociological Theory* 17, no. 3 (1999): 333–48.
26 Patrick Colm Hogan, "Palmer's Anti-Cognitivist Challenge," *Style* 45, no. 2 (2012):
    244; Palmer, "Social Minds in Fiction and Criticism."
27 Daniel M. Wegner, "Transactive Memory: A Contemporary Analysis of the
    Group Mind," *Theories of Group Behavior*, eds. Brian Mullen and George R. Goethals
    (New York: Springer, 1987), 65–89; Robert A. Wilson, *Boundaries of the Mind: The
    Individual in the Fragile Sciences* (Cambridge: Cambridge University Press, 2004).
28 Edwin Hutchins, *Cognition in the Wild* (Cambridge, MA: MIT Press, 1995); Andy
    Clark, *Being There: Putting Brain, Body, and World Together Again* (Cambridge, MA:
    MIT Press, 1997); Philip Robbins and Murat Aydede, *The Cambridge Handbook of
    Situated Cognition* (Cambridge: Cambridge University Press, 2009).
29 Robert A. Wilson, "Collective Memory, Group Minds, and the Extended Mind
    Thesis," *Cognitive Processing* 6, no. 4 (2005): 227–36; Deborah P. Tollefsen, "From
    Extended Mind to Collective Mind," *Cognitive Systems Research* 7, no. 2 (June 2006):
    140–50; Georg Theiner, Colin Allen, and Robert L Goldstone, "Recognizing Group
    Cognition," *Cognitive Systems Research* 11, no. 4 (December 2010): 378–95; Robert
    Rupert, "Empirical Arguments for Group Minds: a Critical Appraisal," *Philosophy
    Compass* 6, no. 9 (2011): 630–39; Bryce Huebner, *Macrocognition* (Oxford: Oxford
    University Press, 2013).
30 Anne Böckler, Gunther Knoblich, and Natalie Sebanz, "Socializing Cognition,"
    Towards a Theory of Thinking, eds. Britt Glatzeider, Vinod Goel, and Albrecht von
    Mueller (London: Springer, 2010), 233–50; Stephen A. Butterfill and Natalie Sebanz,
    "Joint Action: What Is Shared?" *Review of Philosophy and Psychology* 2, no. 2 (2011):
    137–46.
31 Margaret Gilbert, *On Social Facts* (Princeton: Princeton University Press, 1989);
    Philip Pettit, "Groups with Minds of Their Own," *Socializing Metaphysics: The Nature
    of Social Reality*, ed. Frederick Schmitt (Lanham, MD: Rowman & Littlefield, 2003),
    167–94; Philip Pettit and David Schweikard, "Joint Actions and Group Agents,"

Philosophy of the Social Sciences 36, no. 1 (March 2006): 18–39; Christian List and Philip Pettit, *Group Agency: The Possibility, Design, and Status of Corporate Agents* (Oxford: Oxford University Press, 2011).

32 Robert Rupert, "Minding One's Cognitive Systems: When Does a Group of Minds Constitute a Single Cognitive Unit?" *Episteme: A Journal of Social Epistemology* 1, no. 3 (2005): 177–88.

33 Michael Tomasello, *Why We Cooperate* (Cambridge: Cambridge University Press, 2009); Kim Sterelny, *The Evolved Apprentice: How Evolution Made Humans Unique* (Cambridge, MA: MIT Press, 2012).

34 Jürgen Streeck, Charles Goodwin, and Curtis D. LeBaron, *Embodied Interaction: Language and Body in the Material World* (New York: Cambridge University Press, 2011); Sabine C. Koch, Thomas Fuchs, Michela Summa, and Cornelia Müller, *Body Memory, Metaphor and Movement* (Amsterdam: John Benjamins Publishing, 2012); Deborah P. Tollefsen, Rick Dale, and Alexandra Paxton, "Alignment, Transactive Memory, and Collective Cognitive Systems," *Review of Philosophy and Psychology* 4, no. 1 (23 January 2013): 49–64.

35 Daniel M. Wegner, Toni Giuliano, and Paula T. Hertel, "Cognitive Interdependence in Close Relationships," in *Compatible and Incompatible Relationships*, ed. Williams Ickes (New York: Springer, 1985), 253–76.

36 Celia B. Harris and others, "We Remember, We Forget: Collaborative Remembering in Older Couples," *Discourse Processes* 48, no. 4 (2011): 267–303.

37 For an account of "fluent forgetting in the theatre," see Evelyn B. Tribble, *Cognition in the Globe* (New York: Palgrave MacMillan, 2011), 76.

38 David Gallaher and W. J. Stead, *The Complete Rugby Footballer on the New Zealand System* (London: Methuen, 1906), 175.

39 Böckler, Knoblich, and Sebanz, "Socializing Cognition," 242.

40 Frederic C. Bartlett, *Remembering: a Study in Experimental and Social Psychology* (Cambridge: Cambridge University Press, 1932), 201.

41 See Sutton, "Batting, Habit and Memory."

42 Sian Beilock, *Choke* (New York: Free Press, 2011).

43 James Surowiecki, *The Wisdom of Crowds* (New York: Doubleday, 2004); Robert L. Goldstone and Todd M. Gureckis, "Collective Behavior," *Topics in Cognitive Science* 1, no. 3 (2009): 412–38.

44 Clark, *Being There*.

45 Joshua Ferris, *Then We Came to the End: A Novel* (New York: Back Bay Books, 2007).

46 Theiner, Allen, and Goldstone, "Recognizing Group Cognition"; Georg Theiner, "Transactive Memory Systems: A Mechanistic Analysis of Emergent Group Memory," *Review of Philosophy and Psychology* 4, no. 1 (January 2013): 65–89.

47 Carl F. Craver, *Explaining the Brain* (Oxford: Oxford University Press, 2007); William Bechtel, *Mental Mechanisms* (London: Routledge, 2008).

48 William Wimsatt, *Re-Engineering Philosophy for Limited Beings: Piecewise Approximations to Reality* (Cambridge, MA: MIT Press, 2007).

49 Theiner, "Transactive Memory Systems."

50 Jones, *The Book of Fame*, 175; Gallaher and Stead, *The Complete Rugby Footballer on the New Zealand System*, 60. Jones cites from the last sentence of this quotation.

51 Gallaher and Stead, *The Complete Rugby Footballer on the New Zealand System*, 244.

52 Gallaher and Stead, *The Complete Rugby Footballer on the New Zealand System*, 244.

53 Margaret Gilbert, "Walking Together: A Paradigmatic Social Phenomenon," *Midwest Studies in Philosophy* 15 (1990): 1–14; Gilbert, *On Social Facts.*

54 Jones, *The Book of Fame*, 45–7; 65.

55 Marya Schechtman, "The Truth about Memory," *Philosophical Psychology* 7, no. 1 (1994): 7; Peter Goldie, *The Mess Inside: Narrative, Emotion, and the Mind* (Oxford: Oxford University Press, 2012), 44.

10

Reproductive Aesthetics: Multiple Realities in a Seamus Heaney Poem

Stephen Muecke

…the networks of reproduction are too speculative to interest anyone except the most seasoned metaphysicians and the odd poet.

Bruno Latour[1]

In Paris, on a warm summer night, you can join the tourists in observing a remarkably eccentric poet with all his complex apparatus on the Pont Saint Louis, the little bridge that joins the two islands in the Seine. He stands there declaiming, surrounded by things sprouting from his large cart: texts and slogans on sticks and boards, fairy lights illuminating the whole scene with their cool LED glow, a CD player with background music. He will conclude by spruiking and selling you his own CD and texts. Now, *that's* what I call poetry, poetry going about its eccentric, singular business, being an embarrassment (to real poets), creating a scene. It is an event pulling in so much more than the author-text-reader triangle to which we are wont to reduce the practice of poetry. What, I will urge us to wonder in this chapter, are all the heterogeneous things that make a poem come into existence and then help it to stay alive?

I want to explore this question with the Latourian concept of reproduction, for which I need another example. Earlier this year, my friend Toby Miller updated his status with "White Yanqui parthenogenesis" on that most social of social media, Facebook, in reference to an *LA Times* article, "Oscar voters overwhelmingly white, male."[2] Could this support my hypothesis that cultural life is engendered via reproductive technologies? People who vote at the Academy Awards, it seems, have for years been reproducing "white, male" culture (however reductive that may sound) with their power to rank films. And this reproduction would be parthenogenetic because they do it all by themselves, like earthworms, without the need for partners of a different sexuality or race, nor, it is implied, of a different culture.

Such an argument depends on the acceptance of the idea that reproduction is not "simply" biological. The biology of sexual reproduction is immensely complex and, of course, outside the scope of this chapter. Figure 10.1 is a drawing of the translation mechanism of ribonucleic acid (RNA). RNA, along with DNA and proteins, is one of the macromolecules essential to all known forms of life. I have used it here metaphorically,

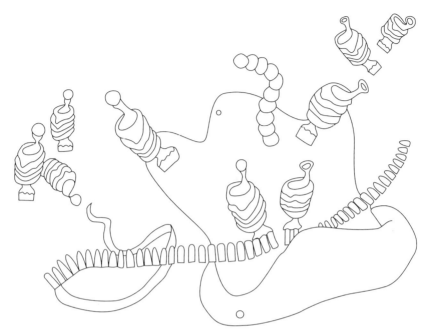

Figure 10.1 Diagram showing the translation of mRNA and the synthesis of proteins by a ribosome
Source: Drawing by Hugo Muecke, 2012.

because it seems to illustrate the complexity of heterogeneous associations at the heart of any kind of reproduction, sexual-biological or bio-cultural. Sexual reproduction can never be purely biological, which means that it cannot be apprehended purely scientifically, through the methods of the disciplines of biology or biochemistry. Leaving aside the fact that biology's procedures, the conditions of existence of that discipline (including methods and technologies, funding bodies, institutions, peer review, contingencies of various sorts), are themselves heterogeneous, it is also the case that animals' reproductive capacities are necessarily linked to the complexities of context—seasons, scents, moods, social pressures, communication and culture—to the point where we cannot deny humans' specific stimulation by bouquets of flowers or bouquets of words. Hence our interest here is in lyric poetry's own conditions of reproduction, or, to put it another way, its form of (continued) existence. Poetry is one of the many ways in which humans foster an interest in each other; the interest in reproduction, we might say, involves the reproduction of interest.

In *Formalism and Marxism* Tony Bennett said that "if production is completed only with consumption, then, so far as literary texts are concerned, their production is never completed. They are endlessly re-produced, endlessly remade with different political consequences and effects."[3] At the time, Bennett's emphasis was largely intertextual, but the *politics* of literature he underscores points to a "context" that this discussion will seek to elaborate. Context often remains under-theorized to the extent that it is seen as the real-world background against which texts play out their variations. This would be the *one* world, the *one* reality, the same one perceived by scientists and sociologists; in fact their *referential* knowledge is often used in literary analysis.

With the help of Bruno Latour, I want to suggest that this context is in fact ontologically plural.[4] There are several worlds: technical ones, referential ones, fictional ones, religious ones and reproductive ones, to mention just a few. They interact with each other without necessarily, or always, going by way of the human perception of the interaction. This throws up the challenge of trying to understand them without such a phenomenological and correlational reduction[5]; there are ways in which a leaf "understands" the sun and the gases in the atmosphere, or the car tire "understands" the bitumen surface of the road, that are supremely indifferent to human presence. We would have to try to find a language that speaks to those relations on their own terms, without the kind of categorical errors we seem to perform all the time: photosynthesis is a scientific issue belonging to the "objective" world of *reference*, right? Why, then, is it so readily made a "subjective" *moral* issue as a part of climate change debates? What is the chain of associations that might link these two different modes of existence, the referential and the moral? What remarkably strange ways we humans have of immersing ourselves in quite different worlds, assuming an omniscient point of view, as if with a little effort the English language could come to grips with, and be a bridge over, just about everything.

Aesthetic objects also have modes of existence that can be understood on their own terms, that is, with the unique sets of relations that they establish with other things, other worlds, other humans and so on. Their peculiarity is in their *relations*, perhaps more than as *things in themselves*, though Graham Harman debates Latour on this point in the second half of *Prince of Networks*, followed recently by articles by himself and Timothy Morton in *New Literary History*.[6] For the proponents of object-oriented philosophy, like Harman, objects have some essential qualities independent of their relations, yet they are not fixed objects either; they are "mortal, ever-changing, built from swarms of subcomponents, and accessible only through oblique allusion" (188). From this position he sets out a limited defense of Cleanth Brooks' (New Critical) autonomy of the poetical text, which like any other object "runs deeper than any coherent meaning" (200). Harman concludes his article in a grand flourish of theoretical utopianism: that this resistant impenetrability of the text objects will assist object-oriented philosophy in its "new" and "liberating" mission.

Rather than this conclusion, where Harman registers his "hope" for a new theory, I prefer his earlier point that "What is truly interesting about 'contexts' is not that they utterly define every entity to the core, but that they open a space where *certain* interactions and effects can take place and not others" (191). Rather than making his essentialism of objects carry the eventual burden of aesthetic profundity and theoretical liberation at the same time (an echo of a long-lasting Kantian theological transcendentalism), I prefer a totally *superficial description* (unburdened by "profundity" as well as any hope of liberation or innovation) of the links both inside and outside a poem, where these specific relations can be seen to extend in transformative chains across different registers of reality, not just from text to text, but text to body, to object, to concepts, to feelings and even to "atmospheres" or "tones." We can experience a poem as we listen to it or read it, and this experience in some ways is both an experience of the poem "itself" and also an experience of its relations; the relations are as real as the thing, as Whitehead asserts.[7] To offer a multirealist reading is to demonstrate that this very experience is not always reducible to human experience. Another way of putting this is to say that the poem has necessary partnerships with virtual humans, things, other texts, history and even the sacred. This is a difficult point to accept for those "correlationists" or phenomenological humanists who follow the orthodoxy that everything in a poem can only be understood via human experience. But if it is true, as object-oriented ontology claims, that an object is never fully present to itself, and manifests in different ways for different other items of reality (wind is different for a sailing boat than it is for a scientist), then the poem–thing relation can take on a causal specificity.[8] A spade should be able to relate to a poem differently to the way it relates to you or me, as in the well-known Heaney poem,

> a clean rasping sound
> When the spade sinks into gravelly ground:
> My father, digging…[9]

Sorry, I can't produce a "bright edge" spade to compare to the "the one in the poem," nor do I want to claim that the poem "captures" the deeper essence of spade. Such a tool simply and superficially manifests in relation to the poem in ways differently to the way it does to me when I do a bit of my own digging. For a start, the poem's spade has the features of not being a pen, and of relating to an earlier Irish potato-digging generation. It is specific in its causal relations.

So what, you may ask, is the advantage in retreating from human centrality in poetic experience—to claim that a poem and a spade might vitalize each other without the human interpretation ready at hand? It is almost the same claim we might make about a blackberry and a cockatoo vitalizing each other, but with poetry, isn't there always devilish language getting in the way, triangulating and threatening to make English speakers, in this case, the center of everything? In order to say no, I have to elaborate the claim that *some poetic relations are not linguistic*. Mine is not the moral eco-critical claim that all sorts of nonhumans deserve a place in the sun, or that Heaney's concern for spuds is ecological. It is actually a cosmic claim in the sense of Stengers' *Cosmopolitics*.[10] It is that "Heaney's world," as we used to say so formulaically about any author, is not just his, but is an ontologically plural world which includes "Heaney," in one corner, as well as all sorts of other things that respond to other kinds of realities. This constructivist approach suggests that attention to spades, spuds, mirth and imperialism offers more to aesthetics, rather than less, when those things are seen as animating life as much as us humans. And from the point of view of the process of creation, it suggests that the poem is a kind of channel for all those things coming together in a composition. And I suspect the composition, in this plural sense, is facilitated by Heaney's loving attitude, dispensed equally for the purposes of the poem, among the spade, his father and the spuds.

Let's continue to read a different Seamus Heaney poem with this kind of ontological plurality in mind.

Fosterage

For Michael McLaverty
"Description is revelation!" Royal
Avenue, Belfast, 1962,
A Saturday afternoon, glad to meet
Me, newly cubbed in language, he gripped
My elbow. "Listen. Go your own way.
Do your own work. Remember Katherine Mansfield—*I will tell*
How the laundry basket squeaked...that note of exile."
But to hell with overstating it:
"Don't have your veins bulging in your biro."
And then, "Poor Hopkins!" I have the Journals
He gave me, underlined, his buckled self
Obeisant to their pain. He discerned
The lineaments of patience everywhere
And fostered me and sent me out, with words
Imposing on my tongue like obols.[11]

My choice of "Fosterage" is not innocent, its title alluding to adoption, care and mentoring. It is about the "schooling" of the poet (it is number five in the six-part sequence of related lyrics titled "Singing School"). I want also to make the case that as readers we "foster" poetry in our reading of it, and that we do this by following the chains of associations that occur both in the mind and across worlds.

The poem is dedicated to Irish novelist Michael McLaverty, who was Headmaster of St. Thomas Intermediate School, Belfast, when Heaney taught there in 1962–63.[12]

Jonathan Allison has done considerable work on the poem, picking up the intertextual links, through the titles of the series and of this poem. He noted a Yeatsian commitment to study as part of the poet's vocation, hence the title of the series, that Allison finds in Yeats:

Nor is there singing school but studying
Monuments of its own magnificence

He also finds the title of our poem in Wordsworth's *The Prelude*: "Fostered alike by beauty and by fear."[13]

The poem is thus thickly embedded in its "monumental" intertext. More obscurely, Allison informs us that the source of the line

I will tell
How the laundry basket squeaked

is an entry from Katherine Mansfield's journal from 22 January 1916. Mansfield and her husband John Middleton Murray were in the South of France at the time; Mansfield is perhaps still mourning the death of her brother, Leslie Heron Beauchamp, who had been killed in action: "you, my little sun of it, are set":

> Oh, I want for one moment to make our undiscovered country leap into the eyes of the Old World. It must be mysterious, as though floating. It must take the breath. It must be "one of those islands..." [*sic*] I shall tell everything, even of how the laundry-basket squeaked at 75. But all must be told with a sense of mystery, a radiance, an afterglow, because you, my little sun of it, are set. You have dropped over the dazzling brim of the world. Now I must play my part.[14]

And "note of exile" refers to Chekhov, as discussed between Heaney and McLaverty, and these examples do not exhaust all the intertextual references in the poem. The intertext is a historical-compositional reality, a weaving together of lines and words remembered or noted by the poet. He later wrote, Allison tells us, in his introduction to a book of McLaverty's short stories, "'Look for the intimate thing,' he would say, and go on to praise the 'note of exile' in Chekhov."[15] The intertext is thus perfectly real, but in a different sense from the referential real. The (inter)textual real depends on repetition and recomposition: that Chekhov once wrote an essay called "In Exile" in 1892, that McLaverty repeated this to Heaney and that this phrase exists as a part of Western literature's cultural capital.

Another register of the real with which the poem is networked is the *referential real*, to which I have referred to a number of times. This does not depend on repetition and recomposition, but on the existence of singular historical events. Michael Parker has confirmed that the central encounter in "Fosterage" takes place in Belfast in 1962, when Heaney was starting to be productive. McLaverty was influencing and "fostering" the poet at this stage, recommending readings, including Katherine Mansfield, Hopkins and Kavanagh.[16] And if Heaney had not encountered McLaverty on Royal Avenue, Belfast, in 1962, would this matter? Not really, but it would matter to the poem's relations to the referential real if McLaverty (the dedicatee) and Royal Avenue did not exist in 1962. Those relations give the poem the power of the "reality effect,"[17] as Barthes called it, an effect in that the words "Royal Avenue" refer precisely to an avenue in Belfast in exactly the same way that they operate as they appear in Belfast city maps. But there is more to be said about this kind of reality effect, and that is the "intimate thing" conjured by the quotation from Katherine Mansfield about the laundry-basket squeaking at 75, a house, most probably, from her New Zealand youth. We all know how a laundry basket squeaks when hefted with damp washing, don't we? It has to be a cane one, not plastic. This is the realist detail that surprises with its observational acuity, an acuity that, in this case, adds a sonorous dimension. It is the "intimate thing" that causes Heaney to exclaim, "Description is revelation!," advice coming from McLaverty, a writer of realist fiction.

So, there are two levels so far in this multirealist (aesthetic) description, which I would claim are essential to the poem's power to reproduce: the historically real and the intertextual-compositional remix. I will go on to add the intersubjective, which I call "partnership," but first I will add a final register of the real, the spiritual. This leaps out in the final word *obols*, a suitably archaic Greek term for the kind of silver coin that would be placed on the tongue to secure one's passage across the Acheron. With this word the ghosts of the classical ancestors are called upon, as if the poet descended from the Greeks in a European tradition, which in a sense he does. The ancestors' "life" is immortal, to the extent that the echoes of their voices are not forgotten, and with the silver words given him, this poet too, it is implied, will pass over into their immortal number. This transcendentalism, this translation from the material to the spiritual, is also a necessary and *real* part of the (multirealist, Western) aesthetic I am attempting to describe; there would be few poems that did not attempt to borrow a bit of this transcendent soul stuff.

The poem, then, is composed of these three different registers of the real, and there may be more in other poems. They are mutually supportive, just as the intersubjective partner relations are essential to a poem's capacity to be produced and reproduced. In "Fosterage," the young poet "newly cubbed in language" receives all sorts of advice: "Go your own way;" "do your own work;" "don't have the veins bulging in your biro." At each reading, the McLaverty–Heaney dyad has added to it the writer–reader one; both are relations of fosterage and influence. Life, and the life-career of poems as they move through the world, cannot be reproduced without partners. These may be human beings, metaphors ("cubbed," above, links to nature, the earthy genealogical opposite to the concluding transcendence), nurturing cultures, concepts and material things like spades.

Because of reproduction, the category of "life" is also central to my scheme. One must be wary of that old Leavisite category that tends to reference an uncritical liberal-humanism,[18] but one can nonetheless conceive of the literary text as existing in an ecology that seeks to sustain itself in a particular place. Under what conditions, one may ask, and with what partners, is the literary text being fostered? We shall have to describe all the things making up this ecology, some of them human, some nonhuman, forming hybrid assemblages that work together in relations of immanence. Reproducibility is about those necessary partnerships that make life (the life of the text, also) flourish: educational institutions and associated bureaucracies, class distinctions, reading groups, literary festivals, publishing houses and so on. Unlike biological reproduction, which can't defer the death of individuals, cultural reproduction seems to have the magical power of sustaining the life of a work for long periods of time if the right cultural mix is maintained.

Bruno Latour's recent work helps us see that this literary life is of a different ontological order to human, animal or plant life—the beings who inhabit the (biological) reproductive order. The life of fictional beings is a separate *mode of existence*. In his discussion of the remarkable work of Etienne Souriau in the 1930s, Latour sets up five modes: phenomena, things, souls, fictional beings and the language of religion. All these modes of existence are not reducible to each other. Irreducibilty is a principle for this *multirealist* perception he is describing. He uses quotations from

Souriau to support, almost in passing, a kind of theory of literature as cultivation. The existence of the work of art depends on it being fostered:

> It is not a matter of following the ontic beyond its attachments to phenomena and to experience, right through to the void; this is the error of so many metaphysicians (and no doubt phenomenology too). It is a matter of inventing or discovering (as in discovering a treasure) positive modes of existence, coming to meet us with their palm fronds, to greet our hopes and aspirations, or our problematic speculations, in order to gather them in and comfort them. All other research is a metaphysical famine.[19]

There is rich material to be mined here for a radically empirical theory of literary reading that asserts relations as real, while denying the metaphysical "void" he refers to. So the premise is that communicative events (like the reading of a poem) do not bridge gaps, but are things that exist to be greeted. Many literary theorists are happy to acknowledge that the text and the process of literary production are dense sets of relations. But they are rarely radical enough, or empirical enough, to follow through the relations, the chains of associations, because most are locked into a representational philosophy that needs gaps. At a crucial point they like to leap in to the void: they call it "the space between"; they evoke forms of transcendence—they call it indeterminacy or ambiguity; they revel in the rich elaboration of potential or possibility and will defend to the end the idea that a text's ultimate unknowability is the justification and the reward of sustained readerly attention.

This negative void is there only because of the SUBJECT—TEXT—OBJECT communicative scenario, with the poverty of its three points and two gaps, giving rise to all that agonizing over representation; how adequately the text represents the world to consciousness, as if there were only two or three different kinds of things that exist: ineffable human subjectivity, dubious objective exteriority and endless attempts at representation in between.

> If by "epistemology" we name the discipline that tries to understand how we manage to bridge the gap between representations and reality, the only conclusion to be drawn about it is that this discipline has no subject matter whatsoever, because we *never* bridge such a gap—not, mind you, because we don't know anything objectively, but because *there is never such a gap*. The gap is an artifact due to the wrong positioning of the knowledge acquisition pathway. We imagine a bridge over an abyss, when the whole activity consists of a drift through a chain of experience where there are many successive event-like termini and many substitutions of heterogeneous media.[20]

So this is why I want to argue that the literary work of art is not a kind of *language bridge* between subject and object. Rather, its tentacles extend in all sorts of directions where the text's relations expand into an *empirical multirealist* world.

Here the text is sustained in a kind of existence, but what kind of existence is this? While a literary text, as an object, is not alive, its existence is defined through its active relations with other things, human and nonhuman, in a complex ecology. This is a space of negotiation and transformation that does not privilege either subject or object. The story or poem does not exist *primarily* in relation to human subjectivities (phenomenology), nor *primarily* in relation to objects (materialism). It has its own existence not reducible to either of those privileged poles in the modernist conceptual architecture. It is not the secondary effect of any primary realities, and cannot be reduced to them, in the manner that a sociology can reduce a religious experience to a set of structures and functions or a religion can assert that evolutionary theory is wrong and the world was created in six days. These sorts of reductions can and are made, more or less convincingly, but through a series of hard-won negotiations, a gathering of allies and transformations from one link in a chain of reference to another. The literary field is replete with such reductions, which we call available *readings*, and they are equally unsatisfactory (a "Marxist reading," or "reading with Butler," for example). These risk crossing the inevitable communicative bridge before they come to it, and they risk taking away the text's own voice. Its "own voice" is what makes it reproducible on its terms, as opposed to a reproduction of a kind of reading. A reading, like a Marxist reading, is sustained through a chain of *reference*, whereas a literary work is sustained by *reproducing* itself. Reference is the domain of knowledge, a separate mode of existence from reproduction. But what has a poem got that a Fredric Jameson critical text lacks? It has a reproducible generic form, and it conjoins language to being to create an event (whereas with literary critical writing, language just refers, and disappears as it goes along). Obviously, the literary work of art never emerges *ex nihilo*: the elements come together, composed through labor, constructed from an intertextual heritage, but not fabricated out of or in relation to the void. Souriau used the word "instauration" to grasp a process of devotional creation that might be experienced by both writer and reader:

> To say, for example, that a fact is "constructed" is inevitably (and they paid me good money to know this) to designate the knowing subject as the origin of the vector, as in the example of God the potter. But the opposite, to say of a work of art that it results from an instauration, is to get oneself ready to see the potter as the one who welcomes, gathers, prepares, explores, and invents the form of a work, just as one discovers or invents a treasure.[21]
>
> But this growing existence is made, we can see, out of a double modality that finally comes together, in the unity of a sole being progressively *invented* in the laboring process. Often there is no warning: the finished work is always up to a certain point a novelty, discovery or surprise. So that's what I was looking for, that's what I was meant to make![22]

Now, in order to "instaure" a text in its own truth ("it is manifested in its entire accomplishment, in its own truth"[23]), my method is to ask two questions of it: *how is it keeping itself alive in its place?* (I am refusing there the modernist universalisms that suggest works of art are ungrounded, that they transcend time and place in a covert Christian reduction perpetuated by Kantianism). Place-based analysis is an implicit or explicit critique of European modernist universals, and proliferates in postcolonial criticism and in eco-criticism, as in the work of Edward Casey, Lucy Lippard and myself.[24] And the second question I ask is: *what are its partners for reproductive purposes?* At this point "the Marxist reading" can be brought back as a partnership, not as a reduction. Or the offer to read "with Butler" is an invitation to go on a date: I can't take this poem out clubbing just by myself; I need another highly desirable partner as well. Two things then: place-based devotion or cultivation, and no reproduction without getting partners to come to the party.

* * *

But as this chapter draws to a close, I feel I have not yet gotten close enough to "Fosterage" to really foster its poetic mode of existence, one that it shares with other lyric poems, and could possibly share with a prose on the way to becoming poetry, a critical prose that breaks, with some alarm, from that distant judgmental perspective that would maintain a pious evenness in the face of creative work,[25] and instead seek out a partnership with that capacity art has to break forth into its own existential style in the face of a Benjaminian historical "emergency."[26] Not determined by context, not reducible to any one or two of its multiply real registers, but coterminous with them, reproducing their forms in transformative imitation, wouldn't you agree, Mr. Heaney, channeling Mr. McLaverty, remembering Mansfield and Hopkins, inventing Chekhov and finding revelation with the Ancients? This is what Taussig calls "the mimetic faculty, the nature that uses culture to create second nature, the faculty to copy, imitate, make models, explore difference, yield into and become Other."[27]

Listen, let me grip your elbow; forget judgment and distance. If you want fosterage, *there is never such a gap.* Let's investigate critical proximity, do the analysis of "Fosterage" without mysterious voids and trace precise relations between real things. The poem is not constructed as a series of benign linguistic equivalences and figures, but as a series of transformative differences that probe always toward alterities. In order for transformations to take place as little events (within the text and in its iterations through various worlds), the text must tempt or try out the Other, to see if it will yield to the point of reproductive partnership. Now, strangely, it is only on this multirealist platform that the poem can speak with its true voice, as its own thing, not reduced to some reading or another, by virtue of the work it has to do trying out its various Others.

You will foster "Fosterage" by sending it out, to your Royal Avenue of the imagination. As soon as you can place it elsewhere, for example, in King Street near my place in Sydney, you have partnered it in that new way and found fertile associations for it in its new location, which are necessary to its continued reproduction. Its lyric existence has the property of proximate linkage, of partnership: neither the historical/referential reduction—"No, no, *not* King St in 2012! It has to be about Royal Avenue, Belfast, in 1962!"—nor the humanist universalism ("Timeless, it speaks to us all"). A *reproductive* mode of existence necessitates specific, working and perhaps unexpected partnerships (which have nothing to do with *representations* which imply a gap, between referent and sign, for example). A poem is now read (or listened to) as traces of life engendered by partners. These are constituted as chains of intimately connected transformations which, working with alterities, generate vitality. There are no metaphors of depth or transcendence, just a ceaseless trying of things out with others. To say that a poem lives in a place, and can go on to live in new places, is to refuse modernist universalisms, and to engage the facts and values of its particular existence as a local voyager.

Notes

1 Bruno Latour, *Enquête sur les modes d'existence: Une anthropologie des Modernes* (Paris: La Découverte, 2012), 196. My translation.
2 "Oscar voters overwhelmingly white, male," *Los Angeles Times*, 19 February 2012.
3 Tony Bennett, *Formalism and Marxism* (London: Methuen, 1979), 136. Thanks to John Frow for reminding me of this quotation.
4 Bruno Latour, *Enquête sur les modes d'existence.*
5 On correlationism, see Quentin Meillassoux, *After Finitude: An Essay on the Necessity of Contingency* (New York: Continuum, 2009).
6 Graham Harman, *Prince of Networks: Bruno Latour and Metaphysics* (Melbourne: re.press, 2007). Graham Harman, "The Well-Wrought Broken Hammer: Object-Oriented Literary Criticism," *New Literary History* 43 (2012): 183–203, hereafter cited in text; Timothy Morton, "An Object-Oriented Defense of Poetry," *New Literary History* 43 (2012): 205–24.
7 Alfred North Whitehead, *Process and Reality: An Essay in Cosmology* (New York: The Free Press, 1978); Morton, "An Object-Oriented Defense of Poetry."
8 Harman, "Well-Wrought Broken Hammer."
9 Seamus Heaney, "Digging," *Death of a Naturalist* (London: Faber and Faber, 1966), 8–9.
10 Isabelle Stengers, *Cosmopolitiques*, 7 vols. (Paris: La Découverte; Les Empêcheurs de Penser en Rond, 1996–97).
11 Seamus Heaney, "Fosterage" from "Singing School," *Opened Ground: Selected Poems 1966–1996*, ed. Seamus Heaney (New York: Farrar, Straus and Giroux, 1998). Copyright © 1998 by Seamus Heaney. Reprinted by permission of the publisher.
12 Jonathan Allison, "'Friendship's Garland' and the Manuscripts of Seamus Heaney's 'Fosterage,'" *The Yearbook of English Studies* 35 (2005): 58–71.
13 Allison, "Friendship's Garland," 61.
14 Cited in Allison, "Friendship's Garland," 63.
15 Allison, "Friendship's Garland," 63n.
16 Michael Parker, *Seamus Heaney: The Making of the Poet* (London: Macmillan, 1993), 29; 149.
17 Roland Barthes, "The Reality Effect," *The Rustle of Language*, trans. Richard Howard (Oxford: Blackwell, 1986), 141–8.
18 Terry Eagleton has narrated the Leavis' use of the concept of "life":
    Scrutiny... represented nothing less than the last-ditch stand of liberal humanism, concerned...with the unique value of the individual and the creative realm of the interpersonal. These values could be summarized as 'Life,' a word which *Scrutiny* made a virtue of not being able to define. If you asked for some reasoned theoretical statement of their case, you had thereby demonstrated that you were

in the outer darkness: either you felt Life or you did not. Great literature was a literature reverently open to Life, and what Life was could be demonstrated by great literature. The case was circular, intuitive and proof against all argument, reflecting the enclosed coterie of the Leavisites themselves.
Eagleton, *Literary Theory: An Introduction* (Oxford: Blackwell, 1996), 36.

19   Etienne Souriau, *Les différents modes d'existence* (Paris: Presses Universitaires de France, 1943), 92.

20   Bruno Latour, "A Textbook Case Revisited: Knowledge as a Mode of Existence," in *The Handbook of Science and Technology Studies*, eds. E. Hackett, O. Amsterdamska, M. Lynch, and J. Wacjman, 3rd ed. (Cambridge, MA: MIT Press, 2007), 83.

21   Bruno Latour, "Reflections on Etienne Souriau's *Les différents modes d'existence*," trans. Stephen Muecke, *The Speculative Turn: Continental Materialism and Realism*, eds. Levi Bryant, Nick Srnicek, and Graham Harman (Melbourne: re.press, 2011), 331.

22   Souriau, cited in Latour, "Reflections on Etienne Souriau," 310.

23   Etienne Souriau, *Avoir une âme* (Lyon: Annales de l'Université de Lyon, 1939).

24   Lucy Lippard, *The Lure of the Local: Sense of Place in a Multicentered Society* (New York: New Press, 1997); Edward Casey, *The Fate of Place: A Philosophical History* (Berkeley, CA: University of California Press, 1997); Stephen Muecke, *Ancient & Modern: Time, Culture and Indigenous Philosophy* (Kensington: University of NSW Press, 2004).

25   Stephen Muecke, "Motorcycles, Snails, Latour: Criticism without Judgement," *Cultural Studies Review* 18, no. 1 (2012): 40–58.

26   Walter Benjamin, "Theses on the Philosophy of History," *Illuminations*, ed. H. Arendt (New York: Harcourt, Brace & World: 1968), 245–55.

27   Michael Taussig, *Mimesis and Alterity: A Particular History of the Senses* (New York: Routledge, 1993), xiii.

11

Distended Moments in the Neuronarrative: Character Consciousness and the Cognitive Sciences in Ian McEwan's *Saturday*

Hannah Courtney

Ian McEwan's 2005 novel *Saturday* is part of a recent surge of novels concerned with the exploration of current scientific theories, particularly the field of the cognitive sciences. This authorial obsession with the scientifically explored human mind manifests itself not just in story content or themes but also in discourse or form. McEwan utilizes an in-depth, thoroughly researched understanding of neuroscience and the cognitive psychological experience of being, which has manifested itself in his early-twenty-first-century writing in a new form of narrative discourse. This chapter will explore how McEwan utilizes the psychological experience of the relativity of time in moments of crisis, and in so doing creates a technical form whereby narrative time is slowed to mimic the experience of story time. McEwan's technical progression thus demonstrates that the science behind narratives like *Saturday* can be used to evolve and mutate discourse as well as story.

In his 2008 article "Consciousness as Content: Neuronarratives and the Redemption of Fiction," Gary Johnson groups *Saturday* with several other recent fictional narratives published from the mid-1990s through the 2000s, including David Lodge's *Thinks...*, Richard Powers' *Galatea 2.2*, Powers' *The Echo Maker*, Jonathan Franzen's *The Corrections* and A. S. Byatt's *A Whistling Woman*. He terms these novels "neuronarratives"—an "emerging subgenre of literature that can provide us with a glimpse of how authors are responding to scientific advances concerning the nature of human consciousness."[1] Johnson defines a neuronarrative as "a work of fiction that has cognitive science as a, or the, main theme," and postulates that the authors of neuronarratives tend to personally battle with, on the one hand, conveying the complex scientific developments of the cognitive sciences to their (probably) literary-minded readership through story content, and, on the other hand, managing to maintain a flowing, un-textbook-like narrative fiction which affirms the place of the humanities (especially creative literature) as important alongside the epistemological breakthroughs of the sciences.[2] Johnson mentions *Saturday* only in passing before going on to analyze *Thinks...* and *Galatea 2.2*, and in this chapter I would like to explore McEwan's novel in relation to Johnson's claim.

Scientific breakthroughs have long inspired the content and thematic nature of fictional works. Indeed, we can look back to Robert Louis Stevenson's 1886 novella *The Strange Case of Dr. Jekyll and Mr. Hyde* as just one famous example of an author's attempt to understand the subconscious mind, to explore the very depths of human character, through a thematic fictional exploration of the "duality" of the mind inspired by the scientific obsession with cognition of the day. Robert Mighall claims Stevenson's work was heavily "reliant upon criminological and psychiatric theories" of the time, the fictional work reading as something of a "case-study in what was known at the time as 'morbid psychology.'"[3] We may now look at Stevenson's understanding of the complexities of cognition as at best primitive, but his work did reflect the scientific ideas concerning cognition of his day, and so we can look at this novella as one among many precursors (I am thinking particularly of the realist branch of science fiction) to the current surge of neuronarratives.

Interestingly, McEwan's *Saturday* does not solely concern itself with the sciences of the *mind*. The author has seen fit to pepper the narrative with references to other scientific theories outside this realm, suggesting that his protagonist (through whose eyes we witness the events of the novel) is not simply a neurosurgeon caught up in his single, narrowly defined area of research but also a well-rounded scientist—one conversant with other branches, such as physics and genetics. Indeed, in the first few pages of the novel, McEwan already has his protagonist wrestling intellectually with Schrödinger's Cat, a physics theory which both allows the scientist to process events he witnesses in terms with which he can grapple (witnessing a burning plane descend into London he muses that the passengers, like the cat in Schrödinger's box, could be both alive *and* dead until the result is known, or that they are already one or the other and "[w]hat then collapses will be his own ignorance") and allows the author to present the very rational, intellectual, epistemologically minded scientific consciousness through whose perspective we will be viewing events for the duration of the novel.[4]

Protagonist Henry Perowne is a card-carrying scientist—a character set up as belonging squarely to one side of the science–humanities dichotomy that Johnson claims is a key feature of many neuronarratives. Johnson maintains that one avenue through which numerous authors choose to educate their readerships on the complex scientific information that that audience may not already possess (yet need to understand in order to fully grasp the narrative content) is "to reopen the two-culture divide within the fictional world of the narrative."[5] Johnson claims this often comes about in order "to facilitate the readers' entry into the 'authorial audience' ... [which] is a construct that is capable of 'getting' the author's intended meaning, even as members of the actual and/or narrative audience might not."[6] This assimilation of real (potentially unknowledgeable) readers into the realm of knowledge can be authorially aided by reanimating the science versus humanities debate so as to give professionally opposed characters the opportunity to explain their differing academic viewpoints to a relatively ignorant outsider. McEwan has chosen to reanimate this dichotomy, seemingly to aid understanding of story content, but more importantly, as a means of tension, to further developments in the story, and to bring about something of a personal crisis for Perowne.

Science versus literature in *Saturday*

In 1959 C. P. Snow gave a now-infamous lecture entitled *The Two Cultures*. This lecture commented upon and lamented the gap that had been forming between the members of two branches of academic knowledge. Snow referred to "[t]wo polar groups: at one pole we have the literary intellectuals...at the other scientists...Between the two a gulf of mutual incomprehension—sometimes (particularly among the young) hostility and dislike, but most of all lack of understanding."[7] This gulf still seems to exist in one form or another today—the stereotypical difference between science and literature, that science knows (or seeks out) facts, whereas literature makes up what is not there, still pervades. However, in *Saturday*, McEwan has sought to question both of these assumptions—prompting us to consider the possibility that what science knows may not be ultimate truth, and that perhaps this may only be understood through the framework of literature. Indeed, literature and science not only intersect in this novel, but they engage with each other, often battling, with no decisive winner at the end. Clearly, since McEwan is an author, he is assigned an automatic prejudice in favor of the literary. However, his dedicated prewriting scientific research reveals an author who is deeply respectful of many different forms of science. In preparation for *Saturday*, McEwan spent two years researching neurosurgery—sitting in on countless operations over the course of that time and keeping up a constant dialogue with one neurosurgeon in particular (gratefully thanked in McEwan's acknowledgments), along with five other doctors and scientists who advised him on the medical elements of the novel. In *Saturday* this respect for and dedication to the cognitive sciences is demonstrated through the creation of a protagonist who is a neurosurgeon. Due to the almost-blanket third-person focalization through Perowne, the events experienced by our protagonist on his single Saturday are delivered to us through his screen of categorization, with diagnostics at the forefront, and scientific references and metaphors, such as the Schrödinger's Cat theory, as his way of understanding or explaining his world.

Yet, through introducing scientific theories into a novel framed by a scientist, and thus by scientific thinking, McEwan is doing more than simply writing a novel about science. He uses his medium to explore the push and pull between literature and science—to question the assumptions based on the binary and allow his readers to make their own conclusions about which side comes out on top. Perowne is (perhaps too overtly) a "science man," not an "arts man"—he believes in the fixed, the facts, rather than interpretation. He is not of a literary bent at all—we learn that his "literate, too literate" daughter Daisy has been "addressing what she believes is his astounding ignorance, guiding his literary education" for a few years, yet he still cannot connect with literature—he cannot see what she sees (6). Indeed, McEwan goes so far as to jest at Perowne's views when his protagonist dismisses magical realist novels as "irksome confections" (67). In a nice postmodern touch, Perowne specifically condemns one such novel in which "[o]ne visionary saw through a pub window his parents as they had been some weeks after his conception, discussing the possibility of aborting him" (67)—a key plot point in McEwan's 1987 novel *The Child in Time*, and a humorous self-reference on the part of the author. McEwan has deliberately contrasted Perowne not just with people who like books, or even with people who like McEwan's books (and thus, many of those reading about Perowne), but also with two extremely literary characters. In addition to his daughter, Daisy, who is just about to release her first collection of poems (a promising achievement from an up-and-coming poet in her early twenties), Perowne's father-in-law, Grammaticus, is a highly successful, world-renowned poet. Perowne does not understand the ability of literature to move people, and so his relatives' striking interest in the literary confounds him. This is all packaged, of course, in the delicious, supreme irony that we only know of Perowne's scientifically bent, antiliterary consciousness through literature—and specifically through the highly aesthetic literary devices caught up in exploring character consciousness within third-person narration.

Throughout the text the big debate that rages in Perowne's mind is that of determinism versus free individual choice, and this comes to represent the larger debate between the ideals of science and those of literature. The narrator introduces Perowne in the first sentence of the novel not as a family man, an amateur squash player, a great maker of fish stew or as one caught up in the throes of world terrorism (all of which apply to our protagonist), but rather as a professional determinist. This first line reads, "[s]ome hours before dawn, Henry Perowne, a neurosurgeon, wakes to find himself already in motion..." (3). He is not in surgery; there is no immediately apparent reason to introduce him as such, except to say that his work defines him—he is a man concerned with how the body forms who we are and what his profession can do to fix that body. McEwan sets out Perowne's thesis—that genetics determine us—early in the novel:

> It's a commonplace of parenting and modern genetics that parents have little or no influence on the characters of their children. You never know who you are going to get. Opportunities, health, prospects, accent, table manners—these might lie within your power to shape. But what really determines the sort of person who's coming to live with you is which sperm finds which egg, how the cards in two packs are chosen, then how they are shuffled, halved and spliced at the moment of recombination. Cheerful or neurotic, kind or greedy, curious or dull, expansive or shy and anywhere in between; it can be quite an affront to parental self-regard, just how much of the work has already been done. On the other hand, it can let you off the hook. The point is made for you as soon as you have more than one child; two entirely different people emerge from their roughly similar chances in life. (25)

Perowne is firmly on the side of cause and effect—our bodies determine who we are because our genes have programmed us just so.

This belief is plainly evidenced during Perowne's encounters with Baxter, the antagonist of the story. Perowne meets Baxter twice during his Saturday—the first time their cars collide and Baxter and his two ruffian friends threaten Perowne's life. It is during this meeting that Perowne observes Baxter and diagnoses the man's neurological disorder—using his scientific knowledge to turn the power tables and escape the situation. The second meeting occurs later that day when Baxter invades

Perowne's home and holds his family at knifepoint. During the post-car crash encounter Perowne observes a "persistent tremor" in Baxter—an "unsteadiness of grip" which "draws Perowne's professional attention" (87). Even as his own life becomes more and more threatened throughout the scene, Perowne sets about clinically analyzing and diagnosing Baxter. Speculating about the cause of Baxter's tremor, agitation, violence and strange head and eye movements "soothes him" and "[p]erversely, he no longer believes himself to be in any great danger" (90). That is, Perowne believes that as soon as he can pinpoint the cause of the disorder that is causing a man to threaten his life, he can predict Baxter's every move and thus be free from harm. In this, Perowne is thoroughly convinced that he is safe because Baxter's actions are determined by his genetic makeup and free choice is therefore not playing a part in his decisions. He claims, "[*i*]*t is written*" (210).

However, rather than simply promoting Perowne's theory of genetic determinism, *Saturday* invites us to question the lead character's assumptions (and thus the extreme, steadfast, unwavering scientific standpoint) by putting forward the possibility of the power of free will. Perowne's determinist theory is questioned deeply in his encounters with Baxter. During the home invasion, Perowne "thinks he's making the right answer" (209) in telling Baxter that Grammaticus is his father, yet his prediction based on determinism is wrong—Baxter's unpredictable free will asserts itself in the form of his breaking Grammaticus' nose. There is, of course, a higher irony here—all of this is unpredictable from the scientific point of view of Perowne, yet highly predictable from the vantage of literature, where revenge and violence commonly run amok to heighten tension, especially in the final dramatic climax. Indeed, if Perowne could only see what we see through the literary angle—that Baxter is a kind of literary cliché of a villain, that his vengeful actions follow a dramatic story arc—then he might indeed be able to predict Baxter's actions. As it is, his scientific standpoint does not allow this and so he constantly faces actions that defy the logic of his science. Once again, though, this irony flips back to wreak havoc on the other "side" of the divide—free will is not predictable through science, yet it is also not possible in literature (the very domain of creativity, and thus, it would seem, free will) where a character's actions are determined by the author. McEwan clearly does not allow an easy victor in this debate.

The author's ultimate toying between determinism and choice—between science and literature—comes in the form of the ill man's reaction to Daisy's recital of Matthew Arnold's poem "Dover Beach." During his invasion of the Perowne home, Baxter demands that she read one of her own poems aloud, but Daisy instead picks Arnold's 1867 work to recite. After this recital Baxter is physically changed (slouching over, loosening his grip on the knife) and it is here that Perowne, amazed and perplexed, wonders whether a poem could indeed invoke a mood swing. Baxter demands that Daisy read it again and following this we see through Perowne's eyes that the ill man "appears suddenly elated" (222). Baxter is thrilled with the poem, amazed at the idea that Daisy actually wrote it, and tells her "[i]t's beautiful" (222). Perowne has witnessed Baxter's transformation "from lord of terror to amazed admirer" (223). It is through Perowne's eyes that we witness the scene, and thus it is through his medical opinion that the events are screened. Perowne wonders at the transformation and is initially amazed by the potential power of literature to induce it, but then quickly reverts to the safety of his scientific standpoint, diagnosing the stages of Baxter's intense high and dismissing the idea of the transformative nature of literature, preferring to believe that Baxter must be determined to respond to the poem in this way while believing himself genetically determined to be unaffected by the same literature. Here McEwan is presenting us with a scientific stereotype: Perowne, even when he sees the transformative power of literature, still rejects this possibility—rejects the arts when they seem to refute the "absolute" knowledge of his own discipline. He goes to bed a determinist, and we, as literary readers, are to "tut" at his closed-mindedness. And yet it is not so simple—Perowne is not a detestable stereotype, but rather a well-rounded character. He is a family man, a loving protector, an admirably intelligent rationalist, a good person. Perowne even proves his worth by performing surgery on his enemy at the conclusion of the novel—a move that can be seen as a compassionate act of self-sacrifice as well as the reassertion of his dominance and power.

Science and determinism are never denigrated for McEwan's audience, but rather used in worthy opposition to his own world, and indeed, presumably to that of many of his readers. The debate in this novel is used to open minds, not close them—to illuminate the opposition. Thus through the internal struggle carried out over the course of *Saturday*, we can see McEwan's great respect for the sciences—a respect that extends not only to interest and thorough research but also to a literary figure viewing the sciences as a worthy enough "adversary" to include the debate between the two fields as a major element of his work. In McEwan's own words, "science parallels literature as a means by which the world can be understood. There are great, noble and ingenious insights which science has brought us and which literature could never equal. Of course, there are many complex facets of experience for which science has no language and literature does."[8] For McEwan, then, science is complementary—not subordinate or superior—to literature.

Character consciousness, narrative time and slowed scene

McEwan's obsession with the cognitive sciences has endowed his early-twenty-first-century works with a new approach to the exploration of character consciousness in crucial moments of crisis. His interest in the cognitive sciences manifests itself in his more recent pieces of fiction not just in story content but also in form, or discourse. As Johnson states, some neuronarratives do, indeed, try to represent cognition while at the same time explaining it. In *Saturday*, McEwan attempts to demonstrate and replicate the cognitive experience of a moment of crisis in a healthy brain. He does this not through simple stream of consciousness followed by an explanation of that brain's processes by a scientific character, but by replicating the experience of this cognition through narrative techniques.

While critics and theorists have been utilizing insights from cognitive neuroscience to decipher literary works for some time, McEwan has been "getting in before his critics," so to speak—applying the insights of the sciences of the mind to the exploration of character consciousness in his writing.[9] McEwan has long been preoccupied with moments of trauma in his characters' lives (murder, rape and incest are among his many favored topics), yet it is how characters *mentally* deal with these crisis moments that has come to the fore in his early-twenty-first-century works. McEwan explains, "I have always thought the defining call of literature is to do with the exploration of human nature, which is also a dominant issue within cognitive and evolutionary psychology. Fundamental notions like consciousness as well as the emotions—surely the novelist's domain—are studied. Emotions like anger, shame and even revenge are studied in beautifully constructed experiments."[10] McEwan has always put his characters through ordeals, and it is through this means that he can explore the human mind in its most extreme state of stress.

It is anecdotally accepted that certain crucial life events where we feel under intense, immediate pressure (and thus where acute anxiety often features) can feel as though they are occurring in a kind of slow motion while our thoughts whir at great speed. This is now commonly associated (conflated) with the theory of the relativity of time. Although not in keeping with the strict boundaries of the physics, we have applied what is commonly understood about the theory to our own experiences—that time is experienced, and can even operate, differently compared to normal experience, depending on the situation in which the subject finds themselves.[11] This has thus become the cognitive application of the physics theory of the relativity of time, and it is this application that McEwan uses in *Saturday* in his exploration of character consciousness in scenes of crisis.

McEwan's early-twenty-first-century works display his fully developed technique for conveying to the reader the importance of a pivotal scene, of "the moment," not just for a character but also for the narrative.[12] The author seems to believe that such an event would undoubtedly result in the cognitive warping of time—an important event would feel weightier, and thus lengthier, and it is this experience that McEwan has attempted to convey through expanded duration of narrative time. These novels convey, in painstaking detail, the myriad, minute thoughts of a character as their mind flits this way and that within a moment of crisis. This is achieved through a third-person narrator focalizing the scene through that character and allowing us detailed access to their thoughts through thought reporting.

McEwan does not simply borrow the well-worn technique of stream of consciousness (often characterized by disjointed or truncated sentence fragments, and an absence of narratorial explanation) from the modernists to do this. Instead, he expands these modernist fragments to full sentences with proper grammar, and it is this detail that conveys the complete character consciousness within the moment. Like that of the modernist stream of consciousness, this character consciousness is undoubtedly raw, fresh and "true"—it contains the immediate human response to a pivotal situation, and in doing so allows an audience to feel the importance of the event and the way in which a character deals with it. However, McEwan's chosen narrative mode of character consciousness exploration resembles more the detailed, flowing, narratorially explained thought-to-thought connections found within traditional character introspection. That is, McEwan's distended moments resemble the detailed character thought exploration found within the novels of Austen, James and Flaubert with one small-but-weighty difference—McEwan's moments occur *in scene* (not on the margins of scenes) in the *moving, timed* moment. This is in direct contrast to those traditional novels where detailed character introspection only occurs in moments of what I have termed "indeterminate duration."

Indeterminate duration occurs when we cannot accurately measure story time because it is unclear or vague. Such indeterminate moments either occur on the edges of story scenes devoid of action markers (which, if present, would indicate story time is progressing), or, more commonly, in moments mid-scene which are not clearly timed—not littered with action markers which allow the reader to fairly accurately ascertain the specific story time over which the narrative is taking place. Such indeterminately timed moments occur, for example, when a character thinks while gazing out a window, or while strolling solitarily around a garden—we know the moment is occurring in time, that the character's thoughts are temporally progressive, yet the absence of clear action markers means we cannot accurately gauge whether they take place over a minute or an hour. These moments do not involve the pressing weight of the moving scene adding to the character's troubles—their minds do not feel the stress of the acute moment putting temporal pressure on their processing. These characters are allowed a long-hand form of thinking (or rather, the narration provides us with the long-hand form of the character's thoughts), where thoughts are allowed to develop in full and where connections between those thoughts are explored in detail, rather than the short hand typically required of temporally urgent narration.

McEwan has taken the lengthy introspection common to moments of indeterminate duration and has placed it in the domain of the modernists' stream of consciousness—in the clearly timed, moving story moment. McEwan's technique allows him to combine the immediacy of the modernists with the detailed introspection of the traditional novelists, delivering us a complex, detailed and easy-to-follow mind in crisis in its slow-motion moment. As a consequence McEwan has developed the simultaneous technique of distending the duration of narrative time, which emphasizes the moment to the reader by expanding the scene, causing the swelling of the moment, and thus replicating the character's cognitive experience. The focus is thereby shifted from the event itself to the way the character is dealing with the event internally.

A smattering of critics has touched on the link between character consciousness and narrative time in McEwan's novels. In his exploration of the relative order (as opposed to my study of duration) of temporality in *The Child in Time*, Dominic Head hints at the concept of a depiction of "personal time" in McEwan's novels.[13] Sebastian Groes claims that McEwan's work has a "distinctive character which explores questions of morality, nationhood and history, sexuality, and *the nature of the imagination and human consciousness.*"[14] Matt Ridley talks about the way McEwan explores character consciousness in his novels: "The novelist's privilege, according to Ian McEwan, is to step inside the consciousness of others, and to lead the reader there like a psychological Virgil. Again and again in McEwan's books, it is the interior monologue of the characters, and that monologue's encounter with the 'truth' in the outside world, that grips us."[15] Ridley claims that McEwan "uses fiction to understand the mind and to explore human nature, as well as uses words to alter readers' consciousness."[16] That is, not only does McEwan explore how a character reacts to their world, but by employing specific textual techniques, he also manipulates the thoughts of the reader into experiencing these character reactions. Laura Marcus claims that "[a]t the heart of all Ian McEwan's fiction is a concern with time and the experience of temporality, from the time of the fiction—narrative duration [...]—to the ways in which characters and readers themselves experience time."[17] Marcus makes reference to McEwan's swelled moments, maintaining that his "signal narrative technique is his representation of the extended temporalities entailed in a singular occurrence."[18] Marcus also briefly mentions the link between time and consciousness in McEwan's fiction. It is my aim to extend what Marcus has touched upon in order to reach an understanding of the link between time and character consciousness so carefully bundled up in McEwan's distended moments.

It is of course necessary to refer here to Gerard Genette's theory on narrative time duration, that is, the length of text detailing a specific story event in relation to its story time duration. In *Narrative Discourse*, Genette famously outlined the four combinations of story time and narrative time he thought possible. Where NT is narrative time, and ST is story time:

$$\text{pause: } NT = n, ST = 0. \text{ Thus: } NT \infty > ST$$
$$\text{scene: } NT = ST$$
$$\text{summary: } NT < ST$$
$$\text{ellipsis: } NT = 0, ST = n. \text{ Thus: } NT < \infty ST.^{[19]}$$

It is immediately plain that there is a missing formula causing an imbalance in Genette's table—that of $NT > ST$, occurring between *pause* and *scene*. Genette claims that although such a duration—something of a slow-motion scene—would be hypothetically possible, it has never been "really actualized in literary tradition"[20]; instead scenes that seem to move slowly are simply made up of *scene* and *pause* switching back and forth. Expanding upon Genette's work, many narratologists have claimed that there *is* such a slow-motion duration—something I will term the *slowed scene* for ease of reference.[21]

Saturday: Three distended moments

Saturday inhabits the mind of just one character, and it is through his eyes in the form of third-person focalization that we witness the events of a single day in his life. In this way, McEwan is intertextually linking his work with that of James Joyce's *Ulysses* and Virginia Woolf's *Mrs Dalloway*—both famous modernist day-in-the-life novels—and so adding his novel to a tradition of time-oriented narratives. Never forgetting the grand sociopolitical setting of the novel amidst the London protests against the Iraq War (which occur in the periphery of Perowne's activity), most of the events which Perowne experiences during his Saturday are normal, everyday, private experiences—playing a game of squash with a friend, preparing for a family meal. These scenes occur in either *scene* or indeterminate duration, as Perowne's mind wanders off exploring thoughts and memories. In his busy, activity-filled day, there are just three scenes that are out-of-the-ordinary events in Perowne's private life and thus sure to have a significant impact on him as he experiences them. These three events reverberate throughout Perowne's day, and it is these scenes that are distended in narrative time.

The first moment of crisis occurs when Perowne, waking in the early hours of the morning and being inexplicably drawn to his bedroom window, witnesses a burning plane flying (or crashing) down into London. Perowne's witnessing of the descent of the plane occurs over the space of six pages—a stretched length of text for such a short activity compared to that given to other longer events in the novel. His mind ranges within that space from one thought to another, constantly referring back to the changing state of the plane in the night sky. It is only from this constant referral back to the moving action of the moment that we can ascertain that Perowne's mind is not drifting from one elongated thought to another—rather, that his mind is frantically racing through a multitude of complex thoughts within a short space of time. The plane's descent thus exposes the narrative time duration of the scene as slowed scene.

We are deliberately requested to view Perowne's thoughts as racing when the narrator states that "[o]nly three or four seconds have passed since he saw this fire in the sky and changed his mind about it twice" (14)—three or four seconds for an extended exploration of Perowne's mind as he wonders what the fireball is, settles on three different hypotheses and even has time to explore his memory and contemplate his own actions in the possibility of waking his wife. Clearly, the duration of narrative time has been greatly extended beyond the duration of story time by the complexity of a mind in a stressed state. The narrator again and again refers to the shortness of time, stating that Perowne thinks "[b]y the time the emergency services have noted and passed on his call, whatever is to happen will be in the past" (17). Perowne's hurriedly sprawling thoughts are littered with references to the position of the plane in the sky— "[i]t's directly south of him now, barely a mile away, soon to pass into the topmost lattice of the bare plane trees, and then behind the Post Office Tower, at the level of the lowest microwave dishes" (14–15), later the plane finally passes "behind the tops of the trees" (16) (those same plane trees referred to in the initial quote), later still the plane "emerges from the trees, crosses a gap and disappears behind the Post Office Tower" (17), and further on in the text the plane finally "passes beyond the Tower" (18) and out of Perowne's view. It is quite clear, then, that this plane scene is constantly moving—at no point does it pause to allow for narratorial physical description—and so it must be concluded that the duration of narrative time has indeed been stretched.

McEwan again employs slowed scene in the second dramatic event of the novel—the post-car crash encounter with Baxter and his two thugs. Following a minor crash, where Baxter (clearly at fault) pulls out into Perowne's car in a deserted street, the four men (including Baxter's cronies, Nark and Nigel) slowly get out of their cars, assess the damage and come together in the street. The scene then follows the same technical pattern as that of the plane crash—short descriptions of action, such as "he turns his whole body towards Perowne" (91), are interspersed with, and thus strung out by, long sections of the full-sentenced and grammatical versions of Perowne's rapid-fire, adrenaline-filled, think-to-save-my-life mental maneuvering through which he desperately diagnoses Baxter's neurological medical condition and uses the man's illness to play the scene to his advantage:

> …Nark is already bunching his right fist. Perowne notes three rings on the index, middle and ring fingers, bands of gold as broad as sawn-off plumbing. He has, he reckons, a few seconds left. Baxter is in his mid-twenties. This isn't the moment to be asking for a family history. If a parent has it, you have a fifty-fifty chance of going down too. Chromosome four. The misfortune lies within a single gene, in an excessive repeat of a single sequence—CAG. Here's biological determinism in its purest form. More than forty repeats of that one little codon, and you're doomed. Your future is fixed and easily foretold. The longer the repeat, the earlier and more severe the onset. Between ten and twenty years to complete the course, from the first small alterations of character, tremors in the hands and face, emotional disturbance, including—most notably—sudden, uncontrollable alterations of mood, to the helpless jerky dance-like movements, intellectual dilapidation, memory failure, agnosia, apraxia, dementia, total loss of muscular control, rigidity sometimes, nightmarish hallucinations and a meaningless end. This is how the brilliant machinery of being is undone by the tiniest of faulty cogs, the insidious whisper of ruin, a single bad idea lodged in every cell, on every chromosome four.
>
> Nark is drawing back his right arm to strike. Nigel seems content to let him go first. Henry has heard that early onset tends to indict the paternal gene. But that may not be right. There's nothing to lose by making a guess. (93–4)

This excerpt reveals the desperation of the scene, during which Perowne is scared for his life. This is adrenaline-filled, rapid-fire thinking with action markers dispersed sporadically throughout the narrative to indicate that the scene is still moving rapidly. And yet the whole interaction is dragged out in the narrative across many pages. The phrases "Nark is already bunching his right fist" and "Nark is drawing back his right arm to strike"—action markers that can be assumed as happening in quick succession—are slowed, distended, squeezed apart by Perowne's complex reasoning as he intensely attempts to diagnose Baxter's condition. By the same token, one cannot imagine Nark pausing in silence with his right arm drawn back ready to strike while Perowne concludes his mental diagnosis, and so we must again deduce that Perowne's thoughts (four complete sentences which involve a weighing up of memories) all occur before Nark's forward motion commences. The duration of narrative time has thus been stretched to the form of slowed scene in order for the reader to witness the minute, fear-filled calculations Perowne makes during this very stressful event.

The third and final distended moment occurs nearing the end of the novel. Baxter and Nigel invade Perowne's home, put a knife to the throat of Perowne's wife Rosalind and hold the entire Perowne family hostage. This scene is incredibly out-of-the-ordinary for real life (though home invasions are quite common in the realms of literary fiction and film) and would be highly traumatic for all involved. Also, for Perowne only, this experience is an extension of his last traumatic event (the post-car crash encounter with Baxter). Yet this time the stakes are higher, with not only his own life threatened but also the lives of his entire family. Just like in that last scene, during this scene we read the rapid-fire mental calculations of Perowne as he attempts to find a way out of this potentially fatal situation by manipulating the expected aspects of Baxter's cognitive disease, and it is these thoughts—detailed in full—which again stretch the duration of narrative time to slowed scene. The excerpt below follows an interaction between Baxter and Perowne which results in Baxter punching Grammaticus and breaking his nose:

> Without a sound, without giving his attacker the satisfaction of a groan, Grammaticus covers his face with his hands. Blood trickles from just below his wristwatch.
>
> Until now, Henry suddenly sees, he's been in a fog. Astonished, even cautious, but not properly, usefully frightened. In his usual manner he's been dreaming—of "rushing" Baxter with [his son] Theo, of pepper sprays, clubs, cleavers, all stuff of fantasy. The truth, now demonstrated, is that Baxter is a special case—a man who believes he has no future and is therefore free of consequences. And that's simply the frame. Within it are the unique disturbances, the individual expression of his condition—impulsiveness, poor self-control, paranoia, mood swings, depression balanced by outbursts of temper, some of this, or all of it and more, would have helped him, stirred him, as he reflected on his quarrel with Henry this morning. And it will be driving Baxter on now. There's no obvious intellectual deterioration yet—the emotions go first, along with the physical coordination. Anyone with significantly more than forty CAG repeats in the middle of an obscure gene on chromosome four is obliged to share this fate in their own particular way. *It is written.* No amount of love, drugs, Bible classes or prison sentencing can cure Baxter or shift him from his course. It's spelled out in fragile proteins, but it could be carved in stone, or tempered steel.
>
> Rosalind and Daisy are converging on John Grammaticus...(209–10)

One cannot imagine a lengthy pause with no action between an elderly man being assaulted and his daughter and granddaughter rushing to his aid, no matter what the circumstances. In fact, had there been this pause (which would have allowed for careful consideration of the situation), calm, strong and intelligent Rosalind and Daisy might have thought such an action ill advised, given the family are being held at knifepoint. As such, one can only assume that the rushing to aid occurs fairly immediately after the breaking of the nose, and yet we have a long paragraph of Perowne's thoughts interrupting the two action markers. These are in-the-moment thoughts—they are temporally progressive, and so do not pause the action of the scene. Instead, Perowne's complex and developing mental maneuvering serves to expand the duration of narrative time, just as he feels this crisis moment expanding around him.

There is one pivotal moment at the conclusion of this scene in which Perowne specifically acknowledges how his experience of story time expands beyond "the normal." Perowne and his son Theo throw Baxter down the stairs and Perowne consciously contemplates in real time the experience of the relativity of time: "There's a moment, which seems to unfold and luxuriously expand, when all goes silent and still, when Baxter is entirely airborne, suspended in time, looking directly at Henry with an expression, not so much of terror, as dismay" (227). The airborne Baxter flying through the air toward near-fatal injury—captured in this moving, yet slowed, moment of "not yet" (but impending) ruin, of terror and dismay—stealthily echoes the opening moment of slowed scene as the plane burns "slowly" to earth. These two scenes, each containing an object moving incredibly slowly through the air, indicate the powerful and ideal story event for slowed scene contained within the depiction of the almost-frozen (yet still-moving) airborne object. It is this floating object—always moving toward its doom, yet resisting such a fate through a perceived slowing—that reveals the power of thought and subjective experience to resist the laws of gravity and momentum, to bend them to the will of the relativity of time. Dramatic and traumatic though the entire home invasion event is as Perowne is experiencing it, it is only in this freed moment—when the immediate threat is removed and so he does not have to speedily calculate for his and his family's futures—that he can acknowledge the stretch of his moment as the characters are slowly thrown toward their inevitable conclusions.

Conclusion

Science has given McEwan much to work with—he obviously greatly respects the discipline and goes out of his way to study it intensely. Yet McEwan does not privilege science above literature in his work, instead choosing in *Saturday* to confound the findings of the one-track scientific mind within the literary form. McEwan has created a protagonist who is steadfastly determinist, yet the author has given him powerful opposition in the arts figures of his family who hail from the world of the experimental, the interpretive, rather than the determined. In placing before us the alternatives of the debate, McEwan's novel suggests that we question Perowne's beliefs—just when Perowne "knows" that he has figured out Baxter, he is surprised by Baxter's choices. Perowne does, in fact, go to bed at the end of the day believing once again in determinism. But we finish the book questioning Perowne's beliefs. For the reader, one man's consciousness has illuminated the debate on determinism versus choice—a consciousness bent on determinism, tantalized by, yet dismissive of, the concept of choice, and this consciousness deliciously delivered to us through literature, through a medium of interpretation, gray areas, and decidedly on the side of free will (and yet, ironically, highly determined by the author). *Saturday* treads the line between the two so-called extremes, bringing them closer through a delicate weaving of scientific and literary themes within the literary form.

It is in his three distended moments that McEwan really reveals his love of scientific theory as well as the literary form. Literature and the sciences have both long been fascinated by the relativity of perception, and the use of slowed scene allows McEwan a technical means through which to explore this converging interest of the two disciplines. These slowed scene moments allow the author to skillfully embed in his text the theory of the relativity of time as experienced by the human mind, using the science to aid his creation of a new variation of the literary techniques associated with the exploration of character consciousness in moments of crisis. McEwan has thus enthusiastically allowed cognitive science to shape his art, to aid his getting more thoroughly into his characters' heads in their traumatic moments, and thus to replicate character experience for his readership through a skillful manipulation of narrative.

In his article on neuronarratives, Johnson stresses content over form for this subgenre, arguing that authors striving to represent consciousness is nothing new (he refers to the modernists as a prime example), but that this new subgenre has come to reflect and explain the advancements of cognitive science through story elements instead. However, McEwan's neuronarrative is not simply an exploration of recent advancements in cognitive science through content or theme. Rather, the author also allows a current scientific understanding of cognition and consciousness to inform his literary preoccupation with the narrative detailing of character perception. McEwan thus imbues *Saturday* with his fascination with this field of cognitive science, using the science to shape the literary discourse as well as the story.

Notes

1 Gary Johnson, "Consciousness as Content: Neuronarratives and the Redemption of Fiction," *Mosaic* 41, no. 1 (2008): 171.
2 Johnson, "Consciousness as Content," 170.
3 Robert Mighall, "Diagnosing Jekyll: The Scientific Context to Dr Jekyll's Experiment and Mr Hyde's Embodiment," *The Strange Case of Dr Jekyll and Mr Hyde and Other Tales of Terror*, ed. Robert Mighall (London: Penguin Books, 2002), 161; 145.
4 Ian McEwan, *Saturday* (London: Vintage Books, 2006), 19. Hereafter cited in text.
5 Johnson, "Consciousness as Content," 174.
6 Johnson, "Consciousness as Content," 174.
7 C. P. Snow, *The Two Cultures* (Cambridge: Cambridge University Press, 2007), 4.
8 Cited in Jon Cook, Sebastian Groes, and Victor Sage, "Journeys without Maps: An Interview with Ian McEwan," *Ian McEwan: Contemporary Critical Perspectives*, ed. Sebastian Groes (London: Continuum, 2009), 128.
9 To cherry-pick a few notable examples: Brian Boyd's use of genetics and evolutionary science (what he calls "evocriticism" (384)); Kay Young and Jeffrey Saver's use of neurobiology; Alan Palmer's use of cognitive psychology and philosophy of mind in his theories of intermental thought and the social mind; Lisa Zunshine's scientifically derived Theory of Mind. See: Brian Boyd, *On the Origin of Stories: Evolution, Cognition, and Fiction* (Cambridge, MA: Belknap Press of Harvard University Press, 2009); Kay Young and Jeffrey Saver, "The Neurology of Narrative," *SubStance* 30, nos. 1–2 (2001): 72–84; Alan Palmer, *Fictional Minds* (Lincoln, NE: University of Nebraska Press, 2004); Lisa Zunshine, *Why We Read Fiction: Theory of Mind and the Novel* (Columbus, OH: Ohio State University Press, 2006).
10 Cited in Cook, Groes, and Sage, "Journeys without Maps," 127.

11 It is not my intention to misappropriate the physics, but rather to explore the implications for a novelist who is genuinely concerned with the human mind and its scientific, phenomenological, cognitive functions. For an exploration of the strict physics of the Theory of Special Relativity, see David Mermin's *Space and Time in Special Relativity* (Prospect Heights, IL: Waveland Press, 1989).

12 Examples of this technique can be found in McEwan's novels, *Atonement* and *Saturday*, and in his novella, *On Chesil Beach*. *Atonement* and *On Chesil Beach* contain one such scene each (the fountain scene as focalized through Cecilia (25–31), and the premature ejaculation scene (104–7), respectively). For an analysis of the distended scenes in these two works, see Hannah Courtney, "Narrative Temporality and Slowed Scene: The Interaction of Event and Thought Representation in Ian McEwan's Fiction," *Narrative* 21, no. 2 (2013): 180–97.

13 Dominic Head, *The Cambridge Introduction to Modern British Fiction, 1950–2000* (Cambridge: Cambridge University Press, 2002), 235.

14 Sebastian Groes, "A Cartography of the Contemporary: Mapping Newness in the Work of Ian McEwan," *Ian McEwan: Contemporary Critical Perspectives*, ed. Sebastian Groes (London: Continuum, 2009), 2. My emphasis added.

15 Matt Ridley, "Foreword: Ian McEwan and the Rational Mind," *Ian McEwan: Contemporary Critical Perspectives*, vii.

16 Ridley, "Foreword," viii.

17 Laura Marcus, "Ian McEwan's Modernist Time: *Atonement* and *Saturday*," *Ian McEwan: Contemporary Critical Perspectives*, 83.

18 Marcus, "Ian McEwan's Modernist Time," 83.

19 Gerard Genette, *Narrative Discourse: An Essay in Method*, trans. Jane E. Lewin (Oxford: Basil Blackwell, 1980), 95.

20 Genette, *Narrative Discourse*, 95.

21 Monika Fludernik mentions "*stretch*," "*slow-down*" and "*time-extending narration*" in her work (33); Mieke Bal refers to the category of "slow-down" (yet hedges by saying it "occurs very seldom … [and it is d]ifficult if not impossible" (106)); Seymour Chatman makes mention of "stretch" (72); Fludernik and Chatman both claim that thoughts or "the portrayal of mental processes" can be the cause of this variation in the duration of narrative time (Fludernik, 33). See: Monika Fludernik, *An Introduction to Narratology*, trans. Patricia Häusler-Greenfield and Monika Fludernik (London: Routledge, 2009); Mieke Bal, *Narratology: Introduction to the Theory of Narrative*, 2nd ed. (Toronto, ON: University of Toronto Press, 1997); Seymour Chatman, *Story and Discourse: Narrative Structure in Fiction and Film* (Ithaca, NY: Cornell University Press, 1978).

12

A Loose Democracy in the Skull:
Characterology and Neuroscience

Julian Murphet

Where is my mind,
Where is my mind,
Where is my mind?

—The Pixies

I

It would be arguable that neuroscience represents the greatest challenge to representations of the subject, the self, since Freud; a claim that immediately provokes the question of whether there has been a Breton, a Buñuel or an Ernst to make good on the challenge. Whatever one thinks about the success or failure of Surrealism, on its own terms it undoubtedly took the gauntlet thrown down by Freud, married it with a bicycle and an ironing board and used the amalgam to assail that great fetish of bourgeois civility, the ego. One of the most productive instigations for artistic innovation ever to have emerged from the *other scene* of science, psychoanalysis sent shock waves across the entire cultural and literary landscape of modernity, and it did so by presenting the psyche as nonunitary, multiple. Where "I" had been, there now went along with it the "it," the "Id," in the midst of whose ferocious pulsions the ego bobbed and tipped like a *bateau ivre*. It provided an exemplary stage on which to present new figurations, new combinations, new rhetorics of a self *uncoincident with itself*. Not confined to effects in Surrealism, this new science of the nonunitary psyche generated a complete reinvention of the representational economy of the subject.

What, then, of today's cognitive sciences? The rather staggering numbers are in:

What do we find in the brain? Billions of neurons (around twenty billion in humans) connected in a network of innumerable links, the synapses. "The human brain," says Changeux, "makes one think of a gigantic assembly of tens of billions of interlacing neuronal 'spider's webs' in which myriads of electrical impulses flash by, relayed from time to time by a rich array of chemical signals." These "spider's webs," neuronal connections also called "arborizations," are constituted progressively over the course of an individual's development.[1]

Confronted with such a dizzying multiple in our very midst and at our very foundation as thinking, feeling and acting beings, what has art, what has literature, to offer? Marco Roth's 2009 article in *n*+1, "Rise of the Neuronovel," provides one somewhat demoralizing answer. Roth's case is that the current spate of novels in awe of the marvels of brain science derives its real tenacity not from the sublime materiality of neural "arborization," but from a cool shift in the intellectual climate of the times, away from "environmental and relational theories of personality back to the study of brains themselves, as the source of who we are."[2] The abandonment of psychoanalysis, sociology and high theory plays into the hands of what he terms a reactionary "new reductionism of mind to brain" that displays two principal coordinates: "it explain[s] proximate causes of mental function in terms of neurochemistry, and ultimate causes in terms of evolution and heredity." Novelists, Roth claims, have contributed to this reductionism in a sequence of works beginning with Ian McEwan's *Enduring Love* (1997; which features Clérambault's syndrome) and progressing through Jonathan Lethem's *Motherless Brooklyn* (1999; Tourette's), Mark Haddon's *Curious Incident of the Dog in the Night Time* (2003; autism), McEwan's own *Saturday* (2005; Huntington's corea), John Wray's *Lowboy* (2009; paranoid schizophrenia) and Richard Powers' *The Echo Maker* (2006; which confronts facial agnosia and Capgras syndrome, and about which I will want to say more in a moment).

Roth's complaints about the "neuronovel" are all fairly standard: the view of human character endorsed by these novels, though troubled by ambivalence here and there, is effectively reductionist in the crude sense, and leaves the vocation of literary style and form little to do but strive to mimic various species of mental disorder and abnormality. Roth concludes that:

> Any possibility of the necessary interpretive leap is disavowed by the pathological premise of the novel itself. By turning so aggressively inward, to an almost cellular level, this kind of novel bypasses the self, let alone society, or history, to arrive at neurology: privacy without individuality. And the deep logic of the story is likewise not one of irony or fate or comeuppance, but simple contingency; the etiology of a neurological condition is biological, not moral. And mere biological contingency has a way of repelling meaning.[3]

But these criticisms are themselves rather naïve and perhaps insensitive to the real lessons at stake in this literary trend. On the one hand, the "cellular level" of the self could turn out to be far more interesting and inspiring to thought and representation than Roth allows. On the other hand, though Roth wants to protect the novel as a form from these incursions from the domain of science, to resist the "diminishing purview" of the novelist's art and to restore the mysteries of selfhood on which the modern novel rested so grandly, it may turn out that the battle was lost long ago.[4] These novels are perhaps confessions of a larger imaginative defeat that is not a matter of personal courage or vision, but seems structural and objective in a manner that I have tried to explain elsewhere.⁵ The dereliction of these writers is not moral or individual, but of the contemporary essence of the novel as an institution: for the novel has nothing further to teach us about "consciousness" at all, and has not for some time. It is time we realized this fact.

Let's look a little more closely at Richard Powers' 2006 National Book Award winner, *The Echo Maker*. It's not a novel that can be faulted for its ambition, since far from wanting to remain trapped at the microscopic level of neural trauma and brain maps, it actively seeks an allegorical correspondence of that terrain with the ecological devastation of unchecked urban development, on the one hand, and the United States' participation in Afghanistan and the second Iraq war, on the other. In that sense, the condition of Capgras syndrome—a disorder in which subjects fail to recognize their loved ones, and violently react to them as body-snatcher-like replicants—is a lively conceit for ecological and geopolitical thinking. America's inability to recognize "the friend" who is the neighbor (be it a Muslim or a magnificent species of crane) is the avowed subject of the book. The accident that renders abattoir-worker Mark Schluter incapable of recognizing his closest family member (his sister) is more or less coterminous with 9/11; and the progress of the syndrome charts a vicious development in the nation's contract with its own citizens, and the economy's with its ecology. But, disappointingly, all of this is made to turn on the arrival and intervention of a world-famous neuroscientist, whose pop-scientific books take an Oliver Sachs-like, wide-eyed and basically affirmative view of the brain's plastic powers of flexible adaptation. It is not that this character, who undergoes his own dissolution as the novel progresses, is made to deliver any final verdict or cure; it is that the cozy neuroscientific optic he brings lends novelistic credence to a view of the human subject that the book wants to endorse as hegemonic, but leave untouched formally. That view is simply this: we now know what the brain is, more or less, and the challenge remaining is to *integrate* that knowledge with the business of narrative and stylistic novel-work. Integration is the key: no importation of knowledge can be allowed to disrupt the mechanisms of plot and characterization so far that these bread-and-butter functions of the novel effectively self-destruct.

But the science knows better than that. There is an extraordinary description of the brain's topography in the novel, voiced internally by the sister, Karin Schluter, who marvels at her own inner constitution by a plurality of brain parts:

> She took the combat inside herself, all possible positions banging around the loose democracy in her skull. How many brain parts had Weber's books described? A riot of free agents; five dozen specialties in the prefrontal bit itself. All those Latin-named life-forms: the olive, the lentil, the almond. Seahorse and shell, spiderweb, snail, and worm. Enough spare body parts to make another creature: breasts, buttocks, knees, teeth, tails. Too many parts for her brain to remember. Even a part named the unnamed substance. And they all had a mind of their own, each haggling to be heard above the others. Of course she was a frenzied mess; everyone was.⁶

What is left of the old humanist "self" in this dispensation? Professor Weber remarks in a lecture that "We think we have access to our own states; everything in neurology tells us that we do not. We think of ourselves as a unified, sovereign nation. Neurology suggests that we are a blind head of state, barricaded in the presidential suite, listening only to handpicked advisors as the country reels through ad hoc mobilizations" (*EM*, 460). At its most inventive, stylistically, the book strives to present for us what it might be to experience this subjectless being-in-the-world on its own terms, without the myth of a "self" to prop it up:

> The self was a painting, traced on that liquid surface. Some thought sent an action potential down an axon. A little glutamate jumped the gap, found a receptor in the target dendrite, and triggered an action potential in the second cell. But then came the *real* fire: the action potential in the receiver cell kicked out a magnesium block from another kind of receptor, calcium flowed in, and all chemical hell broke loose. Genes activated, producing new proteins, which flowed back to the synapse and remodelled it. And that made a new memory, the canyon down which thought flowed. Spirit from matter. Every burst of light, every sound, every coincidence, every random path through space changed the brain, altering synapses, even adding them, while others weakened or fell away from lack of activity. The brain was a set of changes for mirroring change. Use or lose. Use *and* lose. You chose, and the choice unmade you.(*EM*, 484)

This is all very fine, and draws on a dense web of metaphorical conditioning in order to unpack the wonders of Metzinger's, Pinker's, Damasio's and Dennett's work in neuroscience.[7] But is it, after all, a representation of consciousness? Not at all, since "we do not have access" to any of this at the level of subjectivity. The divide between what we know about the brain and what the brain can know about itself at the level of consciousness is absolute, and that is just as well for the novel form, which can then accept this partition as constitutive. Karin's brain, aptly, can't remember how many parts it has. As Todd Feinberg has put it, "There is no way the subject, from the 'inside,' can become aware of his own neurons, from the 'inside.' They can be known only objectively, from the 'outside.' There is no inner eye watching the brain itself, perceiving neurons and glia."[8] What Powers' passage represents is not consciousness, but the mechanics underlying consciousness; here, as everywhere, the "self" goes missing. The scandal of an innermost multiplicity—of brain parts, and beneath them, of axons and dendrites in their several billions, from which a sovereign agency or center of consciousness has been subtracted—is a scandal that confronts the residually humanist novel in its innermost recesses. But the novel refuses that confrontation in its form.

The Echo Maker restages and reneges on this scandal in the form of a nostalgia for the "case history," which is shorthand for the function of narrative, and of language, in both the diagnostic and remedial frames. Professor Weber reminisces about his own coming of intellectual age in a climate of faith in "the talking cure," and thus of language and the literary as such, in the teeth of a new positivist dawn from which language has been violently subtracted. This is, of course, a self-referential, allegorical lament for the fate of the novel and fiction today. But it seems in curiously bad faith, given the radical map of the mind that has been vouchsafed to otherwise capable narrative hands in this novel. There seems to be a threshold of multiplicity beyond which the "talking cure," and the humanist literature that evolved in its wake, cannot meaningfully go: as witness the ultimate form of Powers' own novel, which plays so intriguingly with the limit of this threshold, but recoils into the bland consolations of well-managed plot and seamless affective closure.

Karin's vision of her own inner multitudinousness leaves her, and literature, in an awkward spot: "Too many parts for her brain to remember. Even a part named the unnamed substance. And they all had a mind of their own, each haggling to be heard above the others" (*EM*, 439). This passage is not describing a pathology or a syndrome; it is simply attempting to configure the real absence of what free indirect discourse like this is always presuming in its midst: the locus of a stable point, a "one," or a "she," who is in a position to assemble the parts and make up some singular subject from literary experience. In place of that singularity, we have a brushing against the threshold of an illusion, or what Metzinger calls the "lack of information" that sustains subjectivity: "Phenomenal selfhood results from autoepistemic closure in a self-representing system; it is a lack of information."[9] Karin suddenly grasps the radical lack of information that is her "self"—only she does so externally—at a safe distance from what it might be like actually to inhabit that lack from the inside. That is what the character of her brother is for. Where Powers' novel fails is in its inability to commit itself to that level of destabilization within the space of a single discourse-zone or character, and its decision to bifurcate the lack of information into a brother-object/sister-subject of that lack. Powers opts for a pathology rather than an ontology of the multiple. Stranded in a nostalgia for psychoanalysis, rightly disdainful of pharmaceutical remodeling, *The Echo Makers*, nevertheless, capitulates to a novelistic fail-safe position just outside the "loose democracy" inside the skull of every subject (*EM*, 439).

Now, while I have every sympathy with Fredric Jameson's axiomatic position in *A Singular Modernity* that "consciousness and subjectivity are unrepresentable,"[10] my feeling is that it rather fudges what is at stake in modernity's ambitions and intentions with regard to that impossibility. It is telling that Jameson approaches the question of what the subject *is* from the direction of philosophy—Descartes and Heidegger are his favored examples—but sidesteps the question of what *science* knows about that substance of consciousness. The Cartesian *cogito* and Heidegger's *Dasein*—does anybody really care anymore? If that were all that representation was faced with, I shouldn't wonder that it might turn its back: they are unrepresentable in advance. The thorny question is not how adequate the exhausted *cogito* is to the consciousness it once promised to figure, but, far more radically, what artistic representation is going to make of the figures of subjectivity fashioned by neuroscience; just as it was previously, what art would make of the Unconscious? That is to say, it is indeed *impossible* to produce a meaningful representation of the "arborescence" of neural webs consisting of billions of electrochemical discharges and elegant interconnective glissades across brain-regions each second, let alone of how that transmogrifies into the reflexive self-presence of singular consciousness. And yet, neuroscience has drawn a very rich and compelling picture of that inner world, that *inland empire* of sublime multiplicity, and we are ourselves always in the act of somehow drawing it all together into a composite sense of integrity. Amidst it all, the self exists, and persists. The multiple brain represents itself to itself as "one"; and this representation is its greatest self-preserving act, its "will to power" as an organism of many. In so doing, it raises itself to Hegelian heights, to invoke Malabou:

> the transition from a purely biological entity to a mental entity takes place in the struggle of the one against the other, producing the truth of their relation. Thought is therefore nothing but nature, but a negated nature, marked by its own difference from itself. The world is not the calm prolonging of the biological. The mental is not the wise appendix of the neuronal.
>
> (*WDB*, 81)

The brain's astonishing multiple cancels itself out in the unlikely singular of a human being aware of itself as an integrity, a "loose democracy," a count-as-one.[11] Consequently, there is a vocation for art and literature to work within the space of that insupportable, miraculous, constant act, and find mimetic means for its re-presentation. If there is "no way the subject, from the 'inside,' can become aware of his or her own neurons, from the 'inside,'" that very bar or *no way* opens up strategic possibilities for artistic experimentation.

As we have seen, the novel is not the place for that effort. The institutionalization of its form, its rigid descent into orthodoxy and tired convention, has forced it into an impasse: it must draw intellectual substance from the new frontier of brain science—but our collective resistance to that gives rise to a situation in which "the brain is our work, and we do not know it" (*WDB*, 10). And yet, since it cannot risk its commercially viable form by acceding to what that substance has to teach, the novel "integrates" neuroscience at the level of content, without allowing that science's representations of the psyche, tethered at all points to an organic sublime, to interfere with its insipid and reactionary formal "business as usual."

II

If the novel is not the institutional or artistic space in which to propose genuine representational thoughts about the brain, what is? Some years ago, Gilles Deleuze argued that, despite the novel's constitutive relationship with what we generally take to be the proper domains of thinking—narration, description, characterization—it was postwar cinema that most successfully came to terms with the brain as an *object of thought*. Lauding Stanley Kubrick ("the world itself is a brain, there is identity of brain and world"[12]), Alain Resnais ("a cinema which is cerebral or intellectual but not abstract, because it is clear to what extent feeling, affect, or passion are the principal characters of the brain-world," *C2*, 209–10) and Eisenstein ("the cerebral whole which brought together pathos and the organic," *C2*, 210), Deleuze heralded neuroscience for opening a new and uncertain dominion of thought. He argued, provocatively, that the cinema could be said to have "always already" responded to this domain of thought with apposite imagery. Commenting on what science had disclosed as "cuts in the continuous network of the brain;…micro-fissures which were not simply voids to be crossed, but random mechanisms introducing themselves at each moment between the sending and receiving of an association message" (*C2*, 211), Deleuze hazarded the striking proposition that this "acentered" figuration of the brain-work in science could well have been "obscurely guided" by the way our relationship with our brain had "changed," thanks in large part to the formal lessons of these cinematic masters (*C2*, 212). Though he says nothing on this score, that proposition would find sustenance in the truly extraordinary degree to which brain science, in its public outreach program, is haunted by the metaphor of cinema: as if, in making its path-breaking statements about neural networks, plasticity and autopoiesis, neuroscience had no better figurative resource than the movies. As Slavoj Žižek paraphrases Metzinger on the brain's cinematic autopoesis, "a cave projects itself onto the cave wall, and *it generates-simulates the observer itself*";[13] while Damasio asks, "how the owner of the movie-in-the-brain emerges within the movie."[14]

Perhaps the cinema is the medium in which the "lived brain" first, and best, came to be thought. That is, a brain whose form is that "of a multiple, fragmentary organization, an ensemble of micro-powers more than the form of a central committee" (*WDB*, 36), and experienced immanently as a "continual [process of] relinked parcellings" (*C2*, 213), would have found for itself no better re-presentation than a cinema in which these relinkings and momentary arborescent ensembles are reconfigured as time-images relayed across networks of association, intrareferentiality and transition. This line of thinking cuts directly against the predominant mode of acceptance of the cognitive sciences into film theory, which involves utterly tedious enumerations of forced "correspondences" between narrative events on screen and extrinsic cognitive concepts. Deleuze's arresting point is that film *thinks* brain science immanently, according to its own protocols, and yields for us a working image of the brain as an object of thought. And it does so, of course, at the level of form, not of "content."

This, at least, would be one way of coming to terms with what has been a veritable explosion of contemporary films—at either end of the "artistic" spectrum—concerned with the experience of identity in a mode of crisis, and often unafraid to map that experiential crisis on (bowdlerized) neuroscientific coordinates. Garrett Stewart's remarkable and Deleuzian treatment of this mini-genre in terms of a wholesale transposition of the entire medium from celluloid stock to digital mainframes, in *Framed Time*, is still the go-to reference book for a cinema that projects its mediatic crisis in cognitive dress, and vice versa.[15] I will draw on and query only two points from that study here. First, I would suggest that the "division of labor" that Stewart specifies in this trend toward fractal digitime in world cinema, between the "ontological gothic of American thrillers," on the one hand, and the European art-cinema's "mnemonic uncanny of humanist fantasy," on the other, might be subject to a local deconstruction or two given the brain's contemporary dispersion across multiple, transnational, migratory paths.[16] Second, if "the digital can simulate the death of filmic cinema because it *is* that death" (*FT*, 53), then this, too, has specific repercussions at the level of neuroscience, as we are about to see. Stewart's analysis is the best guide to the contemporary cinema as an immanent *mappa mundi* of our brain-world, but doesn't quite want to admit it. Perhaps that is because he appears not yet to have encountered the artist who would press him to confront the logical consequences of his propositions.

First, however, it remains to establish some coordinates for what will follow. What neither Deleuze nor Stewart seems to have understood is that the brain itself, in its inner constitution, is a kind of infinitely looping media-space, in which the analog and the digital are incessantly passing into and out of one another. Given that (as I'll elaborate later) the "fold" between analog and digital media encourages a leap from a psychoanalytic problematic to a neurological one, it behooves us to focus very intently on this immanent makeup of the brain as a *medium* of thought, caught between a digital and an analog logic. This matters, quite literally, for debates about neuroscience, though it has yet to announce itself as a clarified problematic—thanks to the unquestioned dominance of the digital analogy. As Žižek puts it, "in cognitivism, human thinking itself is conceived as modelled after the functioning of a computer, so that the very gap between understanding (the experience of meaning, of the openness of world) and the 'mute' functioning of a machine potentially disappears."[17] The philosophical debate about whether or not one can legitimately make psychological claims about the brain is related at some outer limit to a for-or-against argument about the brain as the *hard drive* of human consciousness, with consciousness as some kind of epiphenomenal interface. The hard edge of contemporary neuroscience is supposedly dedicated to ridding us of every last illusion about consciousness and the mind as entities distinct from neurological processes, and seeks to transcode all conventional psychology into the digital microphysics of neurology.[18] The fact that this trend is historically coeval with our cultural and informational passage into full digitization should strike nobody as coincidental, since it hinges on an identical faith: in binary number as such, and the furthest extension of the analytic ratio into the very fibers of the human, transforming and transcoding it into data, information and code.

Polemics aside, science shows that the brain is a "unified field" of mixed media. The material substance of the brain (axons, neural somae, dendrites, synapses, etc.) is *continuous with itself*, distributively, characterizing this field as fundamentally *analog* in nature. The brain is analog at the level of its *materiel*: embodied, actual, isomorphic. But the switching process, that determines whether or not a neuron will fire down its axon, is essentially a *digital* matter. We need to pause and take the full measure of this crux. Any cursory understanding of neurological sequences—of the passage of chemical and electrical impulses between neurons in webs of billions and billions, in every central nervous system, all the time—must grasp this intricately woven media system as analog in form, but digital in actuation. What the tree-like dendrites with all their chemoreceptors and voltage-dependent sodium channels *receive* as "information" from other neurons is isomorphic with those signals; or again, the nerve signals that the axons carry away from the somae which have processed that information are similarly isomorphic with it. In either case, we are in the presence of an indexical chain of causality: far from being a distinct or "coded" form of the message they deliver, the chemical and electrical impulses *are* that message. A synapse is thus an analog signal. And yet its pulse mechanism, the critical decision about whether or not any synapse will be enacted at all, is ineluctably digital.

Most advanced artificial intelligence work since the end of the 1980s—and the real collapse then of the digital model—recognizes that analog synapses are the key to long-term emulative success. "A generic circuit, the charge controlled analog synapse (CCAS)...is designed to be the basic building block in microelectronic realizations of large scale artificial neural networks."[19] Such networks are superior to digital networks above all in that they provide memory, dynamic adaptability and all the critical components of intelligence. That they are analog is of the greatest importance. In most ANN (artificial neural network) work being done today, digital counters are still used, but are converted into pulse signals which then serve as the input to what remains a strictly analog synapse circuit—in other words a virtual digital-to-analog converter is in place at all times when digital processes are harnessed to the optimization of the ANN.[20] While researchers often acknowledge the heated competition from the digital environment, and the anachronistic hegemony of the digital as a popular analogy for brain sequencing, they maintain the necessity of remaining within analog circuits, for the most critical reasons: trainability, adaptability and memory. "To be successful while under a highly competitive pressure from the digital world, analog neural networks should not try to transfer digital concepts to the analog world. Instead they should rely on device physics as much as possible to allow an exploitation of the massive parallelism possible in modern VLSI technologies."[21] Even where combining digital information exchange with analog neuron operation, the "massive parallelism" offered by a developed analog neural network is of the utmost value in attaining the best results.

This is really as much to say that, like its most successful models, the brain is inherently a mixture of analog media and digital signals, analog in form but digital in pulse, and organically resistant in its processes, form, architecture and functions to the digital computation that orchestrates its incandescent branching. What neuroscience calls "plasticity," then, involves the capacity to combine analog and digital processes, constantly, in one unending operation of transcoding, allowing biochemical isomorphisms to be conducted by binary code, and vice versa, a trillion times per minute. The "gaps" and "breaks" in neural networks that Deleuze first elevated into film theory and philosophy are at the same time hiatuses at the threshold between discrete media logics: apt figurations, at the cellular level, of where we are with our media, our culture, our worlds.

Before we can launch into an analysis of a contemporary work of art that seems equal to these extraordinary challenges to representation, we need briefly to shift from the micrological to the macrological, to establish an equally important axis for the coordination of what follows. As Malabou perspicaciously elaborates, the profound extension of our understanding of the brain and its works in a networked space coincides historically with an equally profound reconstruction of the space of the social itself. "There is today an exact correlation between descriptions of brain functioning and the political understanding of commanding," Malabou writes (*WDB*, 32), drawing on the work of economic sociologists Luc Boltanski and Eve Chiapello to establish a direct correspondence between neural networks and the "new spirit of capitalism" itself: "neuronal functioning and social functioning interdetermine each other and mutually give each other form…, to the point where it is no longer possible to distinguish them. As though neuronal function were confounded with the natural operation of the world, as though neuronal plasticity anchored biologically—and thereby justified—a certain type of political and social organization" (*WDB*, 9). That organization, of post-Fordist *flexibility*, expects of the human organism an infinitely adaptable responsiveness to sudden shifts in the construction of political and industrial space, a quiescent but ecstatic docility before the administrative and financial terror of multinational capitalism.

What Malabou wants her own Hegelian cognitivism to undertake is a resistance to that flexibility in the name of a productive plasticity. Against what Richard Sennett memorably describes as the "corrosion of character" under a dominating regime of drift, flexibility and risk,[22] Malabou pitches what she sees as the extraordinarily liberating vision of a new "lived brain" implicit in neuroscience despite its frequent capitulation to governing ideologies of docility. The costs of carrying on with this capitulation are the ruin of the human. Sociologists and psychologists seem to concur on this.

> Whatever domain one considers (company, school, family), the rules of the world have changed. They are no longer obedience, discipline, and conformity to morals, but flexibility, change, reaction time, etc. The demand for self-mastery, affective and psychical suppleness, and capacities for action force each person to adapt continuously to a world without continuity, to an unstable, provisional world in flux, and to careers with ups and downs. The legibility of the social and political game is muddied. These institutional transformations give the impression that everyone, including the most fragile, must take up the task of choosing everything and deciding everything.[23]

This exhausting corrosion of the very fibers of a self—the terrible fatigue of being oneself, an inability to forge out of one's inner multiple something resembling a consistent, enduring, resilient core—tips over inevitably into pathology, on the one hand, and social exclusion, on the other. The figure of the interstitial depressive is now typical; Robert Castel thematizes

> the presence, apparently more and more insistent, of individuals who virtually drift about within the social structure, and who populate interstices of society without finding any established position within it. Vague silhouettes, at the margins of labor and at the frontiers of socially consecrated forms of exchange— the long-term unemployed, inhabitants of abandoned suburbs, recipients of a national minimum income, victims of industrial downsizing, young people in search of employment who carry themselves from place to place, from menial jobs to temporary work—who are these people, where did they come from, and what will become of them?[24]

The hazard in what now follows will be that these questions cannot be thought outside a cognitive problematic, which itself cannot be better thought than in the cinema, since it is there that the world and the brain have attained their maximal degree of mutual exposure, and there that the passage between analog and digital is framed at its greatest degree of aesthetic risk.

III

David Lynch's assorted musings on the "self" are not of the most edifying, though they are idiosyncratically synthetic. "The ocean of pure consciousness that Maharishi Mahesh Yogi talks about is also known by modern science as the Unified Field," he writes in *Catching the Big Fish*; and in a phrase that echoes at least something of the neuroscientific postulate of plasticity, he remarks, "It's not the intellectual understanding of the field but the experiencing of it that does everything. You dive within, and by experiencing this field of pure consciousness, you enliven it; you unfold it; it grows."[25] Let us agree, however, that inasmuch as David Lynch *thinks*, he does so as an artist, where these vague and faintly "ridiculous"[26] musings develop into extraordinarily sensitive aesthetic antennae, capable at their most rigorous of materializing this New Age "ocean of consciousness" into its correct neurological version: "constituted by cuts, by voids, by gaps," where "[n]ervous information must cross voids, and something aleatory thus introduces itself between the emission and the reception of a message, constituting the field of action of plasticity" (*WDB*, 36). The unity of the Unified Field, in the brain as in contemporary cinema, consists in intervals, blanks and sudden transferential leaps. Its ground is differential, and so is the self derived from it.

We should immediately observe that the cycle of feature-length works released by Lynch since 1997 (excluding the otherwise fascinating Disney film *The Straight Story*, 1999) consists of a trilogy whose subject is roughly what Garrett Stewart describes as the experience of "temporal paradox" and "temportation" due to subjective trauma (see *FT*, passim). Moreover, this is a trilogy in which the stakes are progressively raised (narratively, characterologically and aesthetically) around the unstated but implicit authorial confrontation with the "death of film" as a representational medium, and the resistless triumph of digital code and processing in the dissemination of visual spectacles. That is to say, the sequence of movies that runs *Lost Highway* (1997), *Mulholland Dr.* (2001) and *INLAND EMPIRE* (2006) stages a dialectic in which an originary "senseless complexity" and "schizophrenic nightmarish delirium with no logic or rules"[27]—the bare residuum of a vanished Surrealism on which Lynch builds the structure of *Lost Highway*—dovetails with an emergent thematic interest in psychological "fugue states," as characterological objects of paradoxical representation, and thence generates a frog-leaping dialectical progression in subsequent works.[28] What is particularly arresting is how, in this progressive radicalization of an already torqued aesthetic space, from film to film across the putative trilogy, the vortex engendered privileges two antinomial functions: the function of the protagonist *self-who-is-not-a-self* (the acentered, split or "fugue" subject) and the function of the *medium* itself (this is an "LA trilogy" that increasingly focuses on its own status as spectacle and "Hollywood"), in a mode of melancholy self-sacrifice and valediction.

The definitive rupture takes place across the border between that most exquisitely beautiful and perfect of Lynch's filmic object-fetishes, *Mulholland Dr.*, and the severe punk anti-aesthetic of *INLAND EMPIRE*, which is simultaneously the rupture between film and digital imaging, and between a psychoanalytic and a neuroscientific map of the brain.[29] The shock of *INLAND EMPIRE*, in the wake of *Mulholland Dr.*, cannot be overemphasized: it is the paradigmatic form of aesthetic disappointment, if your aesthetics are constructed around the category of the beautiful, rather than that of the sublime. The departure from celluloid, as the basis of cinematic beauty, is raised to an absolute. In *Catching the Big Fish*, Lynch writes, "I'm through with film as a medium. For me, film is dead."[30] Making movies with 35 mm film cameras and lighting was, he said at the New York premiere of *INLAND EMPIRE*, his first feature shot on DV, like "swimming through cold molasses."[31] And in *Wired* he put it this way: "Digital video is so beautiful. It's lightweight, modern, and it's only getting better. It's put film into the La Brea Tar Pits."[32] But when David Lynch says "beautiful," he doesn't mean it the way Kant did. What he actually means is that, even if film is "dead," it persists in digitally remediated cinematic form. The beauty of DV is its capacity to capture that undeath, to present itself as a radical kind of hybridity, a "fold" between what it is displacing, and what it, unspeakably, is: code, processing, network, pixel, rather than index, isomorphism, imprint and image. *INLAND EMPIRE* was shot on low-resolution DV, but up-resed and transferred to 35 mm stock for cinema release. It *is* the hybrid form that it is dreaming about, a digi-analog immanence, and in that, not unlike the brain itself.[33]

The brain is very much at issue here, in a manner that is of the greatest philosophical and aesthetic interest. The opening black-and-white close-up shot of an old-fashioned gramophone stylus, over which we hear the first words of the picture—a scratchy radio voice intoning, "Axxon N the longest running radio show in history…"—cuts to a slightly differently angled shot of the same needle superimposed with an obscure organic image of what looks like brain tissue. The digital image thus mediates an image of the brain as an analog storage device, captivated by narrative ("tonight, continuing in the Baltic region…") and thrown into the eerie ether of radio itself. As if that were not enough, this plunge into neuromedial immanence follows the title sequence, a single shot of the words INLAND EMPIRE emerging out of darkness. This induces our sociological unconscious, a dim awareness that Riverside, Ontario and San Bernadino Counties are where LA's "stuff" is stored, in a vast network of warehouses, storage facilities and transportation, and where low-wage working-class and service sector (un-)employment predominates. It further asks us to forge some connection between these two "inland empires," of labor and storage, of transportation and linkage. Indeed, I would argue that this precipitate shift from one order (sociological) to another (neurological) in the space of a single film-thought indicates the presiding rhetorical strategy of the film, connecting it genetically back to a Surrealism with which it wishes to enact both a traditional filiation and a radical break: namely, *anacoluthon*.

In any event, that strange signifier "Axxon N" recurs in the film at key moments of distress and anxiety for the protagonist, who variously goes by the names Nikki

Grace, Susan Blue, "L.B." and other, less defined and more provisional identities (another, characterological, anacoluthon), and whom it is preferable to address as the anonymous "woman in trouble."[34] Indeed, closer inspection reveals that the emergence of this signifier invariably provokes a radical shift in the circuitry of selfhood at work here, so that what Nikki first recalls as the unsettling appearance of this "writin' on metal," in chalk on a door in a back alley of Hollywood, suddenly precipitates her irreversible "fall" into Susan, whom she had until that point merely been playing in a comeback film vehicle, and then again, much later, seals the ultimate fate of Susan's transformation into "L. B.," the doomed Hollywood Boulevard hooker. Beyond that, "Axxon N" also signals the apotheosis in which this woman in trouble, the "owner of the movie-in-the-brain," that is, this movie, at last emerges *within the movie itself*: it is the inscription on the threshold of her own mental cinema. As we have noted, an axon is that long, thread-like part of a nerve cell along which impulses are conducted from the cell body to other cells—that is, it is the active medium between brain cells, the micro-organic "conductor" of impulses between cellular structures. This referential dimension of the cryptic signifier then joins another: the sense in which this sign is *purely material*, effectively a "zero" in the field of signification, a "syntactical plug" which triggers the shift between anacoluthic fragments. This is the stubborn reappearance of *the materiality of the letter* in Lynch's work, on which Michel Chion has written so suggestively.[35] The free-floating letter-scraps of *The Alphabet*, the letters under the fingernails and the "Fire Walk with Me" scrap in *Twin Peaks*, *Blue Velvet*'s love letter and more. Chion links the materiality of the letter, the alphabet system, in Lynch to a bodily fragmentation, a pulling apart of limbs and organs. It is also invariably a "formula" in Deleuze's sense: the letters themselves stutter, repeat and bend the space of inscription and subscription within their film worlds.[36] Their materiality is very literal. In *INLAND EMPIRE*, these letters—Axxon N—create a loop in film space, whereby analog media, electronic media, digital media and neural processing can unfold into each other, even as the woman in trouble cascades from one order of being into another.

Here, however, we are brought up short against an insistent political demand, a Real, which we can now see that the movie is approaching asymptotically. For the glissades of the woman in trouble are unidirectional: from an apex of class security as the wealthy actress-wife of a still wealthier Polish businessman to the far more straitened existence of a lower-middle-class inhabitant of the Inland Empire, still married to a Pole, but this one shabby and impecunious, and inclined to tour the Baltic region with a circus troupe; thence to a truly desperate interstitial figure ("L. B."), alone and having lost both a son and any employment on top of her marital desertion; and finally to a battle-hardened street whore of pure cynicism and *Thanatos*, stabbed to death at Hollywood and Vine with a rusty screwdriver. The logic of this descent is perfectly clear, in relation to what Sennett, Ehrenberg and Castel have to tell us about the "new spirit of capitalism's" emergent population of "vague silhouettes at the margins of labour," drifting casualties of enforced flexibility, who rather than bending have finally broken and imploded in the wreckage of their "psychological suppleness," to join the "increasing number of people who, in modern capitalism, are doomed to fail."[37] The woman in trouble's depressive "psychogenic fugue" state has radicalized to the point where she is literally unable (and we with her) to *coordinate her own being*, to discover a plasticity capable of integrating the ever-dissolving social roles made available to her, and then finally rescinded altogether.

What can we conclude about this extraordinary effort to offer an image of the "world brain" that is simultaneously so sensitive to the vast internal network of neurological sublimity, and to the sociological and economic space in which that immanent plasticity is driven against a merciless wall of "flexibility"? Let us suggest that what this movie gives us is neither a "neuro-realistic" characterization of a woman's experiences in terms of her brain processes (an impossible aim, other than as a meaningless neural map of the arboreal phosphorescence of suffering in a cerebral cortex) nor a "realistic" characterization of the same woman at the level of her objective experience, but something much more interesting and epochal. Namely, we are in an aesthetic space that might be described in terms of the torsion opened up in psychic/neuronal space by the very *transition* from one order of organization to another. That is to say, we see neither the brute organic source of a suffering experience (complex neurological networks) nor the typical "point of view" of a woman's suffering on screen (à la Lars von Trier), but what it might feel like to live on the border between one order of experience (neuronal) and the other (mental, conscious). We are not given anything like cinematic realism (an external view of experience—indeed it should be argued that we never "see" the woman in trouble outside of her own mental projections); instead we are given an entirely new and hypothetical phenomenality, poised on the threshold of its neurological coming-into-being.

This is exactly what Catherine Malabou insists that we are most in need of: a fourth order of plasticity, in which we can begin to speculate about and understand the Hegelian negation of nature that consciousness implies. She asks us to attend to the reality of an "organic tension" in nature itself, self-cancelling, at war with itself, as it rips a hole in its own fabric to admit consciousness. Lynch sets up his cinema at the very point where "*the owner of the movie-in-the-brain emerges within the movie*," and begins the necessary aesthetic work of wondering how that might happen in the first place, in an extremely complex and ambitious allegory. All that we see is immanent, located within the phenomenological self-presencing of an unnamed and (in any traditional sense) "unrepresented" woman in trouble: we do not see *her*; we see the various ways in which she has become a mental self-image. But that phenomenology is not fully adequate either, and in various ways, we feel the violent passage into the phenomenal by the neural itself, as what subtends and enables consciousness, but resists it absolutely. My sense is that this is the most compelling representation to date of the Unconscious, not the psychoanalytic, but the neurological Unconscious, as it were. Lynch's lifelong engagement with Surrealism has sublated itself.

What is more, he takes everything a step further still: he stands firm by his abiding conviction that the greatest power of the "brain" is its capacity for *fantasy*, which is to say, powerful mental phenomena that correspond to no stimuli or "cause" beyond the brain's own self-delight in representing them to itself. No doubt, Lynch's cinema has always been defined by its cast toward fantasy, its exploration of what Todd McGowan calls the "ethics of fantasy": Lynch lets us see "how the insistent devotion to one's fantasy thrusts the subject into the realm of freedom. Rather than being an imaginary retreat from an unpleasant reality, fantasy becomes for Lynch the path that takes us beyond the false limitations that make up our everyday reality. Through an absolute commitment to our fantasies, we change the nature of reality itself."[38] But here in *INLAND EMPIRE* we see something truly unprecedented: fantasy's traversal of the distance between a psychoanalytic and a neurological frame of reference. This is a traversal that enriches rather than impoverishes the form of fantasy. For it is the ultimate affirmation of his masterpiece that fantasy is a far greater power than flexibility—the brain of the woman in trouble finally exhibits an extraordinary plasticity, to the point of resisting death itself, in overcoming its sordid objectness and economic predestination. It passionately seeks a way back up the various layers of its dissociated digi-analog "selfhood," to force a synthesis and a reconciliation that is performed with an affective power far greater than resignation or defeat. She teaches us, in the profoundly moving final credit sequence, what it is possible to *do with our brain*, namely, trigger an explosive and cathartic release of utopian energy just at the point where the logic of domination had determined the death of her body; she musters the last of her body's forces in order to negate it altogether. Where before her dissociation had taken the form of *temporal* seriality, here she is multiplied, luridly and libidinally, into *spatially* cohabiting avatars, most of them women. She enters what we can justly name heaven: her brain's power of overcoming and loving itself, in a desperate, last-ditch stand against what history has made of her humanity, "mere life."

Notes

1   Catherine Malabou, *What Should We Do with Our Brain?* trans. Sebastian Rand (New York: Fordham University Press, 2008), 17–18. Hereafter cited in text as *WDB*.
2   Marco Roth, "Rise of the Neuronovel," nplusonemag.com/rise-neuronovel. Subsequent references are to this site.
3   Roth, "Rise of the Neuronovel."
4   Roth, "Rise of the Neuronovel."
5   See Julian Murphet, "The Mole and the Multiple: A Chiasmus of Character," *New Literary History* 42, no. 2 (Spring 2011): 255–76.
6   Richard Powers, *The Echo Maker* (London: Vintage, 2007), 439. Hereafter cited in text as *EM*.
7   See Thomas Metzinger, *The Ego Tunnel: The Science of the Mind and the Myth of the Self* (New York: Basic Books, 2010); Steven Pinker, *How the Mind Works* (New York: Norton, 2009); Antonio Damasio, *Self Comes to Mind: Constructing the Conscious Brain* (New York: Vintage, 2009); and Daniel C. Dennett, *Consciousness Explained* (New York: Black Bay Books, 1992).
8   Todd Feinberg, cited in Thomas Metzinger, *Being No One: The Self-Model Theory of Subjectivity* (Cambridge, MA: MIT Press, 2004), 177.
9   Metzinger, *Being No One*, 337.
10 Fredric Jameson, *A Singular Modernity: Essay on the Ontology of the Present* (London: Verso, 2002), 55.

11   Alain Badiou details the notion of the count-as-one in his *Being and Event*, trans.
     Oliver Feltham (New York: Continuum, 2005), 89–92; 504.

12   Gilles Deleuze, *Cinema 2: The Time-Image*, trans. Hugh Tomlinson and Robert Galeta
     (London: Athlone, 1989), 205. Hereafter cited in text as *C2*.

13   Slavoj Žižek, *The Parallax View* (Cambridge, MA: MIT Press, 2006), 219.

14   Antonio Damasio, *The Feeling of What Happens: Body and Emotions in the Making of
     Consciousness* (New York: Harcourt, Brace & Co., 1999), 313.

15   See Garrett Stewart, *Framed Time: Towards a Postfilmic Cinema* (Chicago: University
     of Chicago Press, 2007).

16   Stewart, *Framed Time*, 168. Hereafter cited in the text as *FT*.

17   Žižek, *The Parallax View*, 165.

18   Although cf. Catherine Malabou, who rightly asserts that the "cybernetic metaphor
     has... had its day" being dated "to the fifties and reigned until the end of the eighties."
     Malabou, *What Should We Do with Our Brain?*, 34.

19   Aharon J. Agranat, Offer Schwartsglass and Joseph Shappir, "The Charge Controlled
     Analog Synapse," abstract for *Solid-State Electronics* 39, no. 10 (October 1996):
     1435–9.

20   See, for example, Q. Chen, Q. Zheng, and W. Ling, "Implementation of an On-Chip
     Learning Artificial Neural Network," *Neural Network World* 12 (2002): 3–14.

21   Johannes Schemmel, Karlheinz Meier, and Felix Schurmann, "A VLSI Implementation
     of an Analog Neural Network suited for Genetic Algorithms," *ICES '01 Proceedings
     of the 4th International Conference on Evolvable Systems: From Biology to Hardware*
     (2001): 50–61.

22   Richard Sennett, *The Corrosion of Character: The Personal Consequences of Work in
     the New Capitalism* (New York and London: Norton, 1998).

23   Alain Ehrenberg, *La fatigue d'être soi: Dépression et société* (Paris: Odile Jacob, 1998),
     236; cited in Malabou, *What Should We Do with Our Brain?*, 49–50.

24   Robert Castel, *From Manual Workers to Wage Laborers: Transformation of the Social
     Question*, trans. and ed. Richard Boyd (New Brunswick: Transaction Publishers,
     2003), xv.

25   David Lynch, *Catching the Big Fish: Meditation, Consciousness, and Creativity*
     (New York: Jeremy Tarcher/Penguin, 2007), 47–8.

26   Žižek, *The Parallax View*, 159.

27   Slavoj Žižek, *The Art of the Ridiculous Sublime: On David Lynch's* Lost Highway
     (Seattle, WA: Walter Chapin Simpson Center for the Humanities, 2000), 14–15.

28   "And we found this great psychology term—'psychogenic fugue'—describing an event
     where the mind tricks itself to escape some horror. So, in a way, *Lost Highway* is about
     that. And also the fact that nothing can stay hidden forever." David Lynch, *Big Fish*, 109.

29   Lynch shot *INLAND EMPIRE*, himself, on a low-tech, handheld, domestic digi-
     video recorder (Sony PD-150), and constantly refers to its specificity, limitations
     and taboos in the feature. It is remarkable in this context how silent Žižek, Lynch's
     most outspoken Lacanian champion, has been on the subject of *INLAND EMPIRE*,
     evidently an unthinkable and unwatchable object in the frame erected around the
     Lynch corpus by psychoanalysis. But this, for us, is the very magnet of its interest.

30   Lynch, *Big Fish*, 149.

31   S. T. VanAirsdale, "Three Hours of Sleep: Lynch Unveils *INLAND EMPIRE* in
     New York: The vulgar courts the sublime in director's epic Hollywood fever dream,"
     7 October 2006, http://www.thereeler.com/features/three_hours_of_sleep_lynch.php.

32 "David Lynch Interviews–Uncut: Interview with David Lynch No. 1 March 10, 2006," 1 February 2007, http://www.wired.com/culture/lifestyle/news/2007/01/72391?curren tPage=all.

33 Moreover, the movie meditates extensively on analog and electronic media as objects of melancholy digital representation: a recurrent phonograph stylus, cathode-ray TV sets, radio and the apparatus of film production itself.

34 Lynch has referred to Laura Dern's character this way.

35 See Michel Chion, *David Lynch*, trans. Robert Julian, 2nd ed. (London: BFI, 2006), 152.

36 See Gilles Deleuze, "Bartleby; or, The Formula," *Essays Critical and Clinical*, trans. Daniel W. Smith and Michael A. Greco (Minneapolis, MN: University of Minnesota Press, 1997), 68–90.

37 Sennett, *Corrosion of Character*, 135.

38 Todd McGowan, *The Impossible David Lynch* (New York: Columbia University Press, 2007), 223–4.

Afterword: Turn and Turn About

Paul Giles

The central theme of this eclectic and engaging collection of chapters is, as the editors point out on the first page of their introduction, to examine ways in which over recent years "literary critics have increasingly drawn insights from cognitive neuroscience to deepen and clarify our understanding of the value of literature." One key word here is *value*: many of the contributors seek to justify the special qualities of literary creation, implicitly playing this off against a fiscal environment the world over where, for popular political reasons, funding resources are far more frequently being directed toward medicine and other forms of science. This sense of the study of literature as an embattled enterprise lends a certain polemical edge to some of these chapters, as, for example, in Brian Boyd's attempt to validate the affective power of close reading, exemplified for him by the figure of Vladimir Nabokov, to whose texts Boyd attributes a "multilevel awareness of the mind." In his earlier monograph, *On the Origin of Stories: Evolution, Cognition, and Fiction*, Boyd had sought to associate a "biocultural approach to literature" with "a return to the richness of texts and the many-sidedness of the human nature that texts evoke," describing this as "a first truly comprehensive literary theory" in the way it aspired to displace the putatively dehumanizing, noncorporeal abstractions of Boyd's particular *bêtes noires*, French linguistic theorists such as Jacques Derrida or Jacques Lacan. In attempting to reclaim the idea of fiction as "central to human life," Boyd thus seeks to defend "literary studies" against contemporary charges of irrelevance or redundancy, and his contribution to this volume usefully contributes to a pragmatic defense of literary studies as both idea and practice.[1]

Such engaged polemic, however, does inevitably come at a price. The use of the word "origin" in the title of Boyd's book, *On the Origin of Stories*, hints at the kind of unreconstructed essentialism of which many critics have been wary, and his argument also runs the risk of equating "biocultural" narratives with an embodiment of literal truth. Indeed, a few of these chapters risk reading contemporary cognitive neuroscience as if it were a *deus ex machina*, a sudden revelation of immanent purpose in a naughty world. Moreover, the various invocations here of some kind of scientific "turn"—reading through the book, I counted a cognitive turn, a postsecular turn, a posthuman turn, a performative turn, a Heideggerian turn, a theological turn—suggest ways in which literary scholarship has sought increasingly to justify itself in formal terms through a scientific rhetoric of discovery and breakthrough. In the most reductive sense of this formula, individual readings are always subordinated to larger "turns" of one kind or another, just as in the eyes of funding bodies the vagaries of literature are almost by definition subordinated to the harder systems of science. From this perspective, it is easy to infer how science has impacted upon the language as much as the substance of cultural criticism, an event that has occurred, one suspects, for institutional as much as intellectual reasons: in an environment where resources are scarce, researchers in the humanities find it expedient to refer their findings to a discursive framework of scientific progress in an attempt to enhance the value of their academic labor. In a peculiarly Australasian configuration of this issue, John Sutton and Evelyn B. Tribble in this volume suggest analogies between the "situated, distributed, dynamical, and embodied" field of cognitive sciences and the "group agency" typical of "elite sporting teams." For Sutton and Tribble, such group agency would allow us to move beyond "individualist" assumptions to embrace "self-organization in the collective." Probably nothing would please politicians or university administrators more than if literary writers and scholars could be coached and managed as if they were members of the "All Blacks" rugby team intent upon "collective action," as in the Lloyd Jones novel interestingly discussed here. In this sense, the discussion by Sutton and Tribble of *The Book of Fame* in relation to "social ontology and cognitive science" carries some unexpected resonances, touching on relationships between individual consciousness and the social body more generally.

The best work in the area of literature and science—one thinks here of Gillian Beer's exemplary *Darwin's Plots*—has tended to treat these two systems as equipotential, overlapping fictions that elucidate each other in sometimes unexpected ways, as in the intricate textual parallels that Beer traces in her work between the narratives of Darwin and George Eliot.[2] Rather than placing one side of the equation simply in the shadow of its opposite, in other words, Beer treats literature and science as mutually illuminating dialogues, products of their cultural time in equal measure. Several of the contributors to *Mindful Aesthetics* usefully relate contemporary arguments about science to a longer historical trajectory, pointing out, as in Charles T. Wolfe's excellent work, how the irruption of materialism into ossified humanist categories, along with an uncomfortable conception of the human organism itself as a physiological machine, was foreshadowed in the eighteenth-century writings of Denis Diderot and Laurence Sterne that similarly took issue with Cartesian consciousness. Indeed, reading through these chapters I was struck by a sense of how, in intellectual terms, we have for the most part been here before: as Claire Colebrook astutely remarks, this conception of "mindful aesthetics," relating artistic patterns to cerebral reflexes, works specifically as a reversal of the work of Immanuel Kant, for whom aesthetics involved "a way of thinking about a specifically subjective capacity for *form*." But Kant himself was, of course, reacting against the skepticism of David Hume and other eighteenth-century materialists such as Baron d'Holbach and Julien Offray de La Mettrie, who were regarded as scabrous and blasphemous in their own day and for whom rational belief involved an extrapolation or sublimation of irrational instinct and ingrained custom. Rather than a cognitive "turn," as such, it might be argued that what we see in this unfolding historical process is a cognitive turn and turn about, or rather an elaborate and insightful but ineluctably provisional reconceptualization of how contemporary theories of art have been moderated in the light of newly emerging theories of biogenetics.

Despite the ubiquitous pull toward a rhetoric of breakthrough, much of the most convincing recent work in this academic area has actually been historicist in orientation.

One example of this is Alan Richardson's interpretation of Jane Austen's *Emma* in the light of "the most influential psychological thinking of her time," such as Thomas Reid's *Essays on the Intellectual Powers of Man*.[3] Drawing on such discursive parallels, Richardson produces a fine reading of Austen grounded upon an interdisciplinary style of parataxis that opens up genuine new horizons on a familiar literary work. In this light, the more self-consciously polemical aspects of Danta's and Groth's collection struck me as generally less plausible than the various attempts to relate literary texts to specific scientific contexts. There are many instances in this collection of such carefully calibrated and nuanced readings: Anthony Uhlmann's discussion of how J. M. Coetzee represents meaning as generated through relations that are not in themselves representative of human consciousness; Mark Steven's intercalation of William Carlos Williams's poetry with the positivistic kind of medical science fashionable in the mid-twentieth century, grounded as that science was on what was quantifiable and measurable; Stephen Muecke's ingenious association between "reproductive aesthetics," heterogeneous modes of reproduction extending beyond the simply biological and the kind of poetic nexus, as in the poetry of Seamus Heaney, that disperses itself beyond purely linguistic forms; Hannah Courtney's analysis of how Ian McEwan draws deliberately on contemporary descriptions of the human brain—"neuronarratives," in the term she cites here from Gary Johnson—to trace ways in which temporality impacts in differential ways upon human consciousness. Helen Groth's own chapter specifically takes issue with what she calls Lisa Zunshine's blithe "collapse of all literary and literary-critical paradigms into permutations on one transhistorical and transgeneric 'theory of mind.'" By analyzing instead the intellectual correspondences between George Eliot's fiction and James Sully's conception of the psychological function of literature, Groth valuably complicates traditional understandings of Victorian realism by reading Eliot's art, in line with Sully's emphasis on the embedded qualities of memory and dreaming, as "a multichanneled mediation that transmits messages on different frequencies."

On occasions, this disjunction between grand cognitive theory and historicizing practice manifests itself within the structure of individual chapters. In the contribution of Julian Murphet, for instance, there is to my mind a wholly convincing discussion of how the recent films of David Lynch are designed to represent "a neuroscientific map of the brain," a shift both technical and ideological involving a displacement of the psychoanalytic categories of classic cinema into the more amorphous video idiom characteristic of a "digital imaginary." But Murphet allies this analysis with a larger extrapolation derived from Gilles Deleuze that appears much more speculative, suggesting as it does how cinema has superseded the novel as the genre in which such a multifarious picture of the brain might properly be represented. For Murphet, the novel's "rigid descent into orthodoxy and tired convention" makes it "not the institutional or artistic space in which to propose genuine representational thoughts about the brain;" this, incidentally, directly contradicts Ian McEwan's assertion, in a 2005 interview with Zadie Smith, that "cinema is a very inferior, unsophisticated medium" because of what he sees as its structural incapability, unlike fiction, "of being able to enter other people's minds."[4] Of course, McEwan's attachment to a particular version of alterity that he equates with the late liberal-humanist novel carries its own kind of baggage, but his own fiction, moving deftly as it does between conservative and posthumanist perspectives, implies how such prior assumptions about generic scope are always likely to be misleading. One of the great things about Lynch's films is precisely the way in which they reinvent Hollywood cinema in the light of contemporary neurological understandings, just as one of the admirable things about McEwan's novels is the way they interrogate comfortable assumptions about psychological and historical continuity through their projections of social friction and biogenetic rupture. Neither Boyd's polemical valorization of literature nor Murphet's Deleuzian skepticism about its inherent potential seems quite to do justice to the irreducibly *aesthetic* aspects in *Mindful Aesthetics*, the ways in which good art of any kind tends to distinguish itself by its capacity to reorganize conventional patterns—whether religious, ideological or scientific—in challenging new ways.

   Although questions of gender are raised implicitly by Penelope Hone's thoughtful discussion of how George Eliot drew on Victorian scientific understandings of sympathy and psychology in the construction of her fiction, one thing I found slightly surprising about this collection of chapters is that there are relatively few specific interrogations of the extent to which traditional conceptions of science as an exclusionary male preserve have impacted upon the portrayal of gender relations in literature. Without wishing at all to deny the author's mordant brilliance, for example, there would surely be ample scope in any treatment of Nabokov for considering ways in which his various modes of categorization and objectification are mediated by specific gender assumptions, proclivities toward appropriation that the scientist and the fetishist sometimes share. Ultimately, as this critical collection makes clear, the frameworks of cognitive science can usefully be seen as working in parallel to various other forms of cultural materialism that have helped to shape literary and cultural texts. Just as Isobel Armstrong has recently examined ways in which the phenomenon of "glass culture" provided important perspectives for Victorian writers, committed as they were to a "poetics of transparency," so the writers under consideration here relate literary narratives to a neurological capacity to discern patterns.[5] As Colebrook observes, one of the characteristics of cognitive science has been how it has itself been critical of its own cognitive model, so that what we find here is cultural materialism given a reflexive twist, a mirroring idiom that links the discursive strategy inextricably to modes of perception as well as the substance of what is perceived. Yet the dominant philosophical mode here is, as Colebrook also notes, a "return to the body and the lived": a systematic critique of dualistic abstraction and a reference back instead to corporeal embodiment. Although this bears some obvious analogies to the principled critiques of theoretical abstraction that were famously mounted in the late-twentieth century by Richard Rorty, Martha Nussbaum and others, it is by no means the case that an emphasis on the body in itself indicates the rejection of any kind of theoretical compass. Indeed, few domains have come under such sustained theoretical scrutiny in recent times as the human body. Just to take one example, Paul Gilroy in *Between Camps* argued against reified, institutionalized conceptions of racial identity by drawing explicitly on the genetic engineering work of biologists such as Richard Lewontin and Steven Rose to suggest how, given that "we stand on the threshold of a transformed understanding of the visible differences coded inside human bodies," it is possible that "a new, as it were 'postracial' genetic science will appear before long."[6]

In this sense, Paul Sheehan's argument here that "theory and cognitivism are radically incompatible" surely needs to be balanced against a less apocalyptic reading of how history works through loops and spirals. Though theory's "indifference to the biology of mind" may be true of some particular styles of European theory, it is manifestly not true of others. As Sheehan himself allows, scientific assumptions have become internalized and "normalized" in the work of thinkers such as Alain Badiou, and it is not clear that Western culture in the early years of the twenty-first century is actually any more "disillusioned" or "disenchanted" than it was, say, in the wake of World War II, or during the controversies around Darwinian evolution in the 1860s. In the prosperous decade before 9/11, Francis Fukuyama put forward his emollient thesis about "the end of history," suggesting how in the triumphalist new world of neoliberal capitalism all the traumas associated with historical conflict had fallen by the wayside.[7] But the superficiality of such assumptions was soon exposed by external challenges to neoliberal universalism, and contemporary conceptions of "post-theory" seem to be just as misplaced as Fukuyama's faux-utopian vision. There is, ultimately, no such thing as post-theory, any more than there is an "end" to history; there are only different ways in which theoretical concerns are mediated, along with different contexts through which they relate to particular works of culture. In the way they wrestle with the perennial struggle between theoretical abstraction and corporeal matter, all of these chapters testify amply to ways in which dialogues between literature and science continue productively to inform works of the human imagination.

Notes

1   Brian Boyd, *On the Origin of Stories: Evolution, Cognition, and Fiction* (Cambridge, MA: Belknap Press of Harvard University Press, 2009), 2; 384.

2   Gillian Beer, *Darwin's Plots: Evolutionary Narrative in Darwin, George Eliot and Nineteenth-Century Fiction*, 3rd ed. (1983; repr., Cambridge: Cambridge University Press, 2009).

3   Alan Richardson, *The Neural Sublime: Cognitive Theories and Romantic Texts* (Baltimore, MD: The Johns Hopkins University Press, 2010), 92.

4   Ryan Roberts, ed., *Conversations with Ian McEwan* (Jackson, MS: University Press of Mississippi, 2010), 112.

5   Isobel Armstrong, *Victorian Glassworlds: Glass Culture and the Imagination, 1830–1880* (Oxford: Oxford University Press, 2008), 1.

6   Paul Gilroy, *Between Camps: Nations, Cultures and the Allure of Race* (London: Allen Lane/Penguin, 2000), 218.

7   Francis Fukuyama, *The End of History and the Last Man* (New York: Free Press-Simon and Schuster, 1992).

Bibliography

Adams, Frederick, and Kenneth Aizawa. *The Bounds of Cognition.* Oxford: Wiley-Blackwell, 2008.

Adorno, Theodor. *The Positivist Dispute in German Sociology.* Translated by Glyn Adey and David Frisby. London: Heinemann Educational Books, 1976.

Agamben, Giorgio. *The Man without Content.* Translated by Daniel Heller-Roazen. Stanford: Stanford University Press, 1999.

Aggerholm, Kenneth, Ejgil Jespersen, and Lars Tore Ronglan. "Falling for the Feint—An Existential Investigation of a Creative Performance in High-Level Football." *Sport, Ethics, and Philosophy* 5, no. 3 (2011): 343–58.

Agranat, Aharon J., Offer Schwartsglass and Joseph Shappir. "The Charge Controlled Analog Synapse." *Solid-State Electronics* 39, no. 10 (October 1996): 1435–39.

Albright, Daniel. *Quantum Poetics: Yeats, Pound, Eliot, and the Science of Modernism.* Cambridge: Cambridge University Press, 1997.

Alexander, Ian. "Philosophy of Organism and Philosophy of Consciousness in Diderot's Speculative Thought." *Studies in Romance Philology and French Literature presented to John Orr* (Manchester: Manchester University Press, 1953): 1–21.

Allison, Jonathan. "'Friendship's Garland' and the Manuscripts of Seamus Heaney's 'Fosterage.'" *The Yearbook of English Studies* 35 (2005): 58–71.

Altieri, Charles. "Can Modernism Have a Future?" *Modernism/modernity* 7, no. 1 (2000): 127–43.

—— "'Ponderation' in Cézanne and Williams." *Poetics Today* 10, no. 2 (1989): 373–99.

Anderson, Amanda. *The Powers of Distance: Cosmopolitanism and the Cultivation of Detachment.* Princeton: Princeton University Press, 2001.

Anderson, J. R. "Acquisition of Cognitive Skill." *Psychological Review* 89, no. 4 (1982): 369–406.

Armstrong, David M. *A Materialist Theory of the Mind.* London: Routledge, 1968.

Armstrong, Isobel. *Victorian Glassworlds: Glass Culture and the Imagination, 1830–1880.* Oxford: Oxford University Press, 2008.

Armstrong, Nancy. *Desire and Domestic Fiction: A Political History of the Novel.* Oxford: Oxford University Press, 1987.

Attwell, David. *J. M. Coetzee: South Africa and the Politics of Writing.* Los Angeles: University of California Press, 1993.

Jane, Austen. *Northanger Abbey.* Edited by Susan Fraiman. New York: Norton, 2004.

Austin, J. L. *How to Do Things with Words.* Cambridge, MA: Harvard University Press, 1975.

Aziz-Zadeh, Lisa, Stephen M. Wilson, Giacomo Rizzolatti, and Marco Iacoboni. "Congruent embodied representations for visually presented actions and linguistic phrases describing actions." *Current Biology* 16, no. 19 (2006): 1818–23.

Badiou, Alain. *Being and Event.* Translated by Oliver Feltham. New York: Continuum, 2005.

—— *The Century.* Translated by Alberto Toscano. Cambridge: Polity, 2007.

—— *Wittgenstein's Antiphilosophy.* Translated by Bruno Bosteels. London: Verso, 2011.

Bakhtin, M. M. *The Dialogic Imagination: Four Essays.* Translated by Carl Emerson and Michael Holquist. Austin, TX: University of Texas Press, 1981.

—— *Toward a Philosophy of the Act.* Translated by Vadim Liapunov. Austin, TX: University of Texas Press, 1999.

Bal, Mieke. *Narratology: Introduction to the Theory of Narrative.* 2nd ed. Toronto, ON: University of Toronto Press, 1997.

Baldwin, Neil. "Zukofsky, Williams, and *The Wedge*: Toward a Dynamic Convergence." *William Carlos Williams: Man and Poet.* Edited by Carroll Franklin Terrell. Maine: National Poetry Foundation, 1979, 129–42.

Barad, Karen. "Posthumanist Performativity: Toward an Understanding of How Matter Comes to Matter." *Signs: Journal of Women in Culture and Society* 28, no. 3 (2003): 801–31.

Barbieri, Marcello. "Biosemiotics: A New Understanding of Life." *Naturwissenschaften* 95, no. 7 (2008): 577–99.

Barker, Jason. *Alain Badiou: A Critical Introduction.* London: Pluto Press, 2002.

Barsalou, Lawrence W. "Grounded Cognition." *Annual Review of Psychology* 59 (2008): 617–45.

Barthes, Roland. "The Reality Effect." *The Rustle of Language.* Translated by Richard Howard. Oxford: Blackwell, 1986, 141–48.

—— "Réponses." *Tel Quel* 47 (Autumn 1971): 89–107.

Bartlett, Frederic C. *Remembering: A Study in Experimental and Social Psychology.* Cambridge: Cambridge University Press, 1932.

Bataille, George. *Inner Experience.* Translated by Leslie A. Boldt. Albany, NY: SUNY Press, 1988.

Bate, Jonathan. *Song of the Earth.* Cambridge, MA: Harvard University Press, 2000.

Bechtel, William. *Mental Mechanisms.* London: Routledge, 2008.

Beer, Gillian. *Darwin's Plots: Evolutionary Narrative in Darwin, George Eliot and Nineteenth-Century Fiction.* 3rd ed. 1983. Reprint, Cambridge: Cambridge University Press, 2009.

—— *Open Fields: Science in Cultural Encounter.* Oxford: Oxford University Press, 1996.

Beilock, Sian. *Choke.* New York: Free Press, 2011.

Beilock, Sian and Thomas H. Carr. "On the Fragility of Skilled Performance: What Governs Choking under Pressure?" *Journal of Experimental Psychology: General* 130, no. 4 (2001): 701–25.

Benjamin, Walter. "One Way Street." *Selected Writings: 1913–1926,* Volume 1. Edited by Marcus Bullock and Michael W. Jennings. Cambridge, MA: Harvard University Press, 1996, 444–88.

—— "Theses on the Philosophy of History." *Illuminations.* Edited by H. Arendt. New York: Harcourt, Brace & World, 1968, 245–55.

Bergson, Henri. *Creative Evolution.* Translated by Arthur Miller. London: Macmillan, 1911.

Bernstein, J. M. "Readymades, Monochromes, Etc.: Nominalism and the Paradox of Modernism." "Rethinking Beauty." *Diacritics* 32, no. 1 (Spring 2002): 83–100.

Bethlehem, Louise. "*Elizabeth Costello* as Post-Apartheid Text." *J. M. Coetzee in Context and Theory*. Edited by Elleke Boehmer, Katy Iddiols, and Robert Eaglestone. London: Contiuum, 2011, 20–35.

Bickle, John. *Psychoneural Reduction: The New Wave*. Cambridge, MA: MIT Press, 1998.

—— *Philosophy and Neuroscience: A Ruthlessly Reductive Account*. Dordrecht: Kluwer, 2003.

Bickle, John, Pete Mandik, and Andrew Landreth. "The Philosophy of Neuroscience." *Stanford Encyclopedia of Philosophy*. Edited by Edward N. Zalta, 2006. http://plato.stanford.edu/entries/neuroscience/.

Bicknell, Kath. "Feeling Them Ride: Corporeal Exchange in Cross-Country Mountain Bike Racing." *About Performance*, no. 10 (2010): 81–91.

Bizup, Joseph M., and Eugene R. Kintgen. "The Cognitive Paradigm in Literary Studies." *College English* 55, no. 8 (December 1993): 841–57.

Blake, William. *The Marriage of Heaven and Hell*. Edited by Geoffrey Keynes. Oxford: Oxford University Press, 1975.

Blanchot, Maurice. *The Infinite Conversation*. Translated by Susan Hanson. Minneapolis, MN: University of Minnesota Press, 1993.

Bloch, Olivier. *Matière à histoires*. Paris: Vrin, 1998.

Böckler, Anne, Gunther Knoblich, and Natalie Sebanz. "Socializing Cognition." *Towards a Theory of Thinking*. Edited by Britt Glatzeider, Vinod Goel, and Albrecht von Mueller. London: Springer, 2010, 233–50.

Booth, Douglas. "Sites of Truth or Metaphors of Power? Refiguring the Archive." *Sport in History* 26, no. 1 (2006): 91–109.

Bosteels, B. "Radical Antiphilosophy." *Filozofski vestnik* 29, no. 2 (2008): 155–87.

Bourdin, Jean-Claude. "Du *Rêve de D'Alembert* aux *Éléments de physiologie*. Discours scientifique et discours spéculatif dans *Le Rêve de D'Alembert*." *Recherches sur Diderot et sur l'Encyclopédie* 34 (2003): 45–69.

Bowlby, John. *Attachment. Vol. 1, Attachment and Loss*. Harmondsworth: Penguin, 1971.

Boyd, Brian. "Brian Boyd Responds [to Lisa Zunshine]." *Philosophy and Literature* 31, no. 1 (April 2007): 196–99.

—— "Fiction and Theory of Mind." *Philosophy and Literature* 30, no. 2 (2006): 571–81.

—— "Jane, Meet Charles: Literature, Evolution, and Human Nature." *Philosophy and Literature* 22, no. 1 (1998): 1–30.

—— *On the Origin of Stories: Evolution, Cognition, and Fiction*. Cambridge, MA: Belknap Press of Harvard University Press, 2009.

—— "The Origin of Stories: *Horton Hears a Who*." *Philosophy and Literature* 25, no. 2 (2001): 197–214.

Boyle, Robert. *The Works of the Honourable Robert Boyle*. Edited by T. Birch. 6 vols. 1772. Reprint. Hildesheim: Olms, 1966.

Braten, Stein, ed. *On Being Moved: From Mirror Neurons to Empathy*. Amsterdam: John Benjamins Publishing, 2007.

Bruhn, Mark J. "Introduction: Exchange Values: Poetics and Cognitive Science." *Poetics Today* 32, no. 3 (January 2012): 403–60.

Bruya, Brian. *Effortless Attention*. Cambridge, MA: MIT Press, 2010.

Butler, Judith. *Gender Trouble*. New York: Routledge, 1990.

Butterfill, Stephen A., and Natalie Sebanz. "Editorial: Joint Action: What Is Shared?" *Review of Philosophy and Psychology* 2, no. 2 (2011): 137–46.

Cabanis, Pierre Jean George. *On the Relations between the Physical and Moral Aspects of Man*. Translated by Margaret Duggan Saidi. Edited by George Mora. 2 vols. Baltimore, MD: The Johns Hopkins University Press, 1981.

Callus, Ivan and Stefan Herbrechter, eds. *Post-Theory, Culture, Criticism*. Amsterdam: Rodopi, 2004.

Carroll, Joseph. "Poststructuralism, Cultural Constructivism and Evolutionary Biology." *Symplokē* 4, nos. 1–2 (Winter/Summer 1996): 203–19.

—— *Literary Darwinism: Evolution, Human Nature, and Literature*. New York: Routledge, 2004.

—— "What Is Literary Darwinism: An Interview with Joseph Carroll." *Neuronarrative* 2009, http://neuronarrative.wordpress.com/2009/02/27/what-is-literary-darwinism-an-interview-with-joseph-carroll/.

Casey, Edward. *The Fate of Place: A Philosophical History*. Berkeley, CA: University of California Press, 1997.

Castel, Robert. *From Manual Workers to Wage Laborers: Transformation of the Social Question*. Translated and edited by Richard Boyd. New Brunswick: Transaction Publishers, 2003.

Chaffin, Roger, and Topher Logan. "Practicing Perfection: How Concert Soloists Prepare for Performance." *Advances in Cognitive Psychology* 2 (2006): 113–30.

Chatman, Seymour. *Story and Discourse: Narrative Structure in Fiction and Film*. Ithaca, NY: Cornell University Press, 1978.

Chen, Q., Q. Zheng, and W. Ling. "Implementation of an On-Chip Learning Artificial Neural Network." *Neural Network World* 12 (2002): 3–14.

Cheyette, Bryan. *Constructions of "the Jew" in English Literature and Society: Racial Representations, 1875–1945*. Cambridge: Cambridge University Press, 1993.

Chion, Michel. *David Lynch*. Translated by Robert Julian. 2nd ed. London: BFI, 2006.

Clark, Andy. *Being There: Putting Brain, Body, and World Together Again*. Cambridge, MA: MIT Press, 1997.

—— *Natural-Born Cyborgs: Minds, Technologies, and the Future of Human Intelligence*. Oxford: Oxford University Press, 2003.

—— "Reasons, Robots, and the Extended Mind." *Mind and Language* 16 (2001): 121–45.

—— *Supersizing the Mind: Embodiment, Action, and Cognitive Extension*. Oxford: Oxford University Press, 2008.

—— "Where Brain, Body and World Collide." *Material Agency: Towards a Non-Anthropocentric Approach*. Edited by Carl Knappett and Lambros Malafouris. Dordrecht: Springer, 2008, 1–18.

Clark, T. J. *Farewell to an Idea: Episodes from a History of Modernism*. New Haven, CT: Yale University Press, 2001.

Clarke, Edwin, and Charles D. O'Malley. *The Human Brain and Spinal Cord: A Historical Study Illustrated by Writings from Antiquity to the Twentieth Century*. Berkeley, CA: University of California Press, 1968.

Clarke, Samuel. *The Works of Samuel Clarke*. 4 vols. 1738. Reprint. New York: Garland, 1978.

Clarkson, Carroll. *J. M. Coetzee: Countervoices*. London: Palgrave, 2009.

Clemens, Justin. "To Rupture the Matheme with a Poem: A Remark on Psychoanalysis as Antiphilosophy." *Trauma, History, Philosophy*. Edited by Matthew Sharpe, Murray Noonan and Jason Freddi. Newcastle, FL: Cambridge Scholars Press, 2007, 308–12.

Coetzee, J. M. *Doubling the Point: Essays and Interviews*. Edited by David Attwell. Cambridge, MA: Harvard University Press, 1992.
—— *Elizabeth Costello*. New York: Knopf, 2003.
—— "Farm Novel and *Plaasroman* in South Africa." *English in Africa* 13, no. 2 (October 1986): 1–19.
—— *The Lives of Animals*. Princeton: Princeton University Press, 2001.
Cohen, Tom, Barbara Cohen, J. Hillis Miller, and Andrzej Warminsk, eds. *Material Events: Paul de Man and the Afterlife of Theory*. Minneapolis, MN: University of Minnesota Press, 2001.
Colebrook, Claire. *Irony: The New Critical Idiom*. London: Routledge, 1994.
Colombetti, Giovanna. "Varieties of Pre-Reflective Self-Awareness: Foreground and Background Bodily Feelings in Emotion Experience." *Inquiry* 54, no. 3 (June 2011): 293–313.
Connolly, William E. *Neuropolitics: Thinking, Culture, Speed*. Minneapolis, MN: University of Minnesota Press, 2002.
Cooper, Melinda. "Review of Michael Dillon and Julian Reid, *The Liberal Way of War: Killing to Make Life Live*." *Radical Philosophy* 160 (March/April 2010): 52–53.
Courtney, Hannah. "Narrative Temporality and Slowed Scene: The Interaction of Event and Thought Representation in Ian McEwan's Fiction." *Narrative* 21, no. 2 (2013): 180–97.
Craver, Carl F. *Explaining the Brain*. Oxford: Oxford University Press, 2007.
Crews, Frederick. "The End of the Poststructuralist Era." *The Emperor Redressed: Critiquing Critical Theory*. Edited by Dwight Eddins. Tuscaloosa: University of Alabama Press, 1995.
Cunningham, Valentine. *Reading after Theory*. Oxford: Blackwell, 2002.
Daley, Caroline. "The Invention of 1905." *Tackling Rugby Myths: Rugby and New Zealand Society, 1854–2004*, Edited by Greg Ryan. Dunedin: Otago University Press, 2005, 69–87.
Damasio, Antonio R. *Looking for Spinoza: Joy, Sorrow, and the Feeling Brain*. Orlando, FL: Harcourt, 2003.
—— *Descartes' Error: Emotion, Reason, and the Human Brain*. New York: Random House, 1994.
—— *The Feeling of What Happens: Body and Emotions in the Making of Consciousness*. New York: Harcourt, Brace & Co, 1999.
—— *Self Comes to Mind: Constructing the Conscious Brain*. New York: Vintage, 2009.
Dames, Nicholas. *The Physiology of the Novel: Reading, Neural Science, and the Form of Victorian Fiction*. Oxford: Oxford University Press, 2007.
Davis, Colin. *After Poststructuralism*: Reading, Stories and Theory. New York: Routledge, 2004.
Davis, Michael. *George Eliot and Nineteenth-Century Psychology*. Aldershot: Ashgate, 2006.
de Man, Paul. *The Resistance to Theory*. Minneapolis, MN: University of Minnesota Press, 1986.
—— *Aesthetic Ideology*. Edited by Andrzej Warminski. Minneapolis, MN: University of Minnesota Press, 1996.
Deeds Ermarth, Elizabeth. "George Eliot's Conception of Sympathy." *Nineteenth-Century Fiction* 40, no. 1 (June 1985): 23–42.
Deleuze, Gilles. *Cinema 2: The Time-Image*. Translated by Hugh Tomlinson and Robert Galeta. London: Athlone, 1989.
—— *Difference and Repetition*. Translated by Paul Patton. New York: Columbia, 1994.

—— *Essays Critical and Clinical*. Translated by Daniel W. Smith and Michael A. Greco. Minneapolis, MN: University of Minnesota Press, 1997.

—— *Pure Immanence: Essays on a Life*. Translated by Anne Boyman. New York: Zone, 2001.

—— *Dialogues II*. Translated by Hugh Tomlinson and Barbara Habberjam. New York: Continuum, 2006.

Deleuze, Gilles and Félix Guattari. *Qu'est-ce que la philosophie?*. Paris: Minuit, 1991.

—— *What Is Philosophy?*. Translated by Hugh Tomlinson and Graham Burchell. New York: Columbia University Press, 1994.

Dennett, Daniel C. *Consciousness Explained*. New York: Black Bay Books, 1992.

—— "The Self as Center of Narrative Gravity." In *Self and Consciousness: Multiple Perspectives*. Edited by F. J. Kessel, P. Cole, and D. L. Johnson. Hillsdale, NJ: Erlbaum, 1992, 275–78.

Derrida, Jacques. *Limited Inc*. Translated by Alan Bass. Evanston, IL: Northwestern University Press, 1972.

—— *Writing and Difference*. Translated by Alan Bass. Chicago: University of Chicago Press, 1978.

—— *Positions*. Translated by Alan Bass. Chicago: University of Chicago Press, 1981.

—— *Edmund Husserl's Origin of Geometry: An Introduction*. Translated by John P. Leavey Jr. Lincoln, NE: University of Nebraska Press, 1989.

—— *Of Grammatology*. Translated by Gayatri Chakravorty Spivak. Baltimore, MD: The Johns Hopkins University Press, 1998.

—— *On Touching, Jean-Luc Nancy*. Translated by Christine Irizarry. Stanford: Stanford University Press, 2005.

Diderot, Denis. *Œuvres philosophiques*. Edited by Paul Vernière. Paris: Garnier, 1961.

—— *Œuvres complètes*. Edited by H. Dieckmann, J. Proust, and J. Varloot. 25 vols. Paris: Hermann, 1975–2004.

Djikic, Maja, Keith Oatley, Sara Zoeterman, and Jordan B. Peterson. "On Being Moved by Art: How Reading Fiction Transforms the Self." *Creativity Research Journal* 21 (2009): 24–29.

Docherty, Thomas. *After Theory*. Edinburgh: Edinburgh University Press, 1996.

Doidge, Norman. *The Brain That Changes Itself: Stories of Personal Triumph from the Frontiers of Brain Science*. New York: Penguin, 2007.

Downey, Greg. "Balancing between Cultures: Equilibrium in Caporeia." *The Encultured Brain: An Introduction to Neuroanthropology*. Edited by Daniel H. Lende and Greg Downey. Cambridge, MA: MIT Press, 2012, 169–94.

Doyle, Jennifer. *Hold It against Me: Difficulty and Emotion in Contemporary Art*. Durham, NC: Duke University Press, 2012.

Dreyfus, Hubert L. "Intelligence without Representation—Merleau-Ponty's Critique of Mental Representation." *Phenomenology and the Cognitive Sciences* 1, no. 4 (2002): 1–18.

—— "The Return of the Myth of the Mental." *Inquiry* 50, no. 4 (2007): 352–65.

Dreyfus, Hubert L., Stuart E. Dreyfus, and Tom Athanasiou. *Mind over Machine: The Power of Human Intuition and Expertise in the Era of the Computer*. New York: Free Press, 1986.

Dror, Itiel E. and Stevan R. Harnard. *Cognition Distributed: How Cognitive Technology Extends Our Minds*. Amsterdam: John Benjamins Publishing, 2007.

Eagleton, Terry. *After Theory*. New York: Basic Books, 2003.

—— *Literary Theory: An Introduction*. Oxford: Blackwell, 1996.

Easterlin, Nancy and Barbara Reibling, eds. *After Poststructuralism: Interdisciplinarity and Literary Theory*. Evanston, IL: Northwestern University Press, 1993.

Edelman, Gerald. *Bright Air, Brilliant Fire. On the Matter of the Mind*. London: Allen Lane, 1992.

Eich, Eric, John F. Killstrom, Gordon H. Bower, Joseph P. Forgas, and Paula M. Niedenthal. *Counterpoints: Cognition, Memory, and Language*. Oxford: Oxford University Press, 2000.

Eliot, George. *Daniel Deronda*. London: Penguin Books, 1995.

—— *George Eliot's Daniel Deronda Notebooks*. Edited by Jane Irwin. Cambridge: Cambridge University Press, 1996.

—— *The George Eliot Letters*. Edited by Gordon S. Haight. 9 vols. New Haven, CT: Yale University Press, 1955.

—— *Middlemarch*. 1977. Reprint. New York; London: W. W. Norton & Co, 2000.

—— *Selected Essays, Poems and Other Writings*. Oxford: Oxford University Press, 1990.

Feigl, Herbert. *The 'Mental' and the 'Physical'*. 1958. Reprinted with a postscript. Minneapolis, MN: University of Minnesota Press, 1967.

Fenollosa, Ernest. *The Chinese Written Character as a Medium for Poetry*. Edited by Ezra Pound. San Francisco, CA: City Lights Books, 1936.

Ferris, Joshua. *Then We Came to the End: A Novel*. New York: Back Bay Books, 2007.

Fink, Eugen. "The Phenomenological Philosophy of Edmund Husserl and Contemporary Criticism." In *The Phenomenology of Husserl: Selected Critical Readings*. Edited by R. O. Elveton. Chicago: Quadrangle Books, 1970, 73–147.

Flanagan, Owen. *The Problem of the Soul: Two Visions of Mind and How to Reconcile Them*. New York: Basic Books, 2002.

Flesch, William. *Comeuppance: Costly Signaling, Altruistic Punishment and Other Biological Components of Fiction*. Cambridge, MA: Harvard University Press, 2007.

Fludernik, Monika. *An Introduction to Narratology*. Translated by Patricia Häusler-Greenfield and Monika Fludernik. London: Routledge, 2009.

Foot, Philippa. *Natural Goodness*. Oxford: Clarendon Press, 2001.

Foucault, Michel. *The Foucault Reader*. Edited by Paul Rabinow. Harmondsworth: Penguin, 1986.

Freud, Sigmund. *Standard Edition of the Complete Psychological Works*. Translated by James Strachey. 24 vols. London: The Hogarth Press, 1953–74.

—— *The Future of an Illusion, Civilization and Its Discontents, and Other Works*. Edited and translated by James Strachey. London: Vintage, 1961.

Fukuyama, Francis. *The End of History and the Last Man*. New York: Free Press–Simon and Schuster, 1992.

Gallagher, Shaun. *How the Body Shapes the Mind*. Oxford: Clarendon Press, 2005.

Gallaher, David, and W. J. Stead. *The Complete Rugby Footballer on the New Zealand System*. London: Methuen, 1906.

Genette, Gerard. *Narrative Discourse: An Essay in Method*. Translated by Jane E. Lewin. Oxford: Basil Blackwell, 1980.

George Eliot and George Henry Lewes Collection. Beinecke Rare Book and Manuscript Library, Yale University, 1834–1981.

Gilbert, Margaret. *On Social Facts*. Princeton: Princeton University Press, 1989.

—— "Walking Together: A Paradigmatic Social Phenomenon." *Midwest Studies in Philosophy* 15, no. 1 (1990): 1–14.

Gilroy, Paul. *Between Camps: Nations, Cultures and the Allure of Race*. London: Allen Lane/Penguin, 2000.

Ginsberg, Allen. *Howl and Other Poems*. San Francisco, CA: City Lights Books, 1956.

Gleason, Daniel W. "The Visual Experience of Image Metaphor: Cognitive Insights into Imagist Figures." *Poetics Today* 30, no. 3 (Fall 2009): 423–70.

Goldie, Peter. *The Mess Inside: Narrative, Emotion, and the Mind*. Oxford: Oxford University Press, 2012.

Goldstone, Robert L., and Todd M. Gureckis. "Collective Behavior." *Topics in Cognitive Science* 1, no. 3 (2009): 412–38.

Goleman, Daniel. *Social Intelligence: The New Science of Human Relationships*. New York: Bantam, 2006.

Gooch, P. W. "Socratic Irony and Aristotle's 'Eiron': Some Puzzles." *The Phoenix* 41, no. 2 (Summer 1987): 95–104.

Gottschall, Jonathan. *Literature, Science, and a New Humanities*. New York: Palgrave Macmillan, 2008.

Gottschall, Jonathan and David Sloan Wilson, eds. *The Literary Animal: Evolution and the Nature of Narrative*. Evanston, IL: Northwestern University Press, 2005.

Grasseni, Christina. "Skilled Vision: An apprenticeship in breeding aesthetics." *Social Anthropology* 12, no. 1 (2004): 41–55.

Greenblatt, Stephen, ed. *The Norton Anthology of English Literature*. 8th ed. Vol. 2. New York: Norton, 2006.

Greiner, Rae. "Sympathy Time: Adam Smith, George Eliot, and the Realist Novel." *Narrative* 17, no. 3 (October 2009): 291–311.

Groes, Sebastian, ed. *Ian McEwan: Contemporary Critical Perspectives*. London: Continuum, 2009.

Gurjeva, Lyubov G. "James Sully and Scientific Psychology, 1870–1910." *Psychology in Britain: Historical Essays and Personal Reflections*. Edited by G. C. Bunn, A. D. Lovie and G. D. Richards. London: The British Psychological Society, 2001, 72–94.

Gurr, Jens Martin. "Functions of Intertextuality and Metafiction in J. M. Coetzee's *Slow Man*." *Anglistik* 18, no. 1 (March 2007): 95–112.

Habermas, Jurgen. *The Philosophical Discourse of Modernity: Twelve Lectures*. Translated by Frederick Lawrence. Cambridge, MA: MIT Press, 1987.

Hagner, Michael. *Homo cerebralis. Der Wandel vom Seelenorgan zum Gehirn*. Berlin: Berlin Verlag, 1997.

Hansen, Mark. *Embodying Technesis: Technology beyond Writing*. Ann Arbor, MI: University of Michigan Press, 2000.

—— "The Time of Affect, or Bearing Witness to Life." *Critical Inquiry* 30, no. 3 (Spring 2004): 584–626.

Harman, Graham. *Prince of Networks: Bruno Latour and Metaphysics*. Melbourne: re.press, 2007.

—— "The Well-Wrought Broken Hammer: Object-Oriented Literary Criticism." *New Literary History* 43 (2012): 183–203.

Harrington, Anne. *Medicine, Mind, and the Double Brain: A Study in Nineteenth-Century Thought and Culture*. Princeton: Princeton University Press, 1987.

Harris, Celia B., Paul G. Keil, Amanda J. Barnier, John Sutton, and Doris J. F. McIlwain. "We Remember, We Forget: Collaborative Remembering in Older Couples." *Discourse Processes* 48, no. 4 (2011): 267–303.

Harris, Wendell V. ed. *Beyond Poststructuralism: The Speculations of Theory and the Experience of Literature*. University Park: Pennsylvania State University Press, 1996.

Hart, F. Elizabeth. "The Epistemology of Cognitive Literary Studies." *Philosophy and Literature* 25 (2001): 315–34.

—— "The View of Where We've Been and Where We'd Like to Go." *College Literature* 33, no. 1 (Winter 2006): 225–37.

Hartley, David. *Observations on Man, His Frame, His Duty and His Expectations*. 2 vols. London: Richardson, 1749.

Hauser, Marc D. *Moral Minds: How Nature Designed Our Universal Sense of Right and Wrong*. New York: Ecco, 2006.

Hawkes, David. "Against Materialism in Literary Theory." *Early Modern Culture* 9 (2011): http://emc.eserver.org/Hawkes.pdf, forthcoming.

Hayes, Patrick. *J. M. Coetzee and the Novel: Writing and Politics after Beckett*. New York: Oxford University Press, 2010.

Head, Dominic. *The Cambridge Introduction to Modern British Fiction, 1950–2000*. Cambridge: Cambridge University Press, 2002.

Heaney, Seamus. "Digging." *Death of a Naturalist*. London: Faber and Faber, 1966, 8–9.

—— *Opened Ground: Selected Poems 1966–1996*. New York: Farrar, Straus & Giroux, 1998.

Hegel, G. W. F. *Hegel's Logic: Being Part One of the Encyclopedia of the Physical Sciences*. Translated by William Wallace. Oxford: Clarendon Press, 1975.

—— *Phenomenology of Spirit*. Translated by A. V. Miller. Oxford: Oxford University Press, 1977.

Heidegger, Martin. *What Is a Thing?*. Translated by W. B. Barton, Jr. and Vera Deutsch. Chicago: H. Regnery Co, 1967.

—— *Poetry, Language, Thought*. Translated by Albert Hofstadter. New York: Harper and Row, 1971.

Helmholtz, Hermann von. *The Sensations of Tone as a Physiological Basis for the Theory of Music*. New York: Longmans, Green and Co, 1875.

Hering, Ewald. "Über das Gedächtnis als eine allgemeine Function der organisierten Materie." *Almanach der kaiserlichen Akademie der Wissenschaften* 20 (1870): 273–78.

Hickok, Gregory. "Eight Problems for the Mirror Neuron Theory of Action Understanding in Monkeys and Humans." *Journal of Cognitive Neuroscience* 21, no. 7 (July 2009): 1229–43.

Hildebidle, John. "Take off Your Clothes: William Carlos Williams, Science, and the Diagnostic Encounter." *Modern Language Studies* 17, no. 3 (1987): 10–30.

Hogan, Patrick Colm. *The Mind and Its Stories: Narrative Universals and Human Emotion*. Cambridge: Cambridge University Press, 2003.

—— "Palmer's Anti-Cognitivist Challenge." *Style* 45, no. 2 (2012): 244–48.

Horn, Peter. "Michael K: Pastiche, Parody or the Inversion of Michael Kohlhaas." *Current Writing: Text and Reception in Southern Africa* 17, no. 2 (2005): 56–73.

House, Michael K. "Beyond the Brain: Skeptical and Satirical Responses to Gall's Organology." *Neurology and Modernity: A Cultural History of Nervous Systems*. Edited by Laura Salisbury and Andrew Shail. London: Palgrave Macmillan, 2010, 41–58.

Hrdy, Sarah Blaffer. *Mothers and Others: The Evolutionary Origins of Mutual Understanding*. Cambridge, MA: Belknap Press of Harvard University Press, 2009.

Huebner, Bryce. *Macrocognition*. Oxford: Oxford University Press, 2013.

Hutchins, Edwin. *Cognition in the Wild*. Cambridge, MA: MIT Press, 1995.

Huttenlocher, Peter. *Neural Plasticity: The Effects of Environment on the Development of the Cerebral Cortex*. Cambridge, MA: Harvard University Press, 2002.

Iacoboni, Marco. *Mirroring People: The New Science of How We Connect with Others*. New York: Farrar, Straus and Giroux, 2008.

Iriki, Atsushi. "Using Tools: The Moment When Mind, Language, and Humanity Emerged." *RIKEN Research Report* 4, no. 5 (May 2009), http://www.rikenresearch.riken.jp/eng/frontline/5850.

Irwin, Terence. *Aristotle's First Principles*. Oxford: Clarendon Press, 1988.

Israel, Jonathan. *Radical Enlightenment: Philosophy and the Making of Modernity, 1650–1750*. Oxford: Oxford University Press, 2001.

James, Henry. "*Daniel Deronda*: A Conversation." *The Atlantic Monthly* 38, no. 230 (December 1876): 684–94.

Jameson, Fredric. *Marxism and Form: Twentieth-Century Dialectical Theories of Literature*. Princeton: Princeton University Press, 1972.

—— *The Political Unconscious: Narrative as a Socially Symbolic Act*. London: Routledge, 1981.

—— *A Singular Modernity: Essay on the Ontology of the Present*. London: Verso, 2002.

—— *The Modernist Papers*. London: Verso, 2007.

Johnson, Gary. "Consciousness as Content: Neuronarratives and the Redemption of Fiction." *Mosaic* 41, no. 1 (2008): 169–84.

Johnson, Mark. *The Body in the Mind: The Bodily Basis of Meaning, Imagination, and Reason*. Chicago: University of Chicago Press, 1987.

Jones, Lloyd. *The Book of Fame*. New York: Penguin, 2000.

—— *Into the Field of Play*. Auckland: Tandem Press, 1992.

Joyce, James. *Ulysses*. London: Penguin, 1992.

Kaitaro, Timo. "Brain-Mind Identities in Dualism and Materialism: A Historical Perspective." *Studies in History and Philosophy of Biology and Biomedical Sciences* 35 (2004): 627–45.

Karunatilaka, Shehan. *The Legend of Pradeep Mathew*. Minneapolis, MN: Graywolf Press, 2012.

Kassler, Jamie C. "Man—A Musical Instrument: Models of the Brain and Mental Functioning before the Computer." *History of Science* 22 (1984): 59–92.

Kenner, Hugh. *The Pound Era: The Age of Ezra Pound, T. S. Eliot, James Joyce and Wyndham Lewis*. London: Faber and Faber, 1972.

Keysar, Boaz, Yeshayahu Shen, Sam Glucksberg, and William S. Horton. "Conventional Language: How Metaphorical Is It?" *Journal of Memory and Language* 43 (2000): 576–93.

Kitching, Gavin. *The Trouble with Theory: The Educational Costs of Postmodernism*. Sydney: Allen and Unwin, 2008.

Koch, Sabine C., Thomas Fuchs, Michela Summa, and Cornelia Müller. *Body Memory, Metaphor and Movement*. Amsterdam: John Benjamins Publishing, 2012.

Kossew, Sue. *Pen and Power. A Post-Colonial Reading of J. M. Coetzee and Andre Brink*. Amsterdam: Rodopi, 1996.

Kunda, Ziva. *Social Cognition: Making Sense of People*. Cambridge, MA: MIT Press, 1999.

Lacan, Jacques. *Écrits*. Translated by Bruce Fink. New York: Norton, 2006.

Lakoff, George. *Women, Fire, and Dangerous Things: What Categories Reveal about the Mind*. Chicago: University of Chicago Press, 1987.

Lakoff, George, and Mark Johnson. *Metaphors We Live By*. Chicago: University of Chicago Press, 1980.

Lakoff, George, and Mark Turner. *More than Cool Reason: A Field Guide to Poetic Metaphor*. Chicago: University of Chicago Press, 1989.

Lambeth-Climaco, Emily. "'This Rhetoric Is Real': William Carlos Williams's Recalibration of Language and Things." *William Carlos Williams Review* 28, nos. 1–2 (2008): 35–53.

Lange, Friedrich Albrecht. *History of Materialism and Criticism of Its Present Importance*. Translated by E. C. Thomas. 3 vols. 1866. 4th revised edition. London: Kegan Paul, Trench & Trübner, 1892.

Lash, Scott. "Life (Vitalism)." *Theory, Culture & Society* 23, nos. 2–3 (2006): 323–49.

Latour, Bruno. "Cogito ergo sumus! Or Psychology Swept aside Inside Out by the Fresh Air of the Upper Deck..." *Mind, Culture, and Activity: An International Journal* 3, no. 1 (1996): 54–63.

—— "A Textbook Case Revisited: Knowledge as a Mode of Existence." *The Handbook of Science and Technology Studies*. Edited by E. Hackett, O. Amsterdamska, M. Lynch and J. Wacjman. 3rd ed. Cambridge, MA: MIT Press, 2007, 83–112.

—— "Reflections on Etienne Souriau's *Les différents modes d'existence*." Translated by Stephen Muecke. *The Speculative Turn: Continental Materialism and Realism*. Edited by Levi Bryant, Nick Srnicek and Graham Harman. Melbourne: re.press, 2011, 304–33.

Lawrence, D. H. *Lady Chatterley's Lover*. London: Penguin, 1993.

Legrand, Dorothée and Susanne Ravn. "Perceiving Subjectivity in Bodily Movement: The Case of Dancers." *Phenomenology and the Cognitive Sciences* 8, no. 3 (June 2009): 389–408, doi:10.1007/s11097-009-9135-5.

Leslie, Alan. "Pretense and Representation: The Origins of 'Theory of Mind.' " *Psychological Review* 94, no. 4 (1987): 412–26.

Levinas, Emmanuel. *Discovering Existence with Husserl*. Translated by Richard A. Cohen and Michael B. Smith. Evanston, IL: Northwestern University Press, 1998.

Levine, George. *The Realistic Imagination: English Fiction from Frankenstein to Lady Chatterly*. Chicago: University of Chicago Press, 1981.

Lewes, George Henry. *The Physiology of Common Life*. 2 vols. London: Blackwoods, 1859–60.

—— *The Problems of Life and Mind: Third Series, Problem the First: The Study of Psychology, Its Object, Scope and Method*. Boston: Houghton, Osgood and Co, 1879.

Lewis, David. "An Argument for the Identity Theory." *Journal of Philosophy* 63, no. 1 (1966): 17–25.

Lippard, Lucy. *The Lure of the Local: Sense of Place in a Multicentered Society*. New York: New Press, 1997.

List, Christian, and Philip Pettit. *Group Agency: The Possibility, Design, and Status of Corporate Agents*. Oxford: Oxford University Press, 2011.

Locke, John. *An Essay Concerning Human Understanding*. Edited by P. Nidditch. 1690. 5th ed., 1701. Reprint. Oxford: Oxford University Press, 1975.

Loy, Mina. *The Lost Lunar Baedeker*. Edited by Roger L. Conover. New York: Farrar, Straus, and Giroux, 1996.

Luckhurst, Roger. *The Invention of Telepathy: 1870–1901*. Oxford: Oxford University Press, 2002.

Luria, Alexander Romanovich. "Vygotsky and the Problem of Functional Localization" (1967). *Selected Writings of A. R. Luria.* Edited by M. Cole. New York: M. E. Sharpe, 1978.

Lynch, David. *Catching the Big Fish: Meditation, Consciousness, and Creativity.* New York: Jeremy Tarcher/Penguin, 2007.

Lyotard, Jean-François. *Lessons on the Analytic of the Sublime: Kant's Critique of Judgment, Sections 23–29.* Translated by Elizabeth Rottenberg. Stanford: Stanford University Press, 1994.

—— *The Postmodern Condition: A Report on Knowledge.* Translated by Geoff Bennington and Brian Massumi. 1979. Reprint. Manchester: Manchester University Press, 1984.

Malabou, Catherine. *What Should We Do with Our Brain?.* Translated by Sebastian Rand. New York: Fordham University Press, 2008.

Mallarmé, Stéphane. *Selected Letters of Stéphane Mallarmé.* Edited and translated by Rosemary Lloyd. Chicago: Chicago University Press, 1988.

Marcus, Amit. "A Contextual View of Narrative Fiction in the First Person Plural." *Narrative* 16, no. 1 (January 2008): 46–64.

Margolin, Uri. "Telling in the Plural: From Grammar to Ideology." *Poetics Today* 21, no. 3 (Autumn 2000): 591–618.

Martin, Bill. *Matrix and Line: Derrida and the Possibilities of Postmodern Social Theory.* Albany, NY: SUNY Press, 1992.

Matsuno, Koichiro. "Molecular Semiotics towards the Emergence of Life." *Biosemiotics* 1, no. 1 (April 2008): 131–44.

Maturana, Humberto J., and Francisco J. Varela. *The Tree of Knowledge: The Biological Roots of Human Understanding.* Boston: New Science Library, 1987.

Matus, Jill. *Shock, Memory and the Unconscious in Victorian Fiction.* Cambridge: Cambridge University Press, 2009.

Maurseth, Anne Beate. *L'Analogie et le probable: Pensée et écriture chez Denis.* Oxford: Voltaire Foundation, 2007.

McCauley, R. N. and William Bechtel. "Explanatory Pluralism and the Heuristic Identity Theory." *Theory and Psychology* 11 (2001): 736–60.

McConachie, Bruce and F. Elizabeth Hart. *Performance and Cognition: Theatre Studies and the Cognitive Turn.* London: Routledge, 2006.

McDermott, Drew. "Little 'me' (commentary on D. Dennett & M. Kinsbourne, 'Time and the observer')." *Brain and Behavioral Sciences* 15, no. 2 (1992): 217–18.

McEwan, Ian. *Atonement.* London: Vintage Books, 2007.

—— *On Chesil Beach.* London: Vintage Books, 2008.

—— *Saturday.* London: Vintage Books, 2006.

McGowan, Todd. *The Impossible David Lynch.* New York: Columbia University Press, 2007.

McIlwain, Doris, and John Sutton. "Yoga from the Mat Up: How Words Alight on Bodies." *Educational Philosophy and Theory,* (2013): 1–19, forthcoming.

McQuillan, Martin. *Post-Theory: New Directions in Criticism.* Edinburgh: Edinburgh University Press, 1999.

Medawar, Peter. *Pluto's Republic.* Oxford: Oxford University Press, 1982.

Meffen, James. "Elizabeth Costello." *A Companion to the Works of J. M. Coetzee.* Edited by Tim Mehigan. New York: Camden House, 2011, 172–91.

Menary, Richard, ed. *The Extended Mind.* Cambridge, MA: MIT Press, 2010.

Mensching, Günther. "Le matérialisme, une tradition discontinue." In *Materia actuosa…
Mélanges en l'honneur d'Olivier Bloch*. Edited by M. Benítez, A. McKenna and others.
Paris: H. Champion, 2000, 512–25.

Merleau-Ponty, Maurice. *Phenomenology of Perception*. Translated by Donald A. Landes.
London: Routledge, 1962.

Mermin, David N. *Space and Time in Special Relativity*. Prospect Heights, IL: Waveland
Press, 1989.

Métraux, Alexandre. "The Emergent Materialism in French Clinical Brain Research
(1820–1850). A Case Study in Historical Neurophilosophy." *Graduate Faculty
Philosophy Journal* 22, no. 1 (2000): 161–89.

Metzinger, Thomas. *Being No One: The Self-Model Theory of Subjectivity*. Cambridge, MA:
MIT Press, 2004.

—— *The Ego Tunnel: The Science of the Mind and the Myth of the Self*. New York: Basic
Books, 2010.

Mighall, Robert. "Diagnosing Jekyll: The Scientific Context to Dr Jekyll's Experiment and
Mr Hyde's Embodiment." *The Strange Case of Dr Jekyll and Mr Hyde and Other Tales of
Terror*. Edited by Robert Mighall. London: Penguin Books, 2002, 143–61.

Miller, A. H. *The Burdens of Perfection: On Ethics and Reading in Nineteenth-Century
British Literature*. Ithaca, NY: Cornell University Press, 2006.

Miller, James. *The Passion of Michel Foucault*. Cambridge, MA: Harvard University Press,
1994.

Mithen, Steven J. *The Singing Neanderthals: The Origins of Music, Language, Mind and
Body*. London: Weidenfeld and Nicolson, 2005.

Montero, Barbara. "Does Bodily Awareness Interfere with Highly Skilled Movement?"
Inquiry 53, no. 2 (2010): 105–22.

More, Henry. *An Antidote against Atheism* (1653). *A Collection of Several Philosophical
Writings*. 1662. Reprint, New York: Garland, 1978.

Morton, Timothy. "An Object-Oriented Defense of Poetry." *New Literary History* 43
(2012): 205–24.

Muecke, Stephen. *Ancient & Modern: Time, Culture and Indigenous Philosophy*.
Kensington: University of NSW Press, 2004.

—— "Motorcycles, Snails, Latour: Criticism without Judgement." *Cultural Studies Review*
18, no. 1 (2012): 40–58.

Muehlenbein, Michael P. and Mark V. Flinn. "Patterns and Processes of Human Life
History Evolution." *Mechanisms of Life History Evolution: The Genetics and Physiology
of Life History Traits and Trade-offs*. Edited by Thomas Flatt and Andreas Heyland.
New York: Oxford University Press, 2011, 153–68.

Murphet, Julian. "The Mole and the Multiple: A Chiasmus of Character." *New Literary
History* 42, no. 2 (Spring 2011): 255–76.

Nabokov, Vladimir. *The Gift*. Translated by Michael Scammell with the author. New York:
Putnam, 1963.

—— *Bend Sinister*. New York: Time-Life, 1964.

—— *Ada or Ardor: A Family Chronicle*. New York: McGraw-Hill, 1969.

—— *Strong Opinions*. New York: McGraw-Hill, 1973.

—— *Lectures on Russian Literature*. Edited by Fredson Bowers. New York: Harcourt Brace
Jovanovich/Bruccoli Clark, 1981.

Neidich, Warren. *Blow-Up: Photography, Cinema and the Brain*. New York: Distributed Art
Publishers, 2003.

Nietzsche, Friedrich. *Thus Spoke Zarathustra*. Translated by Adrian Del Caro. Cambridge: Cambridge University Press, 2006.

"Novels of the Week, *Daniel Deronda*." *Athenaeum* (29 April 1876): 593.

Nussbaum, Martha C. *Love's Knowledge: Essays on Philosophy and Literature*. New York: Oxford University Press, 1990.

OED Online. Oxford University Press, 2013, http://www.oed.com.

Olick, Jeffrey K. "Collective Memory: The Two Cultures." *Sociological Theory* 17, no. 3 (1999): 333–48.

O'Neill, Joseph. *Netherland*. New York: Vintage, 2009.

Palmer, Alan. *Fictional Minds*. Lincoln, NE: University of Nebraska Press, 2004.

—— "Social Minds in Fiction and Criticism." *Style* 45, no. 2 (Summer 2011): 196–240.

Parker, Michael. *Seamus Heaney: The Making of the Poet*. London: Macmillan, 1993.

Patton, Paul. "Future Politics." *Between Deleuze and Derrida*. Edited by Paul Patton and John Protevi. London: Continuum, 2003.

Michael, Payne and John Schad. *life.after.theory*. London: Continuum, 2003.

Pellow, Kenneth. "Intertextuality and Other Analogues in J. M. Coetzee's *Slow Man*." *Contemporary Literature* 50, no. 3 (Fall 2009): 528–52.

Perez-Alvarez, Frederic, and Carme Timoneda-Gallart. *A Better Look at Intelligent Behavior: Cognition and Emotion*. New York: Nova Science Publishers, 2007.

Pettit, Philip "Groups with Minds of Their Own." *Socializing Metaphysics: The Nature of Social Reality*. Edited by Frederick Schmitt. Lanham: Rowman & Littlefield, 2003.

Pettit, Philip, and David Schweikard. "Joint Actions and Group Agents." *Philosophy of the Social Sciences* 36, no. 1 (March 2006): 18–39.

Piazza, Alberto. "Evolution at Close Range," afterword to *Graphs, Maps, Trees: Abstract Models for Literary History* by Franco Moretti. London: Verso, 2007, 95–113.

Picker, John. *Victorian Soundscapes*. Oxford: Oxford University Press, 2003.

—— "Aural Anxieties and the Advent of Modernity." *The Victorian World*. Edited by Martin Hewitt. New York: Routledge, 2012, 603–19.

Pinker, Steven. *How the Mind Works*. New York: Norton, 2009.

Place, U. T. "Is Consciousness a Brain Process?" *British Journal of Psychology* 47 (1956): 44–50.

—— "We needed the Analytic-Synthetic Distinction to formulate Mind-Brain Identity then: we still do." Paper presented at a symposium on "40 Years of Australian Materialism," Department of Philosophy, University of Leeds, 1997.

Pound, Ezra. *Literary Essays of Ezra Pound*. Edited by T. S. Eliot. New York: New Directions, 1935.

—— "Vortex, Pound." *Blast, No. 1* (June 1914): 153–54.

Powers, Richard. *The Echo Maker*. London: Vintage, 2007.

Price, Leah. *The Anthology and the Rise of the Novel: From Richardson to George Eliot*. Cambridge: Cambridge University Press, 2000.

Prigogine, Ilya and Isabelle Stengers. *Order Out of Chaos*. London: Heinemann, 1984.

Pyle, Forest. "A Novel Sympathy: The Imagination of Community in George Eliot." *NOVEL: A Forum on Fiction* 27, no. 1 (Autumn 1993): 5–23.

Quin, Susan. *Marie Curie: A Life*. United States of America: Perseus Books, 1995.

Rakova, Marina. "The Philosophy of Embodied Realism: A High Price to Pay?" *A Cognitive Linguistics* 13, no. 3 (2003): 215–44.

Ramachandran, V. S. and William Hirstein. "The Science of Art: A Neurological Theory of Aesthetic Experience." *Journal of Consciousness Studies* 6 (1999): 15–51.

Rancière, Jacques. "The Politics of Literature." *SubStance, Issue 103* 33, no. 1 (2004): 10–24.

—— *The Future of the Image.* Translated by Gregory Elliott. London: Verso, 2007.

Ransom, John Crowe. "Criticism, Inc." *Virginia Quarterly Review* 13, no. 4 (Fall 1937): 586–602.

Rapaport, Herman. *The Theory Mess: Deconstruction in Eclipse.* New York: Columbia University Press, 2001.

Rapp, Carl. *William Carlos Williams and Romantic Idealism.* Hanover: Brown University Press, 1984.

Richardson, Alan. *British Romanticism and the Science of Mind.* Cambridge: Cambridge University Press, 2001.

—— *The Neural Sublime: Cognitive Theories and Romantic Texts.* Baltimore, MD: The Johns Hopkins University Press, 2010.

Richardson, Alan and Francis Steen. "Literature and the Cognitive Revolution: An Introduction." *Poetics Today* 23, no. 1 (Spring 2002): 1–8.

Roald, Tone. *Cognition in Emotion: An Investigation through Experiences with Art.* Amsterdam: Rodopi, 2007.

Robbins, Philip and Murat Aydede. *The Cambridge Handbook of Situated Cognition.* Cambridge: Cambridge University Press, 2009.

Roberts, Ryan, ed. *Conversations with Ian McEwan.* Jackson, MS: University Press of Mississippi, 2010.

Robinet, André. *Dom Deschamps, le maître des maîtres du soupçon.* Paris: Seghers, 1974.

Rorty, Richard. *Consequences of Pragmatism: Essays, 1972–1980.* Minneapolis, MN: University of Minnesota Press, 1982.

Roth, Marco. "Rise of the Neuronovel." 14 September 2009. nplusonemag.com/rise-neuronovel.

Rousseau, G. S. *Nervous Acts: Essays on Literature, Culture, and Sensibility.* New York: Palgrave Macmillan, 2004.

Rubery, Matthew. *The Novelty of Newspapers: Victorian Fiction after the Invention of the News.* Oxford: Oxford University Press, 2009.

Rupert, Robert. "Empirical Arguments for Group Minds: A Critical Appraisal." *Philosophy Compass* 6, no. 9 (2011): 630–39.

—— "Minding One's Cognitive Systems: When Does a Group of Minds Constitute a Single Cognitive Unit?" *Episteme: a Journal of Social Epistemology* 1, no. 3 (2005): 177–88.

Ruyer, Raymond. "Ce qui est vivant et ce qui est mort dans le matérialisme." *Revue Philosophique* 116, nos. 7–8 (1933): 28–49.

Ryan, Greg. *The Contest for Rugby Supremacy.* Christchurch: Canterbury University Press, 2005.

Ryan, Judith. *The Vanishing Subject: Early Psychology and Literary Modernism.* London: University of Chicago Press, 1991.

Ryan, Vanessa L. "Living in Duplicate: Victorian Science and Literature Today." *Critical Inquiry* 38, no. 2 (Winter 2012): 411–17.

—— *Thinking without Thinking in the Victorian Novel.* Baltimore, MD: The Johns Hopkins University Press, 2012.

Ryle, Gilbert. *The Concept of Mind*. Chicago: University of Chicago Press, 1949.

Saintsbury, George. "Literature: *Daniel Deronda*." *The Academy* 227 (9 September 1876): 253–54.

Salisbury, Laura and Andrew Shail, eds. *Neurology and Modernity: A Cultural History of Nervous Systems*. London: Palgrave Macmillan, 2010.

Samudra, Jaida Kim. "Memory in Our Body: Thick Participation and the Translation of Kinesthetic Experience." *American Ethnologist* 35, no. 4 (November 2008): 665–81.

Saxe, Rebecca, and Simon Baron-Cohen. *Theory of Mind*. 2006. Reprint. Hove: Psychology Press, 2007.

Schacter, Daniel L. and Donna Rose Addis. "The Cognitive Neuroscience of Constructive Memory: Remembering the Past and Imagining the Future." *Philosophical Transactions of the Royal Society B* 362 (2007): 773–86.

Schechtman, Marya. "The Truth about Memory." *Philosophical Psychology* 7, no. 1 (1994): 3–18.

Schemmel, Johannes, Karlheinz Meier, and Felix Schurmann. "A VLSI Implementation of an Analog Neural Network Suited for Genetic Algorithms." *Evolvable Systems: From Biology to Hardware*. Edited by Yong Liu, Kiyoshi Tanaka, Masaya Iwata, Tetsuya Higuchi and Moritoshi Yasunaga. Berlin: Springer, 2001, 50–61.

Schopenhauer, Arthur. *The Art of Literature*. Translated by T. Bailey Saunders. Mineola, NY: Dover, 2004.

Sennett, Richard. *The Corrosion of Character: The Personal Consequences of Work in the New Capitalism*. New York: Norton, 1998.

Serres, Michel. *Atlas*. Paris: Flammarion, 1997.

—— "Feux et Signaux de Brume: Virginia Woolf's Lighthouse." *SubStance* 116:37, no. 2 (2008): 110–31.

Shatz, Adam. "Desire Was Everywhere." *London Review of Books* 32, no. 24 (16 December 2010): 9–12.

Sheets-Johnstone, Maxine. *The Corporeal Turn*. Exeter: Imprint Academic, 2009.

Smart, J. J. C. "Sensations and Brain Processes." *Philosophical Review* 68, no. 2 (1959): 141–56.

—— "Materialism." *Journal of Philosophy* 60 (1963): 651–62.

Snow, C. P. *The Two Cultures*. Cambridge: Cambridge University Press, 2007.

Sokal, Alan and Jean Bricmont. *Intellectual Impostures: Postmodern Philosophers' Abuse of Science*. London: Profile, 1998.

Souriau, Etienne. *Avoir une âme*. Lyon: Annales de l'Université de Lyon, 1939.

—— *Les différents modes d'existence*. Paris: Presses Universitaires de France, 1943.

Spencer, Herbert. *Principles of Psychology*. 2 vols. New York: D. Appleton, 1906.

Sperber, Dan. "Metarepresentations in an Evolutionary Perspective." *Metarepresentations: A Multidisciplinary Perspective*. Edited by D. Sperber. Oxford: Oxford University Press, 2000, 117–38.

Spinney, Laura. "Tools Maketh the Monkey." *New Scientist* 2677 (2008): 42–45.

Spinoza, Benedictus de. "Preface to *Ethics*." *The Collected Works of Spinoza, Volume 1*. Edited and translated by Edwin Curley. Princeton: Princeton University Press, 1985.

Spolsky, Ellen. "Darwin and Derrida: Cognitive Literary Theory as a Species of Post-Structuralism." *Poetics Today* 23, no. 1 (Spring 2002): 43–62.

——"Preface." *The Work of Fiction: Cognition, Vulture, and Complexity*. Edited by Alan Richardson and Ellen Spolsky. Aldershot: Ashgate, 2004, vii–xiii.

Stengers, Isabelle. *Cosmopolitiques*. 7 vols. Paris: La Découverte; Les Empêcheurs de Penser en Rond, 1996–1997.

Sterelny, Kim. *The Evolved Apprentice: How Evolution Made Humans Unique*. Cambridge, MA: MIT Press, 2012.

Stewart, Garrett. *Framed Time: Towards a Postfilmic Cinema*. Chicago: University of Chicago Press, 2007.

Stiegler, Bernard. "Derrida and Technology: Fidelity at the Limits of Deconstruction and the Prosthesis of Faith." *Jacques Derrida and the Humanities: A Critical Reader*. Edited by Tom Cohen. Cambridge: Cambridge University Press, 2001, 238–70.

Streeck, Jürgen, Charles Goodwin, and Curtis D. LeBaron. *Embodied Interaction: Language and Body in the Material World*. New York: Cambridge University Press, 2011.

Sturrock, John. "Le pauvre Sokal." *London Review of Books* 20, no. 14 (16 July 1998): 8–9.

Suarez, Juan. *Pop Modernism: Noise and the Reinvention of the Everyday*. Urbana, IL: University of Illinois Press, 2007.

Sully, James. "Art and Psychology." *Mind* 1, no. 4 (October 1876): 467–78.

—— "Civilisation and Noise." *Fortnightly Review* 24, no. 143 (November 1878): 704–20.

—— "George Eliot's Art." *Mind* 6, no. 23 (July 1881): 378–94.

—— *Illusions–A Psychological Study*. London: Kegan Paul, Trench & Co, 1887.

—— "The Dream as a Revelation." *Fortnightly Review* 53, no. 315 (March 1893): 354–65.

—— *My Life and Friends: A Psychologist's Memories*. London: T. Fisher Unwin, 1918.

Surowiecki, James. *The Wisdom of Crowds*. New York: Doubleday, 2004.

Sutton, John. *Philosophy and Memory Traces: Descartes to Connectionism*. Cambridge: Cambridge University Press, 1998.

—— "Representation, Levels, and Context in Integrational Linguistics and Distributed Cognition." *Language Sciences* 26, no. 6 (November 2004): 503–24.

—— "Batting, Habit and Memory: The Embodied Mind and the Nature of Skill." *Sport in Society* 10, no. 5 (2007): 763–86.

—— "The Feel of the World: Exograms, Habits, and the Confusion of Types of Memory." *Memento*. Edited by Andrew Kania. New York: Routledge, 2009, 65–86.

—— "Carelessness and Inattention: Mind-Wandering and the Physiology of Fantasy from Locke to Hume." *The Body as Object and Instrument of Knowledge: Embodied Empiricism in Early Modern Science*. Edited by Charles T. Wolfe and Ofer Gal. Dordrecht: Springer, 2010, 243–63.

Sutton, John, Celia B. Harris, Paul G. Keil, and Amanda J. Barnier. "The Psychology of Memory, Extended Cognition, and Socially Distributed Remembering." *Phenomenology and the Cognitive Sciences* 9, no. 4 (December 2010): 521–60.

Sutton, John, Doris McIlwain, Wayne Christensen and Andrew Geeves. "Applying Intelligence to the Reflexes: Embodied Skills and Habits between Dreyfus and Descartes." *Journal of the British Society for Phenomenology* 42, no. 1 (January 2011): 78–103.

Sutton, John and Evelyn B. Tribble. "Materialists Are Not Merchants of Vanishing. Commentary on David Hawkes, 'Against Materialism in Literary Theory.'" *Early Modern Culture* 9, forthcoming.

Symons, Arthur. *Images of Good and Evil*. New York: Woodstock Books, 1996.

Taminiaux, Jacques. *Poetics, Speculation, and Judgment: The Shadow of the Work of Art from Kant to Phenomenology*. Translated by Michael Gendre. Albany, NY: SUNY Press, 1993.

Taussig, Michael. *Mimesis and Alterity: A Particular History of the Senses*. New York: Routledge, 1993.

Theiner, Georg. "Transactive Memory Systems: A Mechanistic Analysis of Emergent Group Memory." *Review of Philosophy and Psychology* 4, no. 1 (January 2013): 65–89.

Theiner, Georg, Colin Allen, and Robert L. Goldstone. "Recognizing Group Cognition." *Cognitive Systems Research* 11, no. 4 (December 2010): 378–95.

Thompson, Evan. *Mind in Life: Biology, Phenomenology, and the Sciences of Mind*. Cambridge, MA: Belknap Press of Harvard University Press, 2007.

Toland, John. *Letters to Serena*. 1704. Reprint. New York: Garland, 1976.

—— *Pantheisticon*. 'Cosmopoli,' 1720.

Tollefsen, Deborah P. "From Extended Mind to Collective Mind." *Cognitive Systems Research* 7, no. 2 (June 2006): 140–50.

Tollefsen, Deborah P., Rick Dale, and Alexandra Paxton. "Alignment, Transactive Memory, and Collective Cognitive Systems." *Review of Philosophy and Psychology* 4, no. 1 (January 2013): 49–64.

Tomasello, Michael. *Origins of Human Communication*. Cambridge, MA: MIT Press, 2008.

—— *Why We Cooperate*. Cambridge: Cambridge University Press, 2009.

Tooby, John, and Leda Cosmides. "Does Beauty Build Adapted Minds? Toward an Evolutionary Theory of Aesthetics, Fiction and the Arts." *SubStance* 30, nos. 1–2 (2001): 6–27.

Tressler, Beth. "Waking Dreams: George Eliot and the Poetics of Double Consciousness." *Victorian Literature and Culture* 39 (2011): 483–98.

Tribble, Evelyn B. *Cognition in the Globe*. New York: Palgrave Macmillan, 2011.

—— "Distributing Cognition in the Globe." *Shakespeare Quarterly* 56, no. 2 (Summer 2005): 135–55.

Tsur, Reuven. *What Is Cognitive Poetics?: Papers in Cognitive Poetics, 1*. Tel Aviv: The Katz Research Institute for Hebrew Literature, Tel Aviv University, 1982.

Turk, Tisha. "Intertextuality and the Collaborative Construction of Narrative: J. M. Coetzee's *Foe*." *Narrative* 19, no. 3 (October 2011): 295–310.

Turner, Mark. *Death Is the Mother of Beauty: Mind, Metaphors, and Criticism*. Chicago: University of Chicago Press, 1987.

—— *Reading Minds: The Study of English in the Age of Cognitive Science*. Princeton: Princeton University Press, 1991.

—— *The Literary Mind*. New York: Oxford University Press, 1996.

Tyndall, John. *Sound: A Course of Eight Lectures Delivered at the Royal Institution of Great Britain*. New York: D. Appleton, 1867.

Uhlmann, Anthony. "Realism and Intertextuality in Coetzee's *Foe*." *Strong Opinions: J. M. Coetzee and the Authority of Contemporary Fiction*. Edited by Chris Danta, Sue Kossew and Julian Murphet. London: Continuum, 2011, 81–95.

—— *Thinking in Literature: Joyce, Woolf, Nabokov*. London: Continuum, 2011.

—— "J. M. Coetzee and the Uses of Anachronism in *Summertime*." *Textual Practice* 26, no. 4 (April 2012): 747–61.

van der Veer, René, and Jaan Valsiner. *Understanding Vygotsky*. London: Blackwell, 1991.

Varela, Francesco J., Evan Thompson, and Eleanor Rosch. *The Embodied Mind: Cognitive Science and Human Experience*. Cambridge, MA: MIT Press, 1992.

Vermeule, Blakey. *Why Do We Care about Literary Characters?*. Baltimore, MD: The Johns Hopkins University Press, 2010.

Vila, Anne C. *Enlightenment and Pathology. Sensibility in the Literature and Medicine of Eighteenth-Century France*. Baltimore, MD: The Johns Hopkins University Press, 1998.

Vogt, Carl. *Physiologische Briefe*. 14th ed. 1847. Reprint. Gießen: Rickersche Buchhandlung, 1874.

Walter, Damien G. "What Neuroscience Tells us about the Art of Fiction." 6 June 2012. http://damiengwalter.com/2012/06/10/what-neuroscience-tells-us-about-the-art-of-fiction/.

Warman, Caroline. *Sade: From Materialism to Pornography*. Oxford: Voltaire Foundation, 2002.

Warner, Marina. *Indigo*. London: Vintage, 1992.

Warner, Nicholas O. "In Search of Literary Science: The Russian Formalist Tradition." *Pacific Coast Philology* 17, nos. 1–2 (November 1982): 69–81.

Wegner, Daniel M. "Transactive Memory: A Contemporary Analysis of the Group Mind." *Theories of Group Behavior*. Edited by Brian Mullen and George R. Goethals. New York: Springer, 1987.

Wegner, Daniel M., Toni Giuliano, and Paula T. Hertel. "Cognitive Interdependence in Close Relationships." *Compatible and Incompatible Relationships*. Edited by Williams Ickes. New York: Springer, 1985, 253–76.

Wellek, René. "The New Criticism: Pro and Contra." *Critical Inquiry* 4, no. 4 (Summer 1978): 611–24.

Wexler, Bruce E. *Brain and Culture: Neurobiology, Ideology, and Social Change*. Cambridge, MA: MIT Press, 2006.

Wheeler, Michael. *Reconstructing the Cognitive World: The Next Step*. Cambridge, MA: MIT Press, 2005.

Wheeler, Michael, and Julia Kiverstein, eds. *Heidegger and Cognitive Science*. New York: Palgrave Macmillan, 2012.

Whitehead, Alfred North. *Process and Reality: An Essay in Cosmology*. New York: The Free Press, 1978.

Williams, William Carlos. "Notes from a Talk on Poetry." *Poetry* 14, no. 2 (1919): 211–16.

—— *Paterson*. Middlesex: Penguin, 1963.

—— *The Autobiography of William Carlos Williams*. New York: New Directions, 1967.

—— *Selected Essays of William Carlos Williams*. New York: New Directions, 1969.

—— *Imaginations*. New York: New Directions, 1971.

—— *The Embodiment of Knowledge*. New York: New Directions, 1974.

—— *The Collected Poems of William Carlos Williams*. 2 vols. New York: New Directions, 1991.

Wilson, Robert A. *Boundaries of the Mind: The Individual in the Fragile Sciences: Cognition*. Cambridge: Cambridge University Press, 2004.

—— "Collective Memory, Group Minds, and the Extended Mind Thesis." *Cognitive Processing* 6, no. 4 (2005): 227–36, doi:10.1007/s10339-005-0012-z.

Wimsatt, William. *Re-Engineering Philosophy for Limited Beings: Piecewise Approximations to Reality*. Cambridge, MA: MIT Press, 2007.

Wittgenstein, Ludwig. *Tractatus Logico-Philosophicus*. London: Routledge, 1961.

Wolfe, Charles T. "Le rêve matérialiste, ou 'Faire par la pensée ce que la matière fait parfois.'" *Philosophiques* 34, no. 2 (2007): 317–28.

—— "From Spinoza to the Socialist Cortex: Steps toward the Social Brain." In *Cognitive Architecture. From Bio-politics to Noo-politics*. Edited by Deborah Hauptmann and Warren Neidich. Rotterdam: 010 Publishers, Delft School of Design, 2010, 184–206.

—— "Forms of Materialist Embodiment." *Anatomy and the Organization of Knowledge, 1500–1850*. Edited by Matthew Landers and Brian Muñoz. London: Pickering and Chatto, 2012, 129–44.

—— "Sensibility as Vital Force or as Property of Matter in Mid-Eighteenth-Century Debates." *Sensibilité: The Knowing Body in the Enlightenment*. Edited by Henry Martyn Lloyd. Oxford: Voltaire Foundation, forthcoming.

Wolfe, Charles T. and Michaela van Esveld. "The Material Soul: Early Modern Epicurean Strategies for Naturalising the Soul." *Conjunctions: Body, Soul and Mind from Plato to Descartes*. Edited by Danijela Kambaskovic-Sawers. Dordrecht: Springer, forthcoming.

Wollheim, Richard. *Freud*. London: Fontana, 1991.

Wood, James. *How Fiction Works*. New York: Farrar, Straus and Giroux, 2008.

Wrathall, Mark and Jeff Malpas, eds. *Heidegger, Coping, and Cognitive Science*. Cambridge, MA: MIT Press, 2000.

Wright, Laurence. "David Lurie's Learning and the Meaning of J. M. Coetzee's *Disgrace*." *J. M. Coetzee's Austerities*. Edited by Graham Bradsaw and Michael Neill. Farnham: Ashgate, 2010, 147–62.

Yeats, W. B. *Selected Poems*. Edited by Timothy Webb. London: Penguin, 1991.

Young, James. *The Texture of Memory: Holocaust, Memorials, and Meaning*. New Haven, CT: Yale University Press, 1993.

Young, Kay and Jeffrey L. Saver. "The Neurology of Narrative." *SubStance* 30, nos. 1–2 (2001): 72–84.

Young, Robert M. *Mind, Brain and Adaptation in the Nineteenth Century: Cerebral Localization and Its Biological Context from Gall to Ferrier*. Oxford: Clarendon Press, 1970. Revised 1990.

Zeki, Semir. *Inner Vision: An Exploration of Art and the Brain*. Oxford: Oxford University Press, 1999.

Žižek, Slavoj. *The Sublime Object of Ideology*. London: Verso, 1989.

—— *The Art of the Ridiculous Sublime: On David Lynch's Lost Highway*. Seattle, WA: Walter Chapin Simpson Center for the Humanities, 2000.

—— "Lacan between Cultural Studies and Cognitivism." *Umbr(a): A Journal of the Unconscious* 4 (2000): 9–32.

—— *The Parallax View*. Cambridge, MA: MIT Press, 2006.

Zukofsky, Louis. *Prepositions: The Collected Critical Essays of Louis Zukofsky, Expanded Edition*. New York: Horizon Press, 1967.

Zunshine, Lisa. *Why We Read Fiction: Theory of Mind and the Novel*. Columbus, OH: The Ohio State University Press, 2006.

—— "Fiction and Theory of Mind: An Exchange." *Philosophy and Literature* 31 (2007): 189–95.

Index